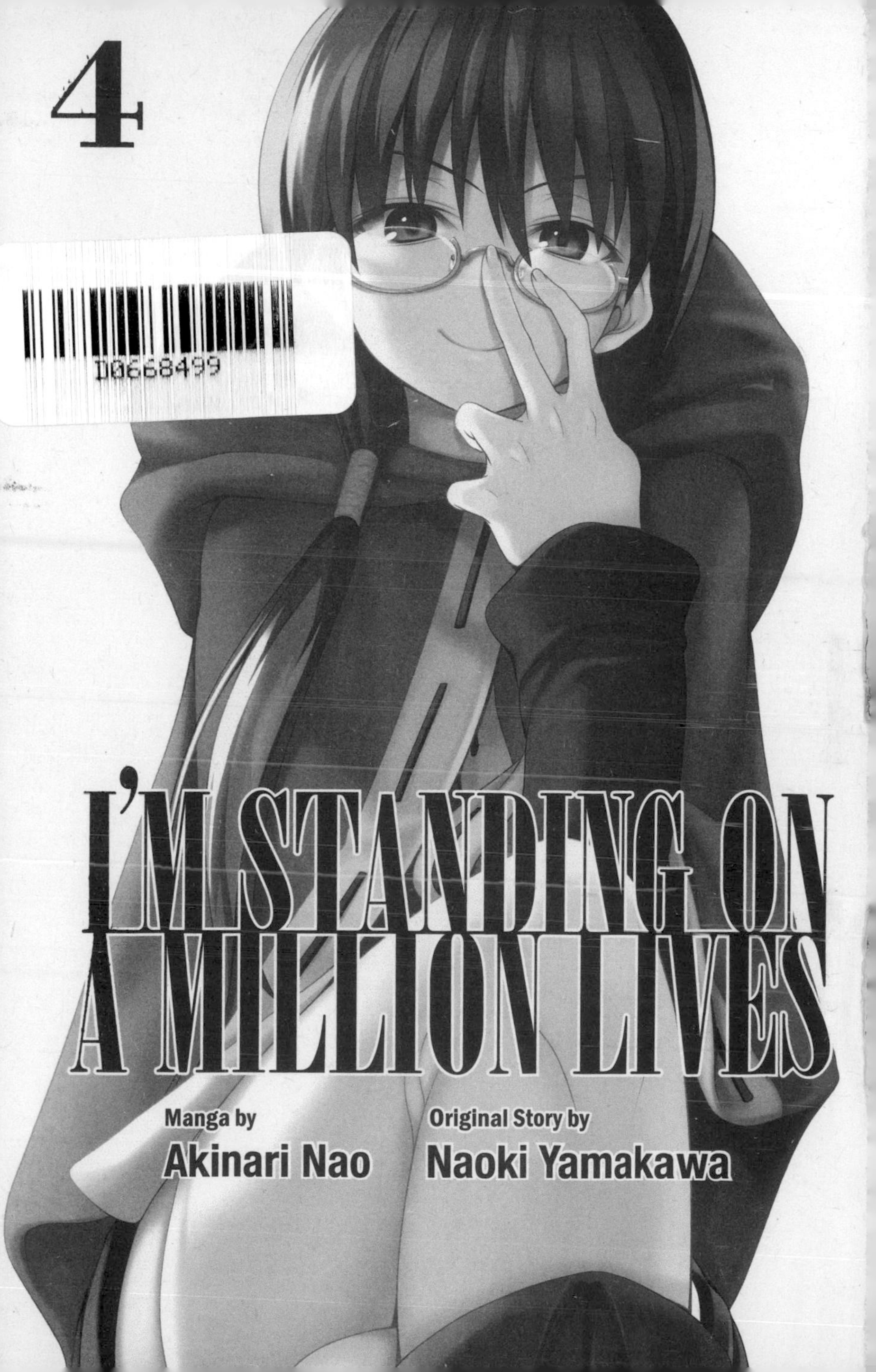
4
I'M STANDING ON A MILLION LIVES
Manga by
Akinari Nao
Original Story by
Naoki Yamakawa

❧ CONTENTS ❧

#15: The Papier-Mâché Paradise

003

#16: The Mega-Stake & the Surprise Attack

039

#17: Flight from Glory & Glory to the Fleeing

079

#18: All They Could Do Was Look Up

115

#19: Descendants of the Island of Disasters

151

#15 The Papier-Mâché Paradise

FOR FARMERS, THE MORNINGS...

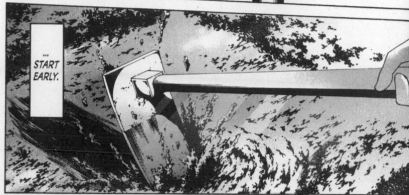

...START EARLY.

BOOST THAT LEVEL! GOTTA CHANGE MY OCCUPATION!

I NEED A WEAPON TO FIGHT THE ORCS!

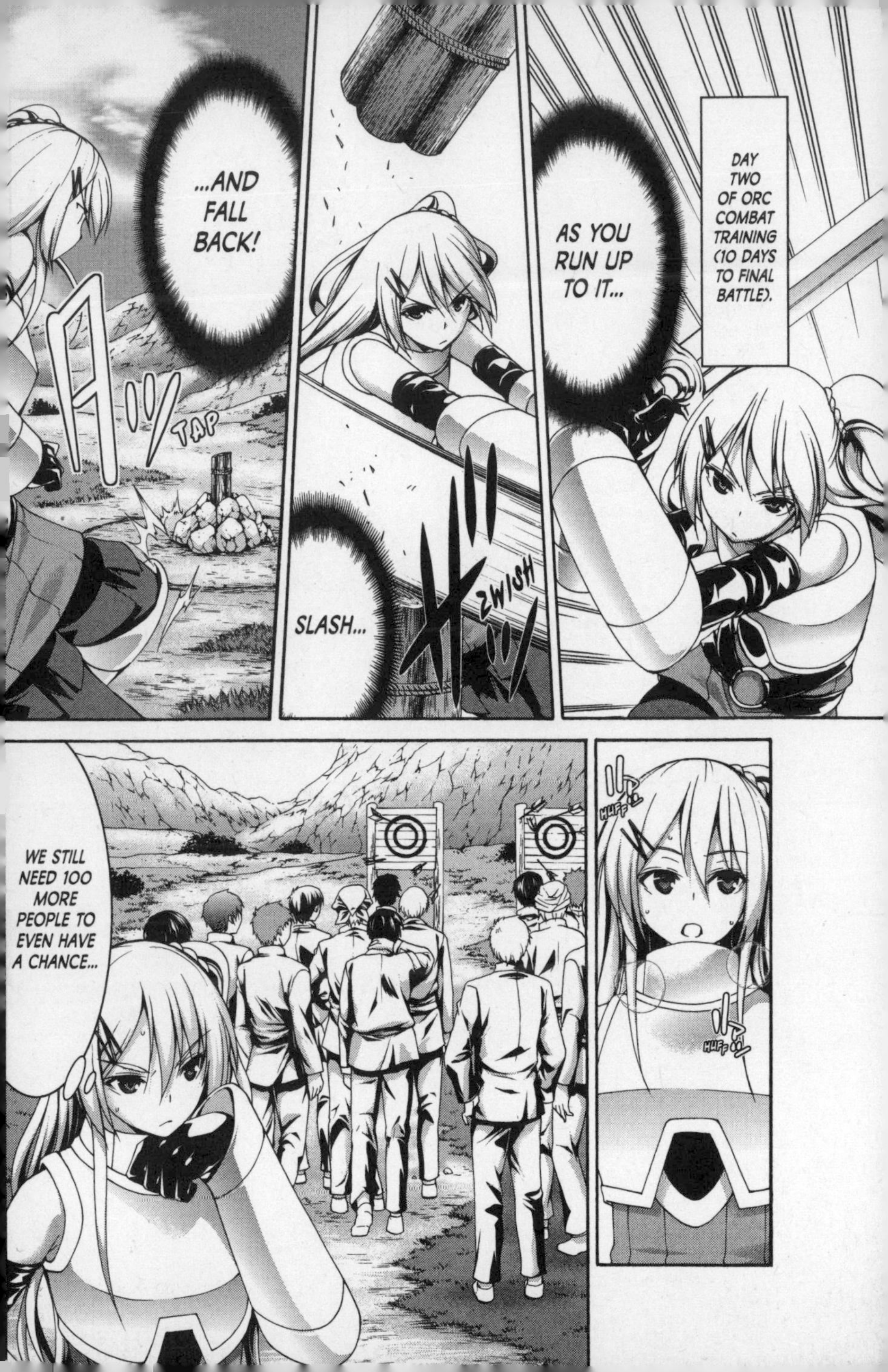
DAY TWO OF ORC COMBAT TRAINING (10 DAYS TO FINAL BATTLE).
AS YOU RUN UP TO IT...
SLASH...
SWISH
...AND FALL BACK!
TAP
HUFF
HUFF
WE STILL NEED 100 MORE PEOPLE TO EVEN HAVE A CHANCE...

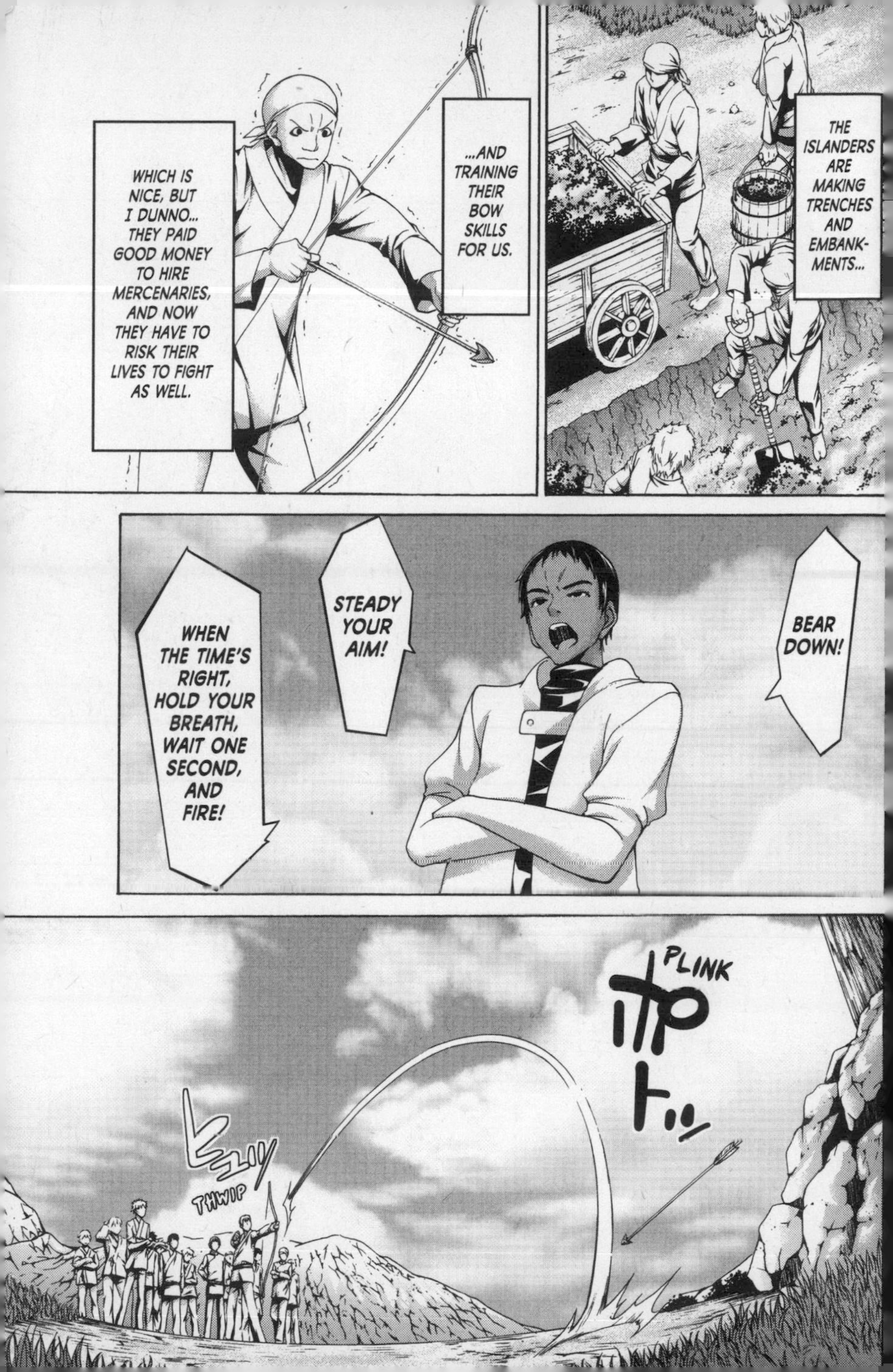
THE ISLANDERS ARE MAKING TRENCHES AND EMBANK-MENTS...
...AND TRAINING THEIR BOW SKILLS FOR US.
WHICH IS NICE, BUT I DUNNO... THEY PAID GOOD MONEY TO HIRE MERCENARIES, AND NOW THEY HAVE TO RISK THEIR LIVES TO FIGHT AS WELL.
BEAR DOWN!
STEADY YOUR AIM!
WHEN THE TIME'S RIGHT, HOLD YOUR BREATH, WAIT ONE SECOND, AND FIRE!
PLINK
THWIP

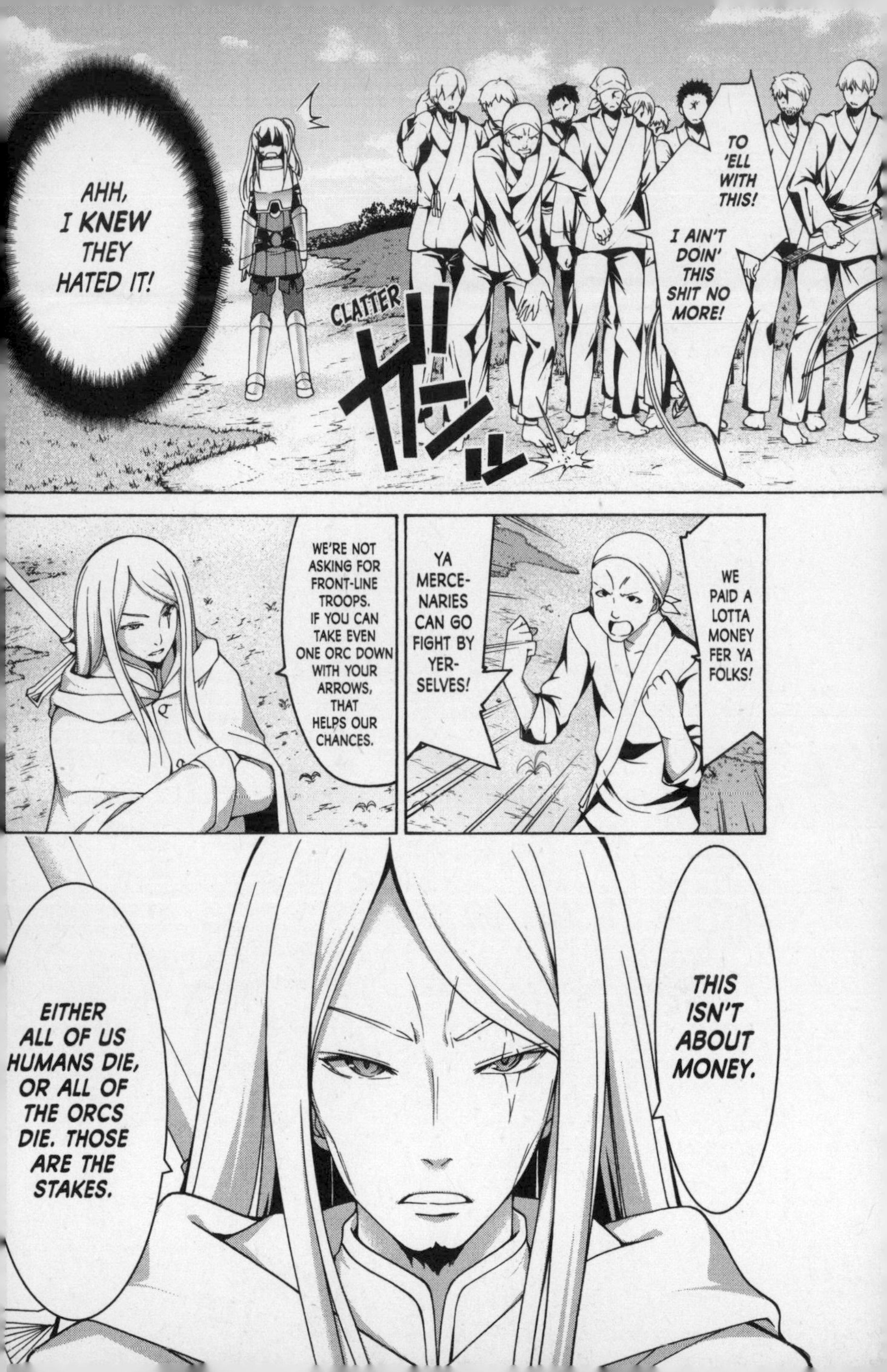
TO 'ELL WITH THIS!
I AIN'T DOIN' THIS SHIT NO MORE!
CLATTER
AHH, I KNEW THEY HATED IT!
WE PAID A LOTTA MONEY FER YA FOLKS!
YA MERCE-NARIES CAN GO FIGHT BY YER-SELVES!
WE'RE NOT ASKING FOR FRONT-LINE TROOPS. IF YOU CAN TAKE EVEN ONE ORC DOWN WITH YOUR ARROWS, THAT HELPS OUR CHANCES.
THIS ISN'T ABOUT MONEY.
EITHER ALL OF US HUMANS DIE, OR ALL OF THE ORCS DIE. THOSE ARE THE STAKES.

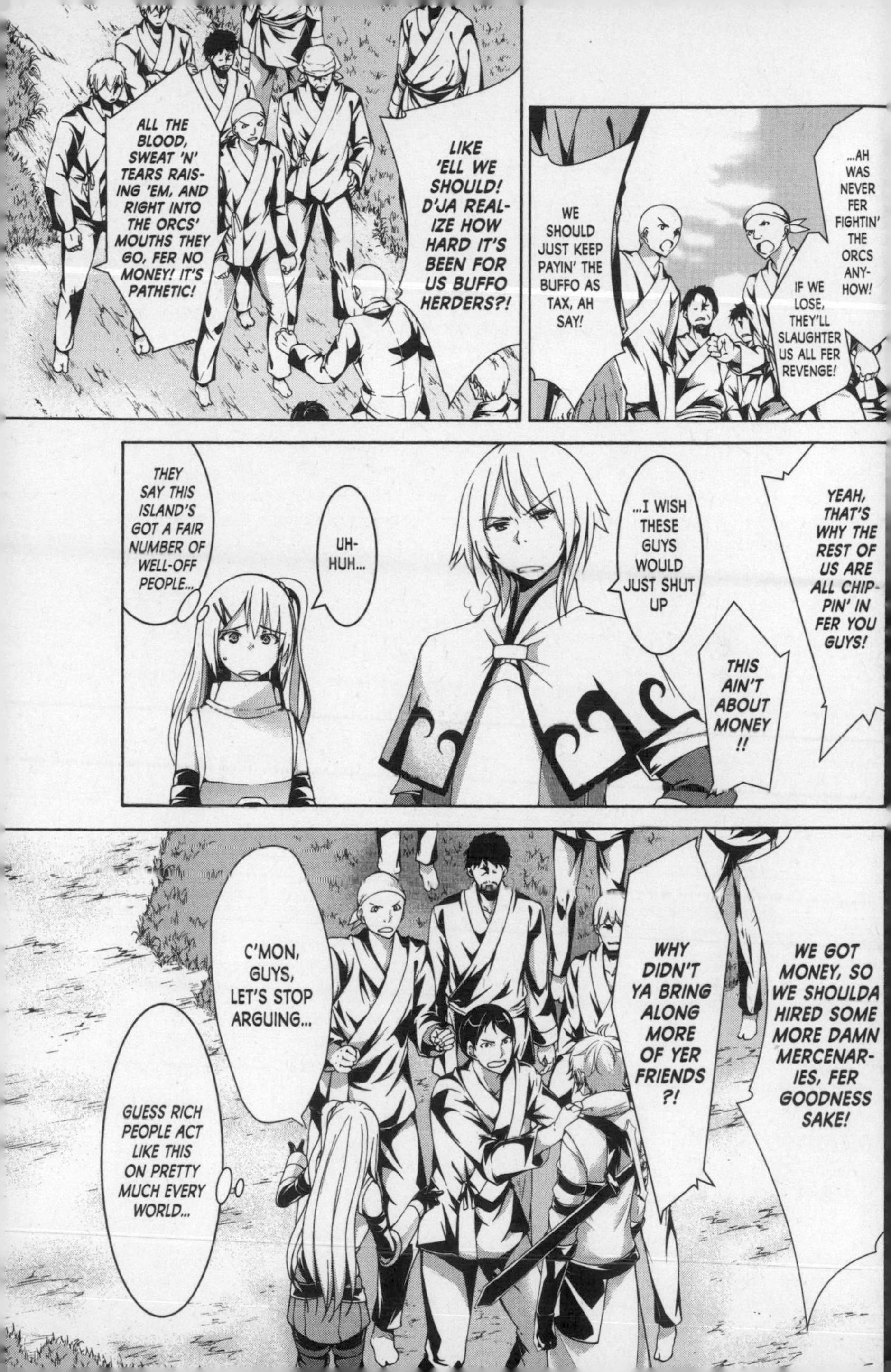
...AH WAS NEVER FER FIGHTIN' THE ORCS ANYHOW!
IF WE LOSE, THEY'LL SLAUGHTER US ALL FER REVENGE!
WE SHOULD JUST KEEP PAYIN' THE BUFFO AS TAX, AH SAY!
LIKE 'ELL WE SHOULD! D'JA REALIZE HOW HARD IT'S BEEN FOR US BUFFO HERDERS?!
ALL THE BLOOD, SWEAT 'N' TEARS RAISING 'EM, AND RIGHT INTO THE ORCS' MOUTHS THEY GO, FER NO MONEY! IT'S PATHETIC!
YEAH, THAT'S WHY THE REST OF US ARE ALL CHIPPIN' IN FER YOU GUYS!
THIS AIN'T ABOUT MONEY!!
...I WISH THESE GUYS WOULD JUST SHUT UP
UH-HUH...
THEY SAY THIS ISLAND'S GOT A FAIR NUMBER OF WELL-OFF PEOPLE...
WE GOT MONEY, SO WE SHOULDA HIRED SOME MORE DAMN MERCENARIES, FER GOODNESS SAKE!
WHY DIDN'T YA BRING ALONG MORE OF YER FRIENDS?!
C'MON, GUYS, LET'S STOP ARGUING...
GUESS RICH PEOPLE ACT LIKE THIS ON PRETTY MUCH EVERY WORLD...

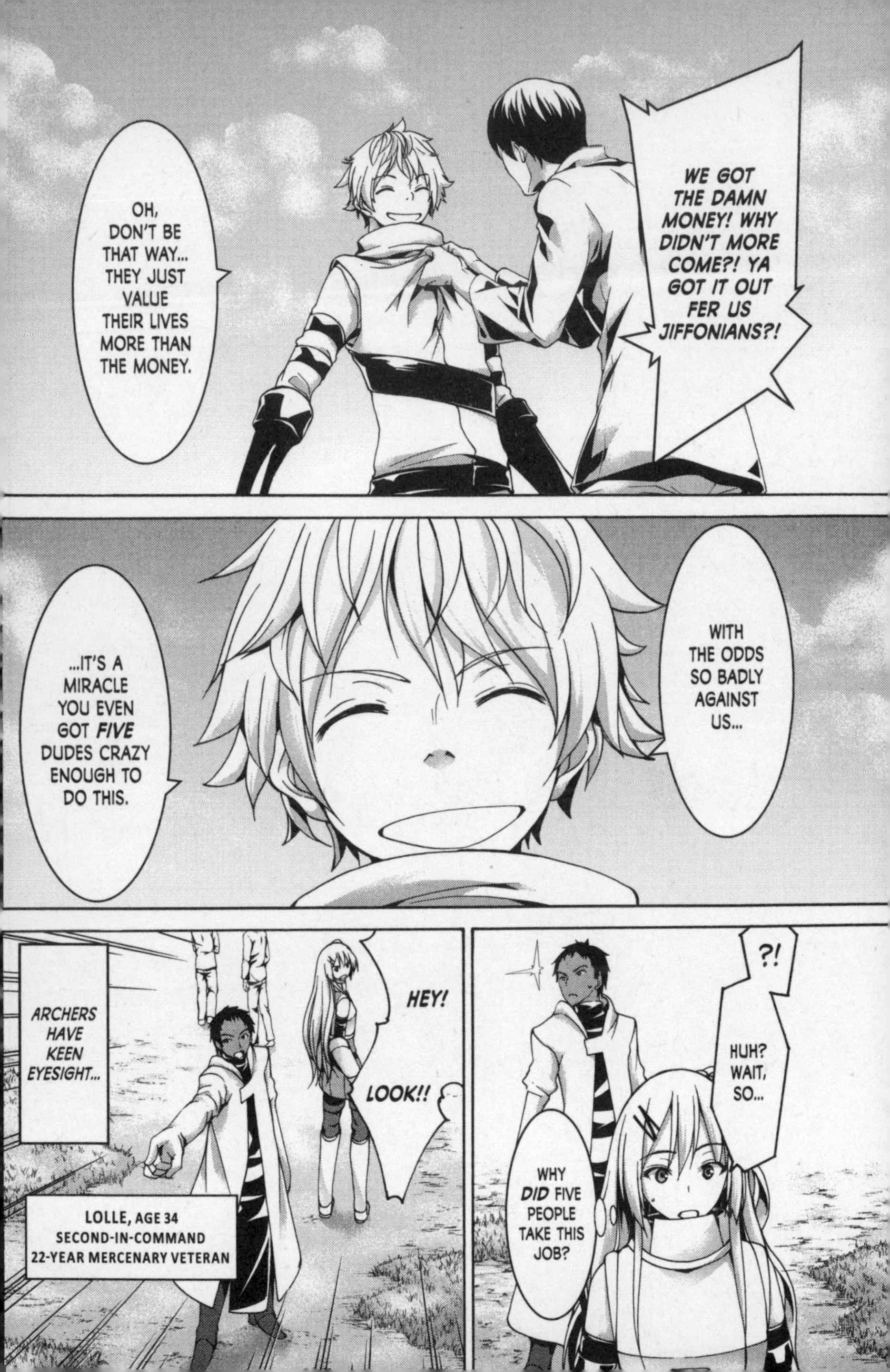
WE GOT THE DAMN MONEY! WHY DIDN'T MORE COME?! YA GOT IT OUT FER US JIFFONIANS?!
OH, DON'T BE THAT WAY... THEY JUST VALUE THEIR LIVES MORE THAN THE MONEY.
WITH THE ODDS SO BADLY AGAINST US...
...IT'S A MIRACLE YOU EVEN GOT *FIVE* DUDES CRAZY ENOUGH TO DO THIS.
?!
HUH? WAIT, SO...
WHY *DID* FIVE PEOPLE TAKE THIS JOB?
HEY!
LOOK!!
ARCHERS HAVE KEEN EYESIGHT...
LOLLE, AGE 34
SECOND-IN-COMMAND
22-YEAR MERCENARY VETERAN

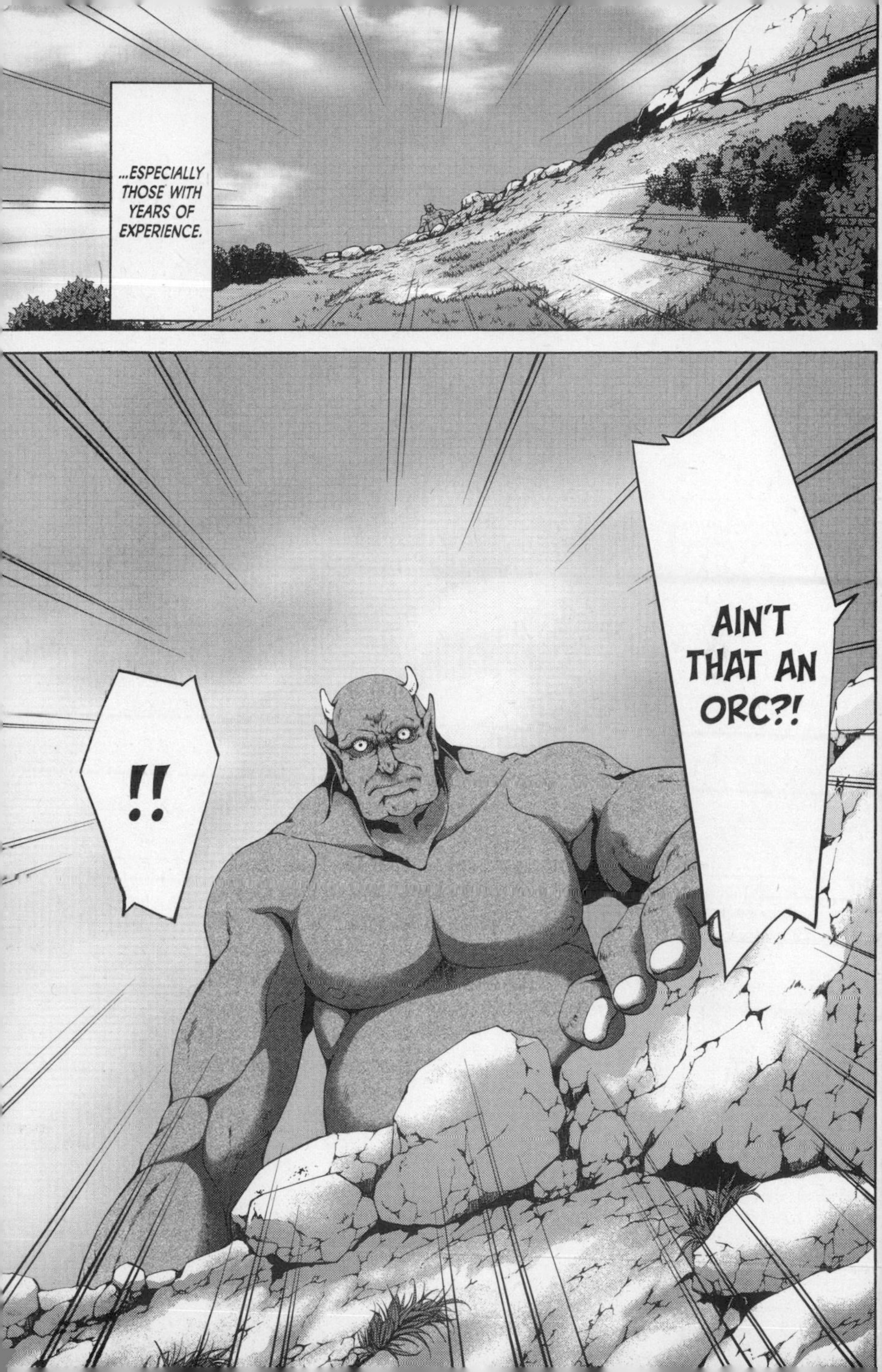
...ESPECIALLY THOSE WITH YEARS OF EXPERIENCE.
AIN'T THAT AN ORC?!
!!

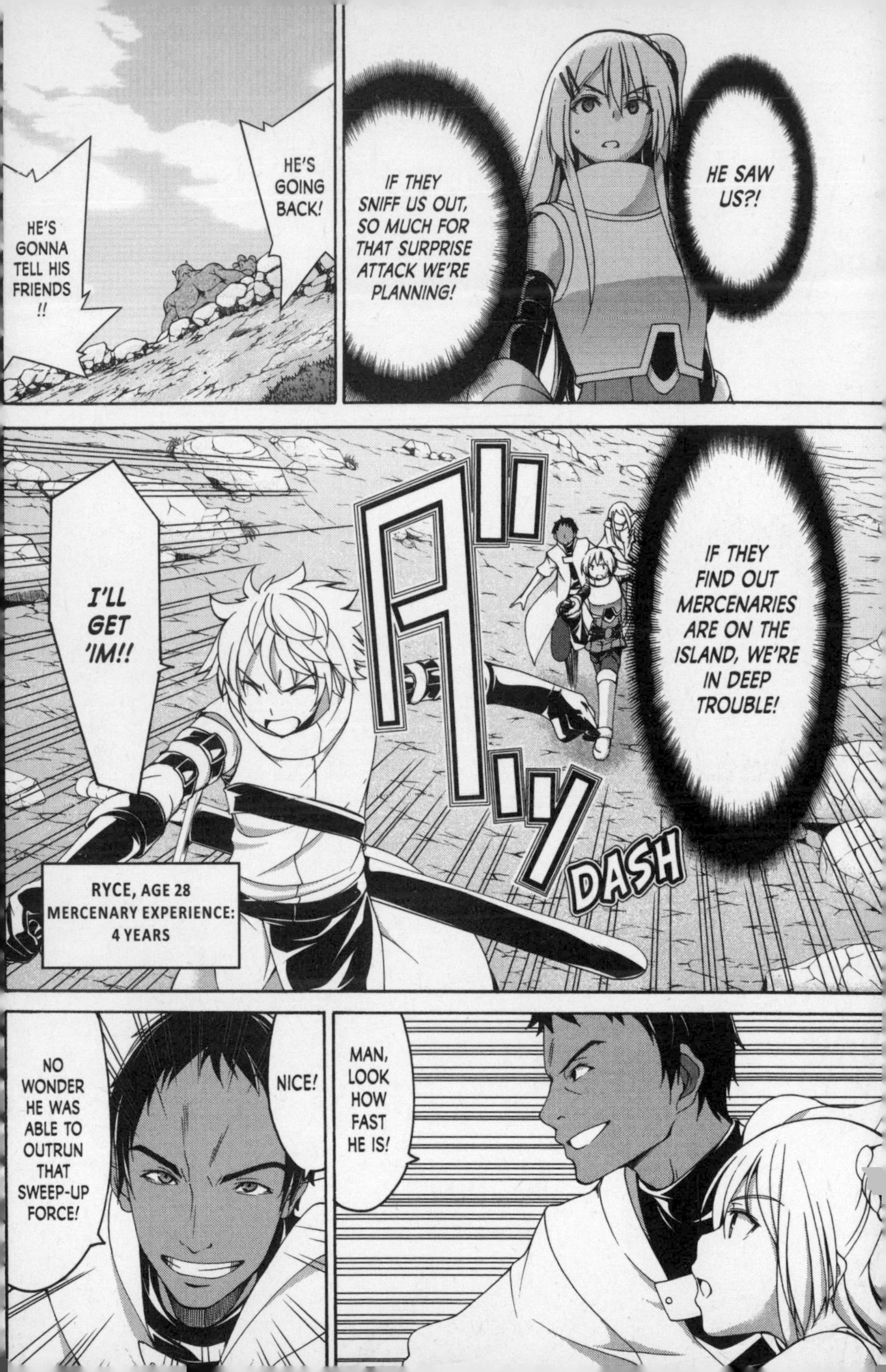
HE SAW US?!
IF THEY SNIFF US OUT, SO MUCH FOR THAT SURPRISE ATTACK WE'RE PLANNING!
HE'S GOING BACK!
HE'S GONNA TELL HIS FRIENDS !!
IF THEY FIND OUT MERCENARIES ARE ON THE ISLAND, WE'RE IN DEEP TROUBLE!
DASH
I'LL GET 'IM!!
RYCE, AGE 28 MERCENARY EXPERIENCE: 4 YEARS
MAN, LOOK HOW FAST HE IS!
NICE!
NO WONDER HE WAS ABLE TO OUTRUN THAT SWEEP-UP FORCE!

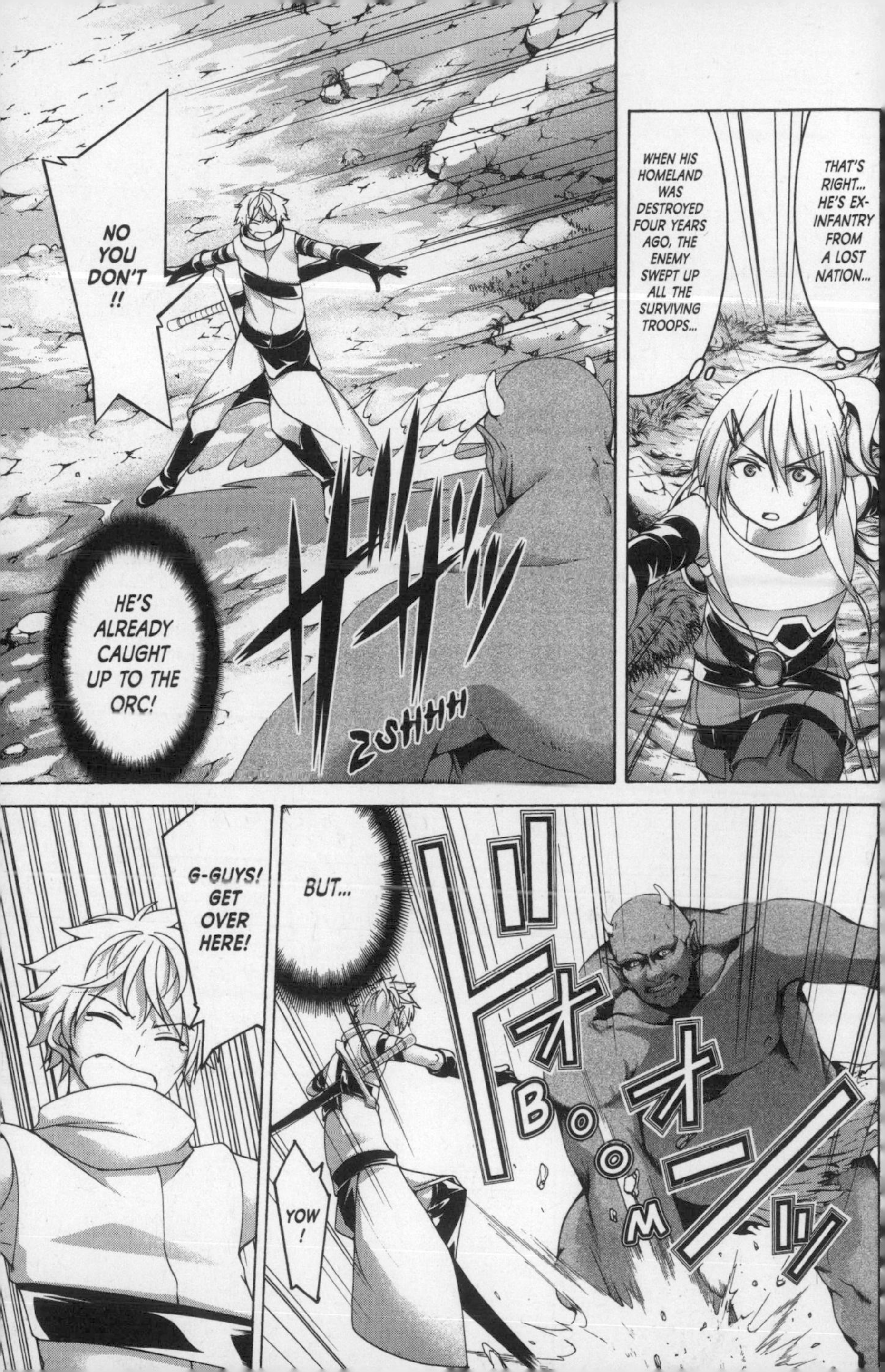
THAT'S RIGHT... HE'S EX-INFANTRY FROM A LOST NATION...
WHEN HIS HOMELAND WAS DESTROYED FOUR YEARS AGO, THE ENEMY SWEPT UP ALL THE SURVIVING TROOPS...
NO YOU DON'T !!
HE'S ALREADY CAUGHT UP TO THE ORC!
ZSHHH
BUT...
BOOM
YOW!
G-GUYS! GET OVER HERE!

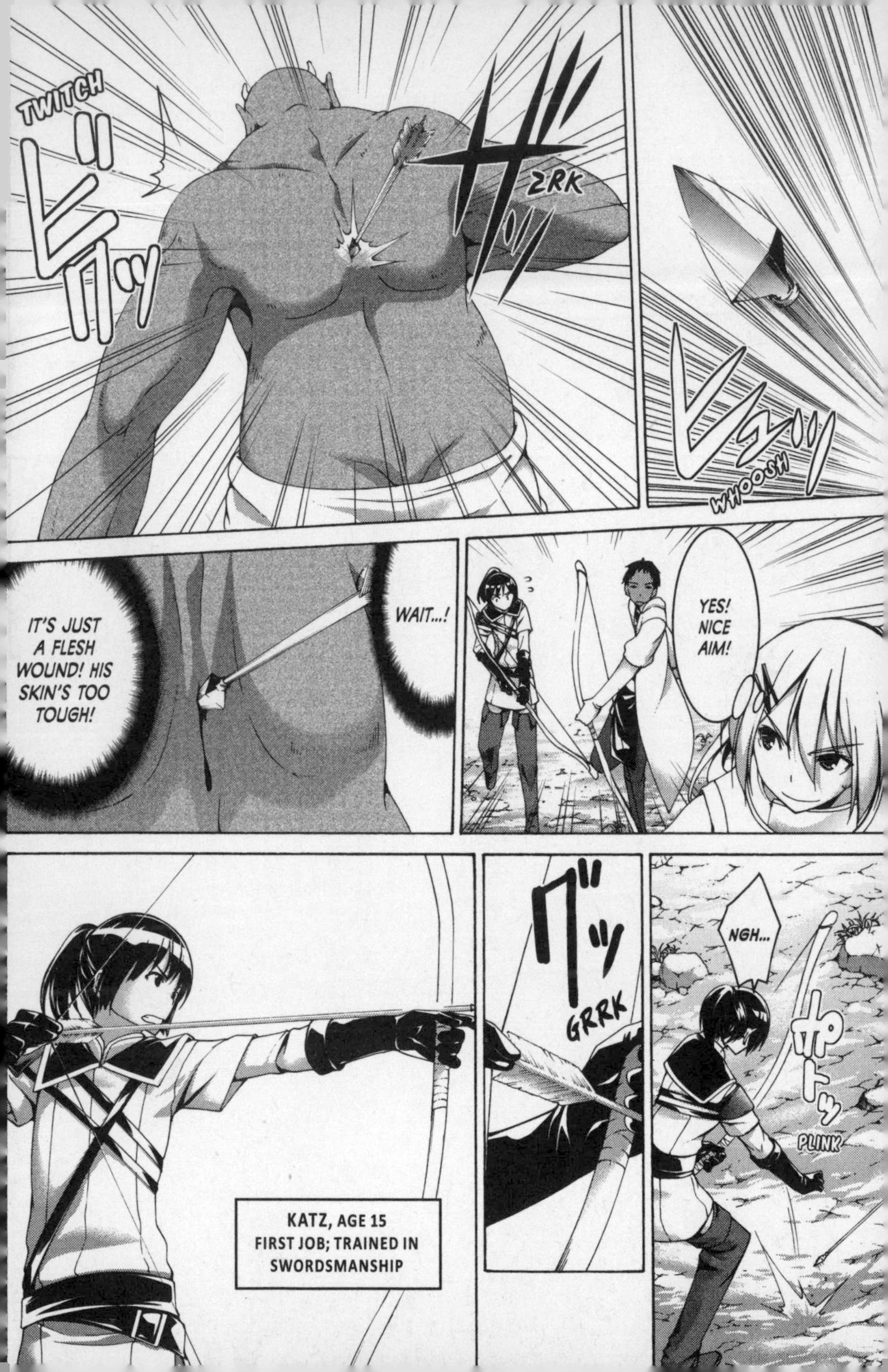
WHOOSH
ZRK
TWITCH
YES! NICE AIM!
WAIT...!
IT'S JUST A FLESH WOUND! HIS SKIN'S TOO TOUGH!
NGH...
PLINK
GRRK
KATZ, AGE 15
FIRST JOB; TRAINED IN SWORDSMANSHIP

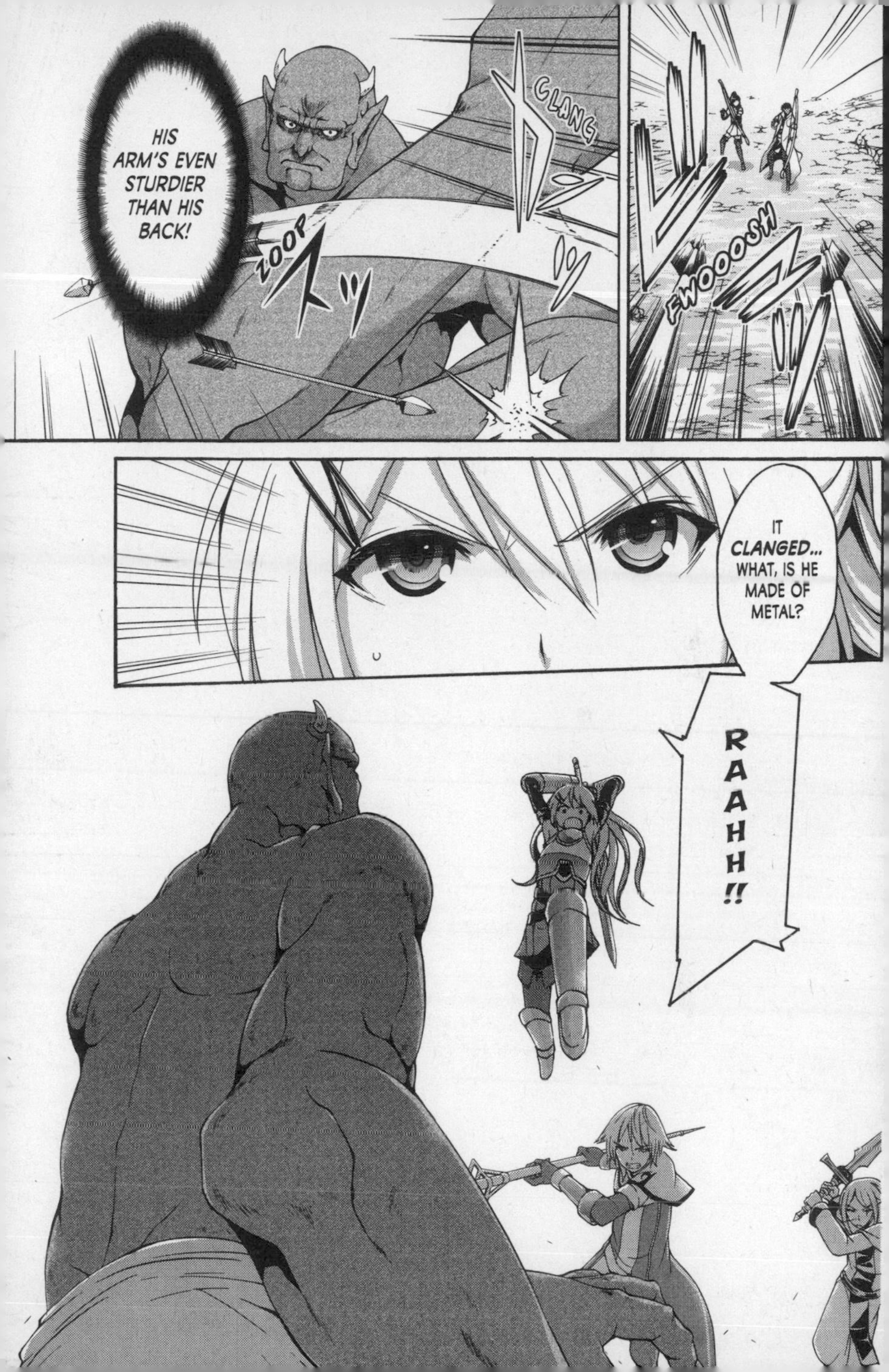
FWOOOSH
CLANG
ZOOP
HIS ARM'S EVEN STURDIER THAN HIS BACK!
IT CLANGED... WHAT, IS HE MADE OF METAL?
RAAHH!!

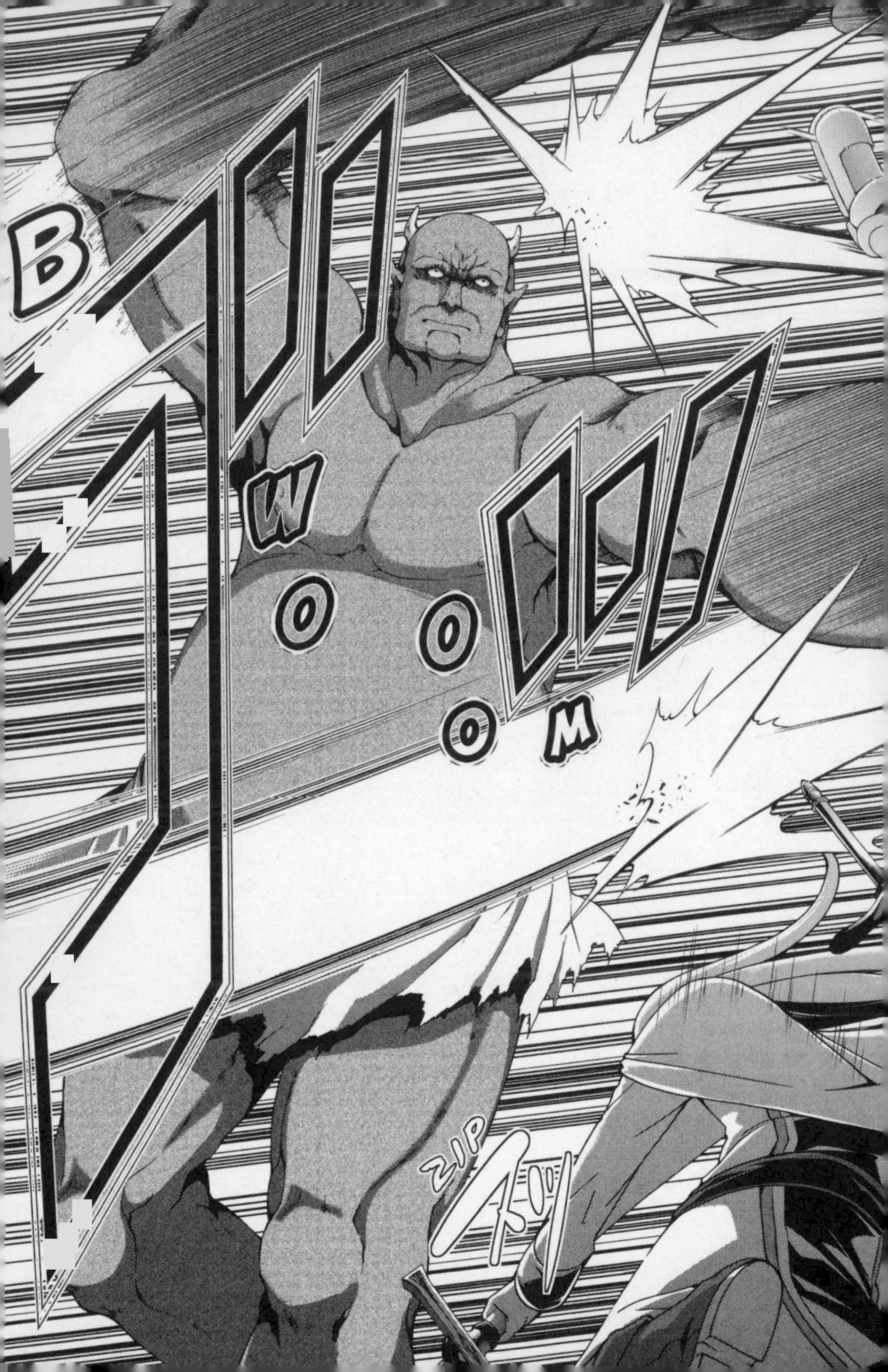
BWOOOOM
ZIP

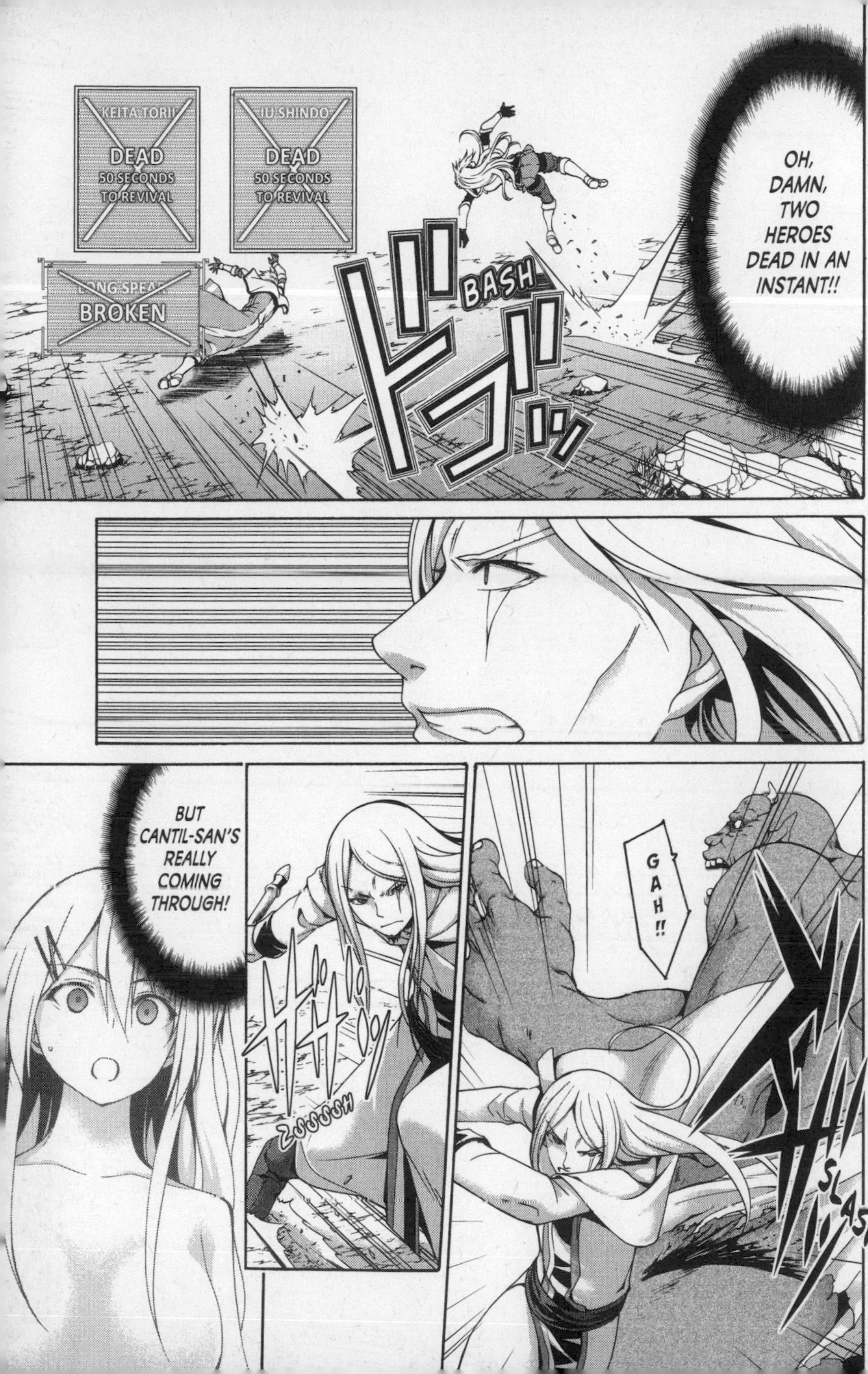
OH, DAMN, TWO HEROES DEAD IN AN INSTANT!!
BASH
IU SHINDO
DEAD
50 SECONDS TO REVIVAL
KEITA TORII
DEAD
50 SECONDS TO REVIVAL
BROKEN
GAH!!
SLASH
BUT CANTIL-SAN'S REALLY COMING THROUGH!

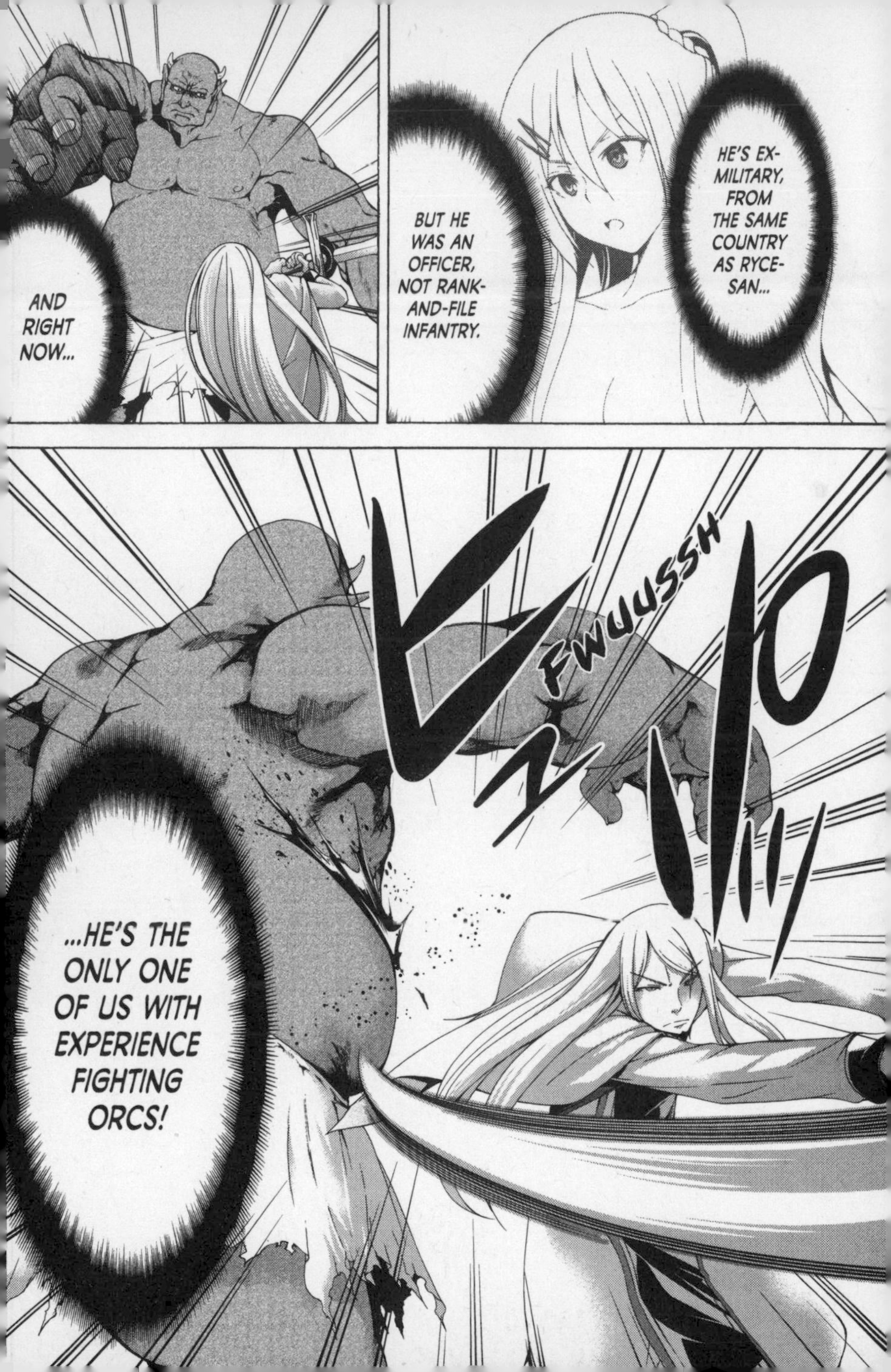
HE'S EX-MILITARY, FROM THE SAME COUNTRY AS RYCE-SAN...
BUT HE WAS AN OFFICER, NOT RANK-AND-FILE INFANTRY.
AND RIGHT NOW...
FWUUSSH
...HE'S THE ONLY ONE OF US WITH EXPERIENCE FIGHTING ORCS!

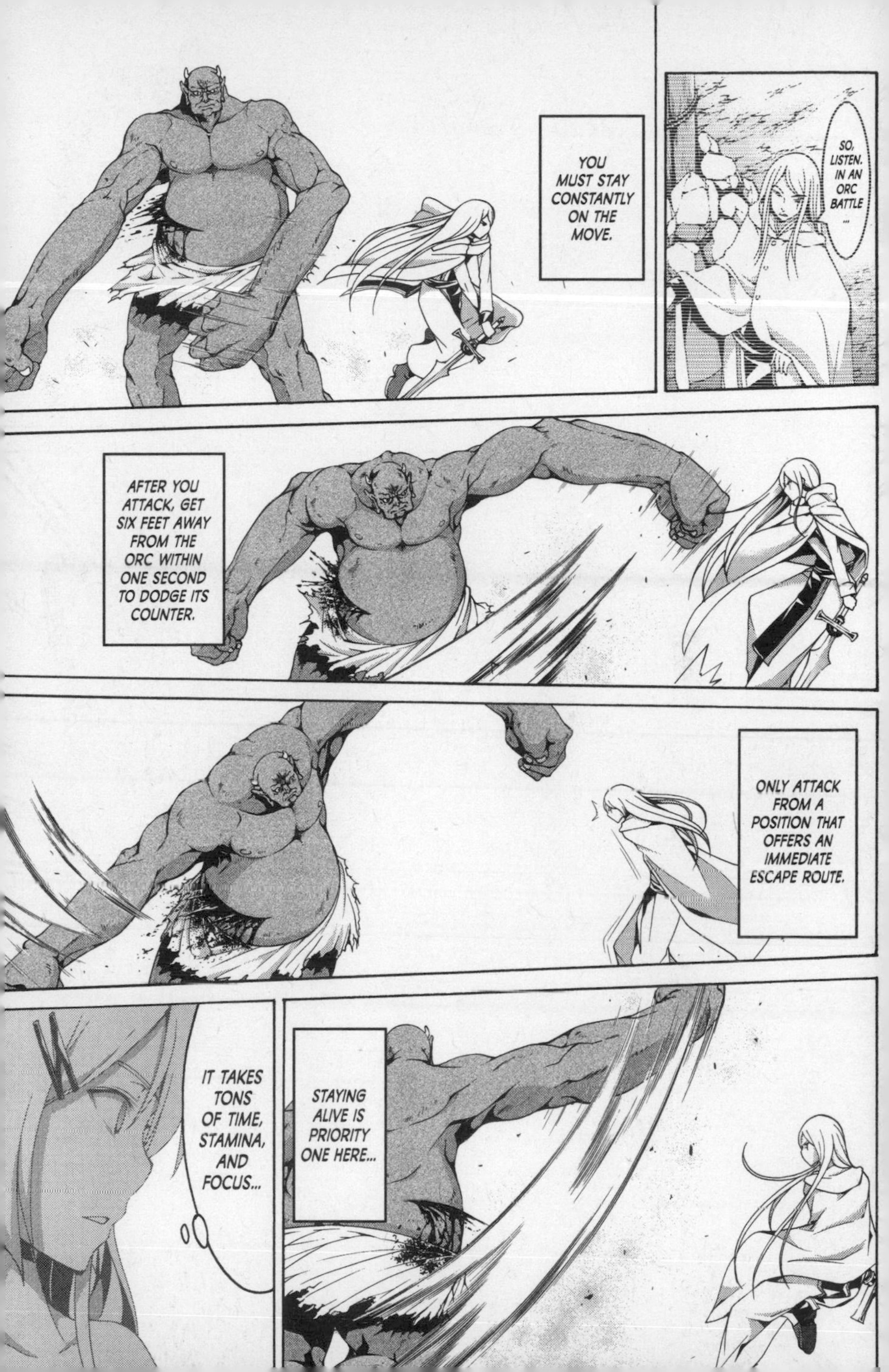
SO, LISTEN. IN AN ORC BATTLE ...
YOU MUST STAY CONSTANTLY ON THE MOVE.
AFTER YOU ATTACK, GET SIX FEET AWAY FROM THE ORC WITHIN ONE SECOND TO DODGE ITS COUNTER.
ONLY ATTACK FROM A POSITION THAT OFFERS AN IMMEDIATE ESCAPE ROUTE.
STAYING ALIVE IS PRIORITY ONE HERE...
IT TAKES TONS OF TIME, STAMINA, AND FOCUS...

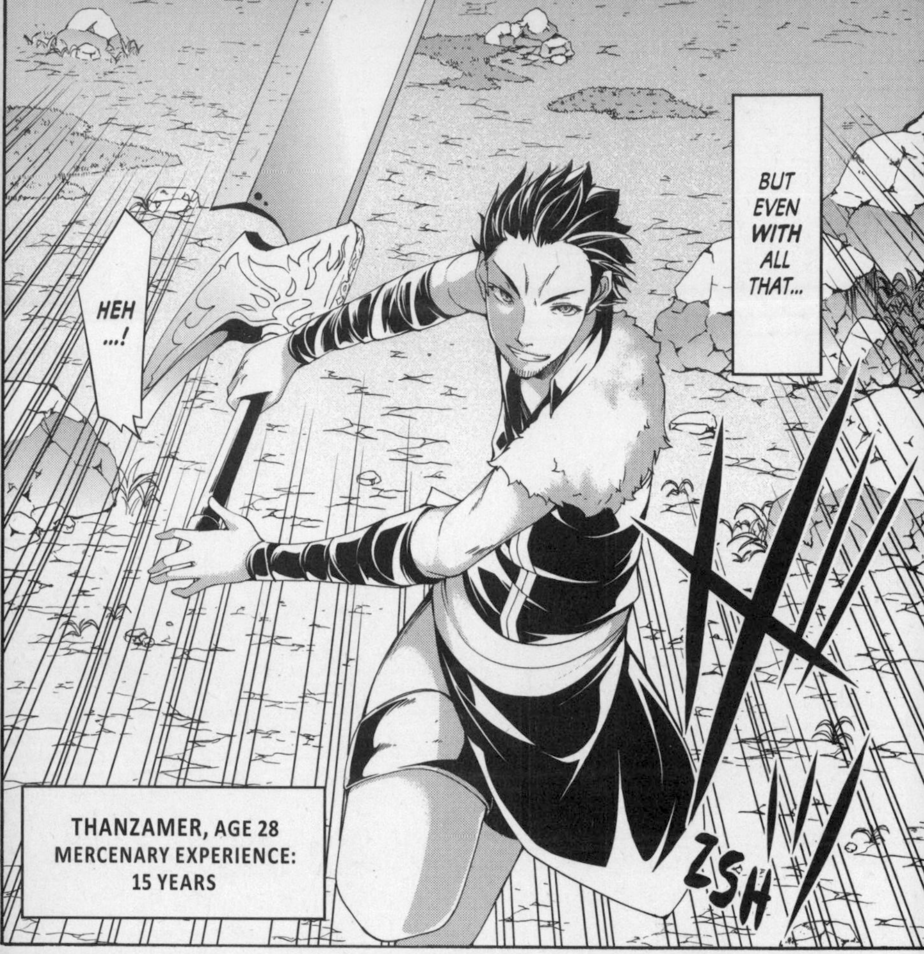
BUT EVEN WITH ALL THAT...
HEH ...!
THANZAMER, AGE 28
MERCENARY EXPERIENCE: 15 YEARS
ZSH

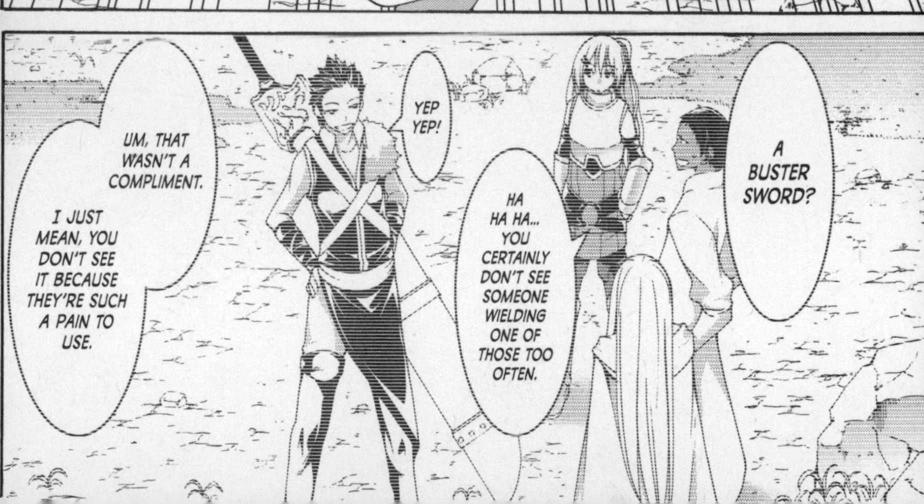
A BUSTER SWORD?
HA HA HA... YOU CERTAINLY DON'T SEE SOMEONE WIELDING ONE OF THOSE TOO OFTEN.
YEP YEP!
UM, THAT WASN'T A COMPLIMENT.
I JUST MEAN, YOU DON'T SEE IT BECAUSE THEY'RE SUCH A PAIN TO USE.

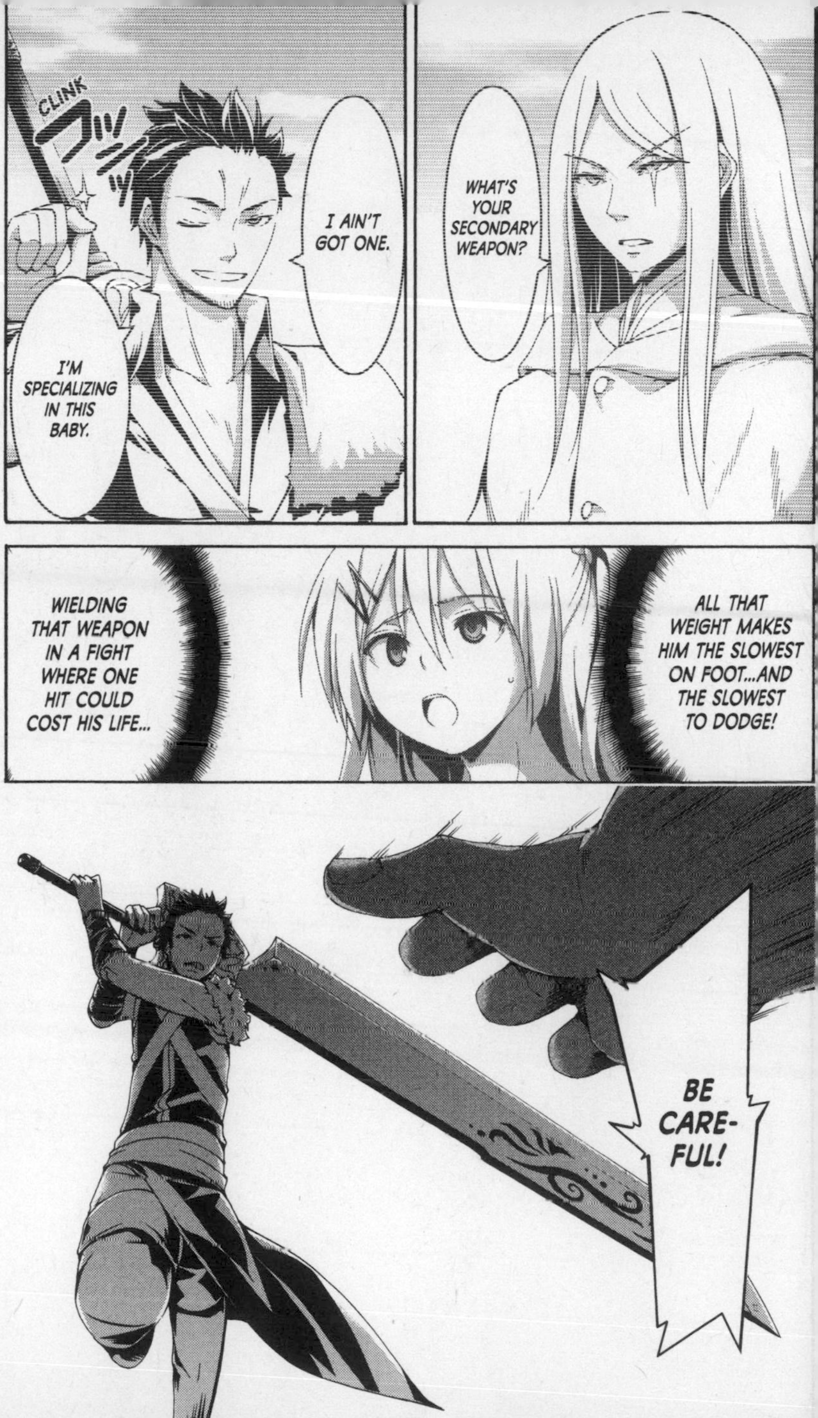
WHAT'S YOUR SECONDARY WEAPON?
CLINK
I AIN'T GOT ONE.
I'M SPECIALIZING IN THIS BABY.
ALL THAT WEIGHT MAKES HIM THE SLOWEST ON FOOT...AND THE SLOWEST TO DODGE!
WIELDING THAT WEAPON IN A FIGHT WHERE ONE HIT COULD COST HIS LIFE...
BE CARE-FUL!

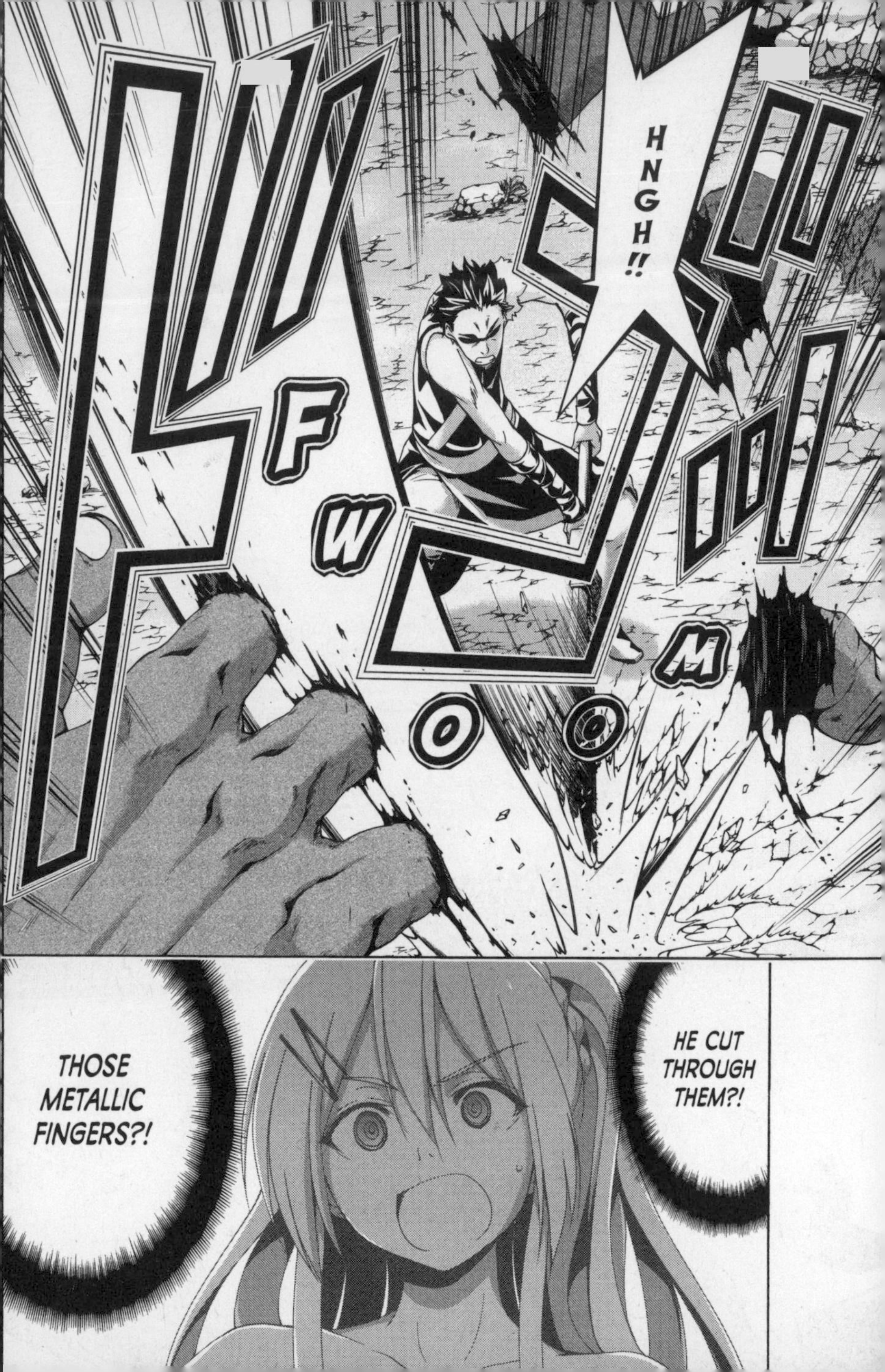
HNGH!!
FWOOM
HE CUT THROUGH THEM?!
THOSE METALLIC FINGERS?!

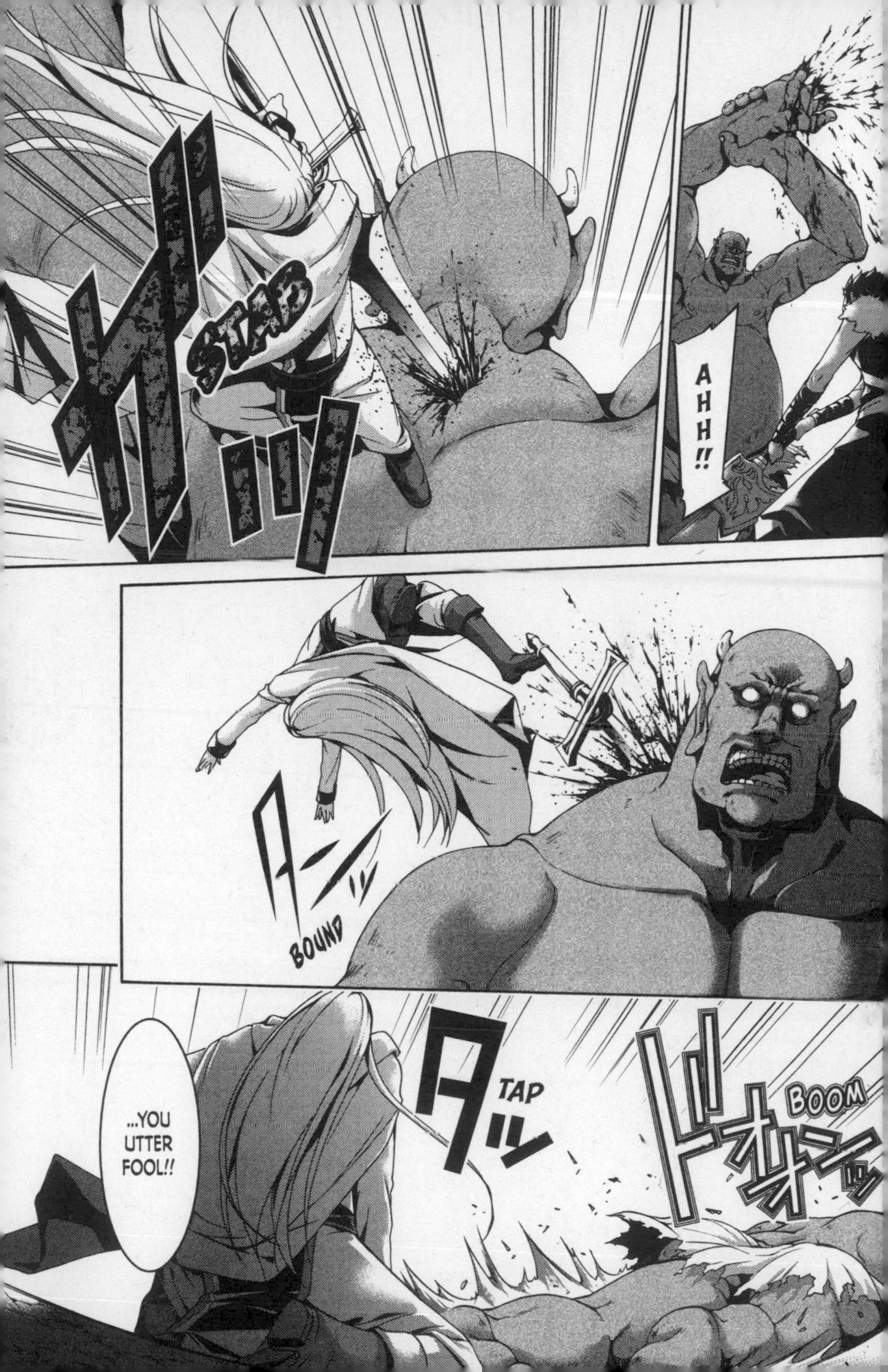
AHH!!
STAB
BOUND
BOOM
TAP
...YOU UTTER FOOL!!

AH...

IF THAT HADN'T GONE CLEAN THROUGH, YOU'D BE DEAD!

BUT IT *DID*, DIDN'T IT?

IU SHINDO

REVIVED

0 SECONDS

KEITA TORII

REVIVED

0 SECONDS

ZOOOP

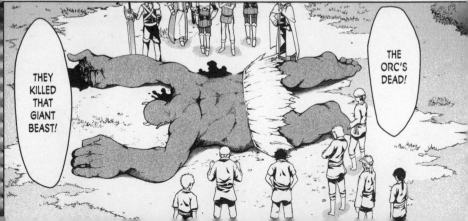

THEY KILLED THAT GIANT BEAST!

THE ORC'S DEAD!

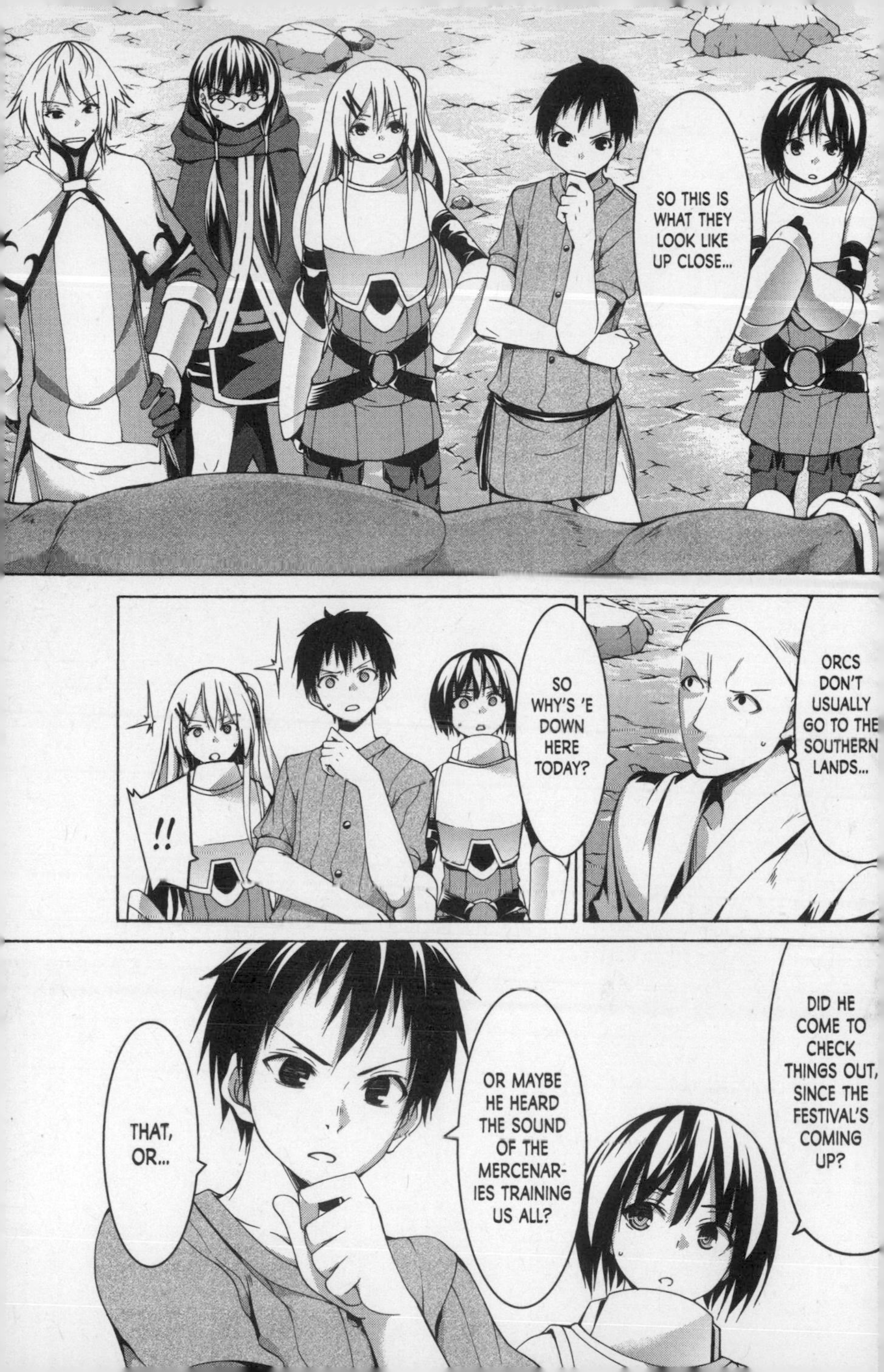
SO THIS IS WHAT THEY LOOK LIKE UP CLOSE...
ORCS DON'T USUALLY GO TO THE SOUTHERN LANDS...
SO WHY'S 'E DOWN HERE TODAY?
!!
DID HE COME TO CHECK THINGS OUT, SINCE THE FESTIVAL'S COMING UP?
OR MAYBE HE HEARD THE SOUND OF THE MERCENAR-IES TRAINING US ALL?
THAT, OR...

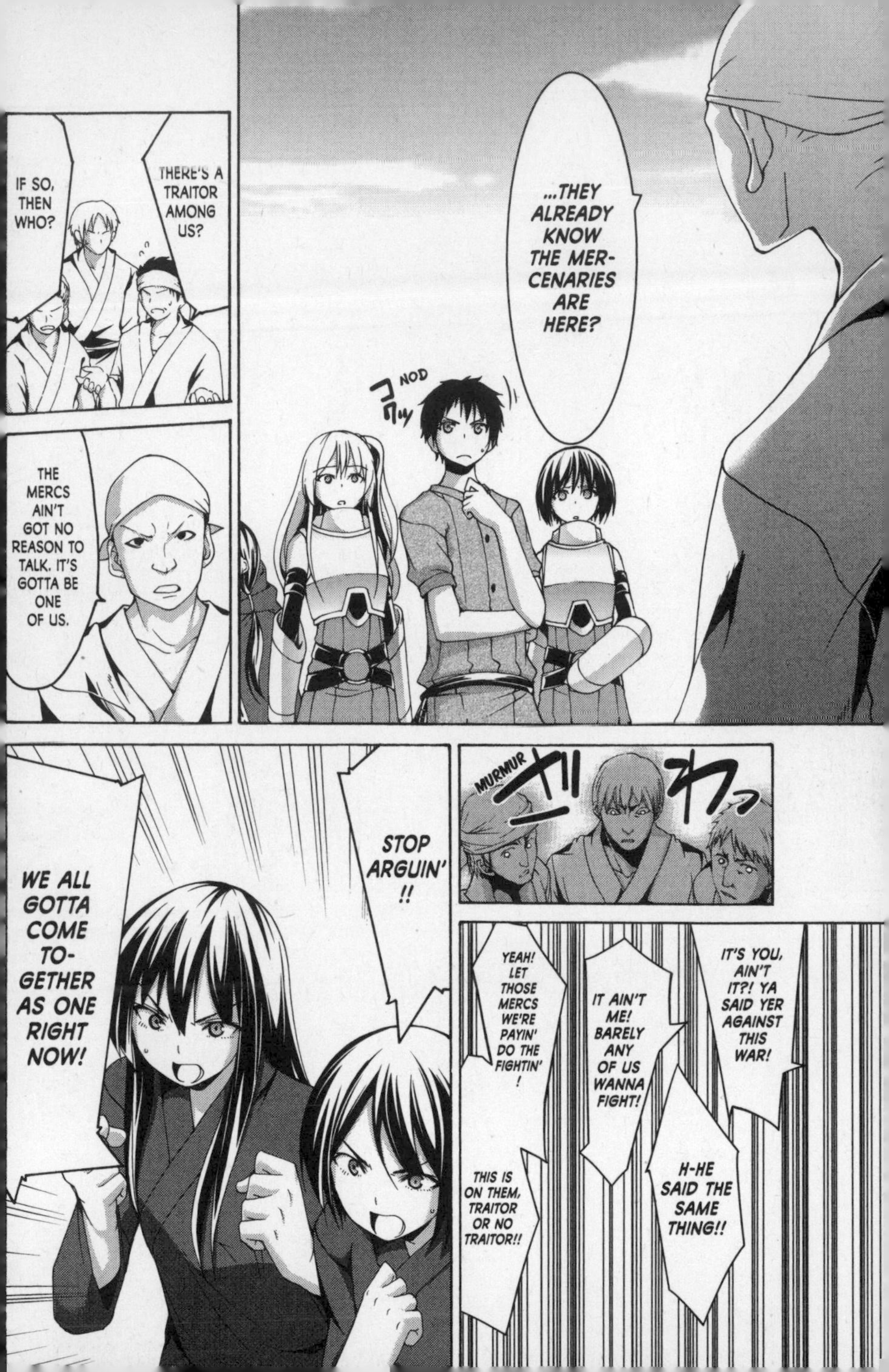
...THEY ALREADY KNOW THE MER-CENARIES ARE HERE?
NOD
THERE'S A TRAITOR AMONG US?
IF SO, THEN WHO?
THE MERCS AIN'T GOT NO REASON TO TALK. IT'S GOTTA BE ONE OF US.
MURMUR
IT'S YOU, AIN'T IT?! YA SAID YER AGAINST THIS WAR!
H-HE SAID THE SAME THING!!
IT AIN'T ME! BARELY ANY OF US WANNA FIGHT!
YEAH! LET THOSE MERCS WE'RE PAYIN' DO THE FIGHTIN'!
THIS IS ON THEM, TRAITOR OR NO TRAITOR!!
STOP ARGUIN'!!
WE ALL GOTTA COME TO-GETHER AS ONE RIGHT NOW!

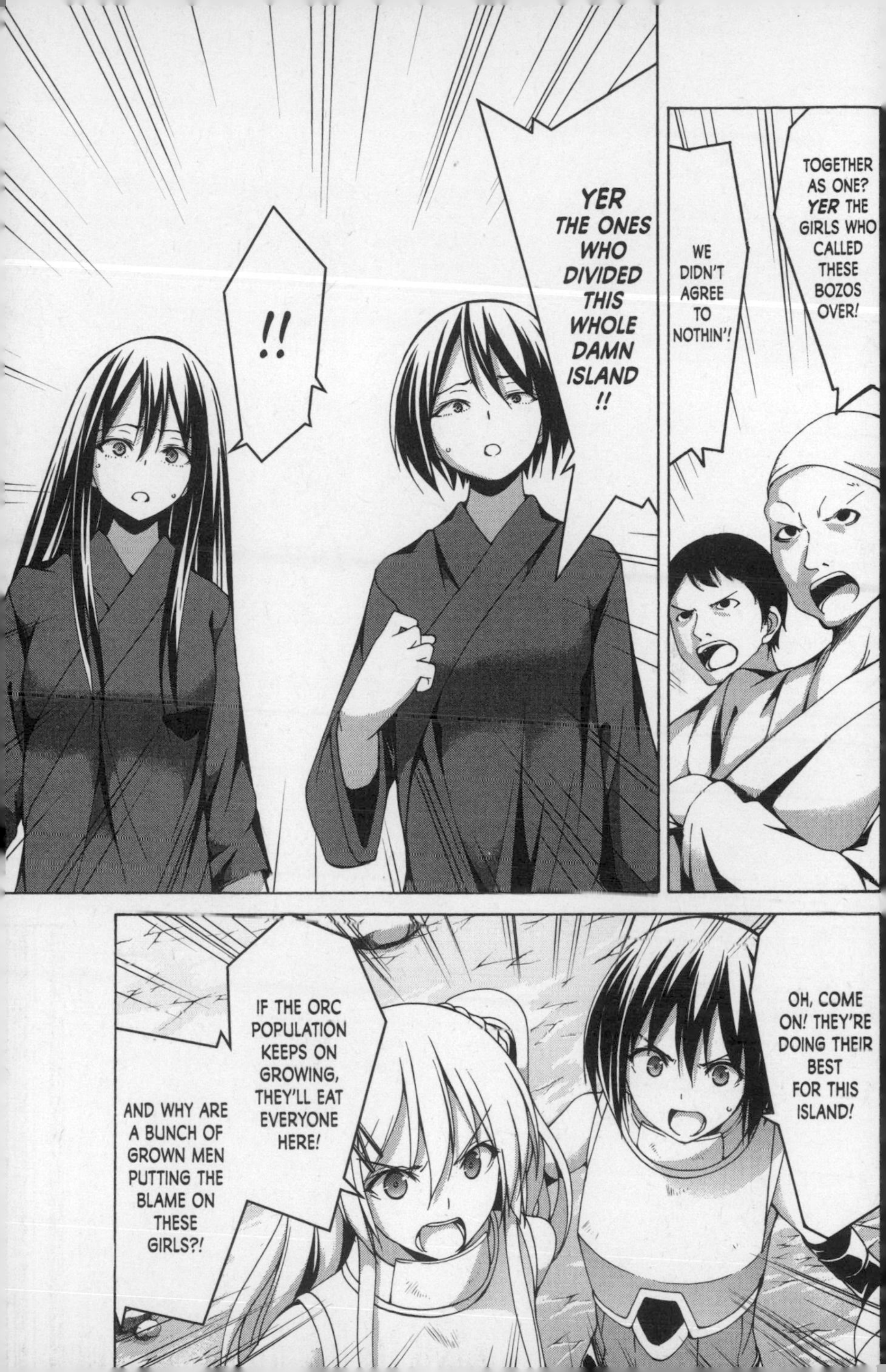
TOGETHER AS ONE? YER THE GIRLS WHO CALLED THESE BOZOS OVER!
WE DIDN'T AGREE TO NOTHIN'!
YER THE ONES WHO DIVIDED THIS WHOLE DAMN ISLAND !!
!!
OH, COME ON! THEY'RE DOING THEIR BEST FOR THIS ISLAND!
IF THE ORC POPULATION KEEPS ON GROWING, THEY'LL EAT EVERYONE HERE!
AND WHY ARE A BUNCH OF GROWN MEN PUTTING THE BLAME ON THESE GIRLS?!

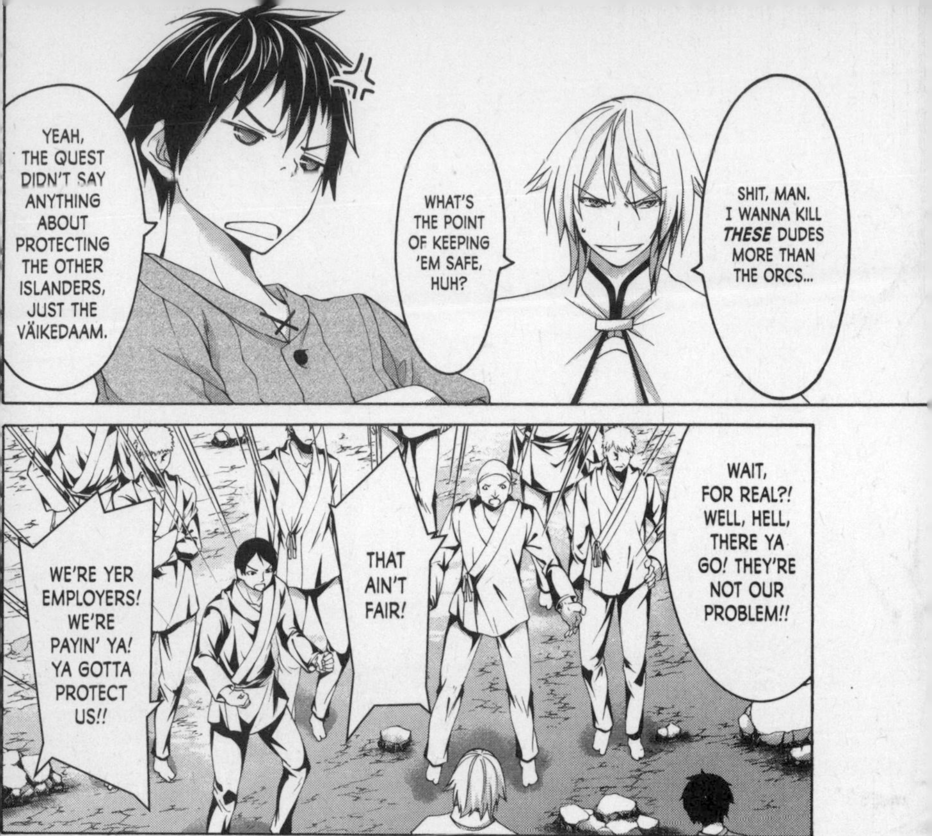
SHIT, MAN. I WANNA KILL *THESE* DUDES MORE THAN THE ORCS...
WHAT'S THE POINT OF KEEPING 'EM SAFE, HUH?
YEAH, THE QUEST DIDN'T SAY ANYTHING ABOUT PROTECTING THE OTHER ISLANDERS, JUST THE VÄIKEDAAM.
WAIT, FOR REAL?! WELL, HELL, THERE YA GO! THEY'RE NOT OUR PROBLEM!!
THAT AIN'T FAIR!
WE'RE YER EMPLOYERS! WE'RE PAYIN' YA! YA GOTTA PROTECT US!!

*The Players aren't actually planning to collect the reward, since money doesn't carry over to the next quest.

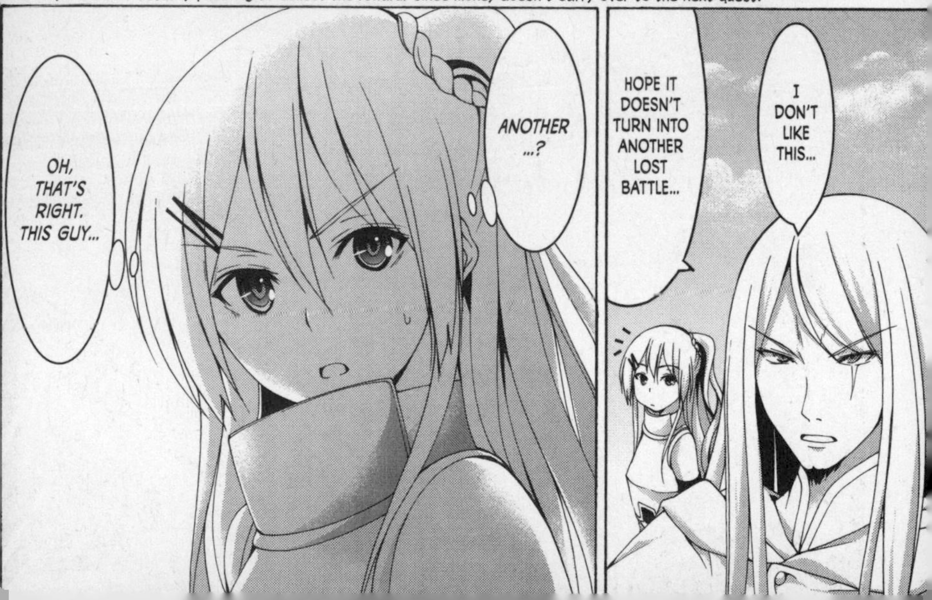
I DON'T LIKE THIS...
HOPE IT DOESN'T TURN INTO ANOTHER LOST BATTLE...
ANOTHER ...?
OH, THAT'S RIGHT. THIS GUY...

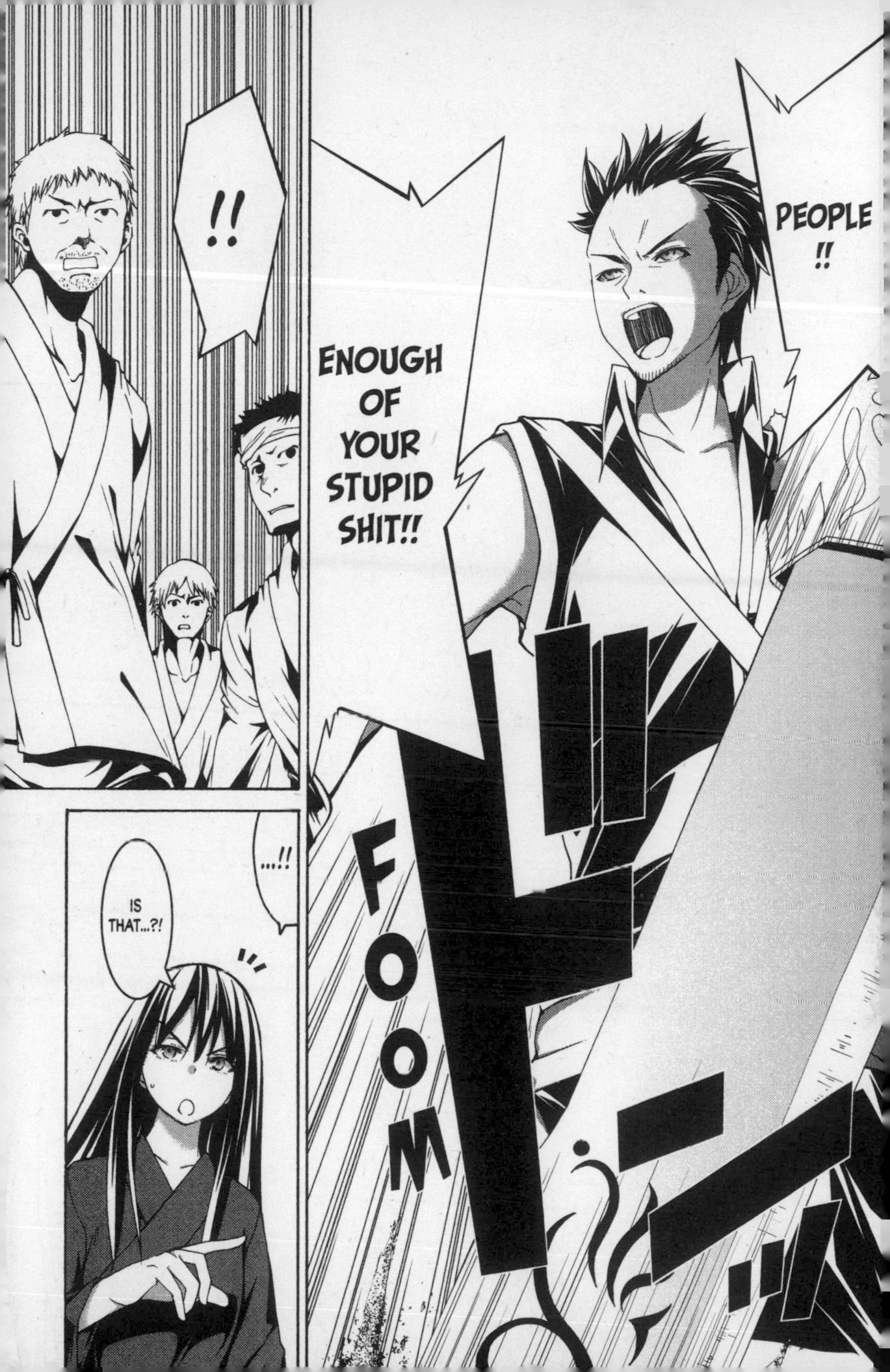
PEOPLE !!
ENOUGH OF YOUR STUPID SHIT!!
FOOM
!!
...!!
IS THAT...?!

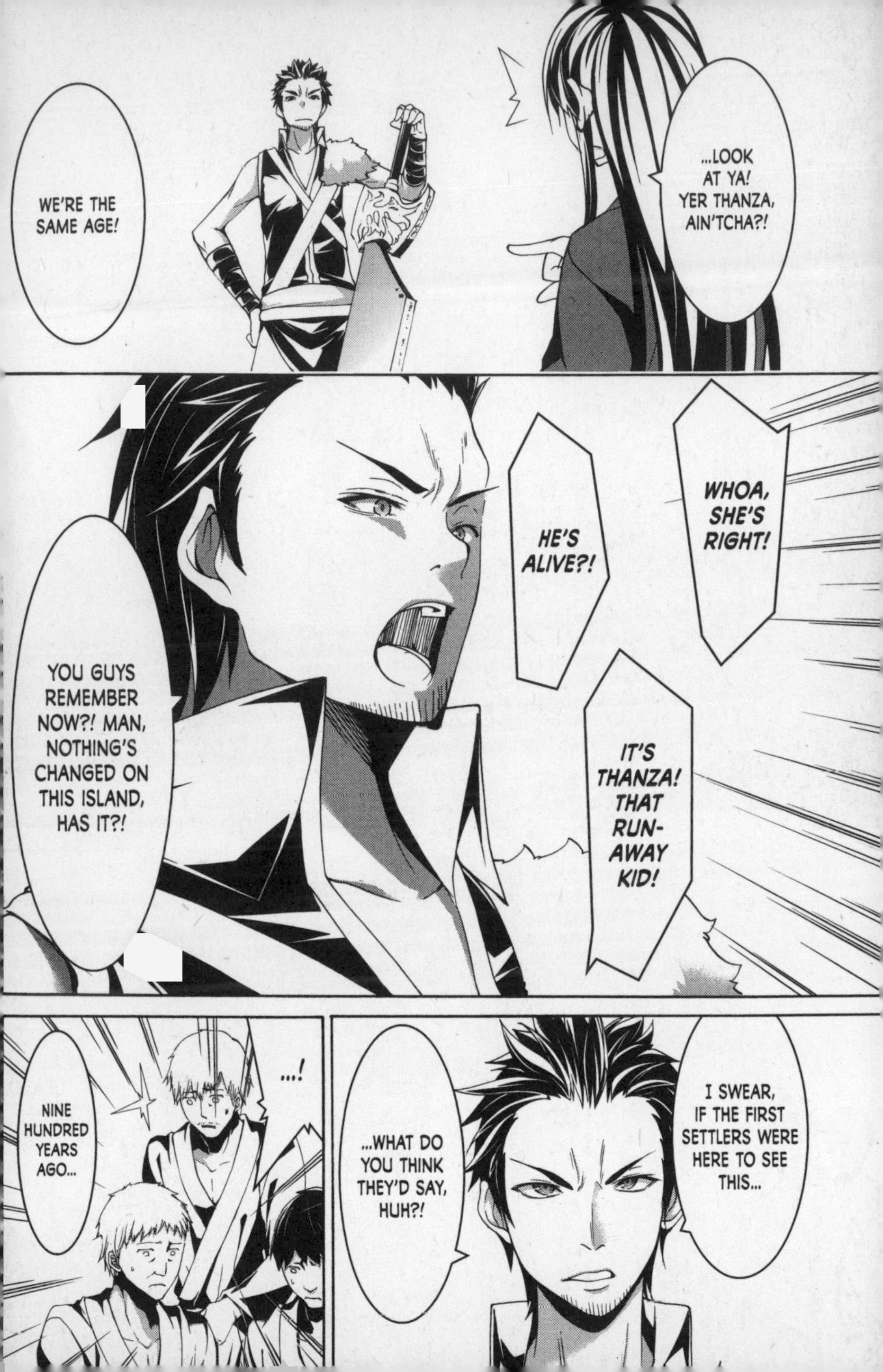
...LOOK AT YA! YER THANZA, AIN'TCHA?!
WE'RE THE SAME AGE!
WHOA, SHE'S RIGHT!
HE'S ALIVE?!
IT'S THANZA! THAT RUN-AWAY KID!
YOU GUYS REMEMBER NOW?! MAN, NOTHING'S CHANGED ON THIS ISLAND, HAS IT?!
I SWEAR, IF THE FIRST SETTLERS WERE HERE TO SEE THIS...
...WHAT DO YOU THINK THEY'D SAY, HUH?!
...!
NINE HUNDRED YEARS AGO...

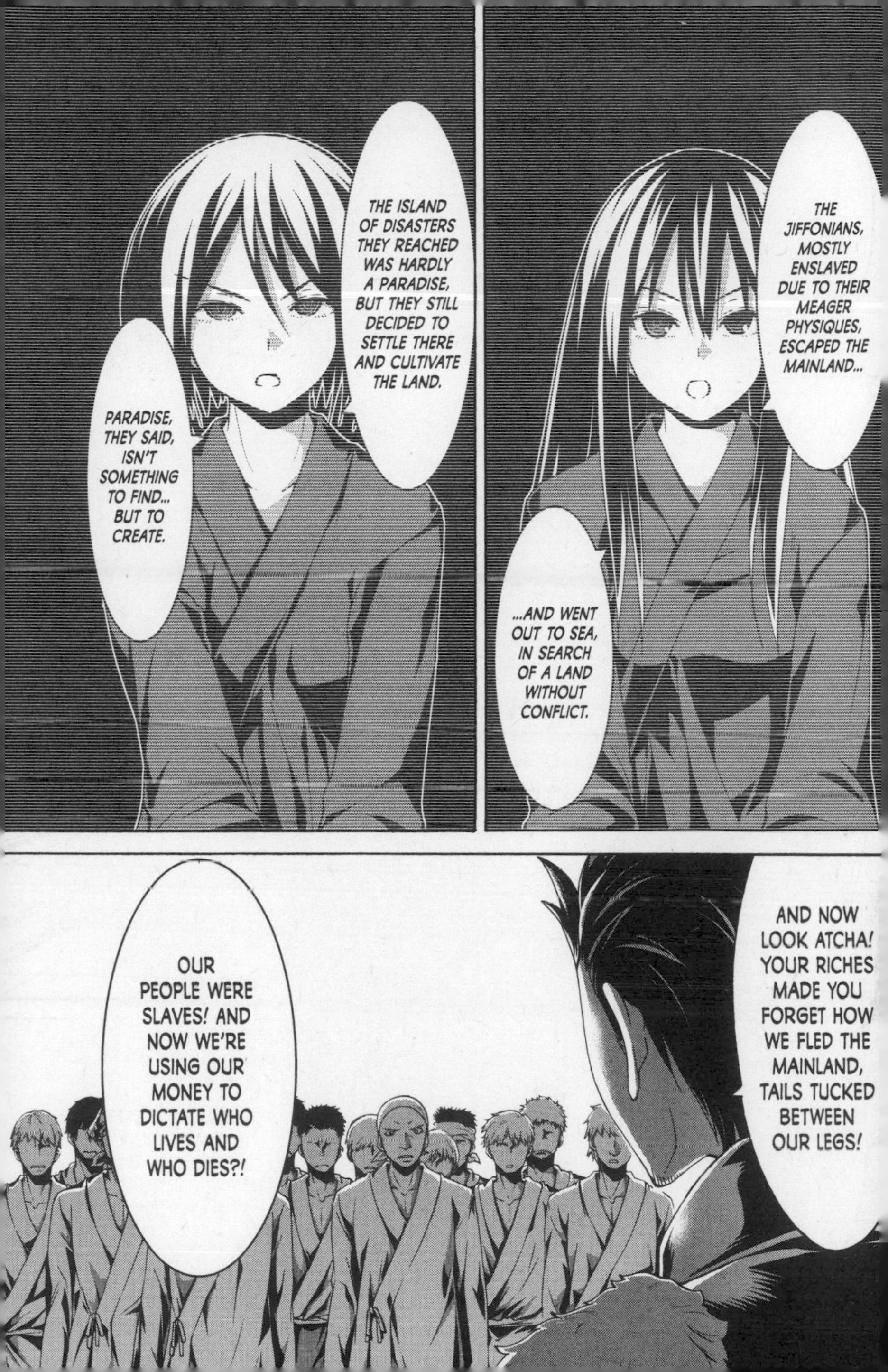
THE JIFFONIANS, MOSTLY ENSLAVED DUE TO THEIR MEAGER PHYSIQUES, ESCAPED THE MAINLAND...
...AND WENT OUT TO SEA, IN SEARCH OF A LAND WITHOUT CONFLICT.
THE ISLAND OF DISASTERS THEY REACHED WAS HARDLY A PARADISE, BUT THEY STILL DECIDED TO SETTLE THERE AND CULTIVATE THE LAND.
PARADISE, THEY SAID, ISN'T SOMETHING TO FIND... BUT TO CREATE.
AND NOW LOOK ATCHA! YOUR RICHES MADE YOU FORGET HOW WE FLED THE MAINLAND, TAILS TUCKED BETWEEN OUR LEGS!
OUR PEOPLE WERE SLAVES! AND NOW WE'RE USING OUR MONEY TO DICTATE WHO LIVES AND WHO DIES?!

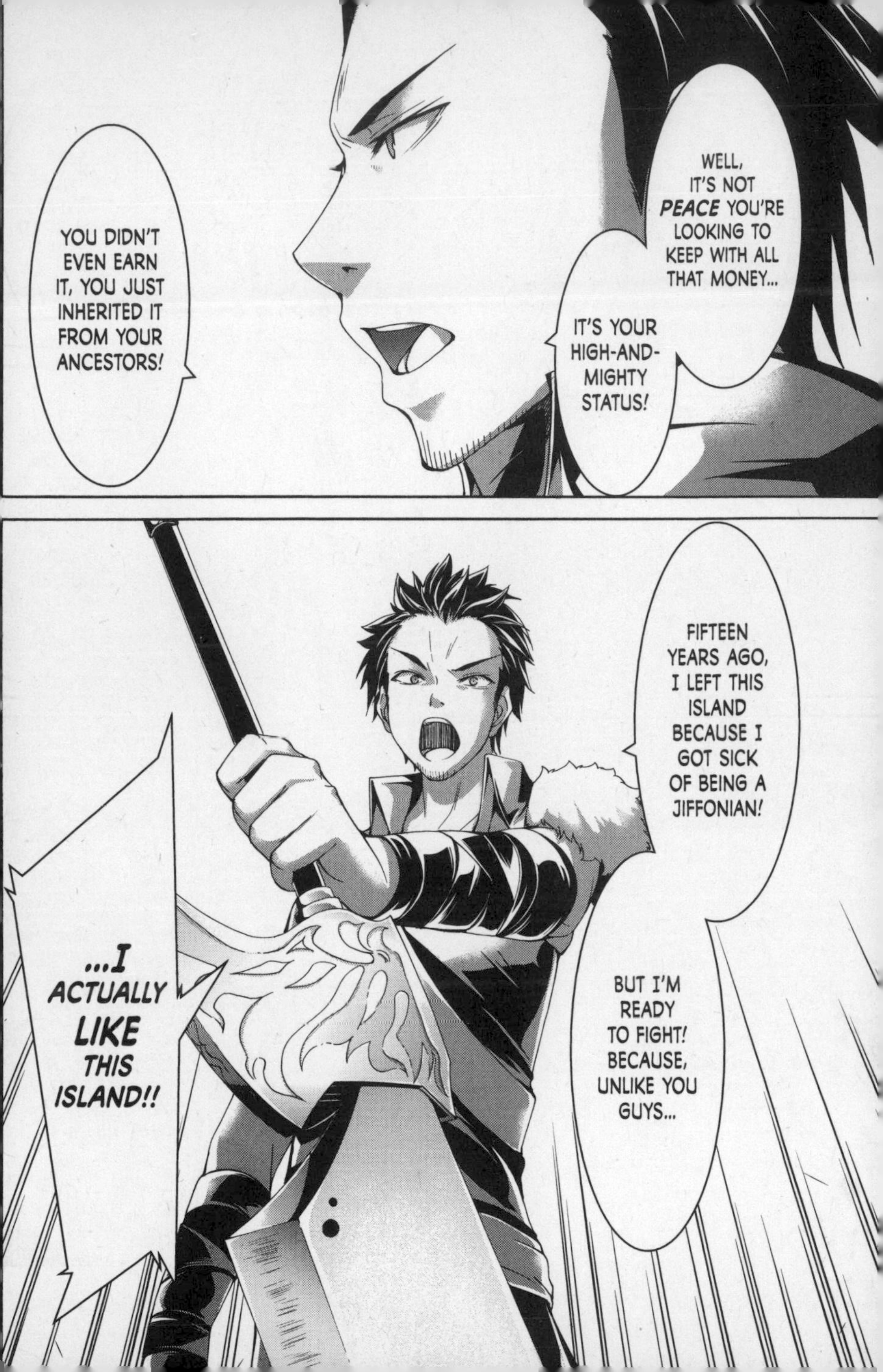
WELL, IT'S NOT *PEACE* YOU'RE LOOKING TO KEEP WITH ALL THAT MONEY...
IT'S YOUR HIGH-AND-MIGHTY STATUS!
YOU DIDN'T EVEN EARN IT, YOU JUST INHERITED IT FROM YOUR ANCESTORS!
FIFTEEN YEARS AGO, I LEFT THIS ISLAND BECAUSE I GOT SICK OF BEING A JIFFONIAN!
BUT I'M READY TO FIGHT! BECAUSE, UNLIKE YOU GUYS...
...I ACTUALLY **LIKE** THIS ISLAND!!

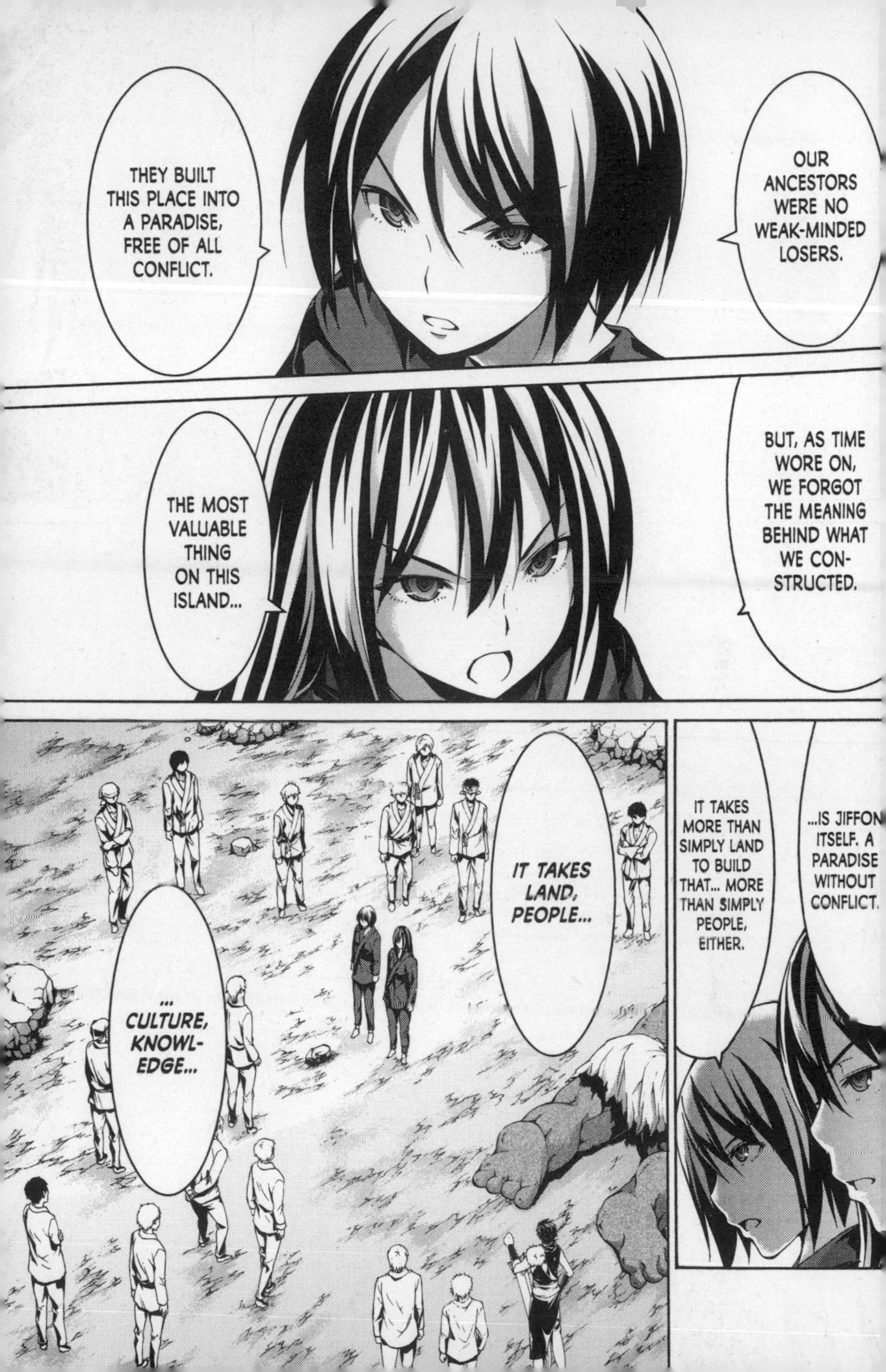
OUR ANCESTORS WERE NO WEAK-MINDED LOSERS.
THEY BUILT THIS PLACE INTO A PARADISE, FREE OF ALL CONFLICT.
BUT, AS TIME WORE ON, WE FORGOT THE MEANING BEHIND WHAT WE CONSTRUCTED.
THE MOST VALUABLE THING ON THIS ISLAND...
...IS JIFFON ITSELF. A PARADISE WITHOUT CONFLICT.
IT TAKES MORE THAN SIMPLY LAND TO BUILD THAT... MORE THAN SIMPLY PEOPLE, EITHER.
IT TAKES LAND, PEOPLE...
...CULTURE, KNOWLEDGE...

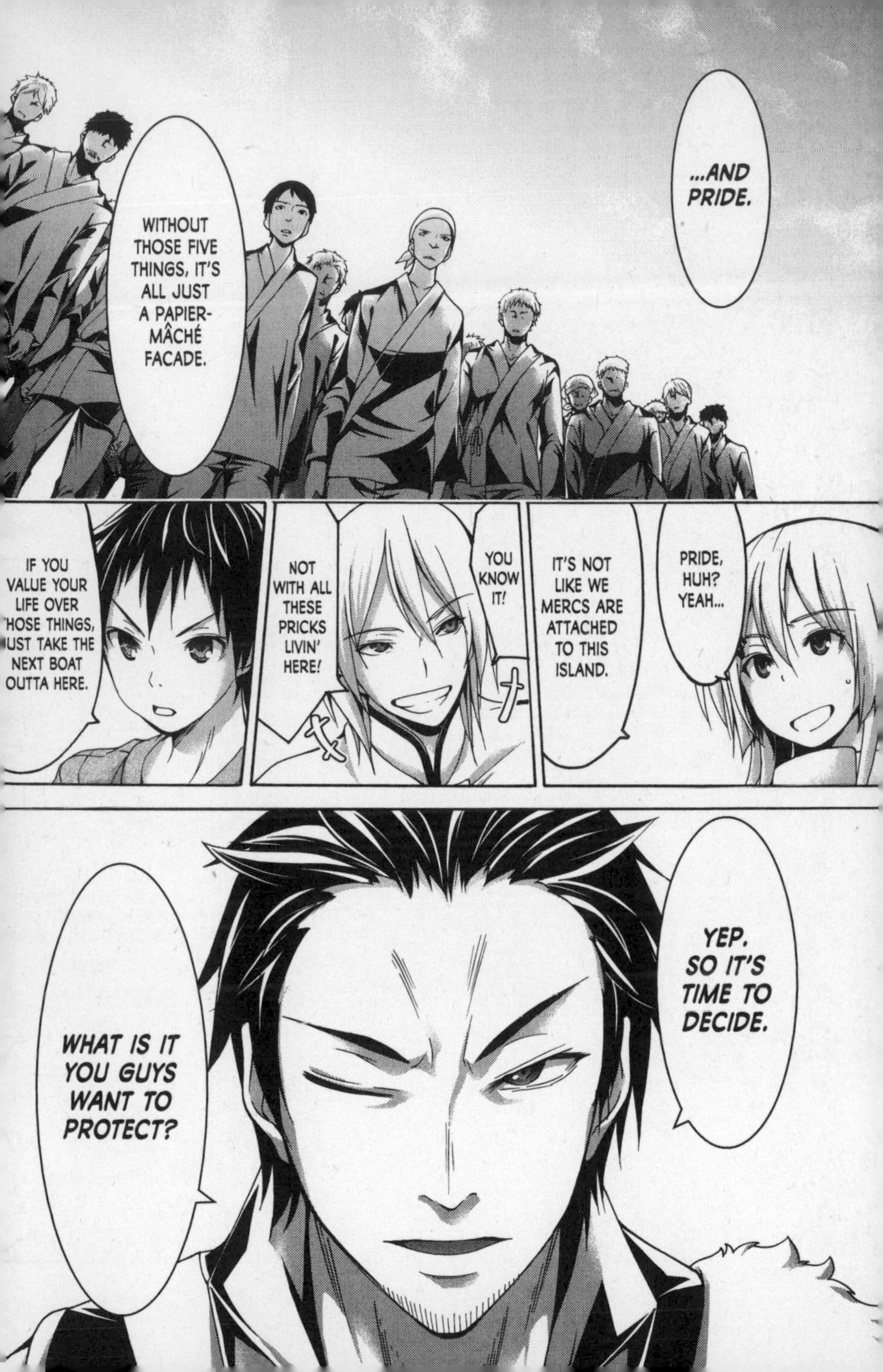
...AND PRIDE.
WITHOUT THOSE FIVE THINGS, IT'S ALL JUST A PAPIER-MÂCHÉ FACADE.
PRIDE, HUH? YEAH...
IT'S NOT LIKE WE MERCS ARE ATTACHED TO THIS ISLAND.
YOU KNOW IT!
NOT WITH ALL THESE PRICKS LIVIN' HERE!
IF YOU VALUE YOUR LIFE OVER THOSE THINGS, JUST TAKE THE NEXT BOAT OUTTA HERE.
YEP. SO IT'S TIME TO DECIDE.
WHAT IS IT YOU GUYS WANT TO PROTECT?

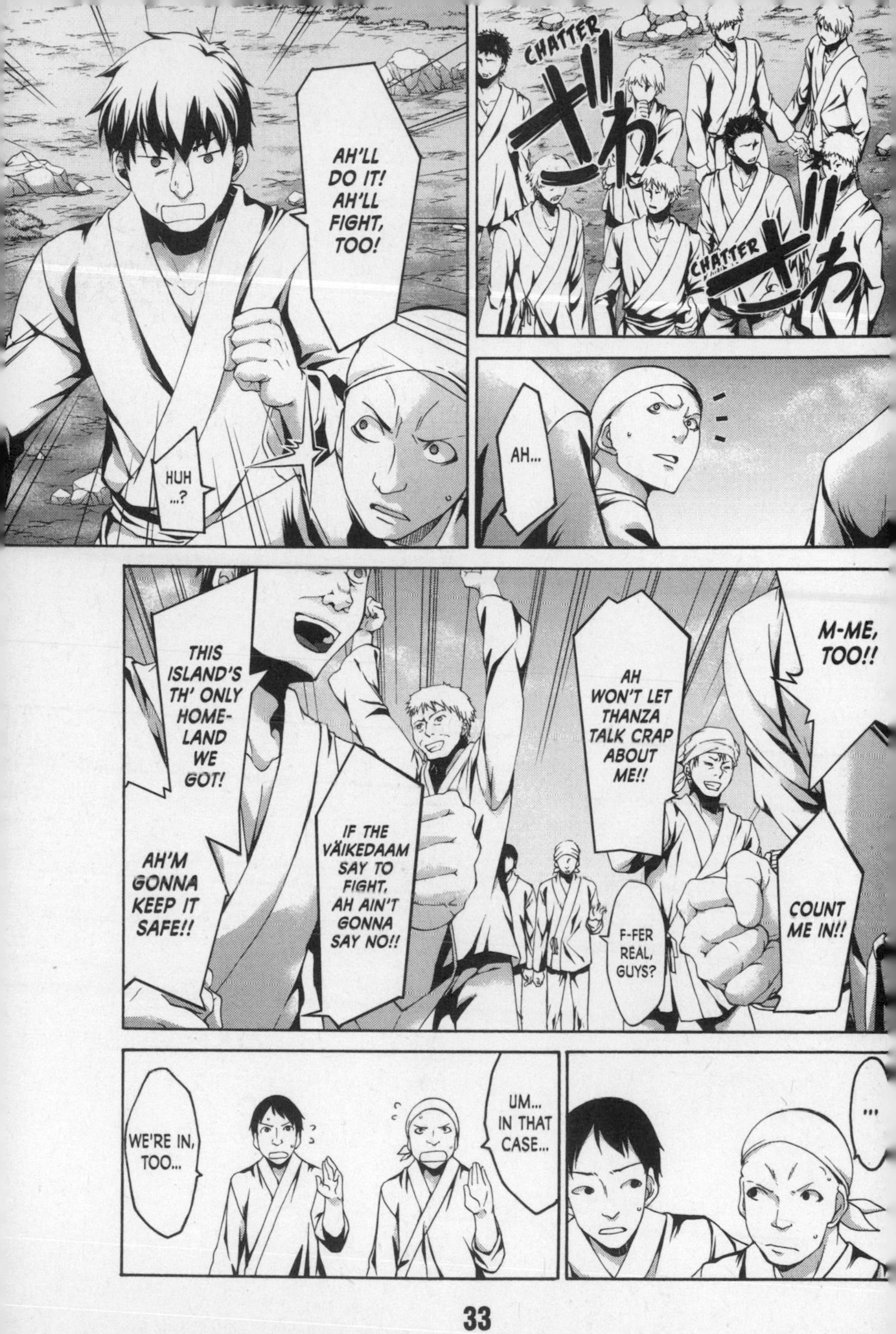
CHATTER
ざわ
CHATTER
ざわ
AH...
AH'LL DO IT! AH'LL FIGHT, TOO!
HUH ...?
M-ME, TOO!!
AH WON'T LET THANZA TALK CRAP ABOUT ME!!
COUNT ME IN!!
F-FER REAL, GUYS?
IF THE VÄIKEDAAM SAY TO FIGHT, AH AIN'T GONNA SAY NO!!
THIS ISLAND'S TH' ONLY HOME-LAND WE GOT!
AH'M GONNA KEEP IT SAFE!!
...
UM... IN THAT CASE...
WE'RE IN, TOO...

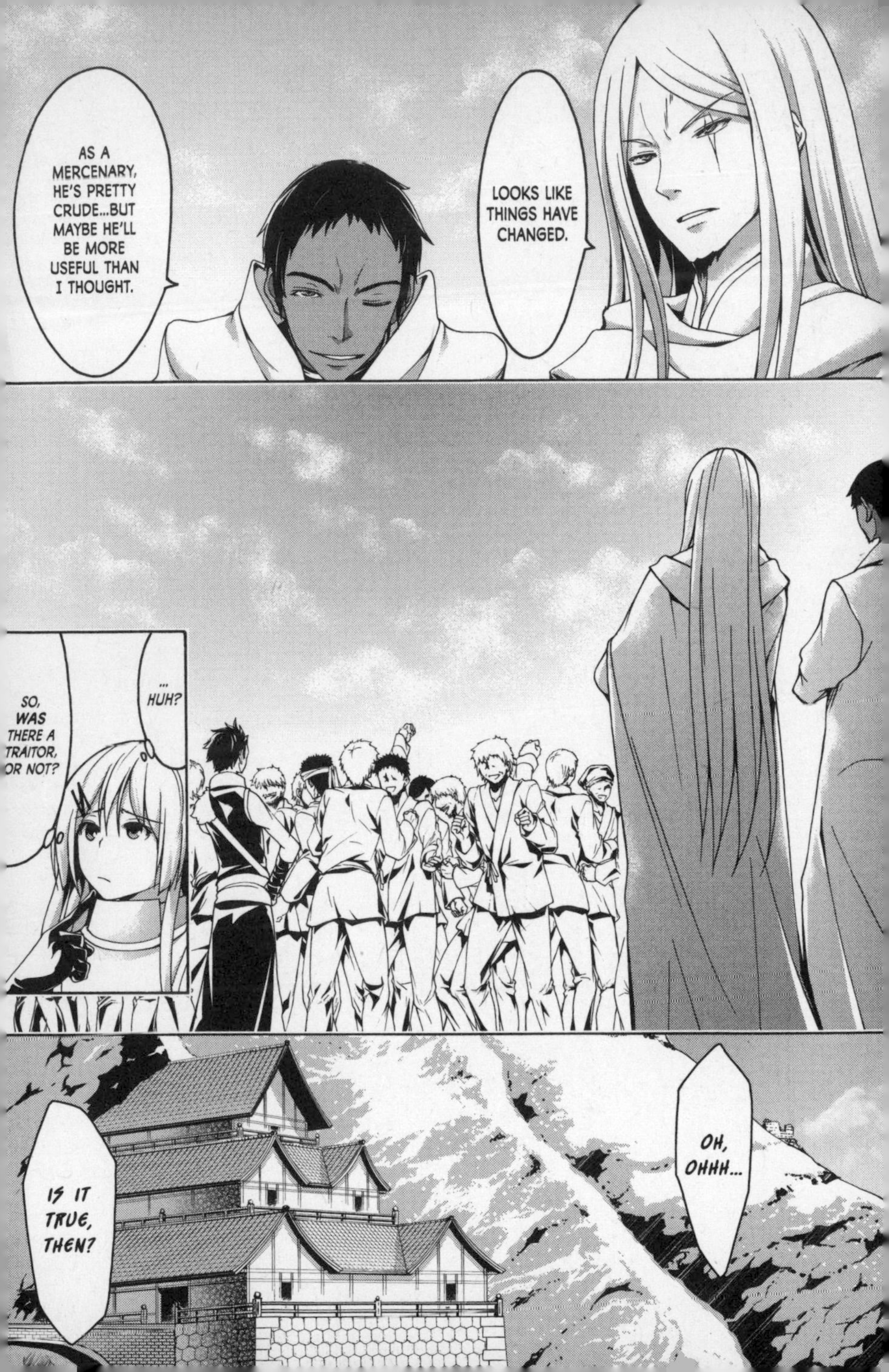
LOOKS LIKE THINGS HAVE CHANGED.
AS A MERCENARY, HE'S PRETTY CRUDE...BUT MAYBE HE'LL BE MORE USEFUL THAN I THOUGHT.
...HUH?
SO, WAS THERE A TRAITOR, OR NOT?
OH, OHHH...
IS IT TRUE, THEN?

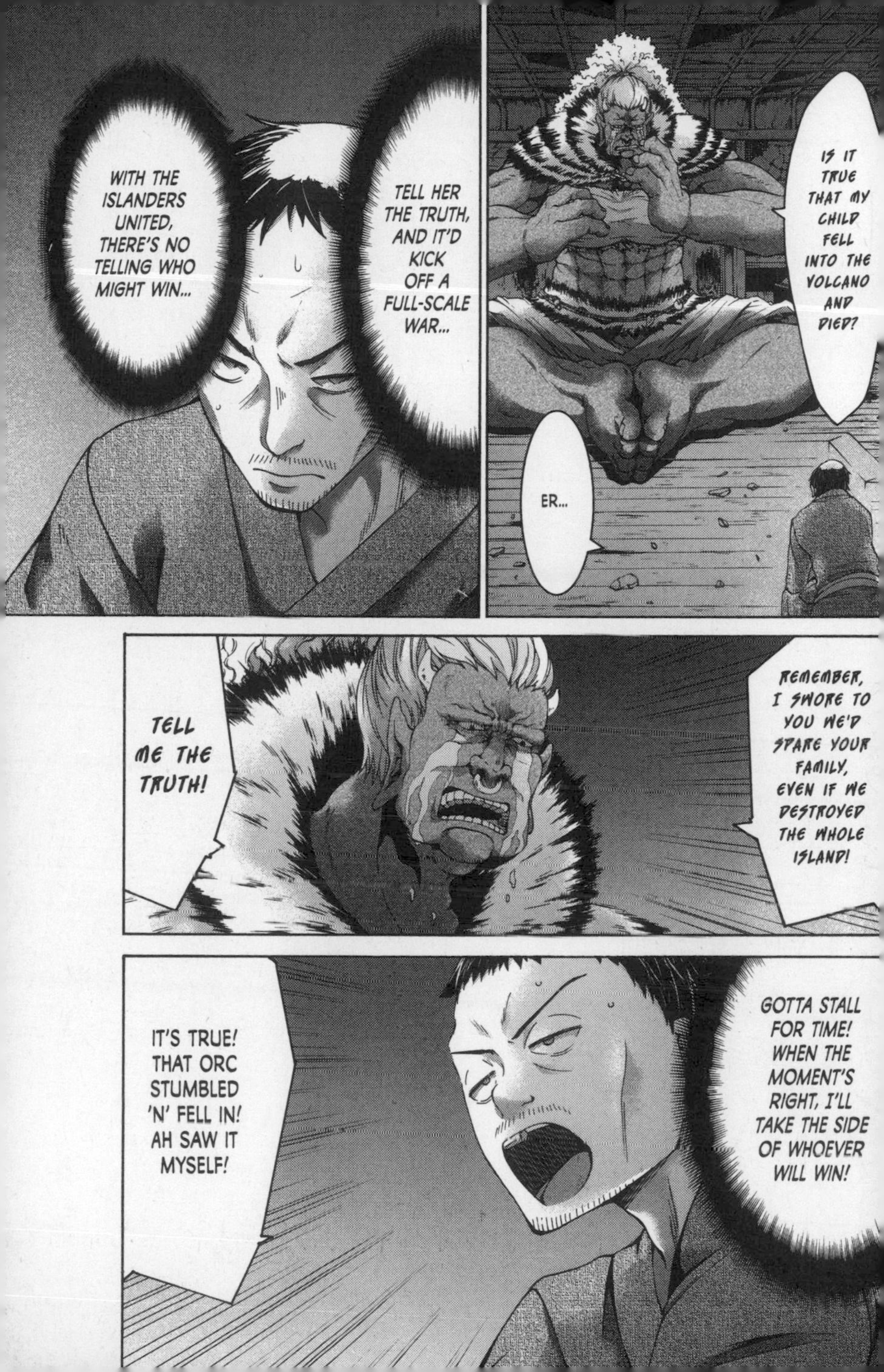
IS IT TRUE THAT MY CHILD FELL INTO THE VOLCANO AND DIED?
ER...
TELL HER THE TRUTH, AND IT'D KICK OFF A FULL-SCALE WAR...
WITH THE ISLANDERS UNITED, THERE'S NO TELLING WHO MIGHT WIN...
REMEMBER, I SWORE TO YOU WE'D SPARE YOUR FAMILY, EVEN IF WE DESTROYED THE WHOLE ISLAND!
TELL ME THE TRUTH!
GOTTA STALL FOR TIME! WHEN THE MOMENT'S RIGHT, I'LL TAKE THE SIDE OF WHOEVER WILL WIN!
IT'S TRUE! THAT ORC STUMBLED 'N' FELL IN! AH SAW IT MYSELF!

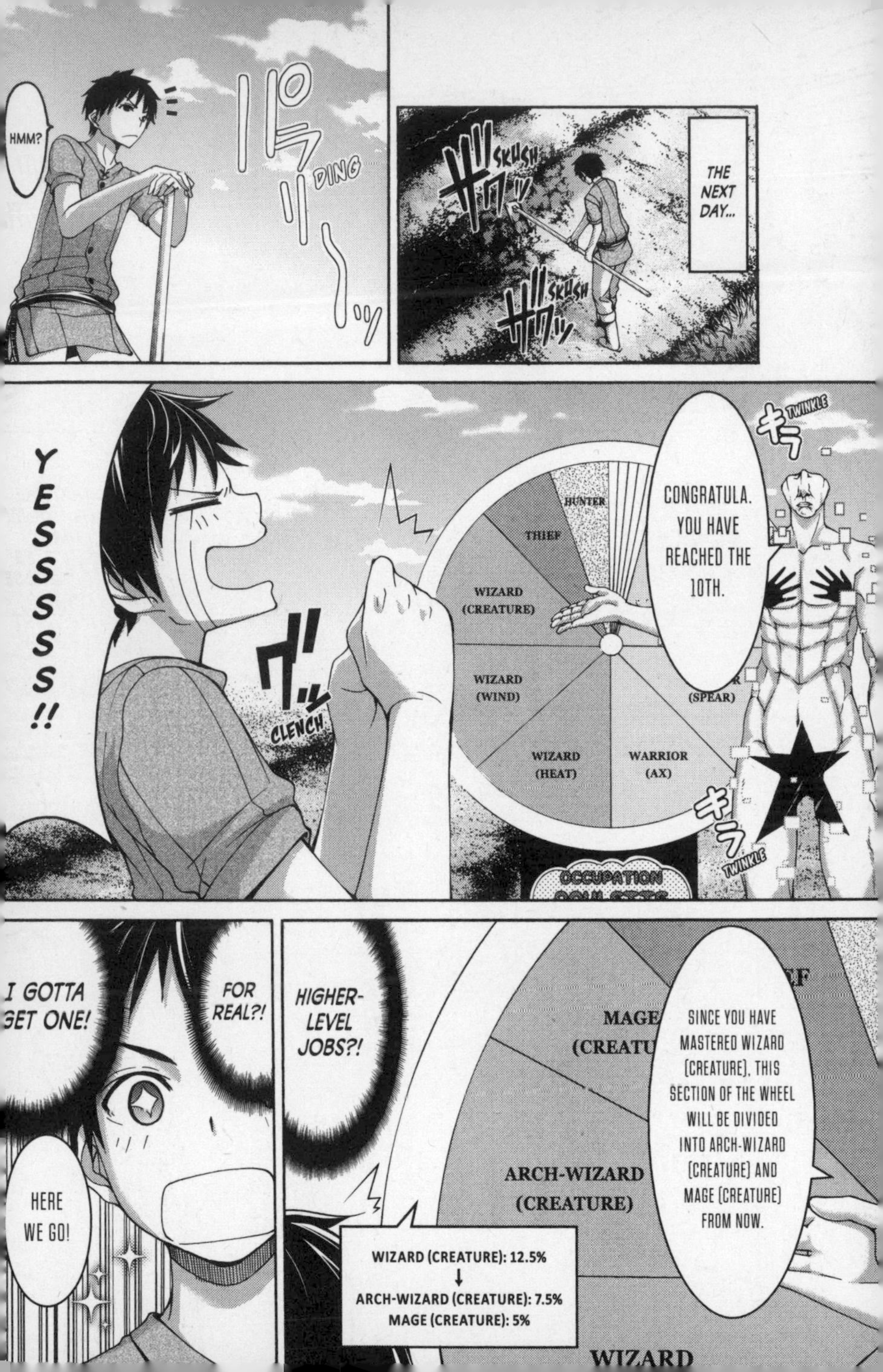
THE NEXT DAY...
SKUSH
SKUSH
HMM?
DING
TWINKLE
CONGRATULA. YOU HAVE REACHED THE 10TH.
HUNTER
THIEF
WIZARD (CREATURE)
WIZARD (WIND)
WIZARD (HEAT)
WARRIOR (AX)
(SPEAR)
TWINKLE
CLENCH
YESSSSSS!!
OCCUPATION
SINCE YOU HAVE MASTERED WIZARD (CREATURE), THIS SECTION OF THE WHEEL WILL BE DIVIDED INTO ARCH-WIZARD (CREATURE) AND MAGE (CREATURE) FROM NOW.
MAGE
(CREATU
ARCH-WIZARD (CREATURE)
WIZARD
WIZARD (CREATURE): 12.5%
↓
ARCH-WIZARD (CREATURE): 7.5%
MAGE (CREATURE): 5%
HIGHER-LEVEL JOBS?!
FOR REAL?!
I GOTTA GET ONE!
HERE WE GO!

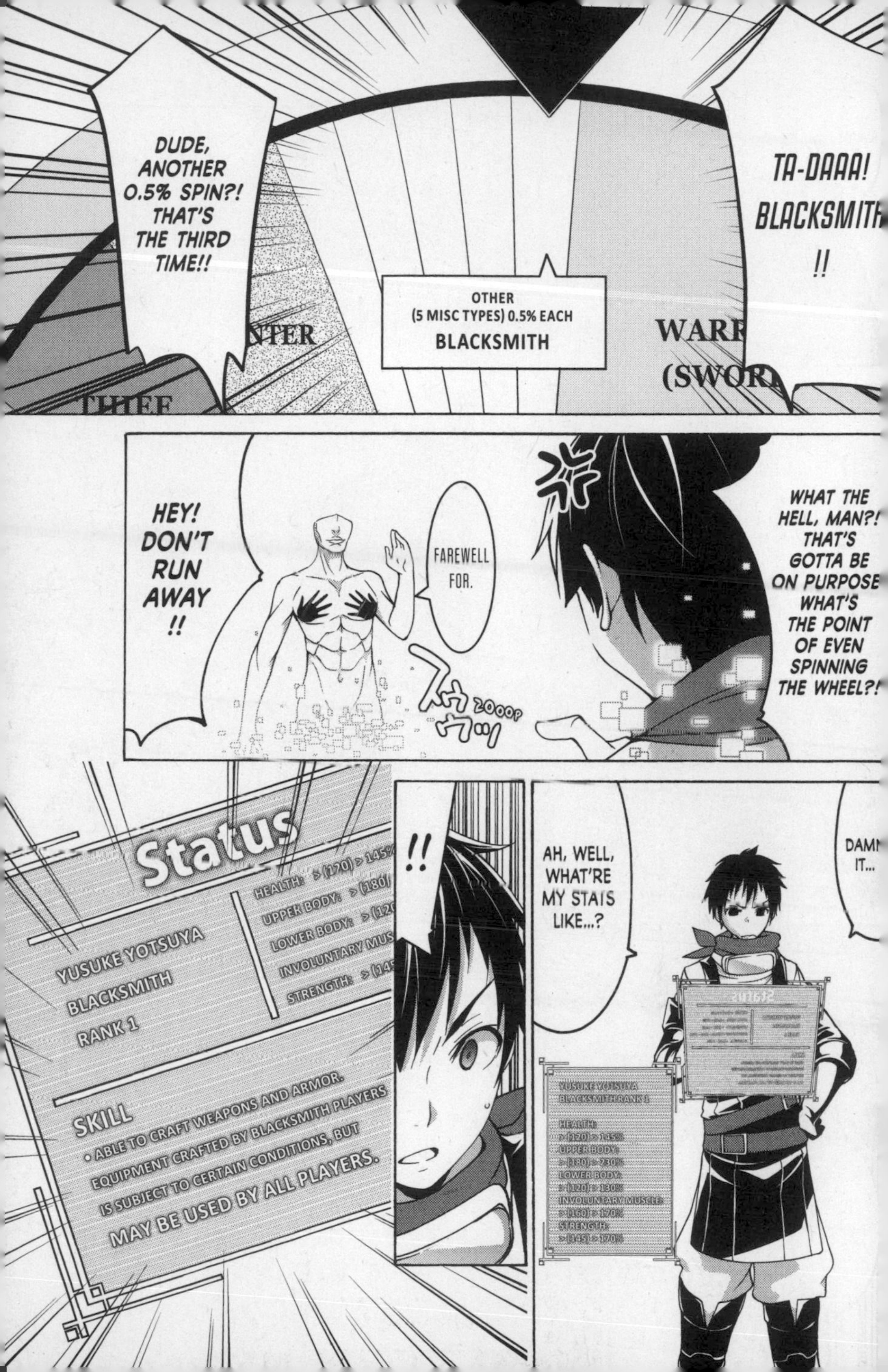

TA-DAAA! BLACKSMITH!!
DUDE, ANOTHER 0.5% SPIN?! THAT'S THE THIRD TIME!!
OTHER
(5 MISC TYPES) 0.5% EACH
BLACKSMITH
WHAT THE HELL, MAN?! THAT'S GOTTA BE ON PURPOSE
WHAT'S THE POINT OF EVEN SPINNING THE WHEEL?!
FAREWELL FOR.
HEY! DON'T RUN AWAY!!
ZOOOP
DAMN IT...
AH, WELL, WHAT'RE MY STATS LIKE...?
YUSUKE YOTSUYA
BLACKSMITH RANK 1
HEALTH: > (120) > 145%
UPPER BODY: > (180) > 230%
LOWER BODY: > (120) > 130%
INVOLUNTARY MUSCLE: > (160) > 170%
STRENGTH: > (145) > 170%
!!
Status
YUSUKE YOTSUYA
BLACKSMITH
RANK 1
SKILL
• ABLE TO CRAFT WEAPONS AND ARMOR.
EQUIPMENT CRAFTED BY BLACKSMITH PLAYERS
IS SUBJECT TO CERTAIN CONDITIONS, BUT
MAY BE USED BY ALL PLAYERS.

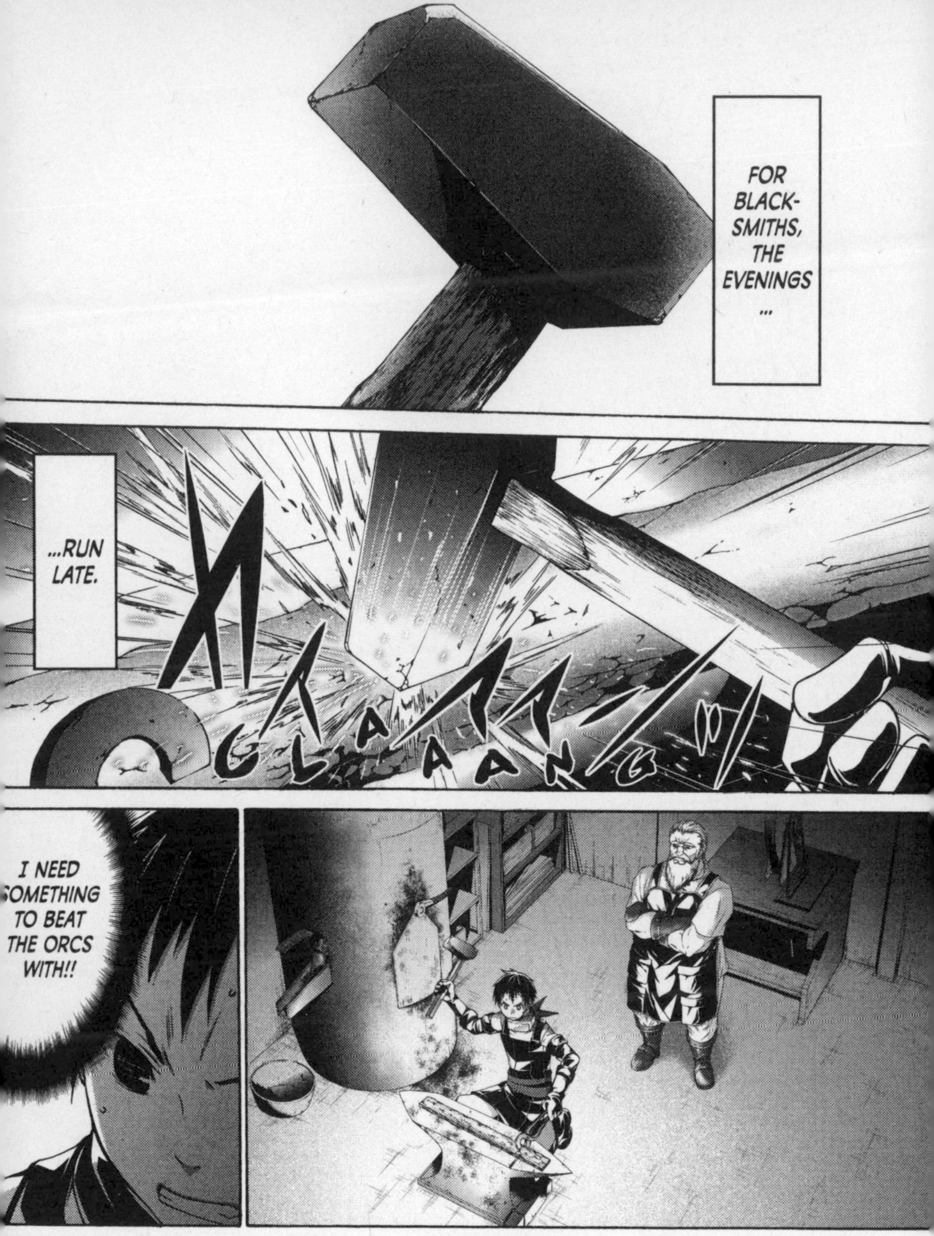
FOR BLACK-SMITHS, THE EVENINGS ...
...RUN LATE.
CLAAANG!!
I NEED SOMETHING TO BEAT THE ORCS WITH!!

9 DAYS TO HARVEST FESTIVAL / 14 ORCS LEFT
REMAINING QUEST TIME: APPR. 10 DAYS AND 2 HOURS

#16 The Mega-Stake & the Surprise Attack

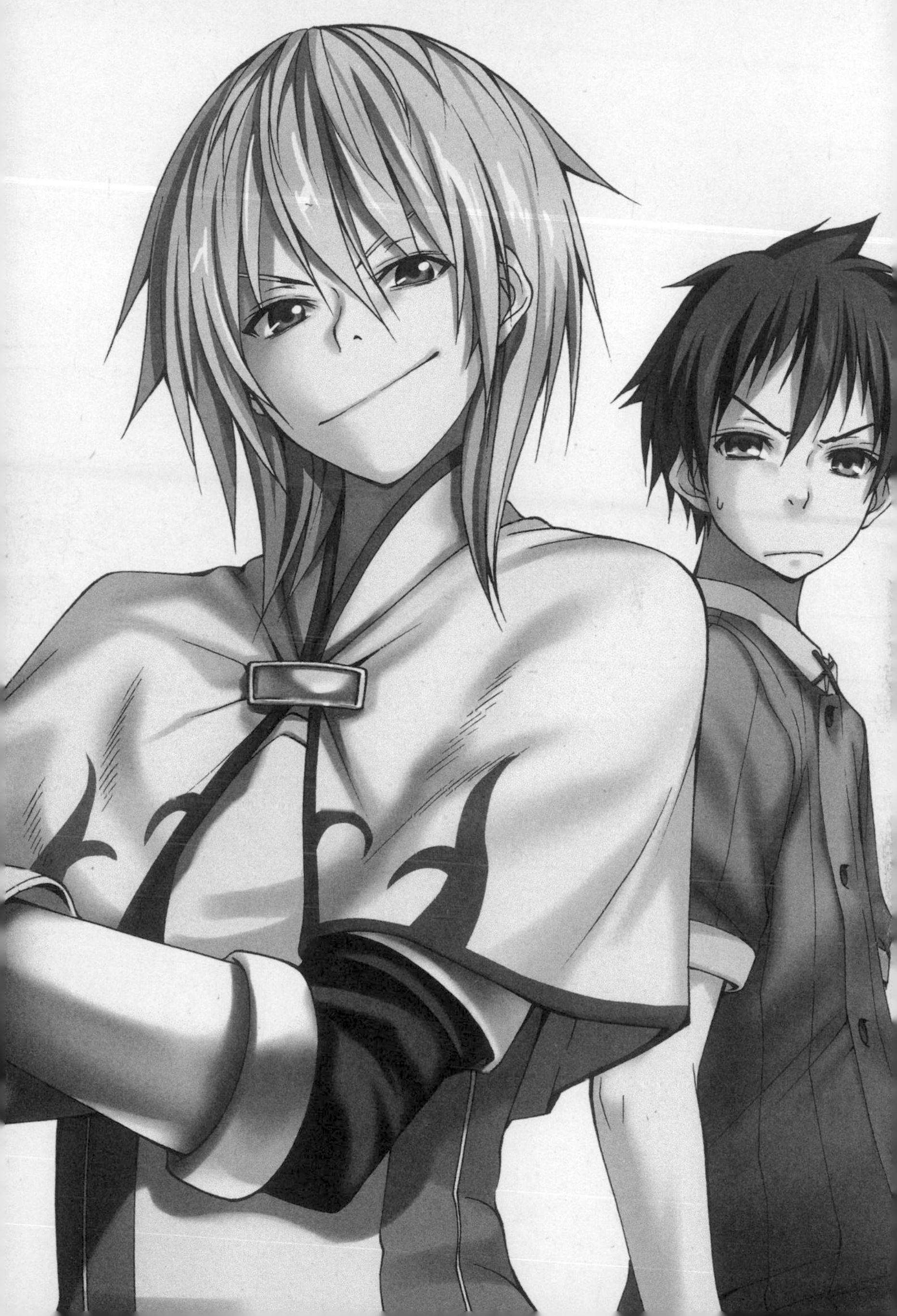

I'M STANDING ON
A MILLION LIVES

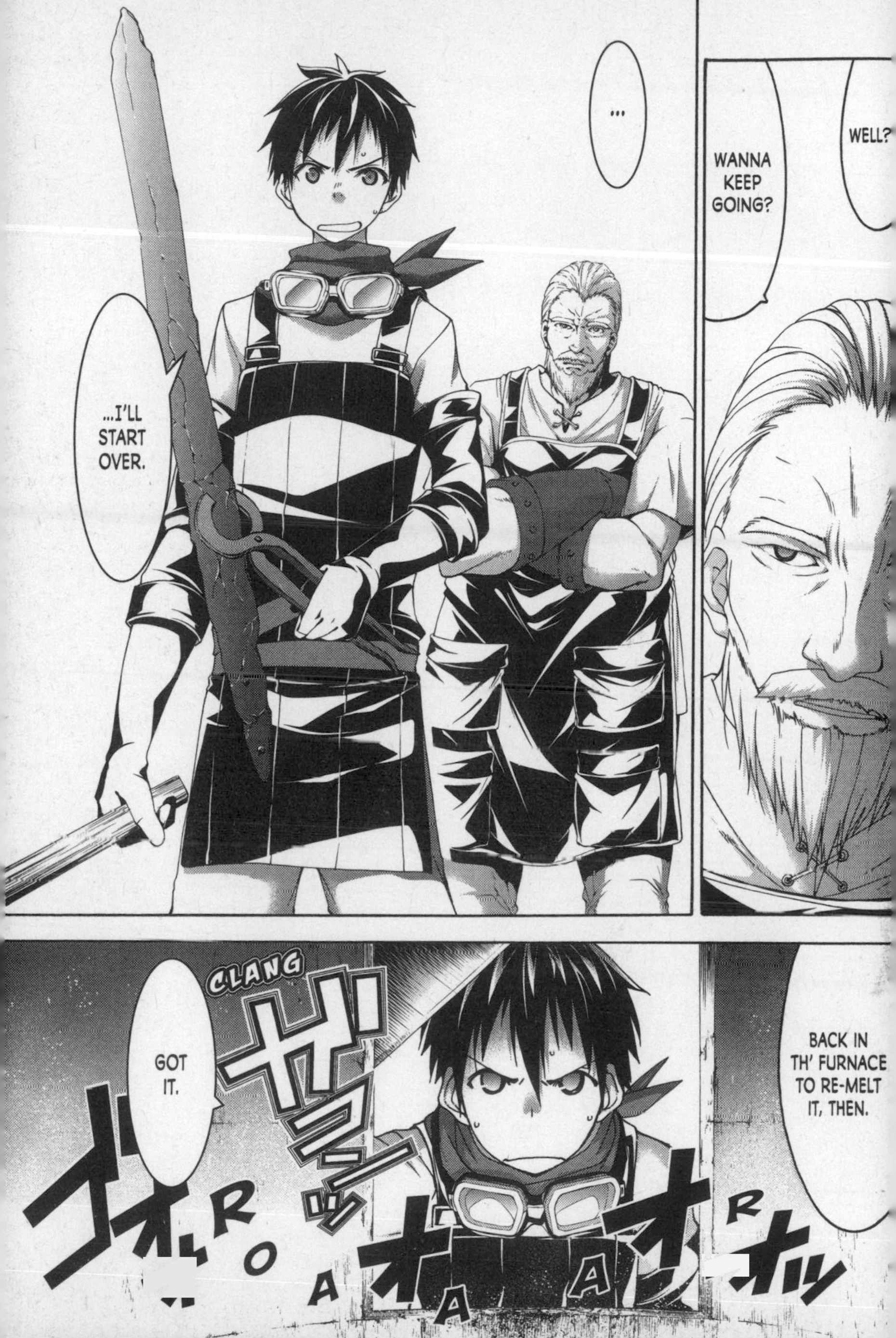
WELL?
WANNA KEEP GOING?
...
...I'LL START OVER.
BACK IN TH' FURNACE TO RE-MELT IT, THEN.
CLANG
GOT IT.

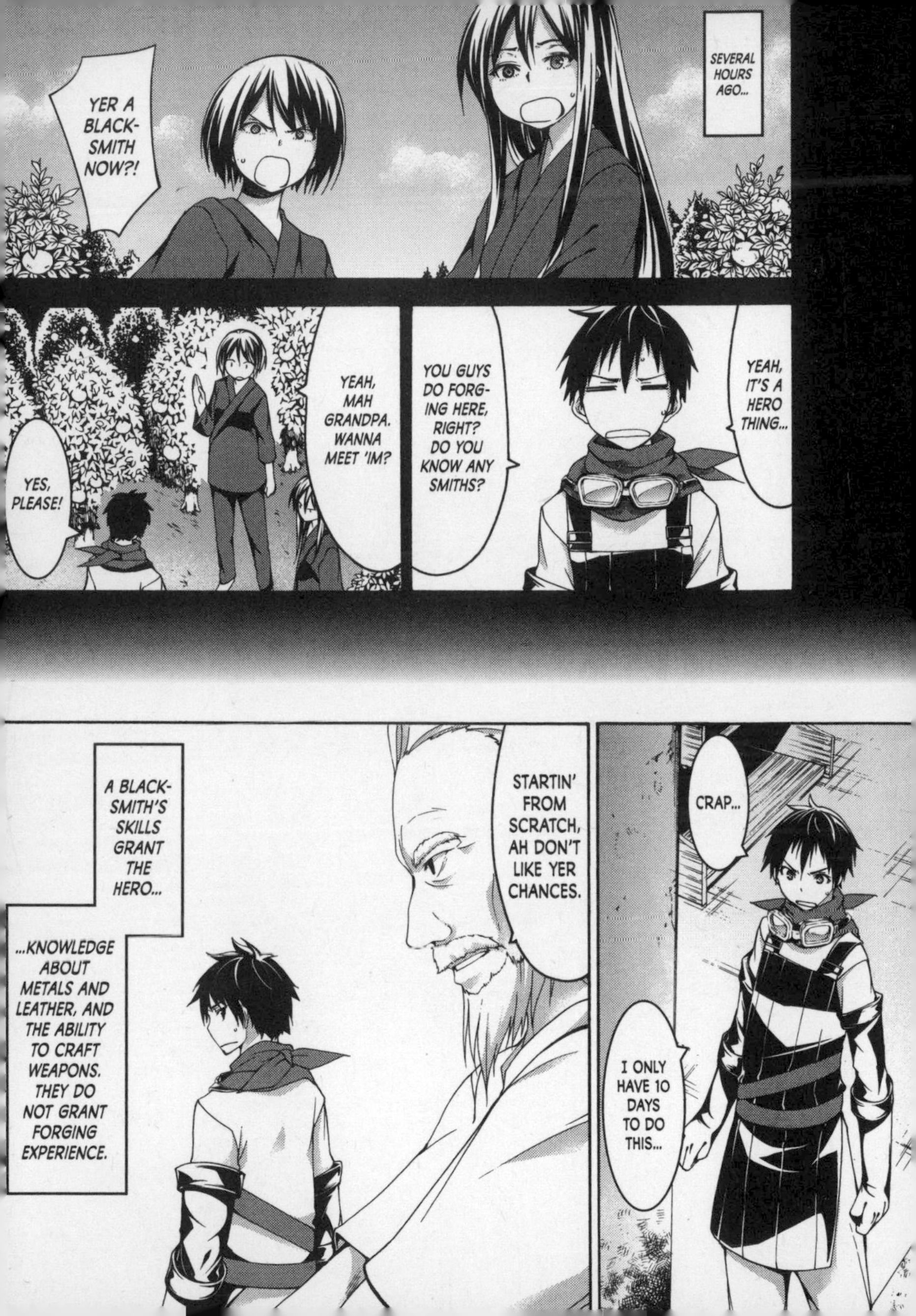
SEVERAL HOURS AGO...
YER A BLACK-SMITH NOW?!
YEAH, IT'S A HERO THING...
YOU GUYS DO FORG-ING HERE, RIGHT? DO YOU KNOW ANY SMITHS?
YEAH, MAH GRANDPA. WANNA MEET 'IM?
YES, PLEASE!
CRAP...
I ONLY HAVE 10 DAYS TO DO THIS...
STARTIN' FROM SCRATCH, AH DON'T LIKE YER CHANCES.
A BLACK-SMITH'S SKILLS GRANT THE HERO...
...KNOWLEDGE ABOUT METALS AND LEATHER, AND THE ABILITY TO CRAFT WEAPONS. THEY DO NOT GRANT FORGING EXPERIENCE.

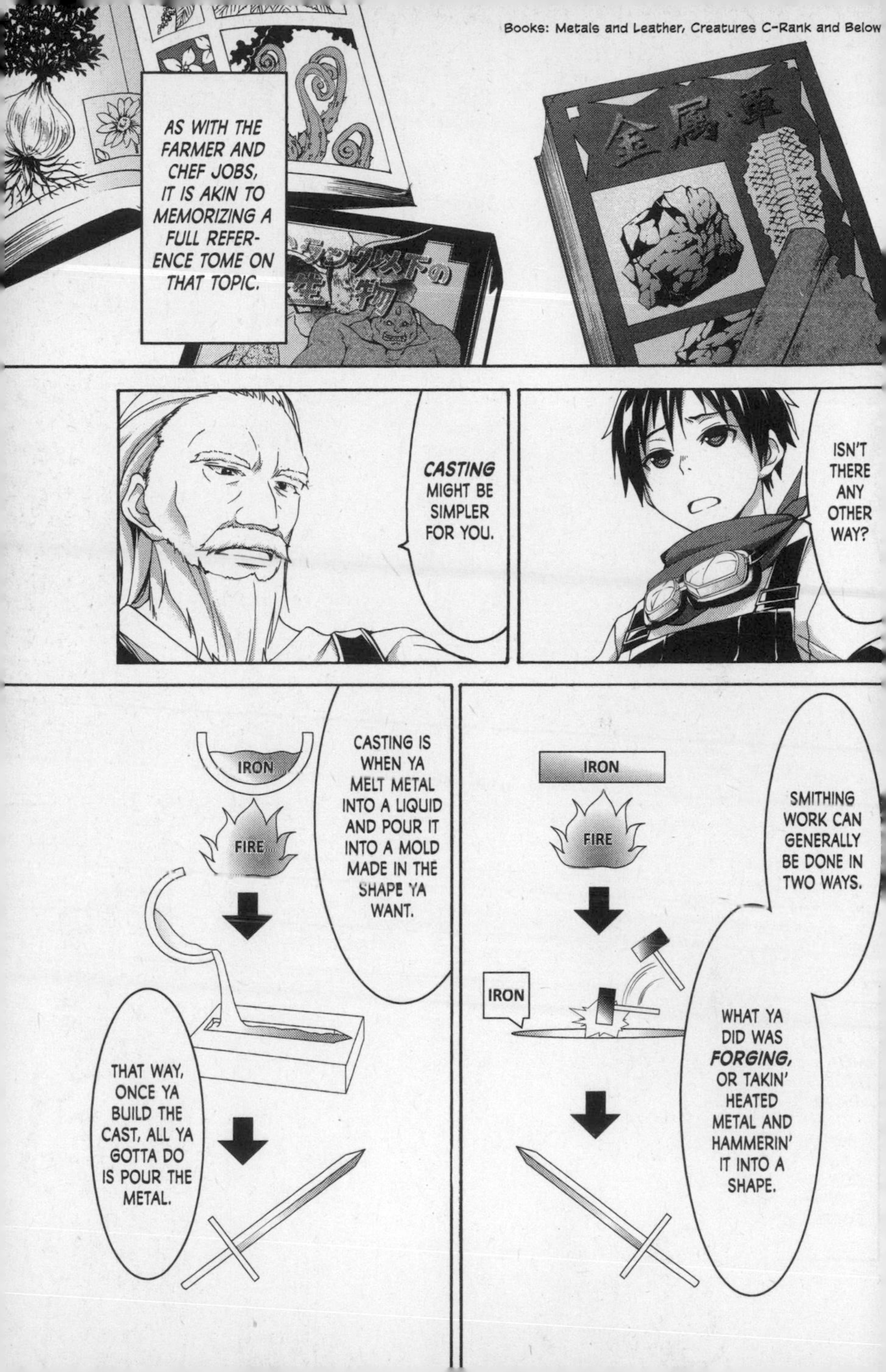
Books: Metals and Leather, Creatures C-Rank and Below
金属・革
AS WITH THE FARMER AND CHEF JOBS, IT IS AKIN TO MEMORIZING A FULL REFERENCE TOME ON THAT TOPIC.
ISN'T THERE ANY OTHER WAY?
CASTING MIGHT BE SIMPLER FOR YOU.
SMITHING WORK CAN GENERALLY BE DONE IN TWO WAYS.
IRON
FIRE
IRON
WHAT YA DID WAS *FORGING*, OR TAKIN' HEATED METAL AND HAMMERIN' IT INTO A SHAPE.
CASTING IS WHEN YA MELT METAL INTO A LIQUID AND POUR IT INTO A MOLD MADE IN THE SHAPE YA WANT.
IRON
FIRE
THAT WAY, ONCE YA BUILD THE CAST, ALL YA GOTTA DO IS POUR THE METAL.

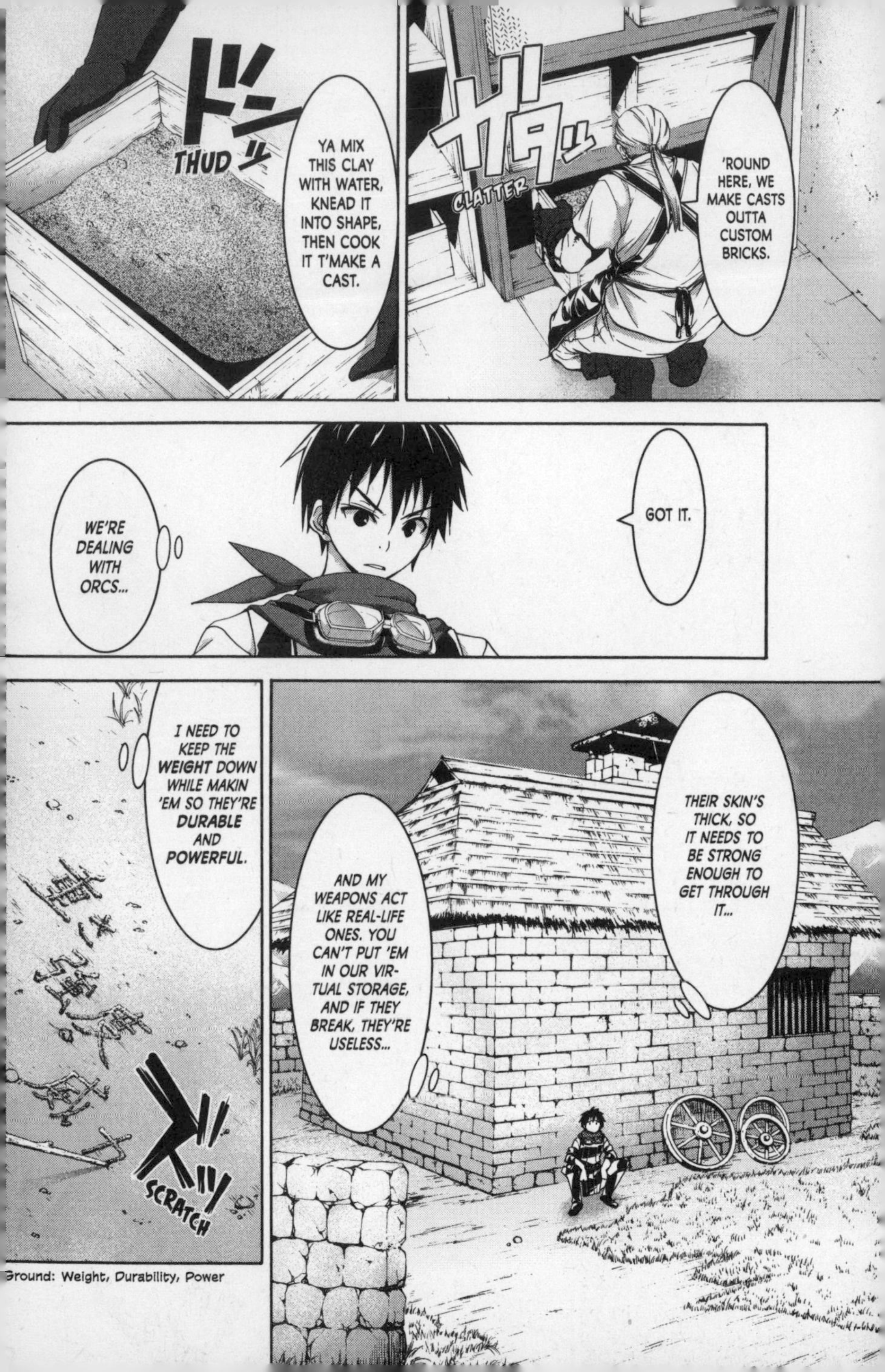
CLATTER
'ROUND HERE, WE MAKE CASTS OUTTA CUSTOM BRICKS.
THUD
YA MIX THIS CLAY WITH WATER, KNEAD IT INTO SHAPE, THEN COOK IT T'MAKE A CAST.
GOT IT.
WE'RE DEALING WITH ORCS...
THEIR SKIN'S THICK, SO IT NEEDS TO BE STRONG ENOUGH TO GET THROUGH IT...
AND MY WEAPONS ACT LIKE REAL-LIFE ONES. YOU CAN'T PUT 'EM IN OUR VIR-TUAL STORAGE, AND IF THEY BREAK, THEY'RE USELESS...
I NEED TO KEEP THE **WEIGHT** DOWN WHILE MAKIN 'EM SO THEY'RE **DURABLE** AND **POWERFUL**.
SCRATCH
Ground: Weight, Durability, Power

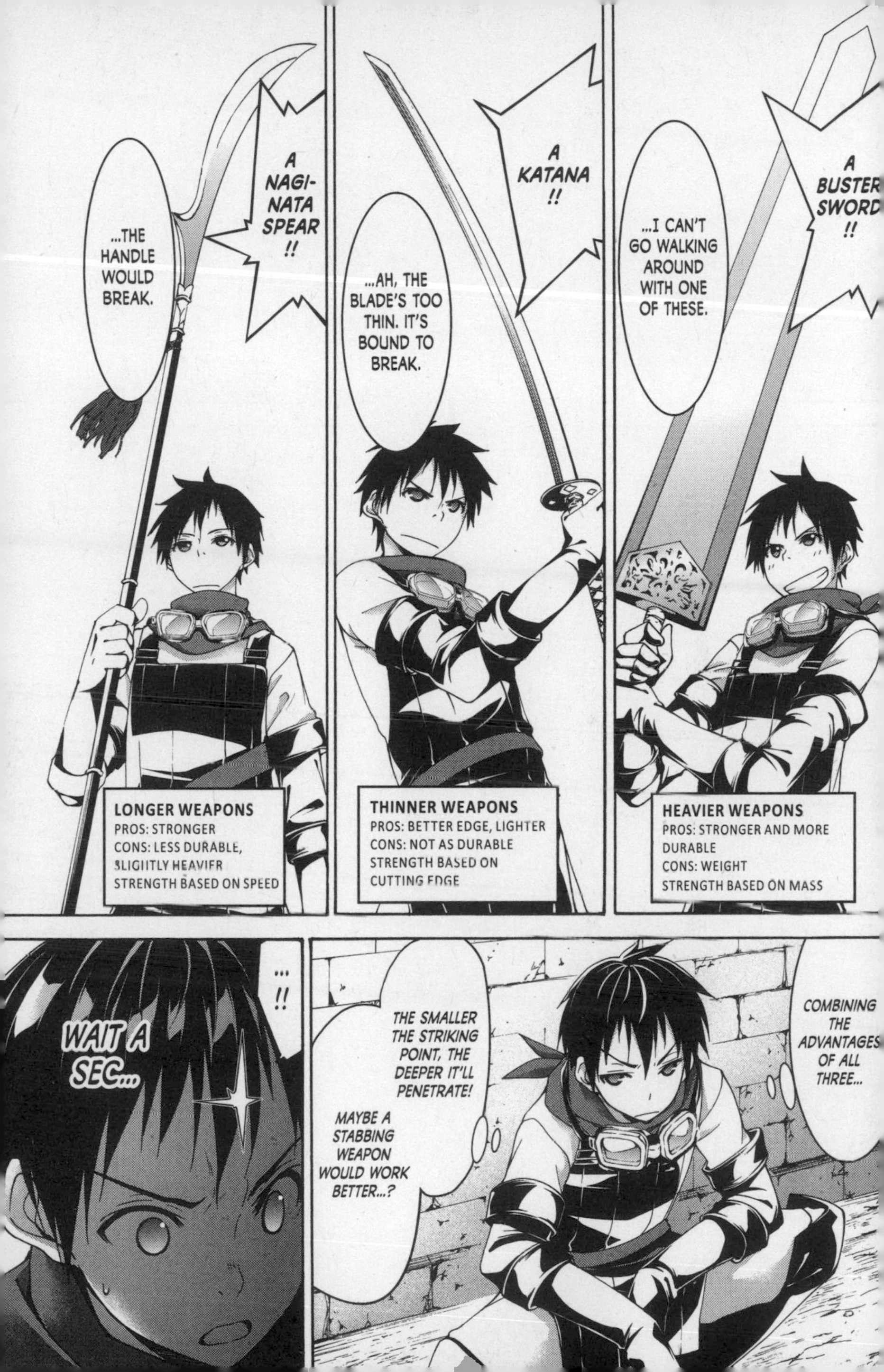
A BUSTER SWORD!!
...I CAN'T GO WALKING AROUND WITH ONE OF THESE.
HEAVIER WEAPONS
PROS: STRONGER AND MORE DURABLE
CONS: WEIGHT
STRENGTH BASED ON MASS
A KATANA!!
...AH, THE BLADE'S TOO THIN. IT'S BOUND TO BREAK.
THINNER WEAPONS
PROS: BETTER EDGE, LIGHTER
CONS: NOT AS DURABLE
STRENGTH BASED ON CUTTING EDGE
A NAGINATA SPEAR!!
...THE HANDLE WOULD BREAK.
LONGER WEAPONS
PROS: STRONGER
CONS: LESS DURABLE, SLIGHTLY HEAVIER
STRENGTH BASED ON SPEED
COMBINING THE ADVANTAGES OF ALL THREE...
THE SMALLER THE STRIKING POINT, THE DEEPER IT'LL PENETRATE!
MAYBE A STABBING WEAPON WOULD WORK BETTER...?
...!!
WAIT A SEC...

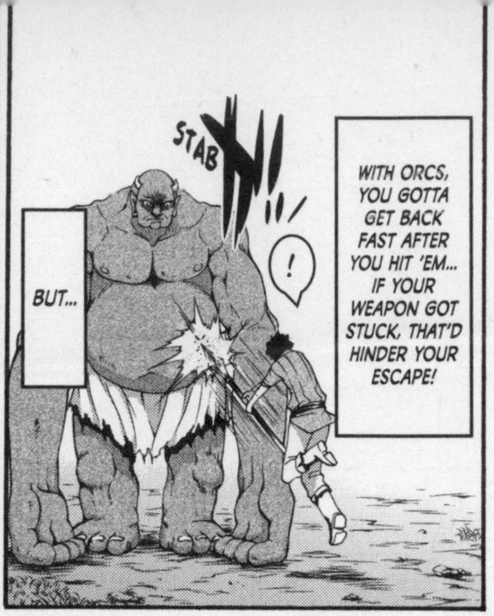
WITH ORCS, YOU GOTTA GET BACK FAST AFTER YOU HIT 'EM... IF YOUR WEAPON GOT STUCK, THAT'D HINDER YOUR ESCAPE!
STAB
!
BUT...

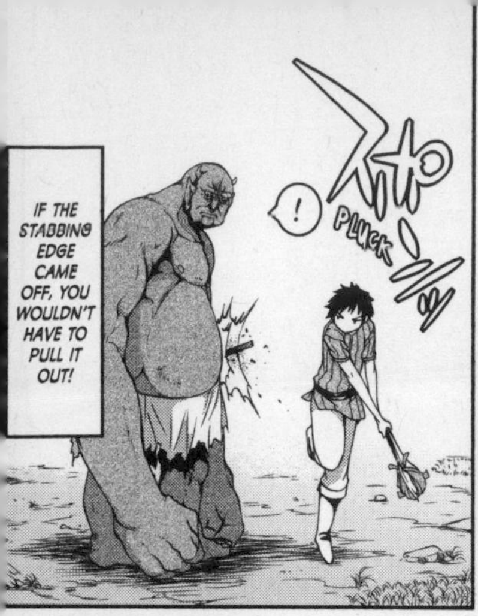
PLUCK
!
IF THE STABBING EDGE CAME OFF, YOU WOULDN'T HAVE TO PULL IT OUT!

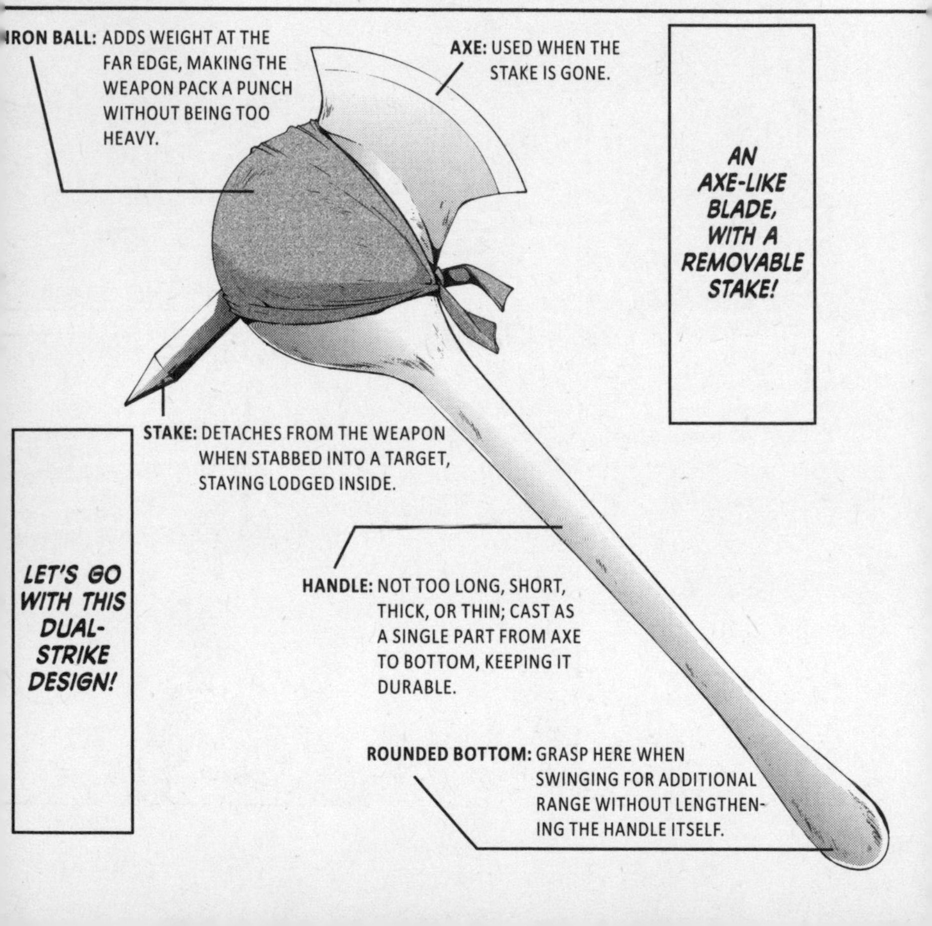
AN AXE-LIKE BLADE, WITH A REMOVABLE STAKE!
AXE: USED WHEN THE STAKE IS GONE.
IRON BALL: ADDS WEIGHT AT THE FAR EDGE, MAKING THE WEAPON PACK A PUNCH WITHOUT BEING TOO HEAVY.
STAKE: DETACHES FROM THE WEAPON WHEN STABBED INTO A TARGET, STAYING LODGED INSIDE.
HANDLE: NOT TOO LONG, SHORT, THICK, OR THIN; CAST AS A SINGLE PART FROM AXE TO BOTTOM, KEEPING IT DURABLE.
ROUNDED BOTTOM: GRASP HERE WHEN SWINGING FOR ADDITIONAL RANGE WITHOUT LENGTHEN-ING THE HANDLE ITSELF.
LET'S GO WITH THIS DUAL-STRIKE DESIGN!

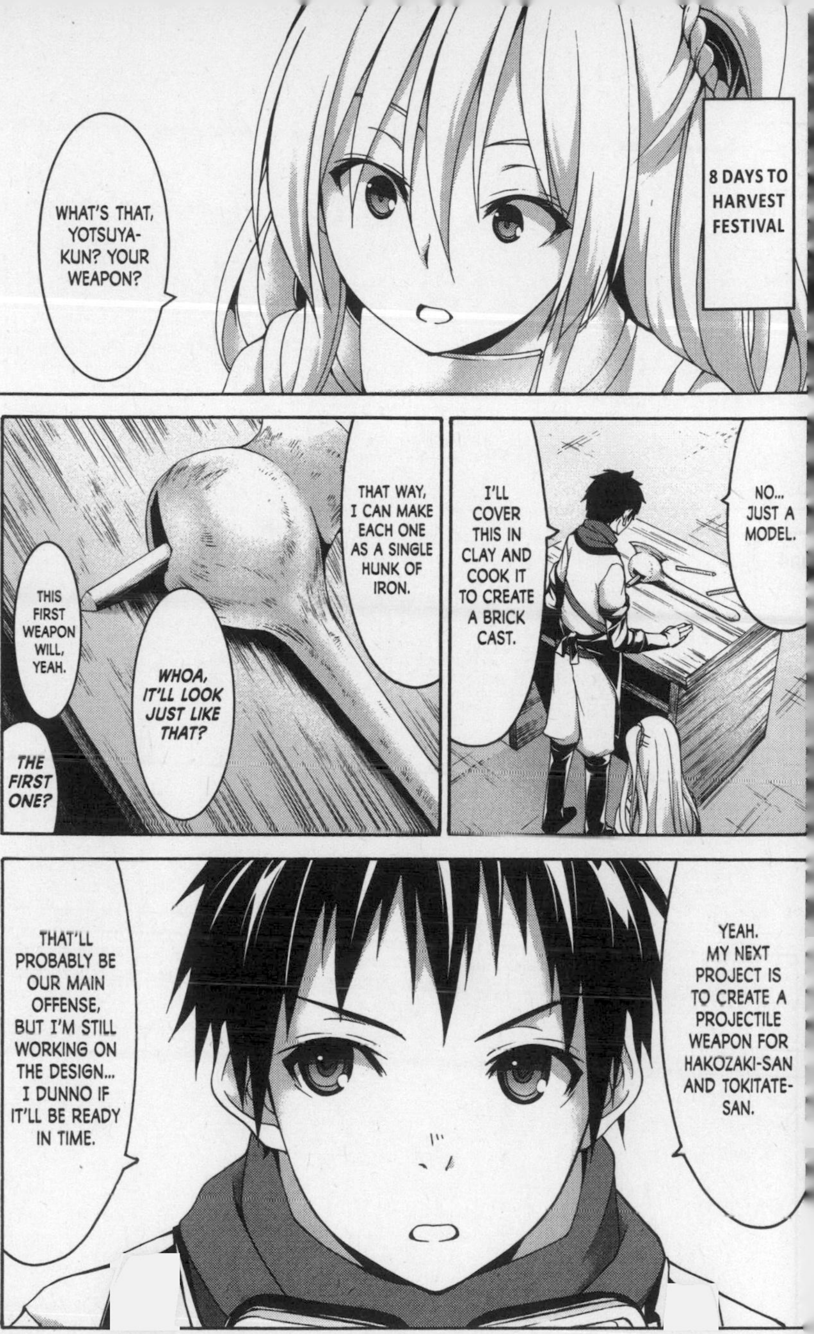
8 DAYS TO HARVEST FESTIVAL
WHAT'S THAT, YOTSUYA-KUN? YOUR WEAPON?
NO... JUST A MODEL.
I'LL COVER THIS IN CLAY AND COOK IT TO CREATE A BRICK CAST.
THAT WAY, I CAN MAKE EACH ONE AS A SINGLE HUNK OF IRON.
WHOA, IT'LL LOOK JUST LIKE THAT?
THIS FIRST WEAPON WILL, YEAH.
THE FIRST ONE?
YEAH. MY NEXT PROJECT IS TO CREATE A PROJECTILE WEAPON FOR HAKOZAKI-SAN AND TOKITATE-SAN.
THAT'LL PROBABLY BE OUR MAIN OFFENSE, BUT I'M STILL WORKING ON THE DESIGN... I DUNNO IF IT'LL BE READY IN TIME.

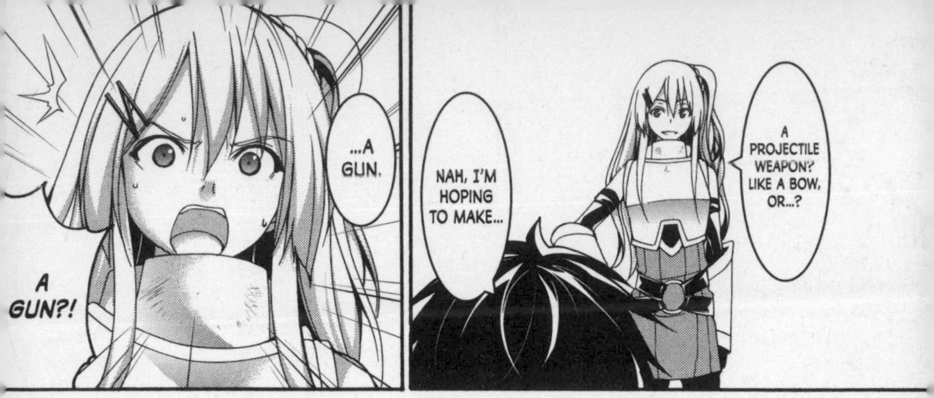
A PROJECTILE WEAPON? LIKE A BOW, OR...?
NAH, I'M HOPING TO MAKE...
...A GUN.
A GUN?!

7 DAYS TO HARVEST FESTIVAL

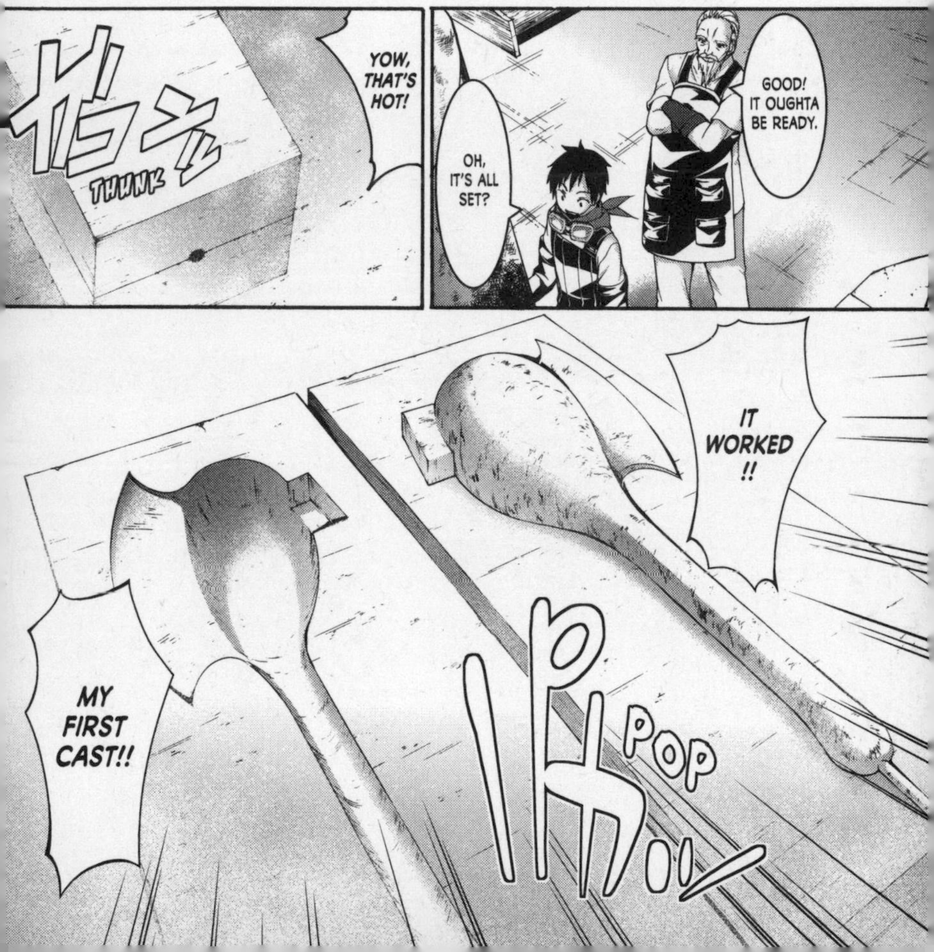
GOOD! IT OUGHTA BE READY.
OH, IT'S ALL SET?
YOW, THAT'S HOT!
THUNK
IT WORKED !!
POP
MY FIRST CAST!!

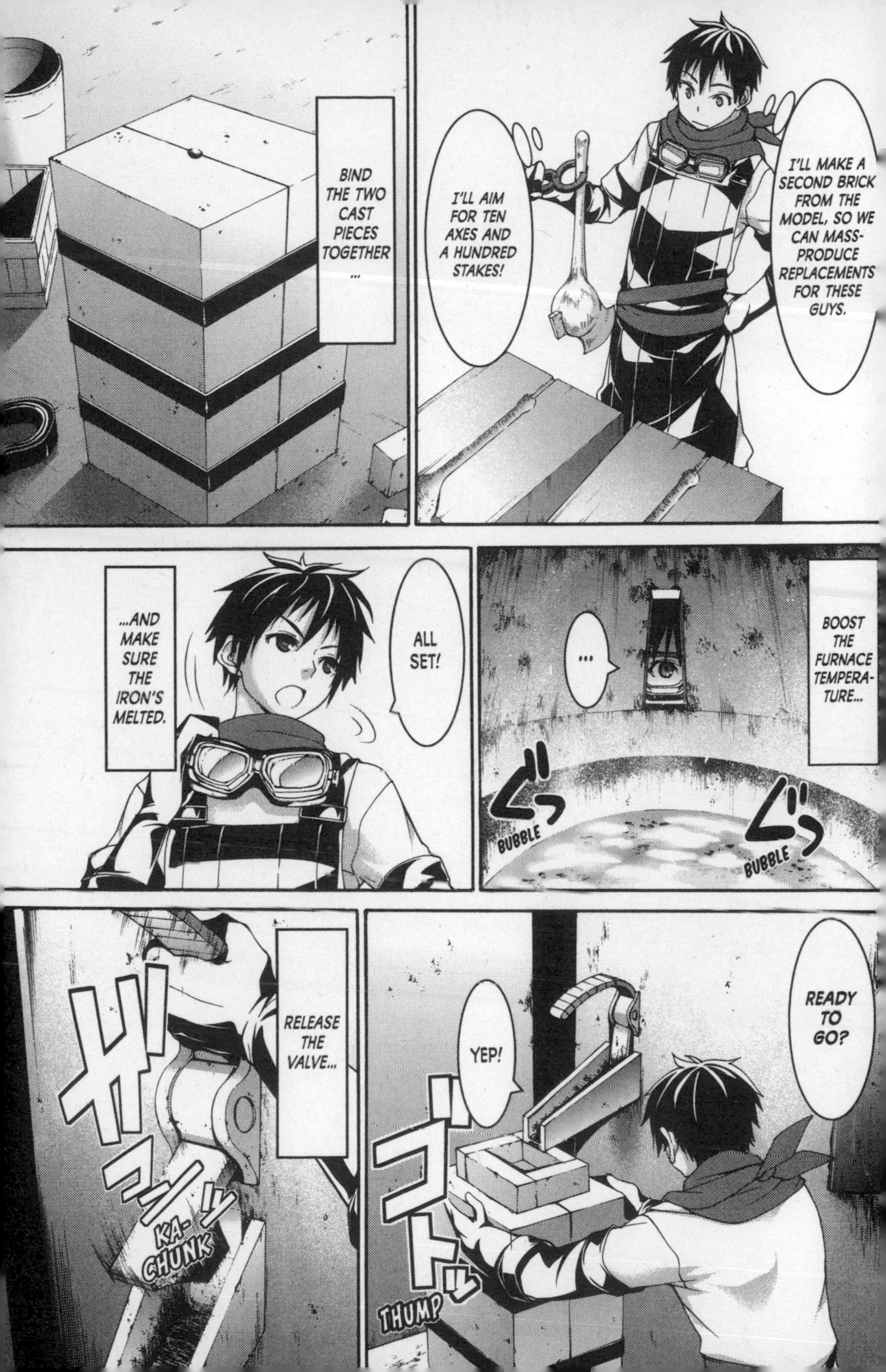
I'LL MAKE A SECOND BRICK FROM THE MODEL, SO WE CAN MASS-PRODUCE REPLACEMENTS FOR THESE GUYS.
I'LL AIM FOR TEN AXES AND A HUNDRED STAKES!
BIND THE TWO CAST PIECES TOGETHER ...
BOOST THE FURNACE TEMPERA-TURE...
...
BUBBLE
BUBBLE
ALL SET!
...AND MAKE SURE THE IRON'S MELTED.
READY TO GO?
YEP!
THUMP
RELEASE THE VALVE...
KA-CHUNK

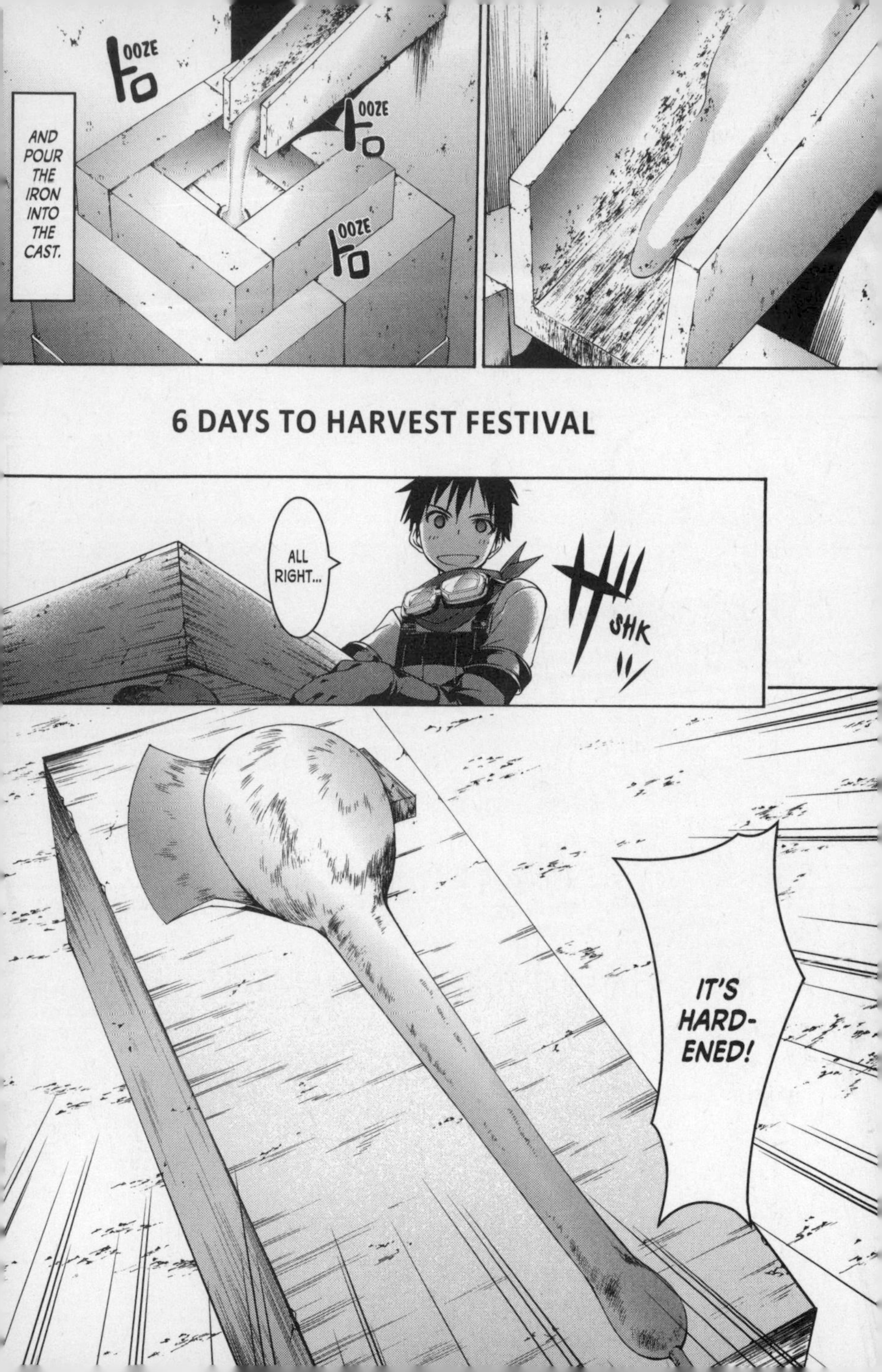
OOZE
OOZE
AND POUR THE IRON INTO THE CAST.
OOZE
6 DAYS TO HARVEST FESTIVAL
SHK
ALL RIGHT...
IT'S HARD-ENED!

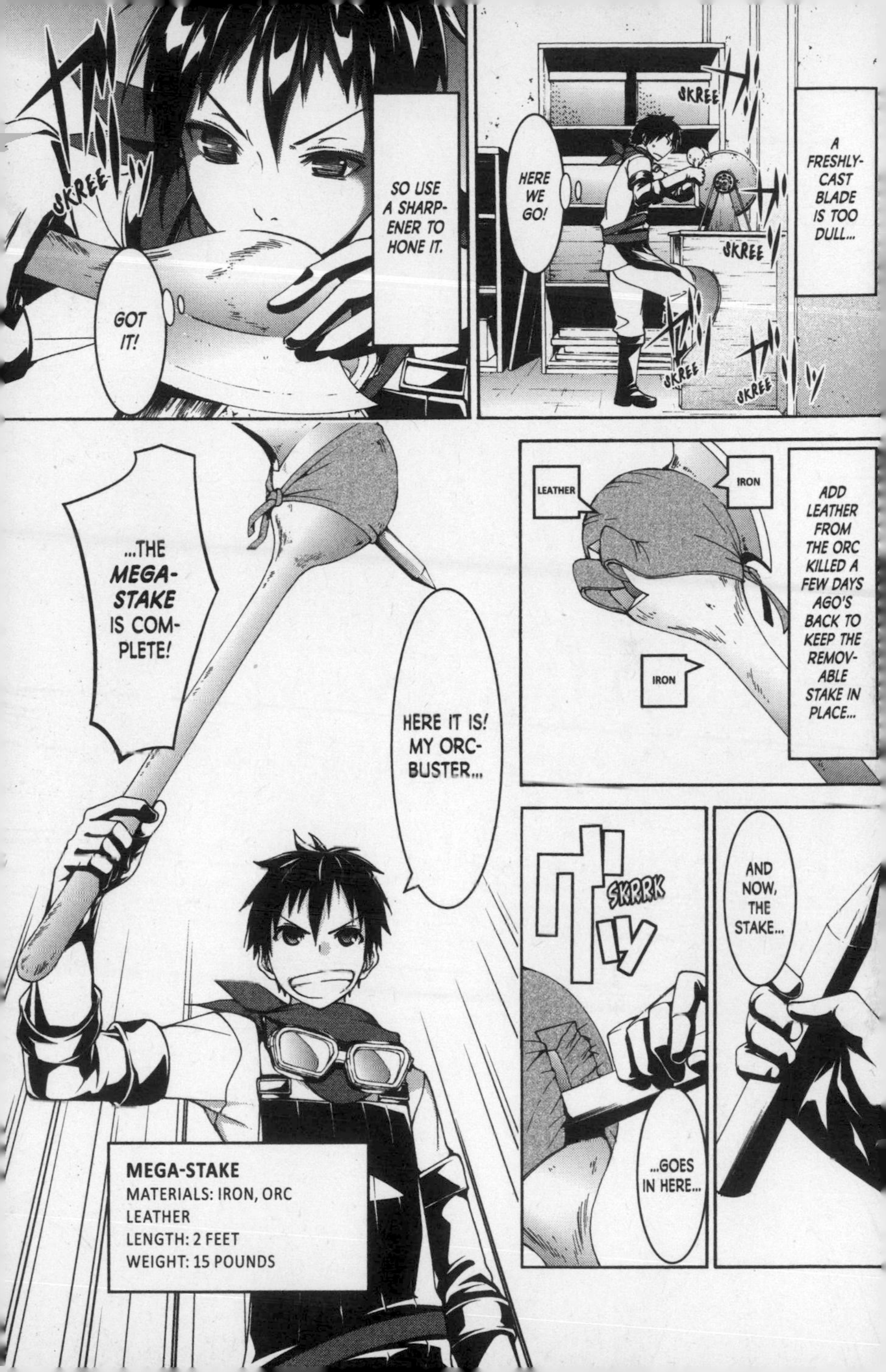
A FRESHLY-CAST BLADE IS TOO DULL...
SKREE
HERE WE GO!
SKREE
SKREE
SKREE
SO USE A SHARPENER TO HONE IT.
SKREE
GOT IT!
ADD LEATHER FROM THE ORC KILLED A FEW DAYS AGO'S BACK TO KEEP THE REMOVABLE STAKE IN PLACE...
IRON
LEATHER
IRON
AND NOW, THE STAKE...
SKRRK
...GOES IN HERE...
HERE IT IS! MY ORC-BUSTER...
...THE MEGA-STAKE IS COMPLETE!
MEGA-STAKE
MATERIALS: IRON, ORC LEATHER
LENGTH: 2 FEET
WEIGHT: 15 POUNDS

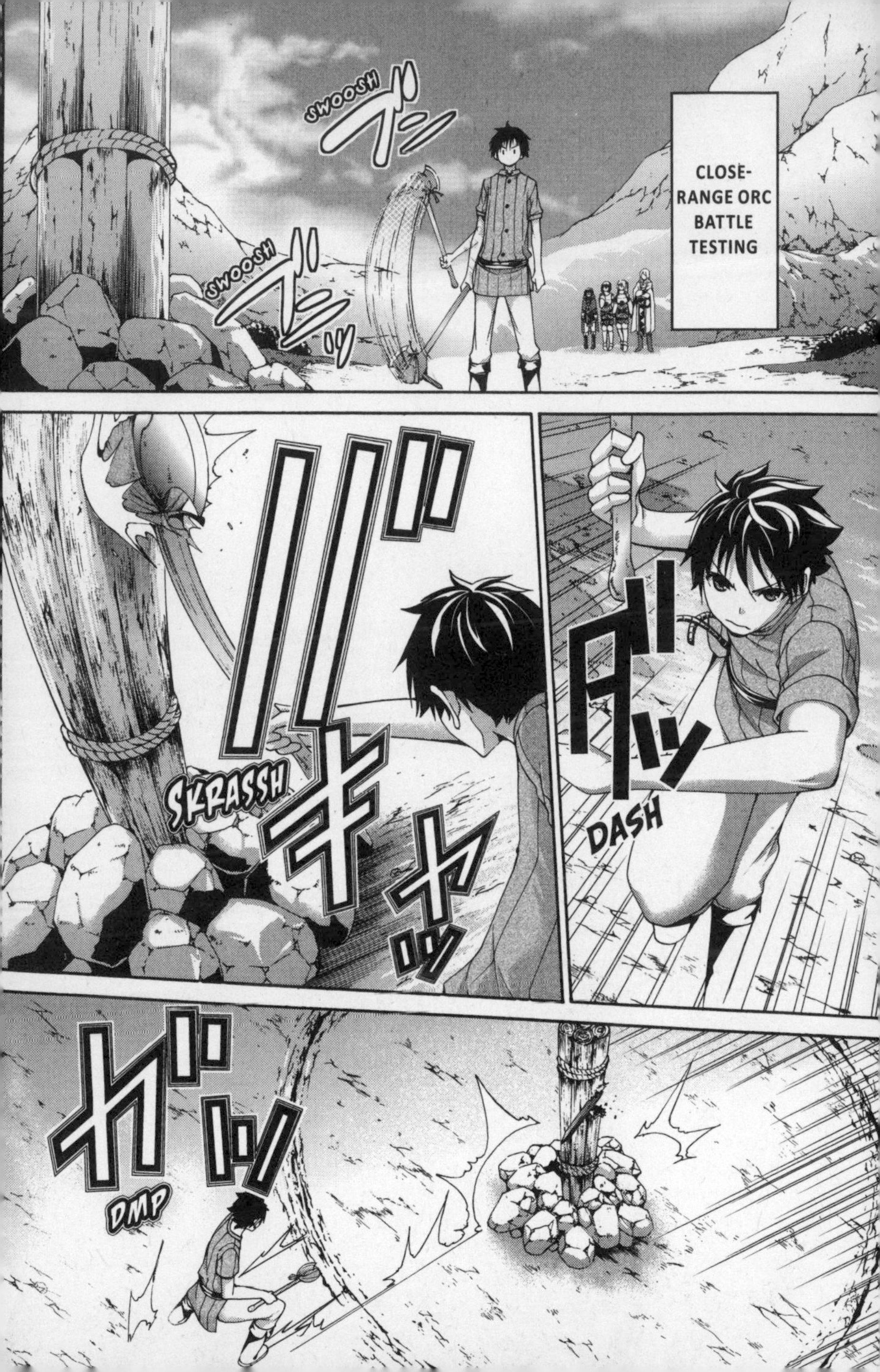
CLOSE-RANGE ORC BATTLE TESTING
SWOOSH
SWOOSH
DASH
SKRASSH
DMP

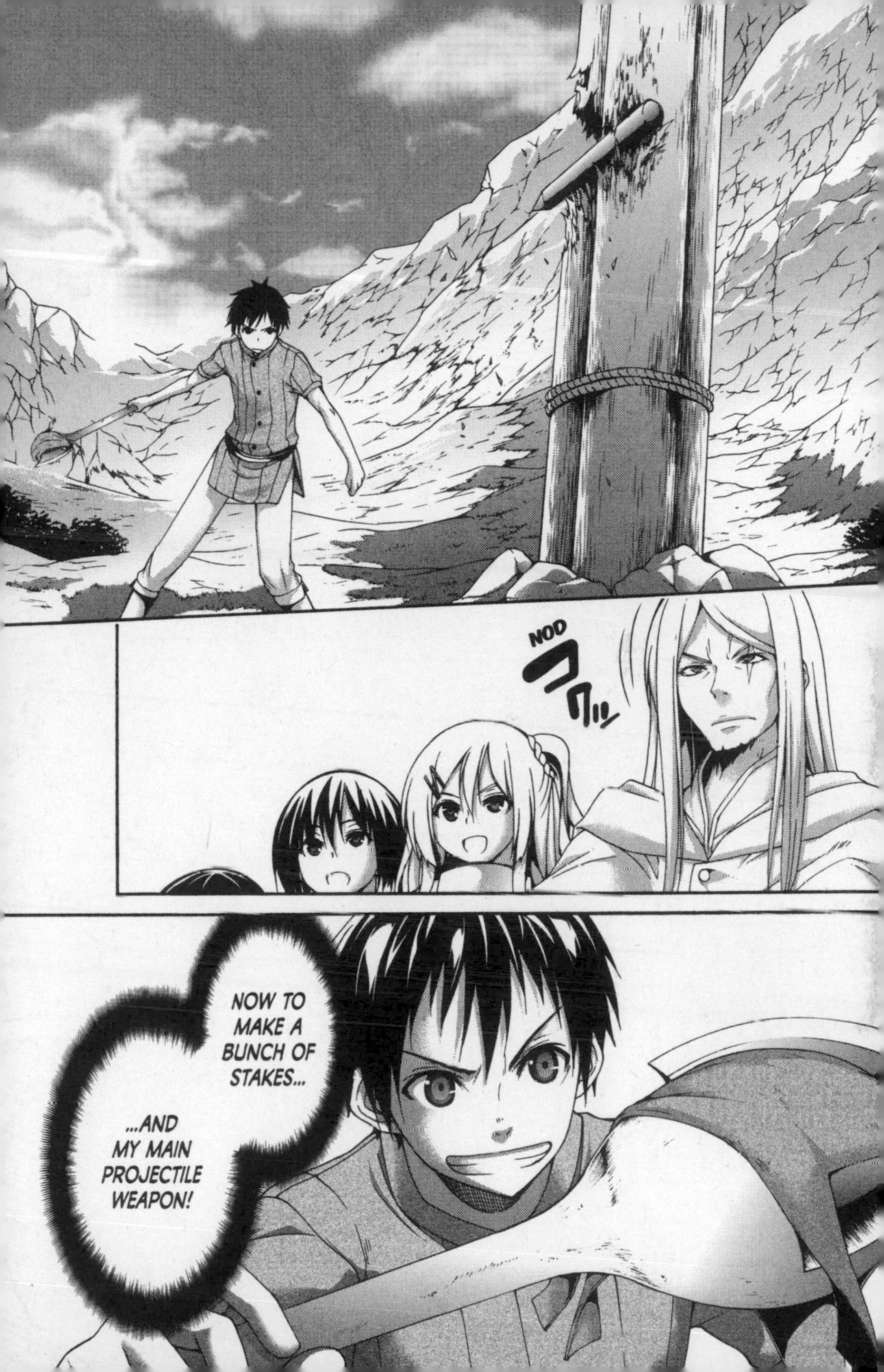
NOD
NOW TO MAKE A BUNCH OF STAKES...
...AND MY MAIN PROJECTILE WEAPON!

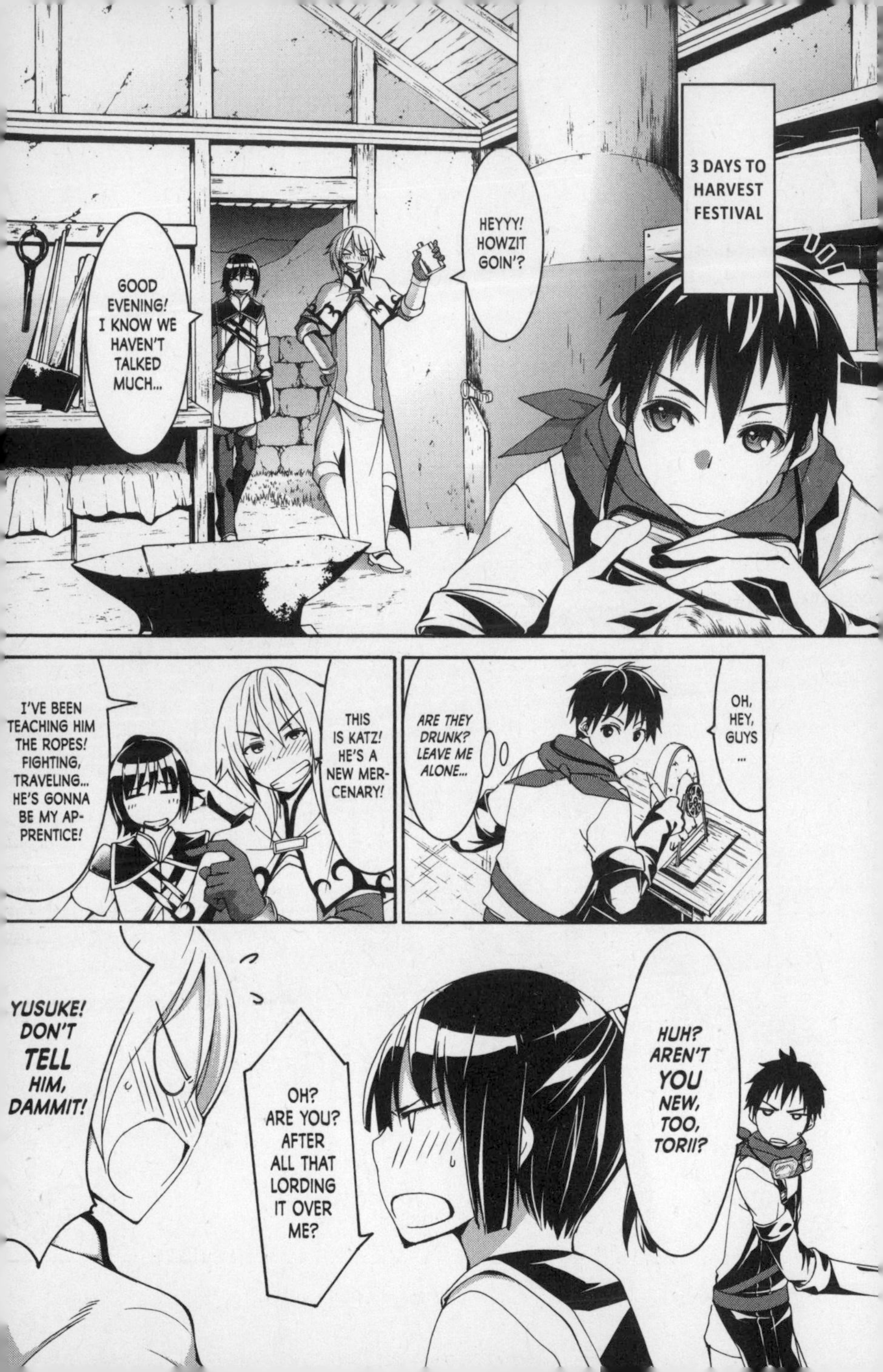
3 DAYS TO HARVEST FESTIVAL
HEYYY! HOWZIT GOIN'?
GOOD EVENING! I KNOW WE HAVEN'T TALKED MUCH...
OH, HEY, GUYS ...
ARE THEY DRUNK? LEAVE ME ALONE...
THIS IS KATZ! HE'S A NEW MER-CENARY!
I'VE BEEN TEACHING HIM THE ROPES! FIGHTING, TRAVELING... HE'S GONNA BE MY AP-PRENTICE!
HUH? AREN'T YOU NEW, TOO, TORII?
OH? ARE YOU? AFTER ALL THAT LORDING IT OVER ME?
YUSUKE! DON'T TELL HIM, DAMMIT!

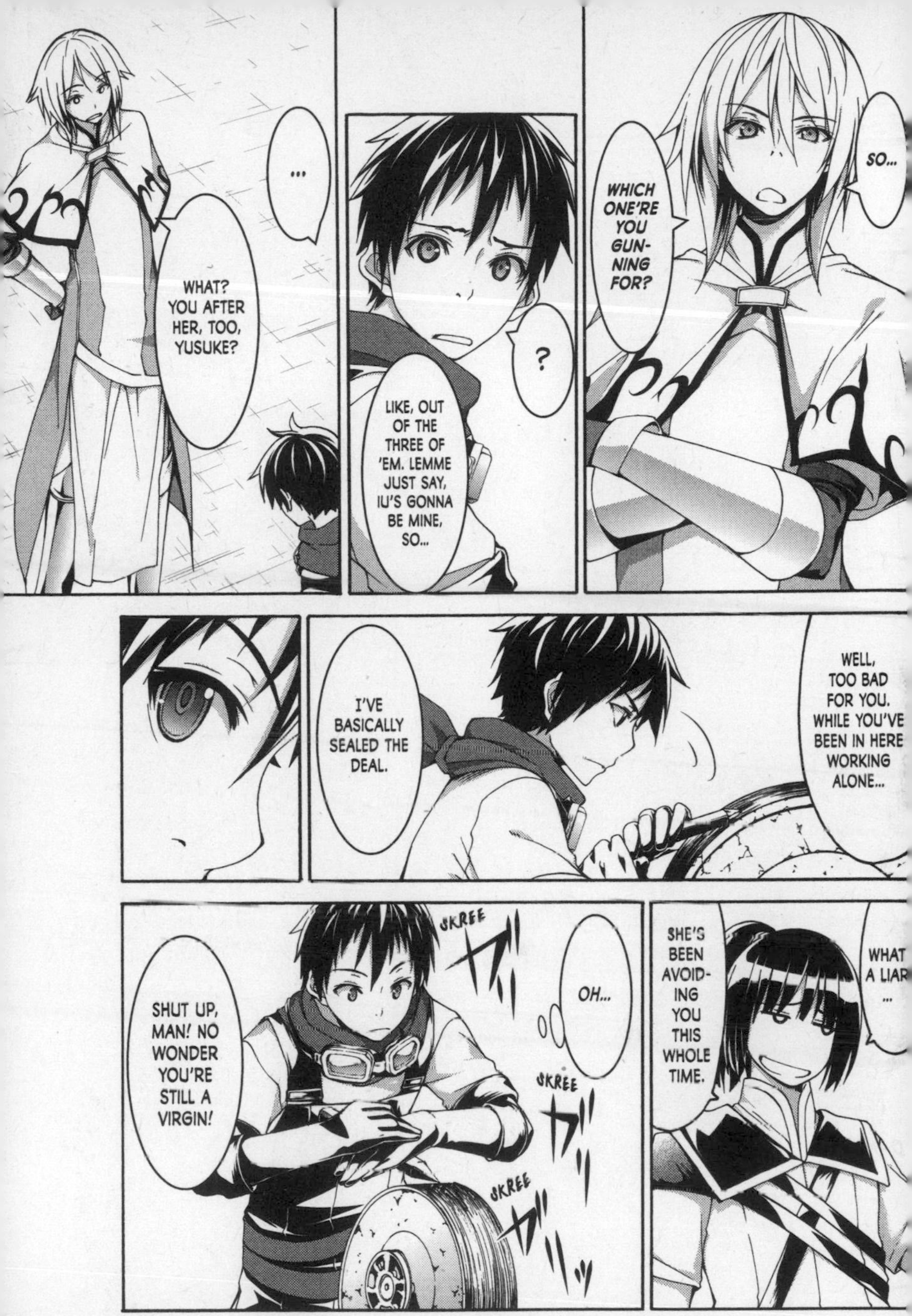
SO...
WHICH ONE'RE YOU GUN-NING FOR?
?
LIKE, OUT OF THE THREE OF 'EM. LEMME JUST SAY, IU'S GONNA BE MINE, SO...
...
WHAT? YOU AFTER HER, TOO, YUSUKE?
WELL, TOO BAD FOR YOU. WHILE YOU'VE BEEN IN HERE WORKING ALONE...
I'VE BASICALLY SEALED THE DEAL.
WHAT A LIAR ...
SHE'S BEEN AVOID-ING YOU THIS WHOLE TIME.
OH...
SKREE
SKREE
SKREE
SHUT UP, MAN! NO WONDER YOU'RE STILL A VIRGIN!

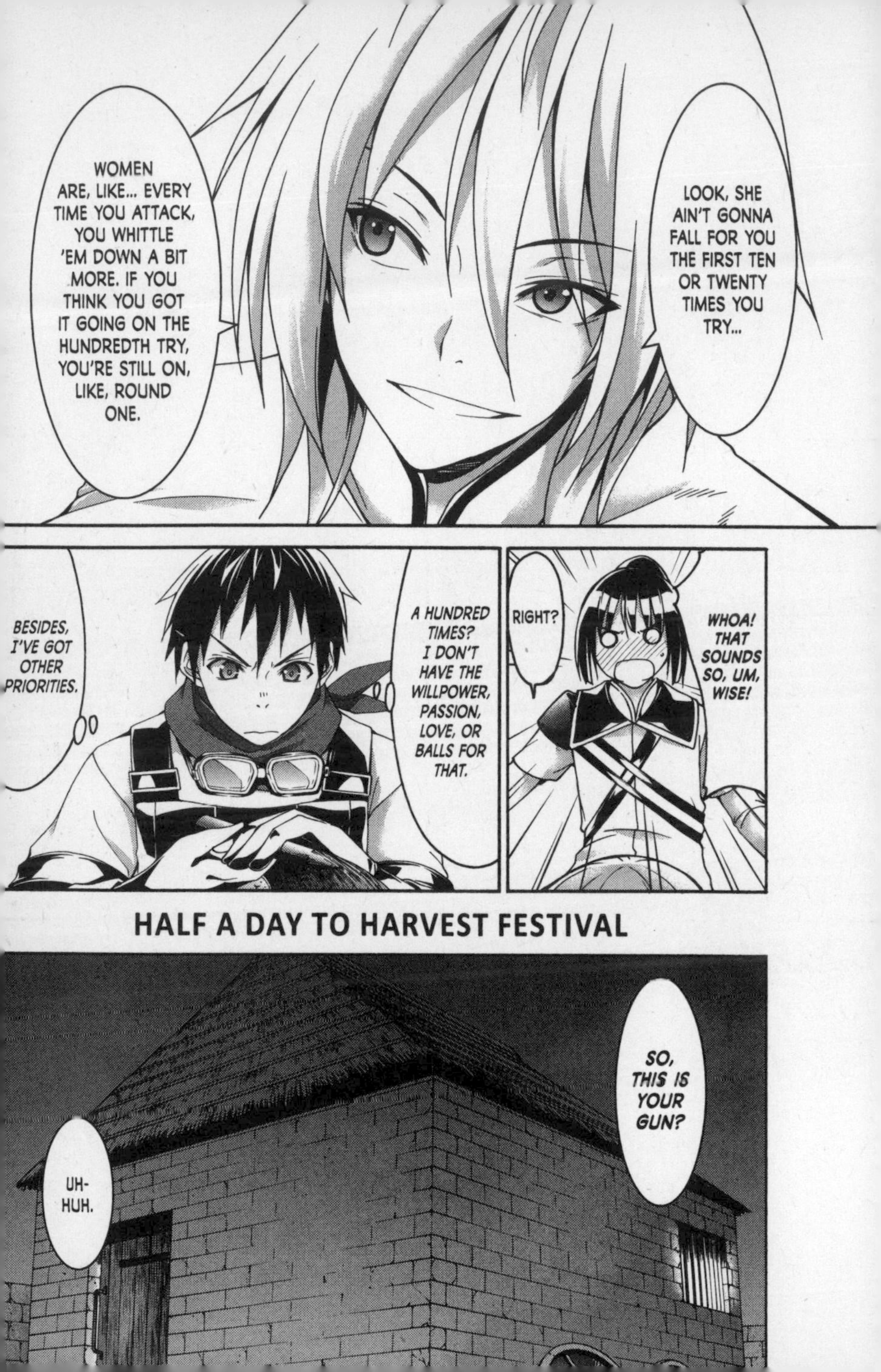
LOOK, SHE AIN'T GONNA FALL FOR YOU THE FIRST TEN OR TWENTY TIMES YOU TRY...
WOMEN ARE, LIKE... EVERY TIME YOU ATTACK, YOU WHITTLE 'EM DOWN A BIT MORE. IF YOU THINK YOU GOT IT GOING ON THE HUNDREDTH TRY, YOU'RE STILL ON, LIKE, ROUND ONE.
WHOA! THAT SOUNDS SO, UM, WISE!
RIGHT?
A HUNDRED TIMES? I DON'T HAVE THE WILLPOWER, PASSION, LOVE, OR BALLS FOR THAT.
BESIDES, I'VE GOT OTHER PRIORITIES.
HALF A DAY TO HARVEST FESTIVAL
SO, THIS IS YOUR GUN?
UH-HUH.

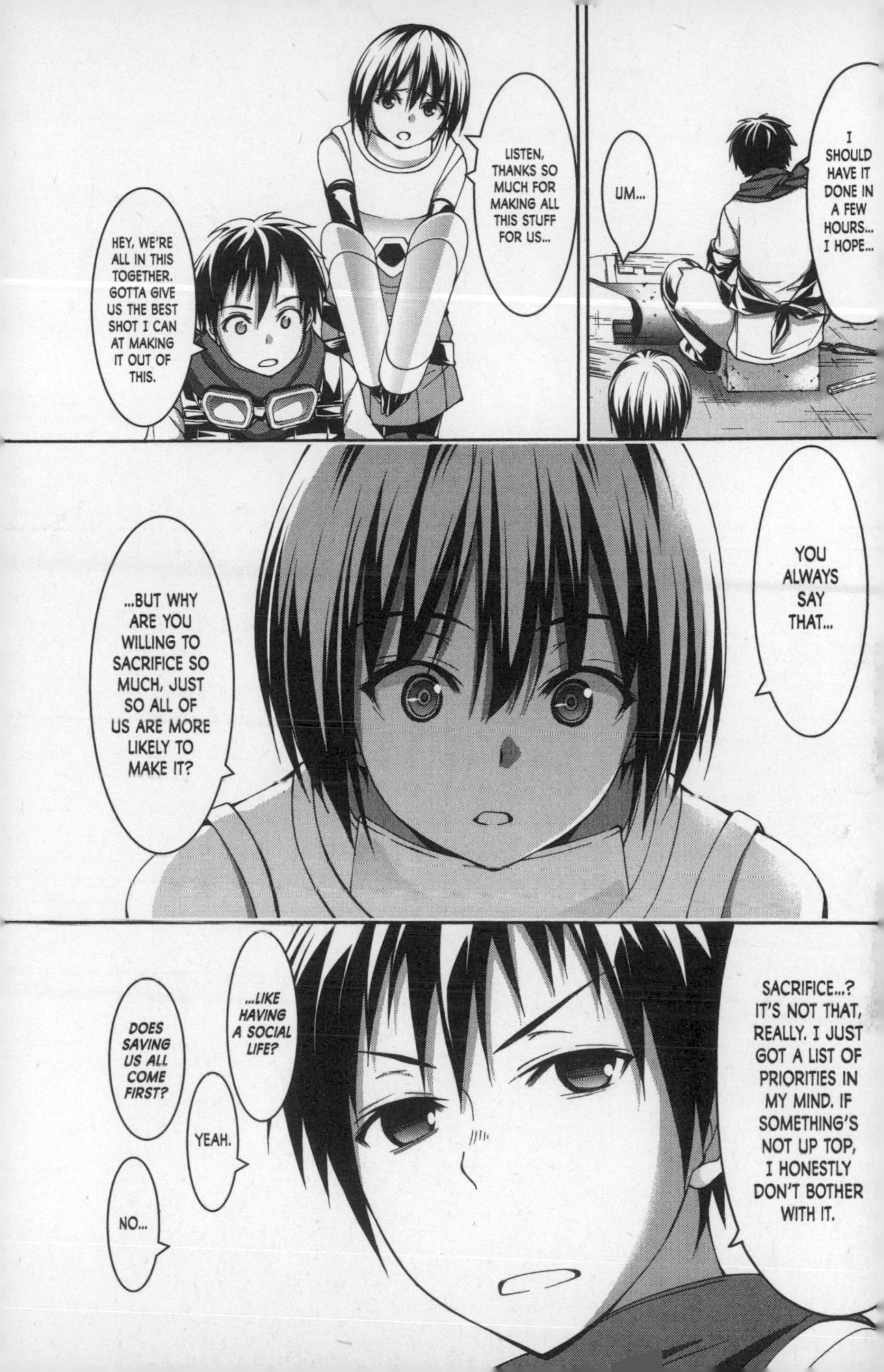
I SHOULD HAVE IT DONE IN A FEW HOURS... I HOPE...
UM...
LISTEN, THANKS SO MUCH FOR MAKING ALL THIS STUFF FOR US...
HEY, WE'RE ALL IN THIS TOGETHER. GOTTA GIVE US THE BEST SHOT I CAN AT MAKING IT OUT OF THIS.
YOU ALWAYS SAY THAT...
...BUT WHY ARE YOU WILLING TO SACRIFICE SO MUCH, JUST SO ALL OF US ARE MORE LIKELY TO MAKE IT?
SACRIFICE...? IT'S NOT THAT, REALLY. I JUST GOT A LIST OF PRIORITIES IN MY MIND. IF SOMETHING'S NOT UP TOP, I HONESTLY DON'T BOTHER WITH IT.
...LIKE HAVING A SOCIAL LIFE?
DOES SAVING US ALL COME FIRST?
YEAH.
NO...

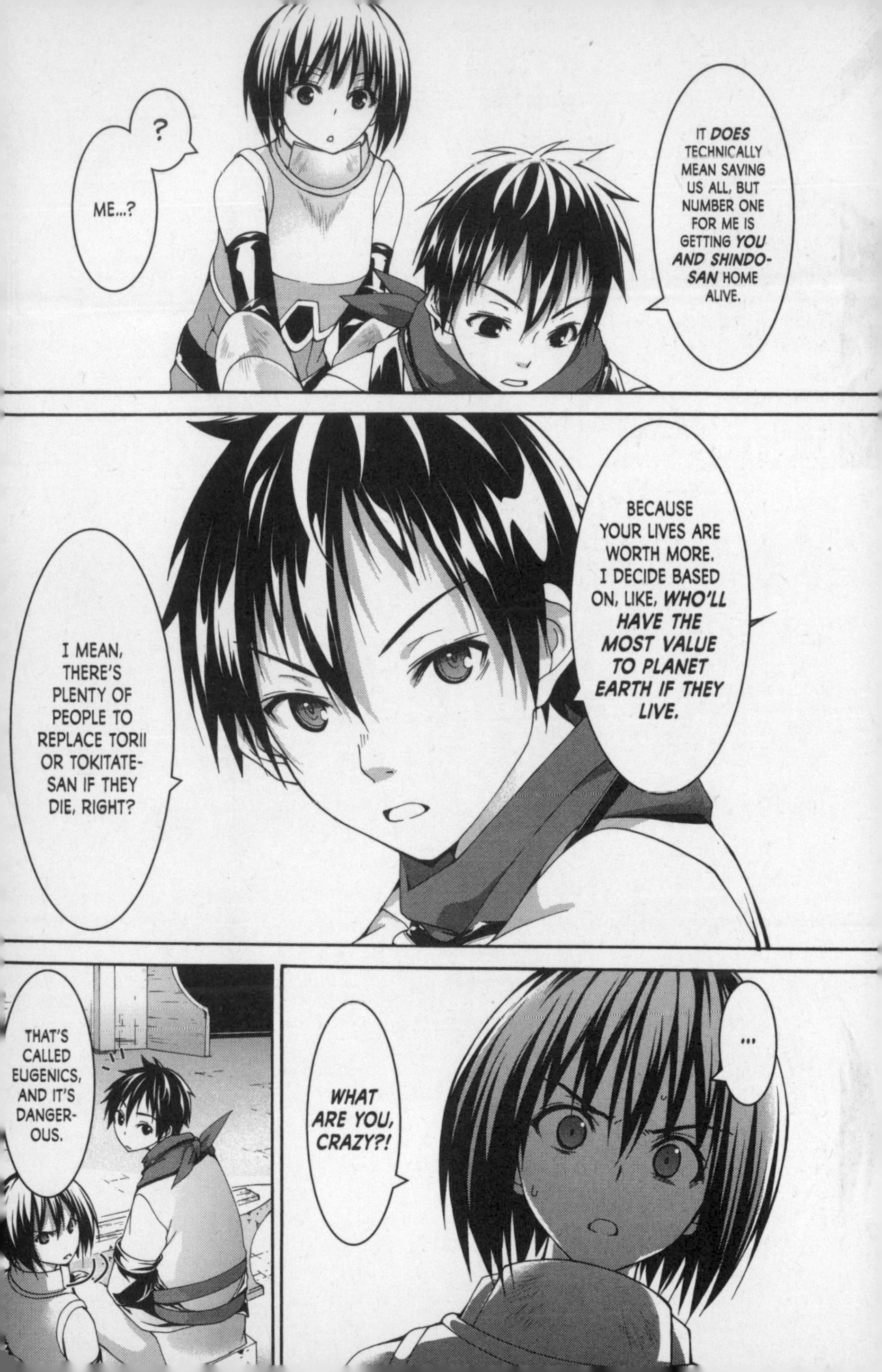
IT DOES TECHNICALLY MEAN SAVING US ALL, BUT NUMBER ONE FOR ME IS GETTING YOU AND SHINDO-SAN HOME ALIVE.
?
ME...?
BECAUSE YOUR LIVES ARE WORTH MORE. I DECIDE BASED ON, LIKE, WHO'LL HAVE THE MOST VALUE TO PLANET EARTH IF THEY LIVE.
I MEAN, THERE'S PLENTY OF PEOPLE TO REPLACE TORII OR TOKITATE-SAN IF THEY DIE, RIGHT?
...
WHAT ARE YOU, CRAZY?!
THAT'S CALLED EUGENICS, AND IT'S DANGER-OUS.

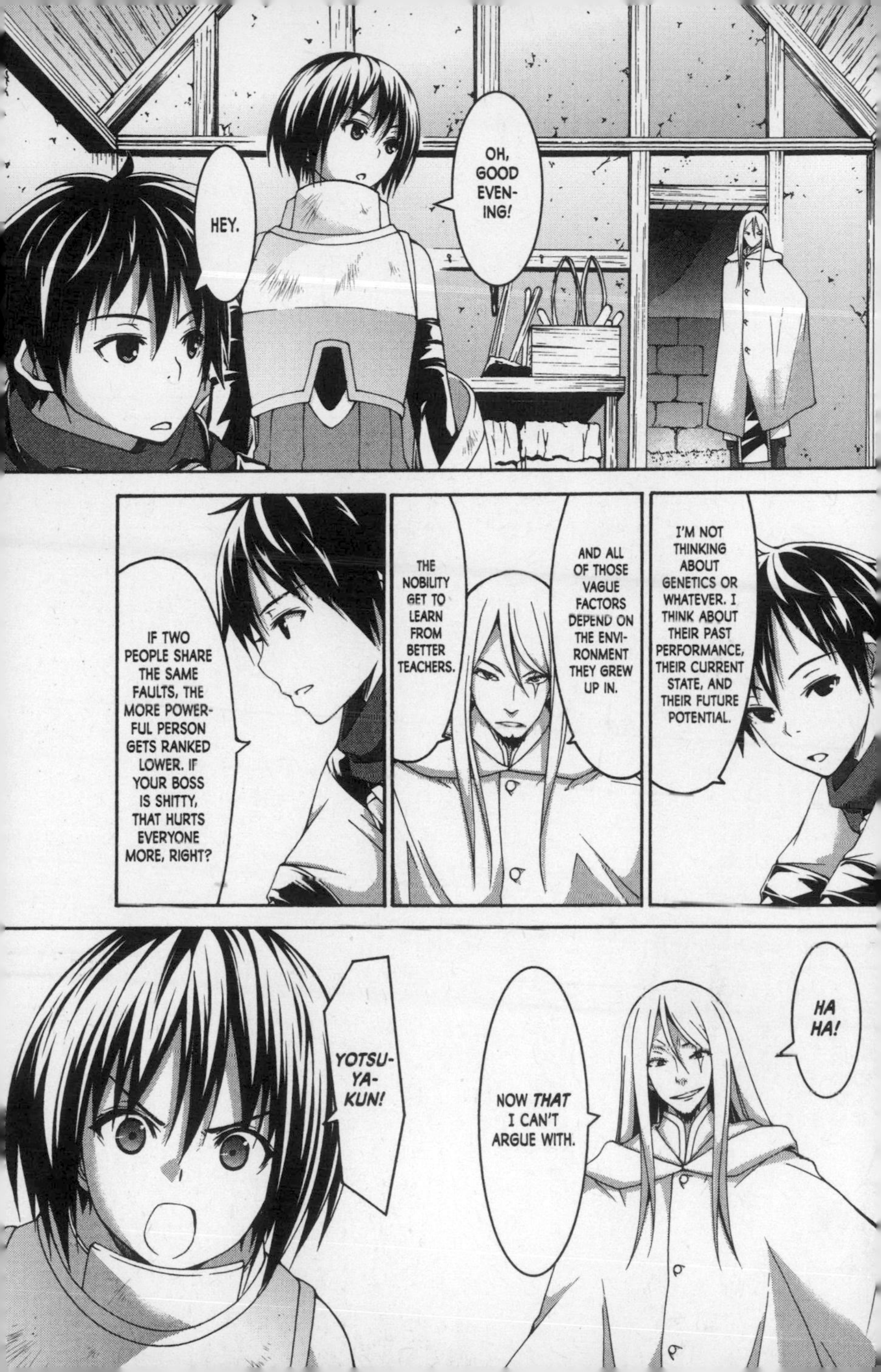
OH, GOOD EVEN-ING!
HEY.
I'M NOT THINKING ABOUT GENETICS OR WHATEVER. I THINK ABOUT THEIR PAST PERFORMANCE, THEIR CURRENT STATE, AND THEIR FUTURE POTENTIAL.
AND ALL OF THOSE VAGUE FACTORS DEPEND ON THE ENVI-RONMENT THEY GREW UP IN.
THE NOBILITY GET TO LEARN FROM BETTER TEACHERS.
IF TWO PEOPLE SHARE THE SAME FAULTS, THE MORE POWER-FUL PERSON GETS RANKED LOWER. IF YOUR BOSS IS SHITTY, THAT HURTS EVERYONE MORE, RIGHT?
HA HA!
NOW *THAT* I CAN'T ARGUE WITH.
YOTSU-YA-KUN!

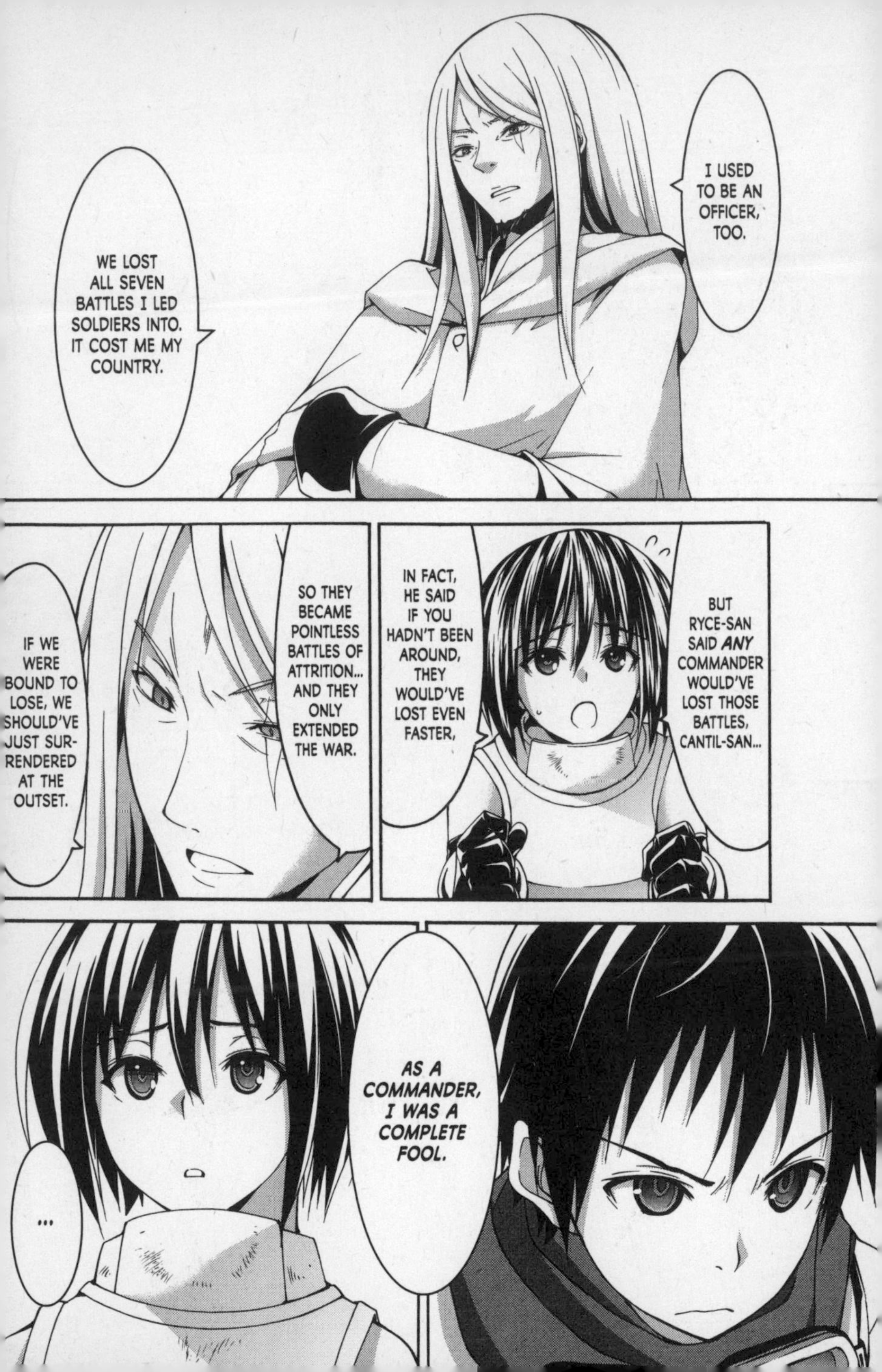
I USED TO BE AN OFFICER, TOO.
WE LOST ALL SEVEN BATTLES I LED SOLDIERS INTO. IT COST ME MY COUNTRY.
BUT RYCE-SAN SAID *ANY* COMMANDER WOULD'VE LOST THOSE BATTLES, CANTIL-SAN...
IN FACT, HE SAID IF YOU HADN'T BEEN AROUND, THEY WOULD'VE LOST EVEN FASTER,
SO THEY BECAME POINTLESS BATTLES OF ATTRITION... AND THEY ONLY EXTENDED THE WAR.
IF WE WERE BOUND TO LOSE, WE SHOULD'VE JUST SUR-RENDERED AT THE OUTSET.
AS A COMMANDER, I WAS A COMPLETE FOOL.
...

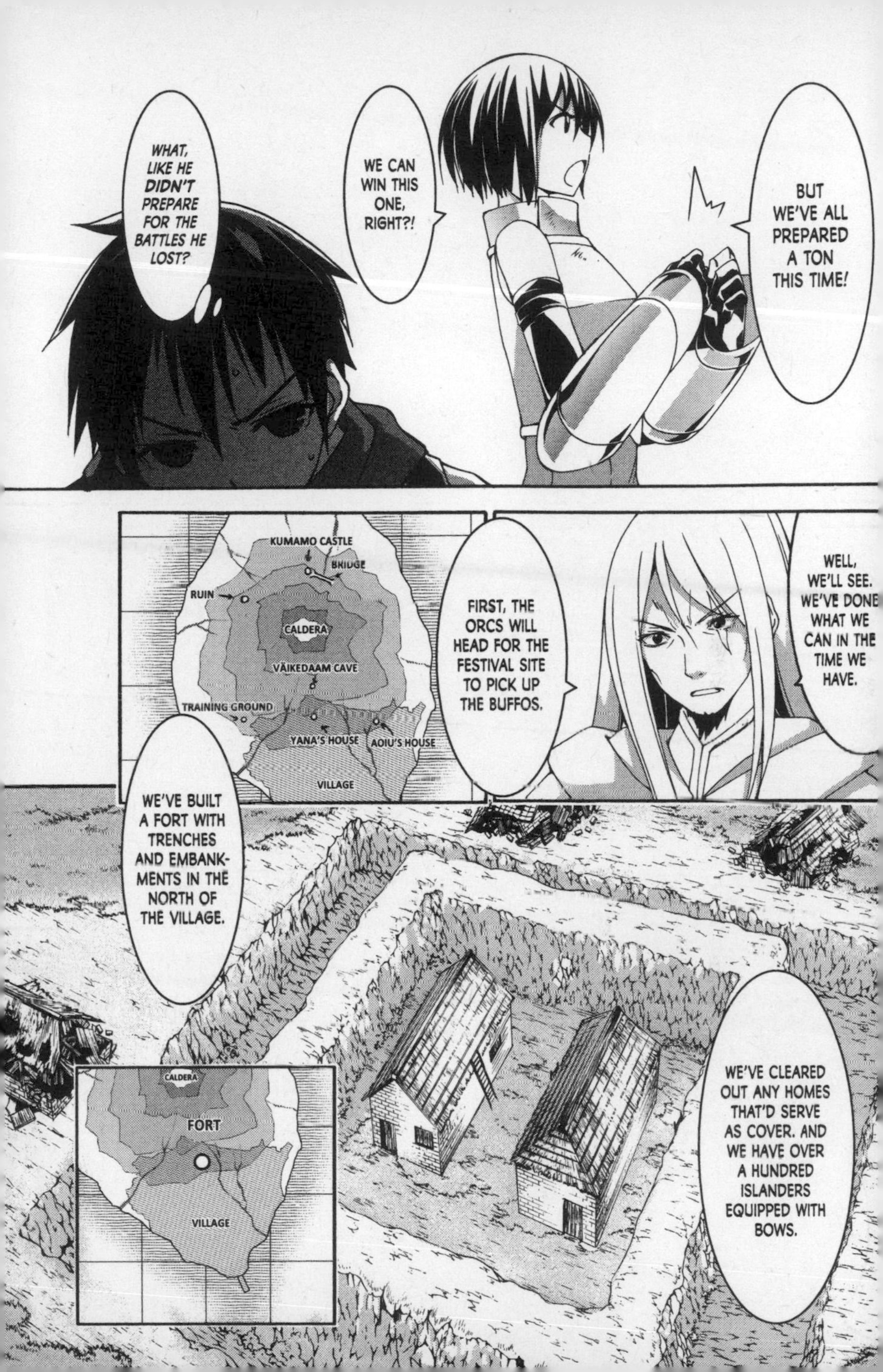
BUT WE'VE ALL PREPARED A TON THIS TIME!
WE CAN WIN THIS ONE, RIGHT?!
WHAT, LIKE HE DIDN'T PREPARE FOR THE BATTLES HE LOST?
WELL, WE'LL SEE. WE'VE DONE WHAT WE CAN IN THE TIME WE HAVE.
FIRST, THE ORCS WILL HEAD FOR THE FESTIVAL SITE TO PICK UP THE BUFFOS.
KUMAMO CASTLE
BRIDGE
RUIN
CALDERA
VÄIKEDAAM CAVE
TRAINING GROUND
YANA'S HOUSE
AOIU'S HOUSE
VILLAGE
WE'VE BUILT A FORT WITH TRENCHES AND EMBANK-MENTS IN THE NORTH OF THE VILLAGE.
WE'VE CLEARED OUT ANY HOMES THAT'D SERVE AS COVER. AND WE HAVE OVER A HUNDRED ISLANDERS EQUIPPED WITH BOWS.
CALDERA
FORT
VILLAGE

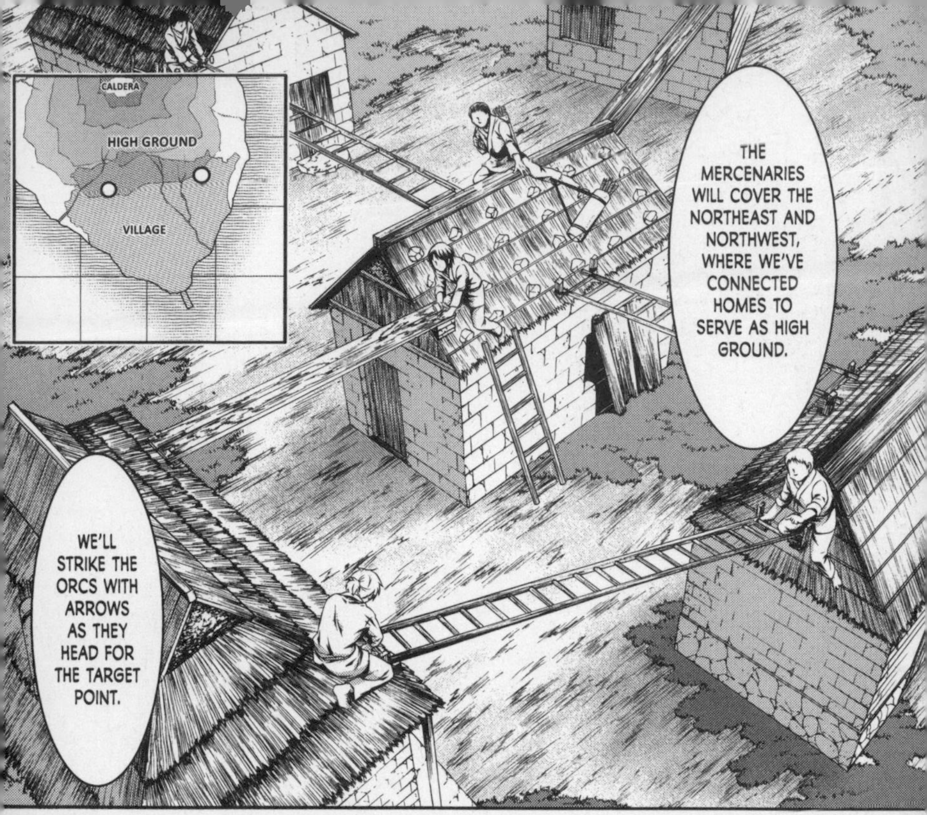
THE MERCENARIES WILL COVER THE NORTHEAST AND NORTHWEST, WHERE WE'VE CONNECTED HOMES TO SERVE AS HIGH GROUND.
WE'LL STRIKE THE ORCS WITH ARROWS AS THEY HEAD FOR THE TARGET POINT.
CALDERA
HIGH GROUND
VILLAGE

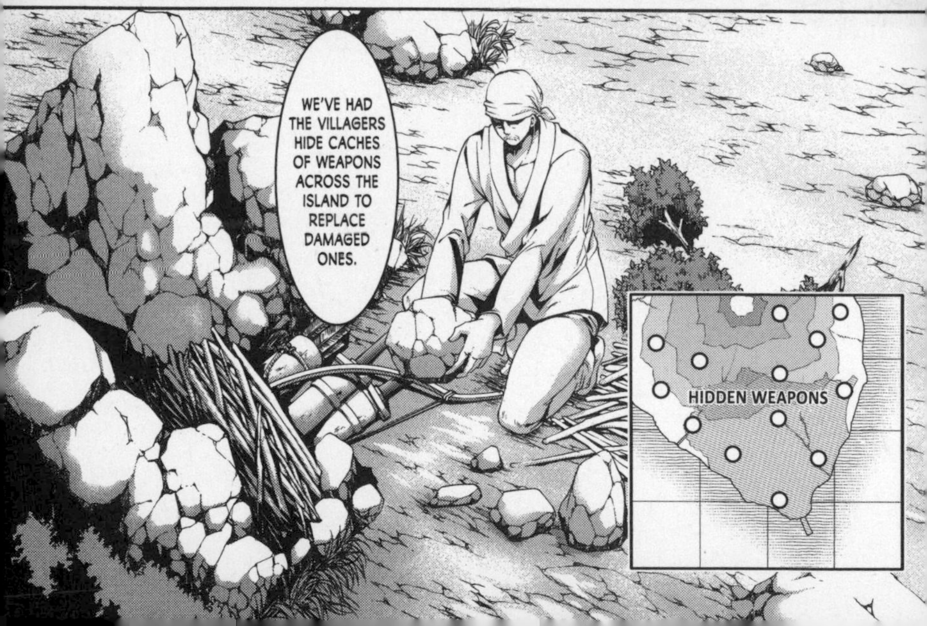
WE'VE HAD THE VILLAGERS HIDE CACHES OF WEAPONS ACROSS THE ISLAND TO REPLACE DAMAGED ONES.
HIDDEN WEAPONS

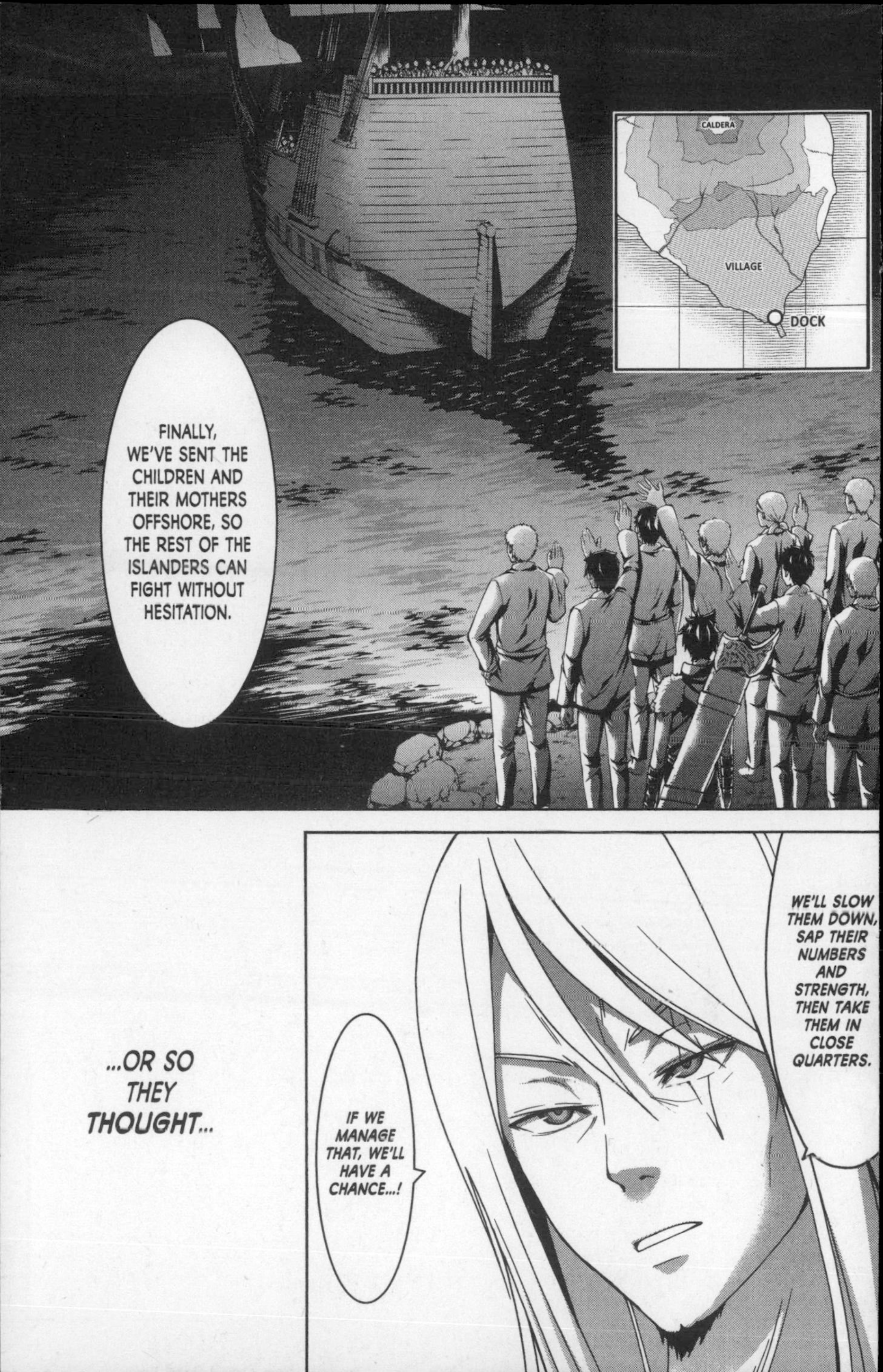
CALDERA
VILLAGE
DOCK
FINALLY, WE'VE SENT THE CHILDREN AND THEIR MOTHERS OFFSHORE, SO THE REST OF THE ISLANDERS CAN FIGHT WITHOUT HESITATION.
WE'LL SLOW THEM DOWN, SAP THEIR NUMBERS AND STRENGTH, THEN TAKE THEM IN CLOSE QUARTERS.
IF WE MANAGE THAT, WE'LL HAVE A CHANCE...!
...OR SO THEY THOUGHT...

HALF A DAY TO HARVEST FESTIVAL / START OF BATTLE...

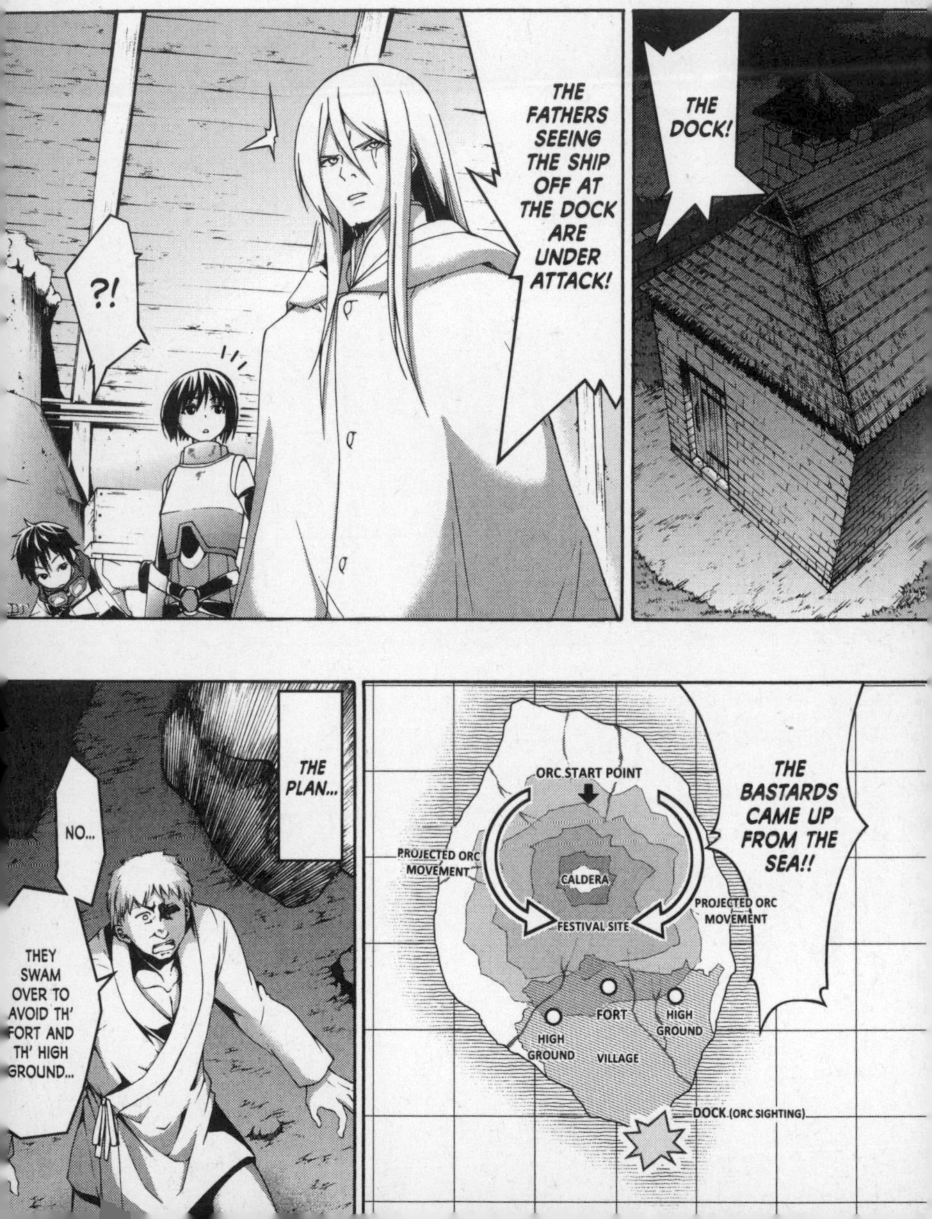

THE DOCK!
THE FATHERS SEEING THE SHIP OFF AT THE DOCK ARE UNDER ATTACK!
?!
THE BASTARDS CAME UP FROM THE SEA!!
ORC START POINT
PROJECTED ORC MOVEMENT
CALDERA
PROJECTED ORC MOVEMENT
FESTIVAL SITE
FORT
HIGH GROUND
HIGH GROUND
VILLAGE
DOCK (ORC SIGHTING)
THE PLAN...
NO...
THEY SWAM OVER TO AVOID TH' FORT AND TH' HIGH GROUND...

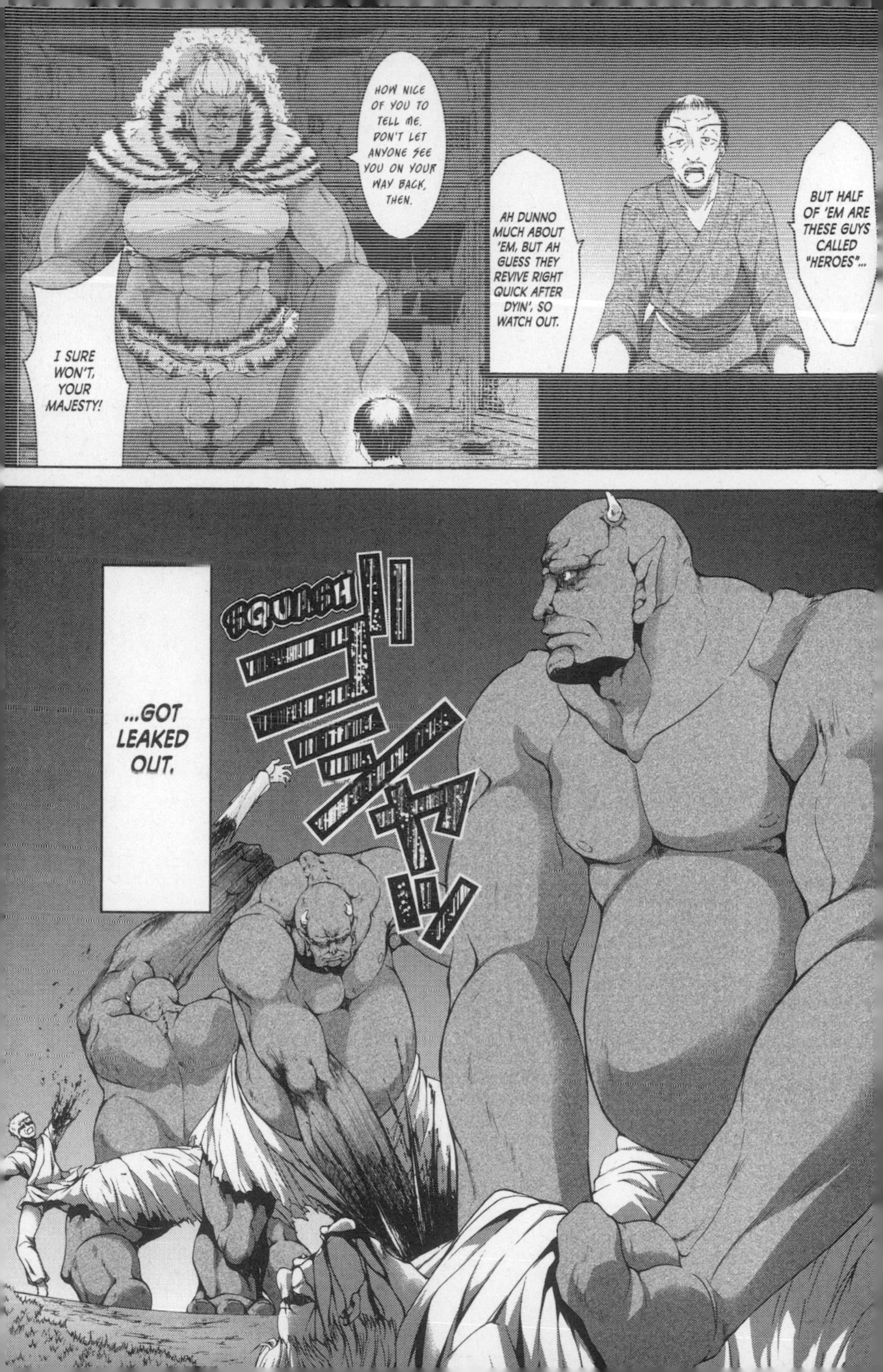
BUT HALF OF 'EM ARE THESE GUYS CALLED "HEROES"...
AH DUNNO MUCH ABOUT 'EM, BUT AH GUESS THEY REVIVE RIGHT QUICK AFTER DYIN', SO WATCH OUT.
HOW NICE OF YOU TO TELL ME. DON'T LET ANYONE SEE YOU ON YOUR WAY BACK, THEN.
I SURE WON'T, YOUR MAJESTY!
SQUASH
...GOT LEAKED OUT.

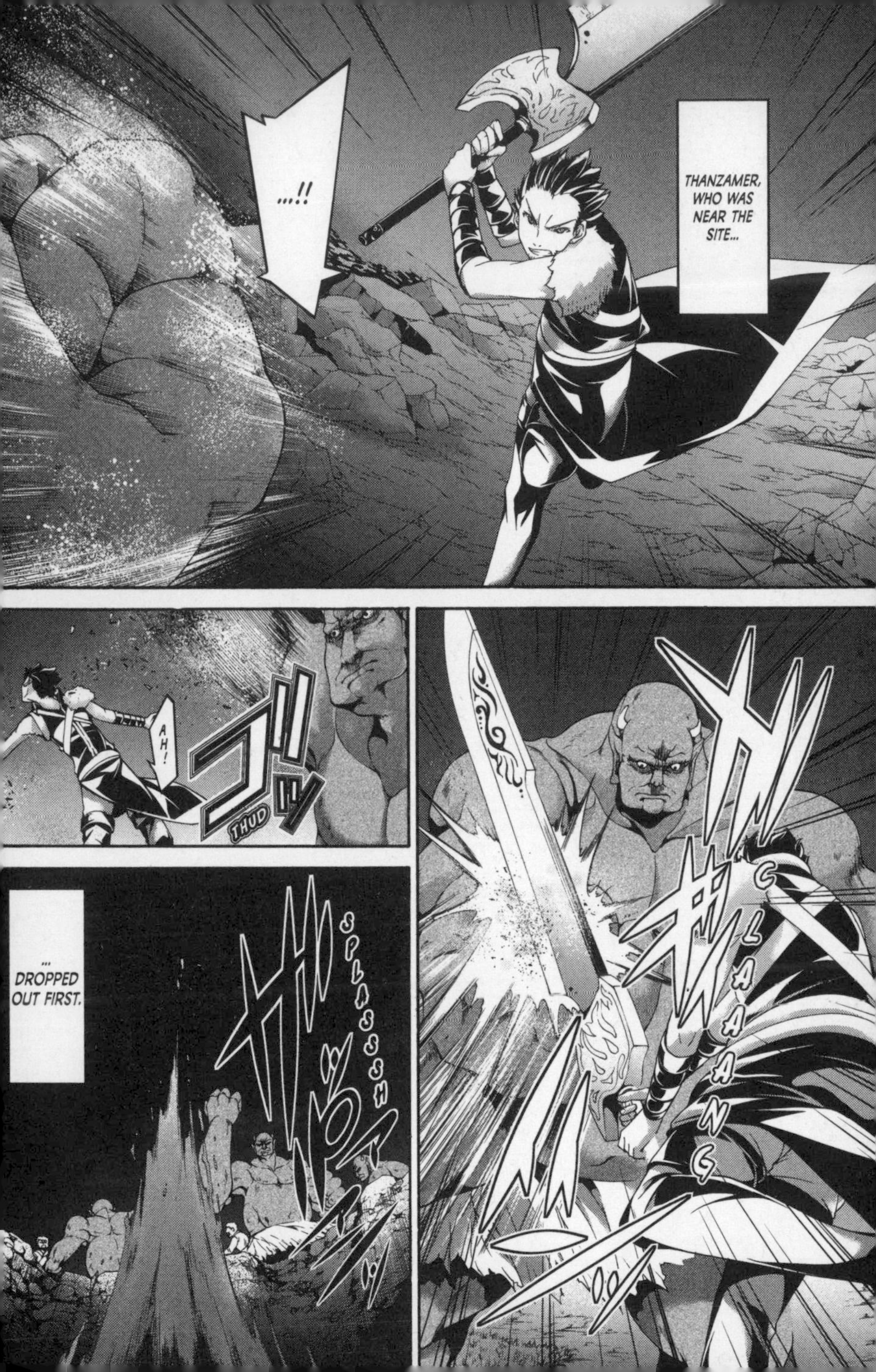
THANZAMER, WHO WAS NEAR THE SITE...
...!!
CLAAANG
AH!
THUD
... DROPPED OUT FIRST.
SPLASSSH

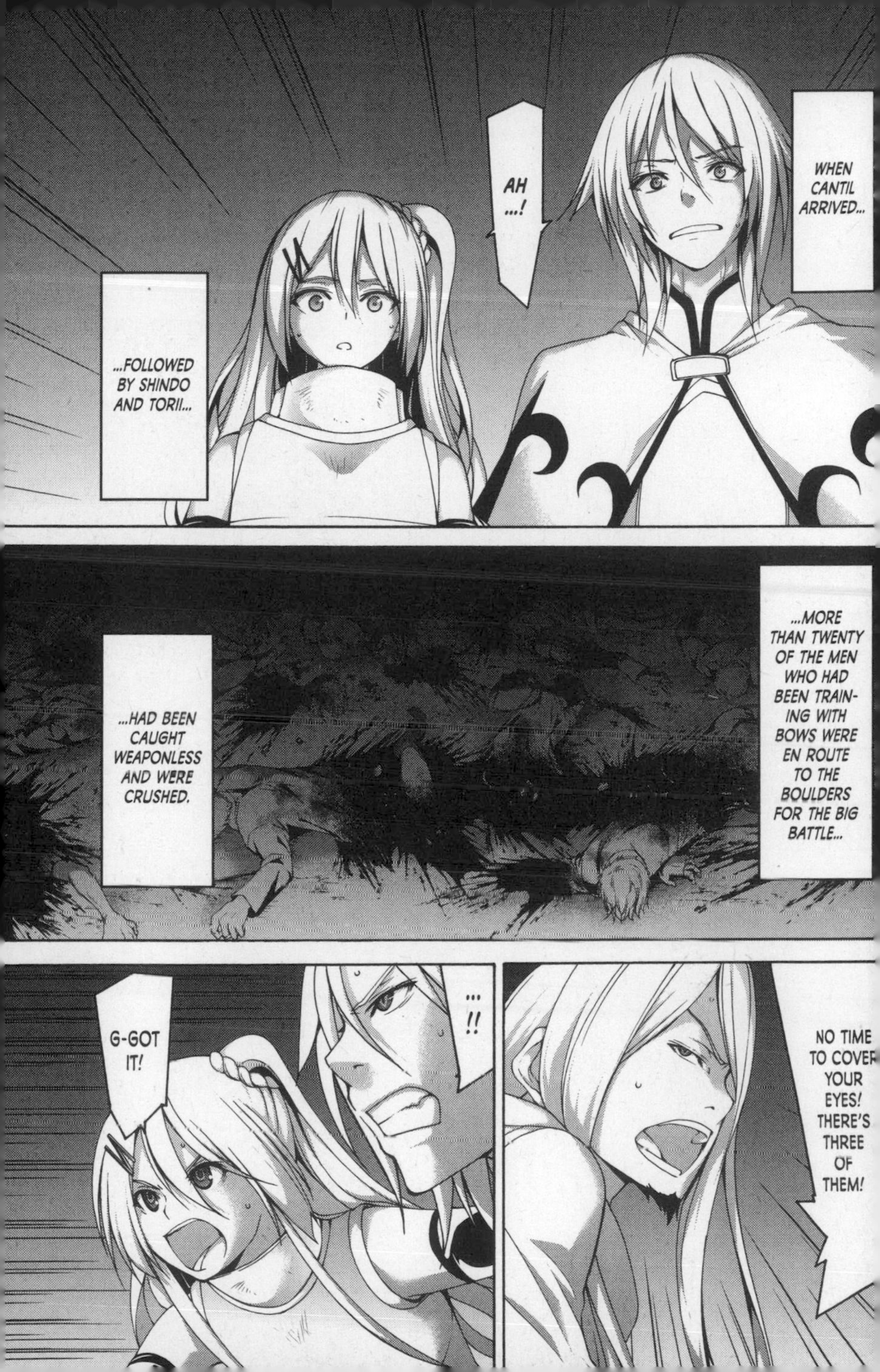
WHEN CANTIL ARRIVED...
AH ...!
...FOLLOWED BY SHINDO AND TORII...
...MORE THAN TWENTY OF THE MEN WHO HAD BEEN TRAIN-ING WITH BOWS WERE EN ROUTE TO THE BOULDERS FOR THE BIG BATTLE...
...HAD BEEN CAUGHT WEAPONLESS AND WERE CRUSHED.
NO TIME TO COVER YOUR EYES! THERE'S THREE OF THEM!
...!!
G-GOT IT!

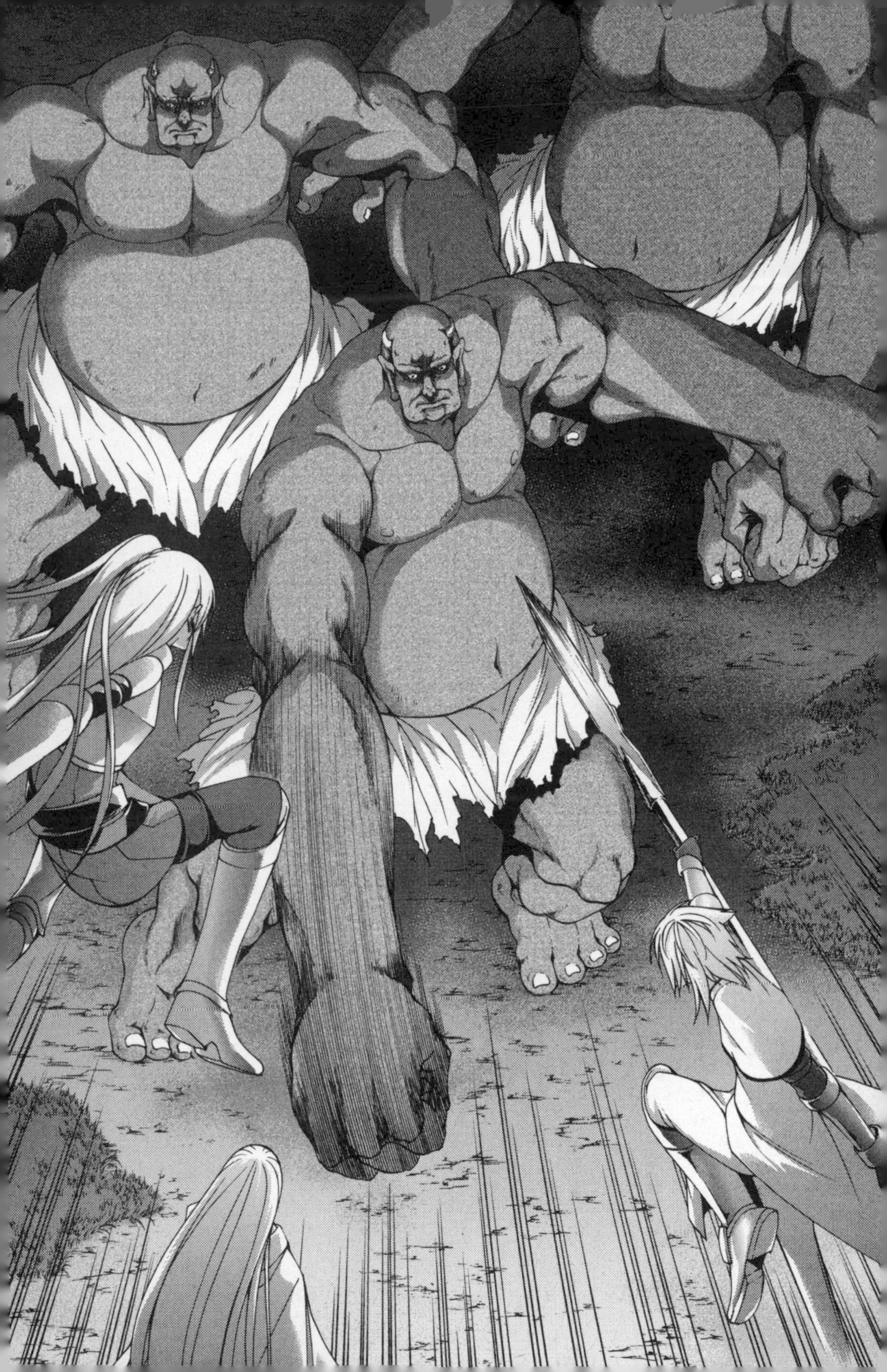

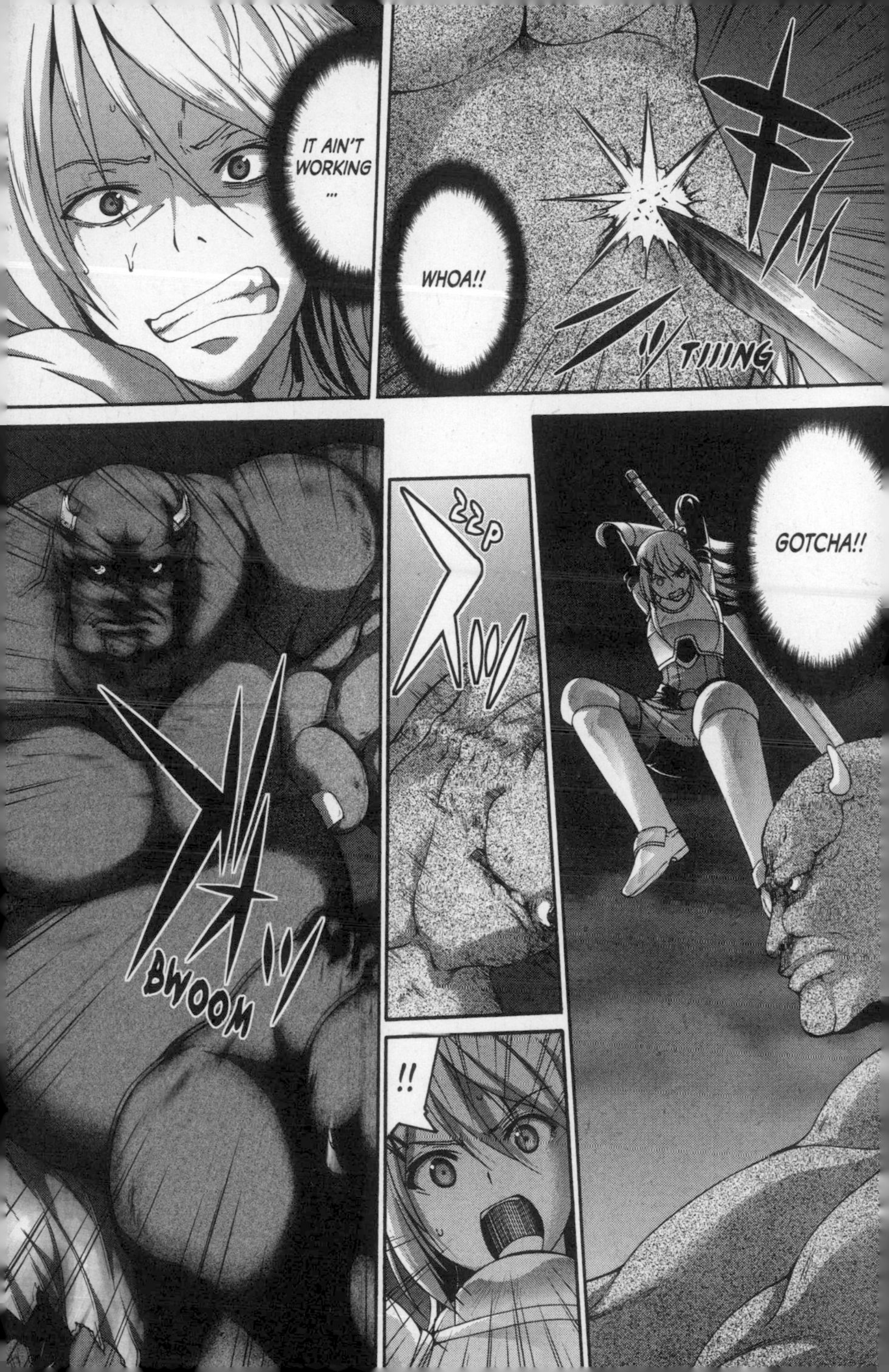
WHOA!!
TIIING
IT AIN'T WORKING ...
GOTCHA!!
!!
BWOOM

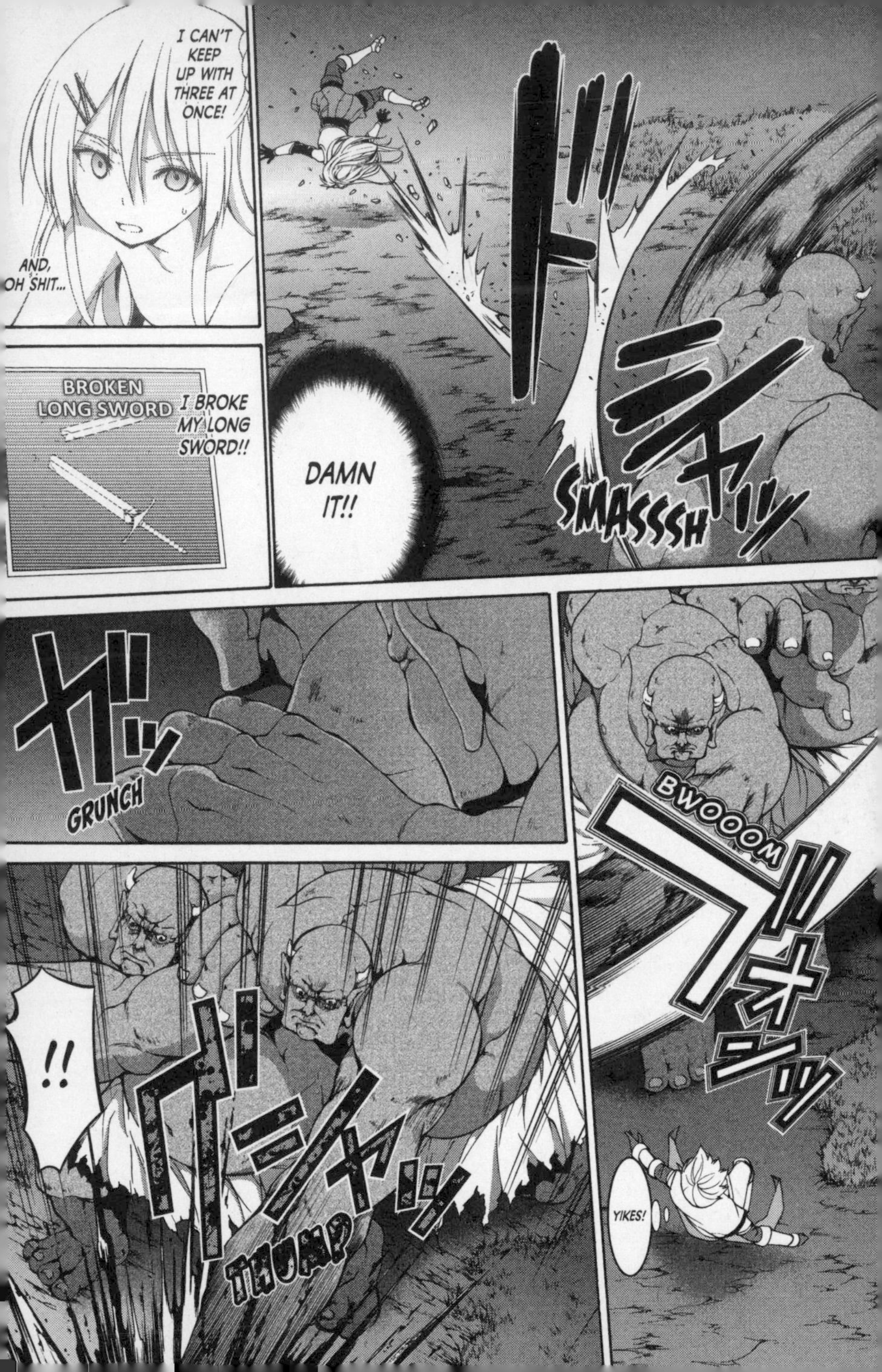
SMASSSH
DAMN IT!!
I CAN'T KEEP UP WITH THREE AT ONCE!
AND, OH SHIT...
BROKEN LONG SWORD
I BROKE MY LONG SWORD!!
BWOOOM
YIKES!
GRUNCH
!!
THUMP

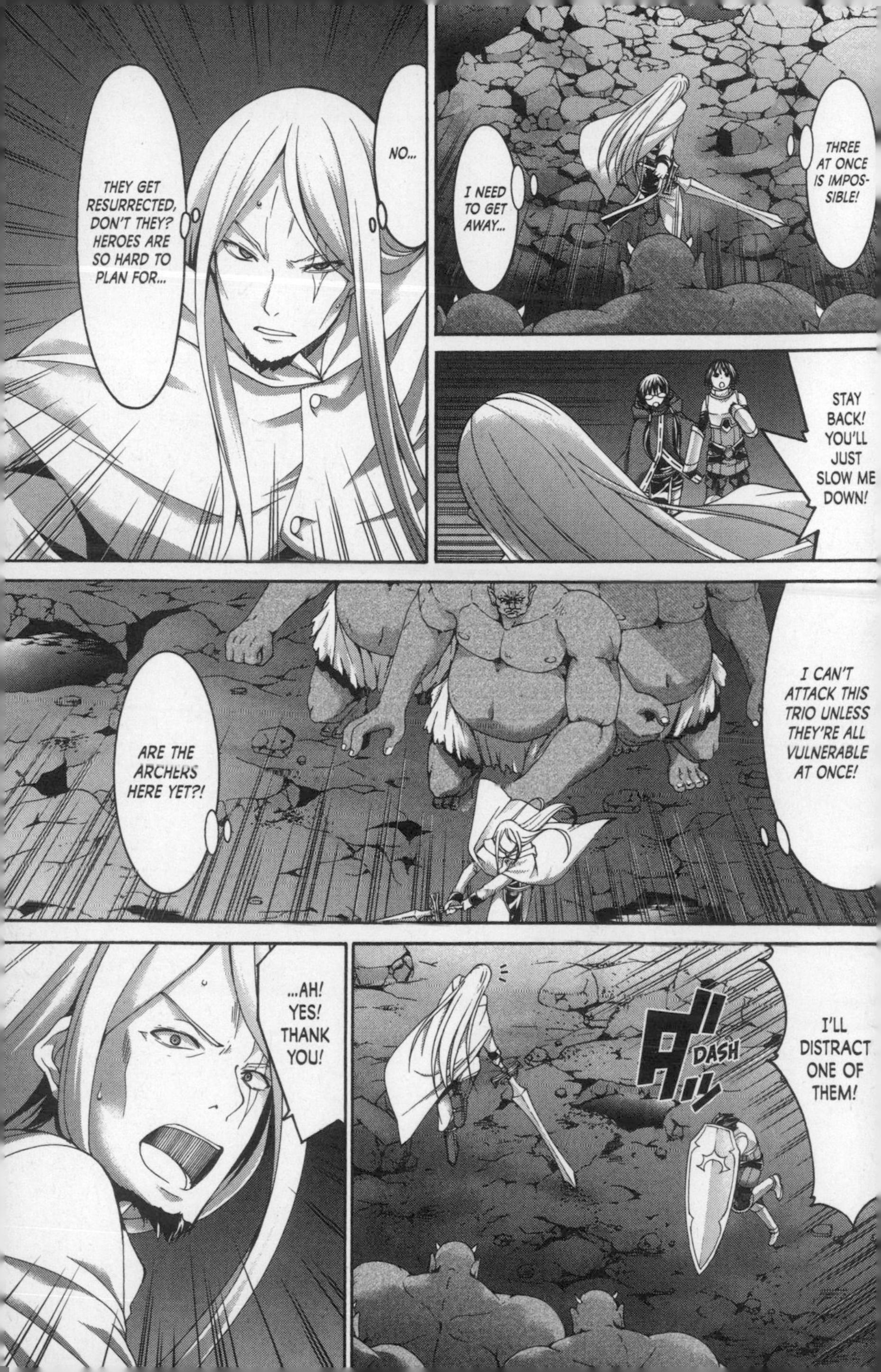
THREE AT ONCE IS IMPOSSIBLE!
I NEED TO GET AWAY...
STAY BACK! YOU'LL JUST SLOW ME DOWN!
NO...
THEY GET RESURRECTED, DON'T THEY? HEROES ARE SO HARD TO PLAN FOR...
I CAN'T ATTACK THIS TRIO UNLESS THEY'RE ALL VULNERABLE AT ONCE!
ARE THE ARCHERS HERE YET?!
I'LL DISTRACT ONE OF THEM!
ダッ
DASH
...AH! YES! THANK YOU!

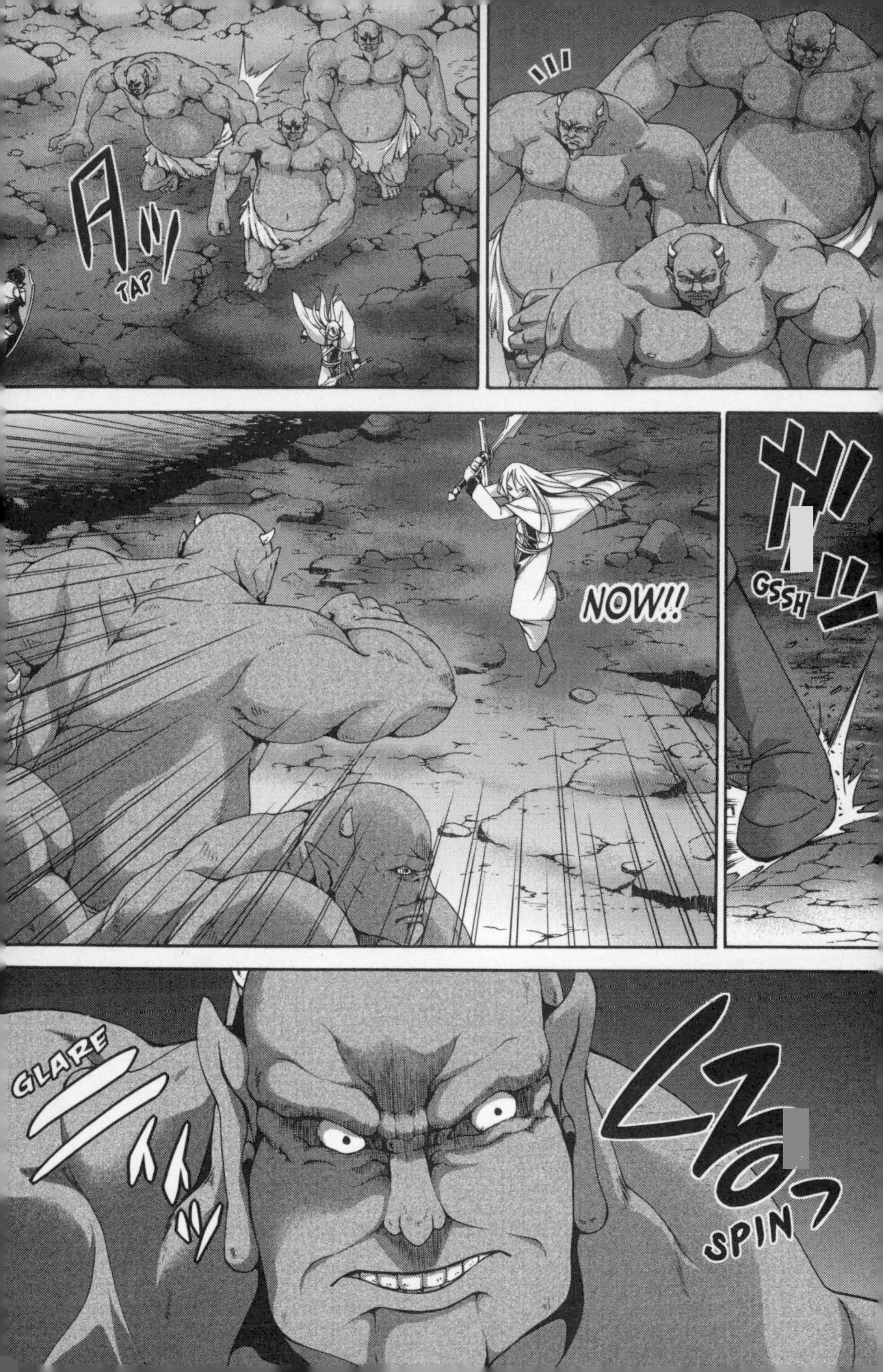
TAP
GSSH
NOW!!
SPIN
GLARE

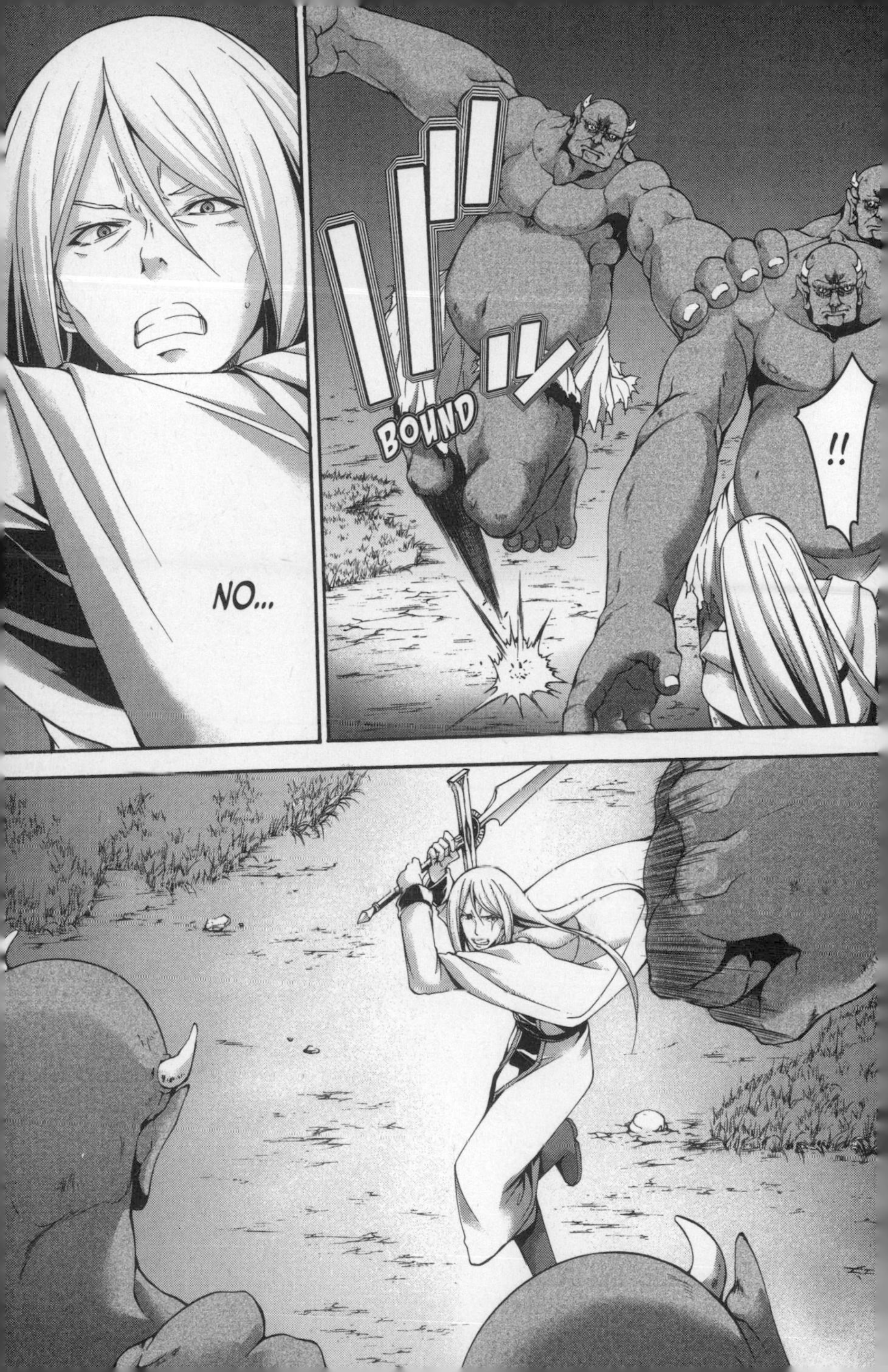
BOUND
!!
NO...

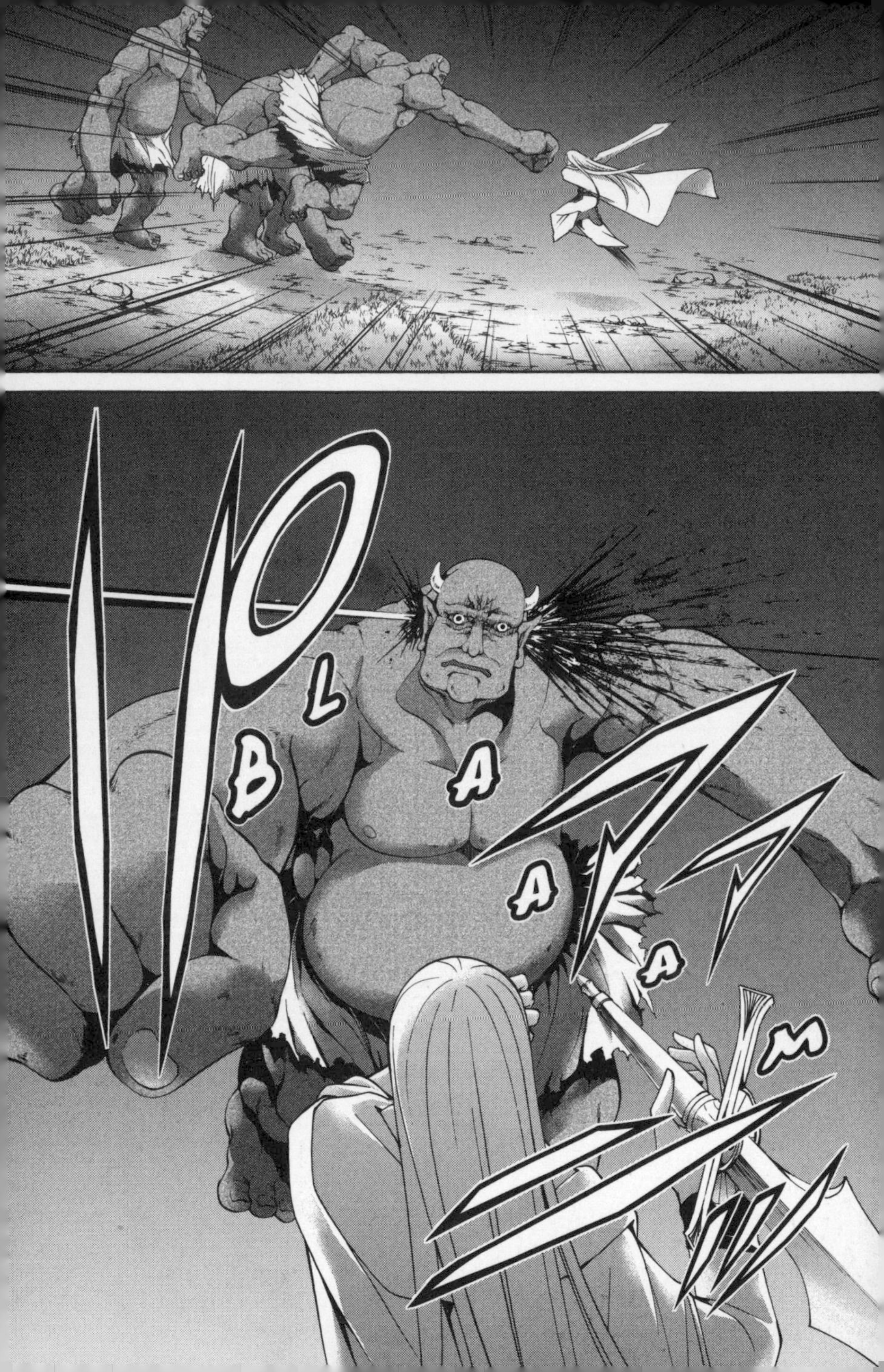
BLAAAM

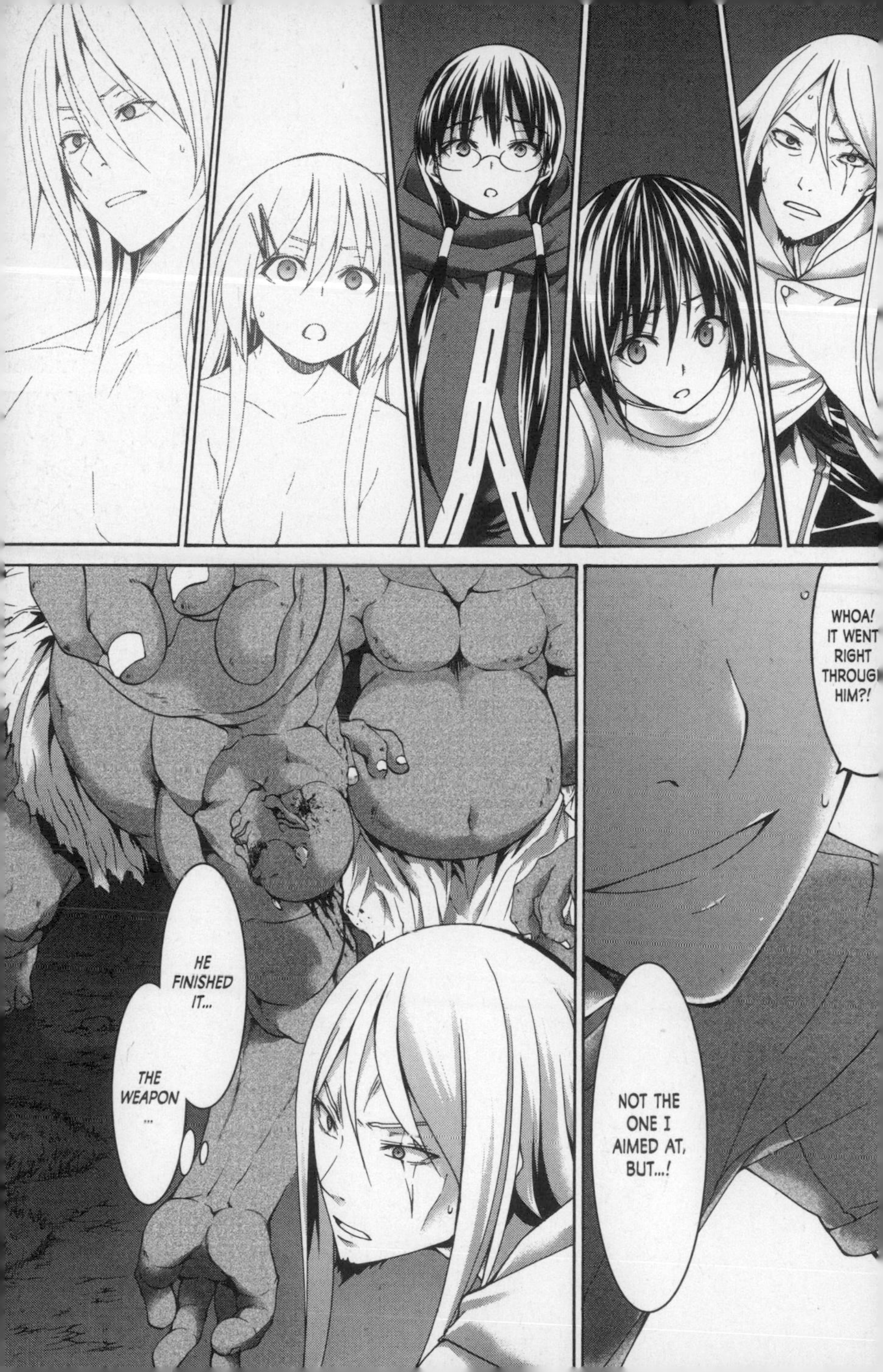
WHOA! IT WENT RIGHT THROUGH HIM?!
NOT THE ONE I AIMED AT, BUT...!
HE FINISHED IT...
THE WEAPON...

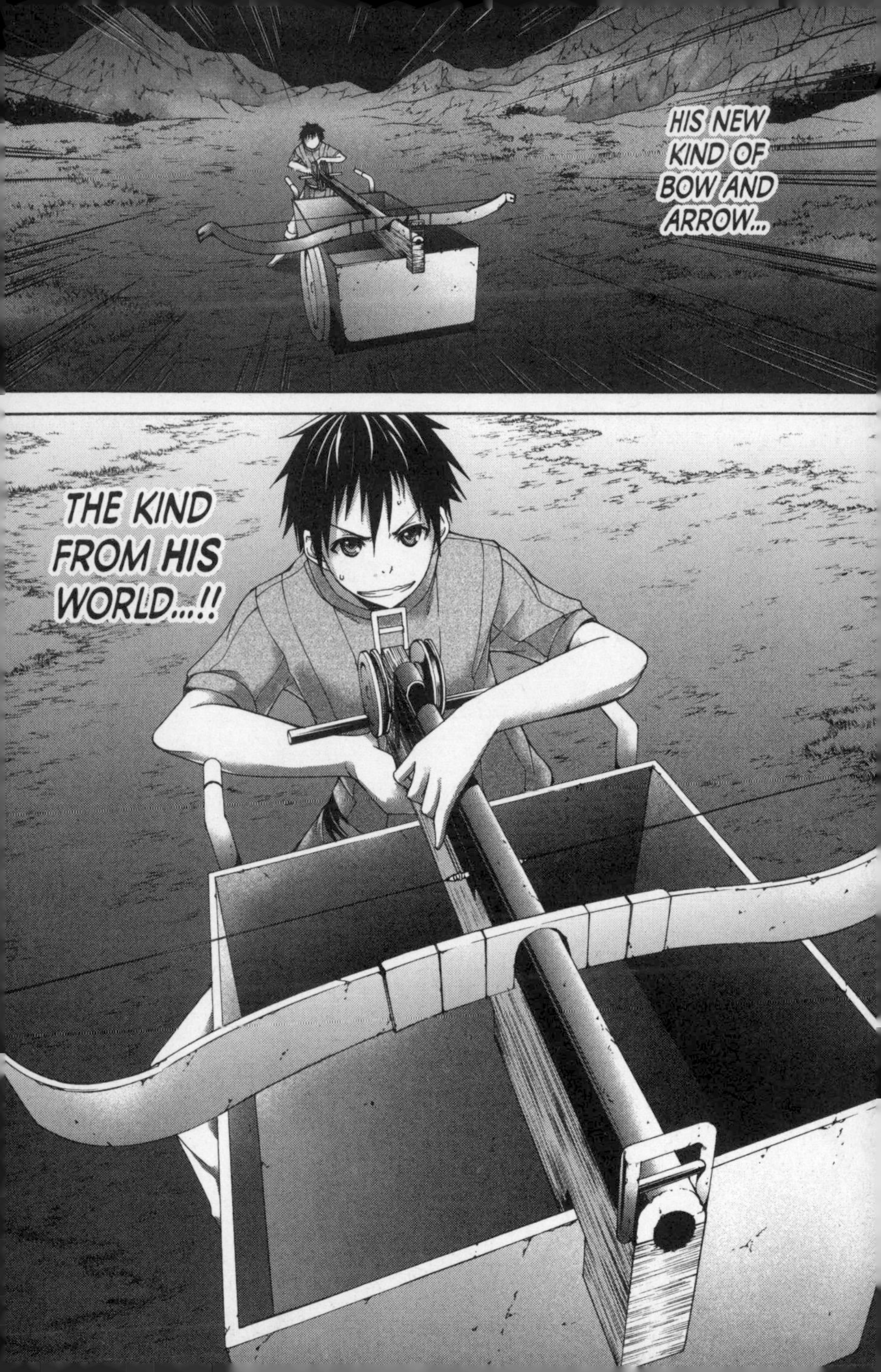
HIS NEW KIND OF BOW AND ARROW...
THE KIND FROM HIS WORLD...!!

I'M STANDING ON A MILLION LIVES

I'M STANDING ON A MILLION LIVES.

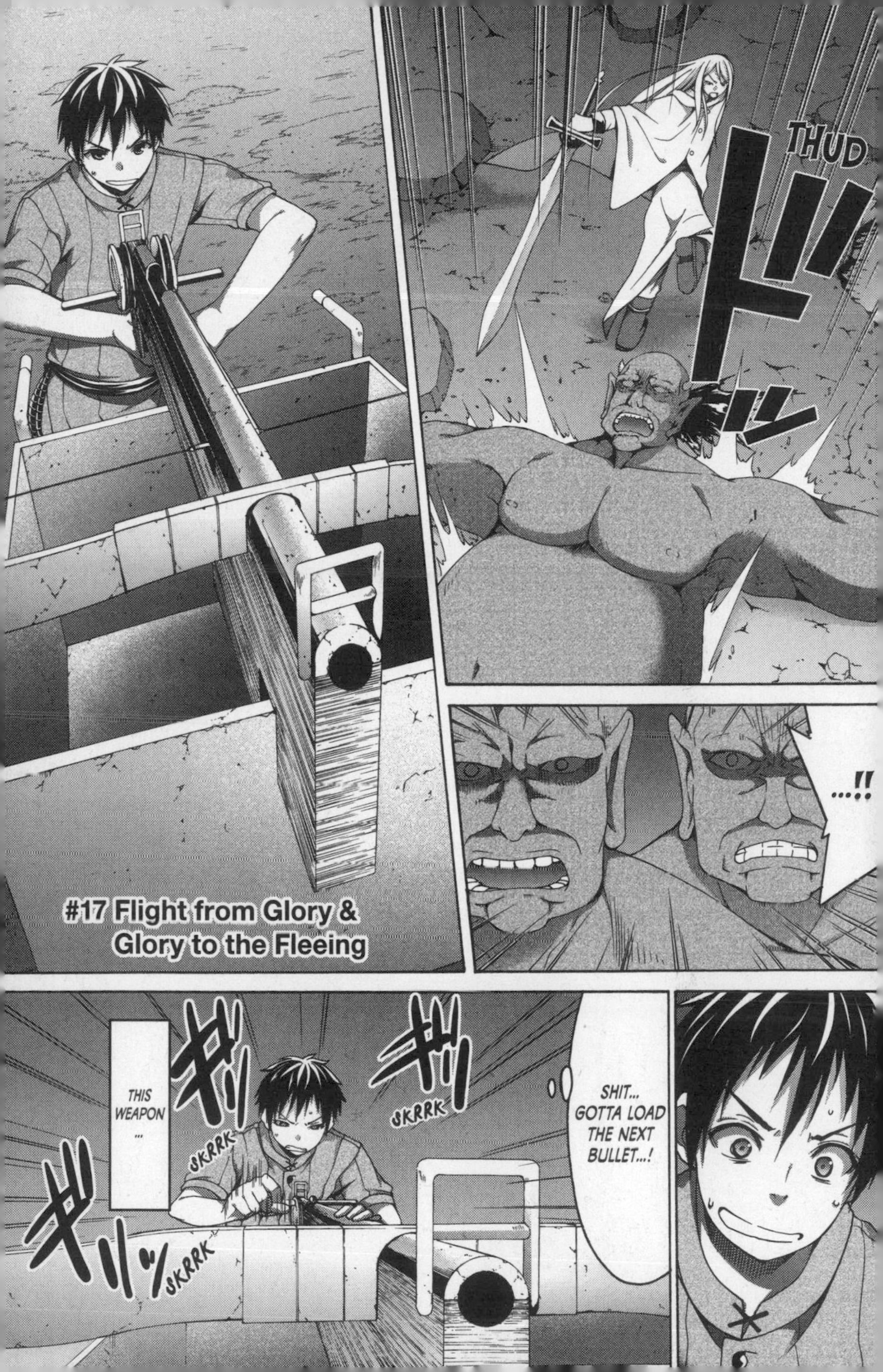

THUD
ドドッ
...!!
#17 Flight from Glory & Glory to the Fleeing
SHIT... GOTTA LOAD THE NEXT BULLET...!
THIS WEAPON ...
SKRRK
SKRRK
SKRRK

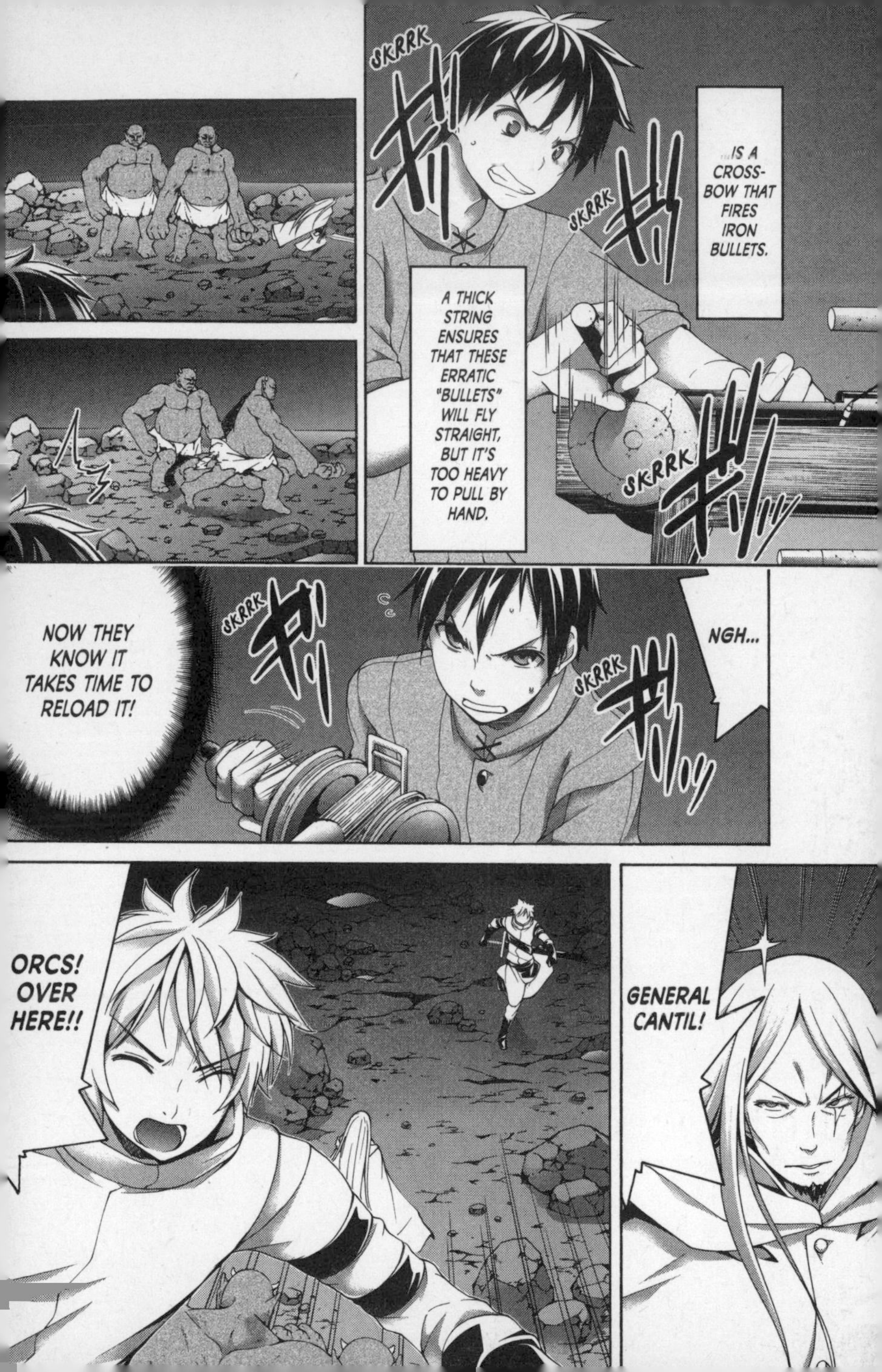
...IS A CROSS-BOW THAT FIRES IRON BULLETS.
SKRRK
SKRRK
A THICK STRING ENSURES THAT THESE ERRATIC "BULLETS" WILL FLY STRAIGHT, BUT IT'S TOO HEAVY TO PULL BY HAND.
SKRRK
NGH...
SKRRK
SKRRK
NOW THEY KNOW IT TAKES TIME TO RELOAD IT!
GENERAL CANTIL!
ORCS! OVER HERE!!

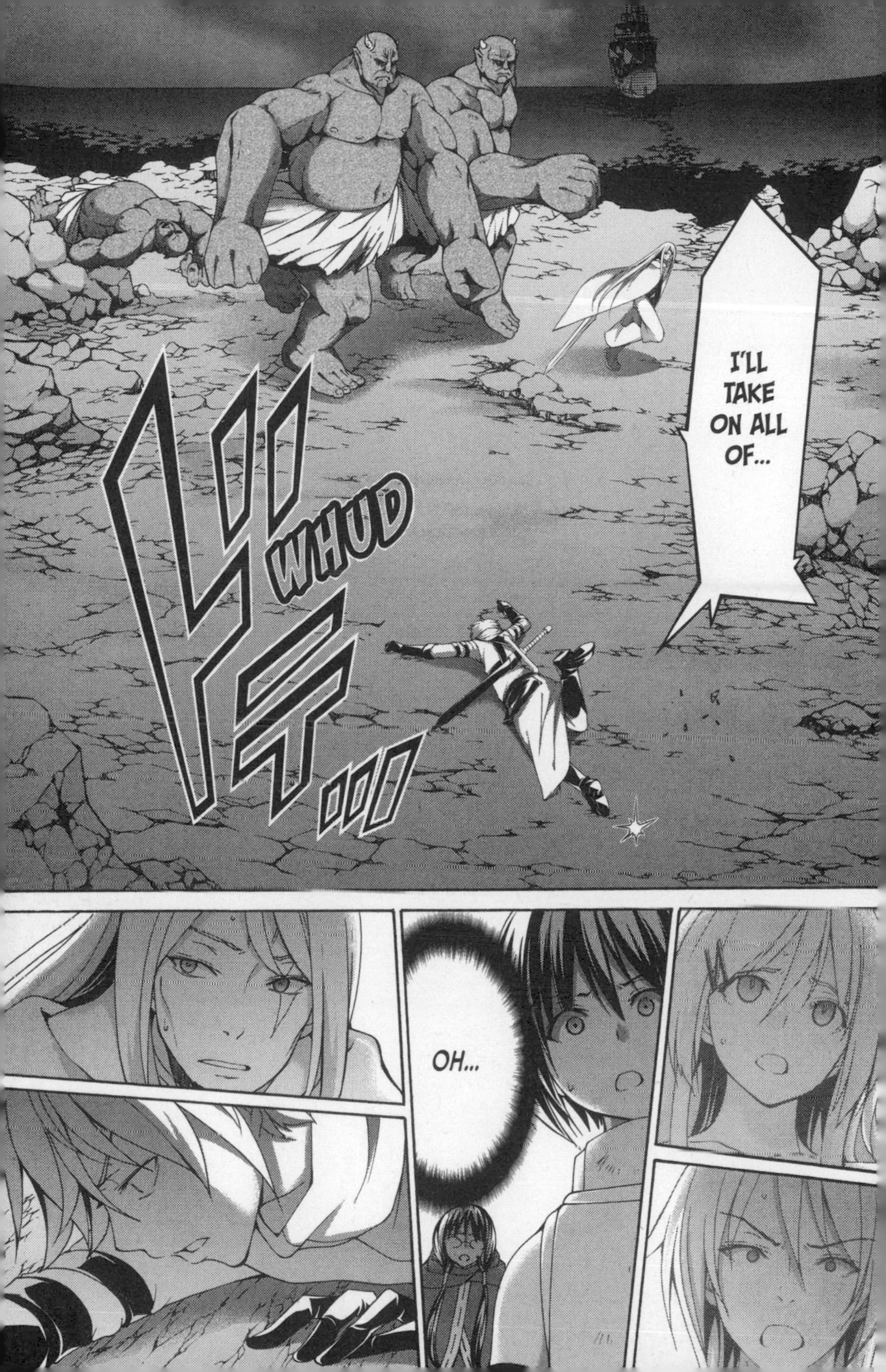
I'LL TAKE ON ALL OF...
WHUD
OH...

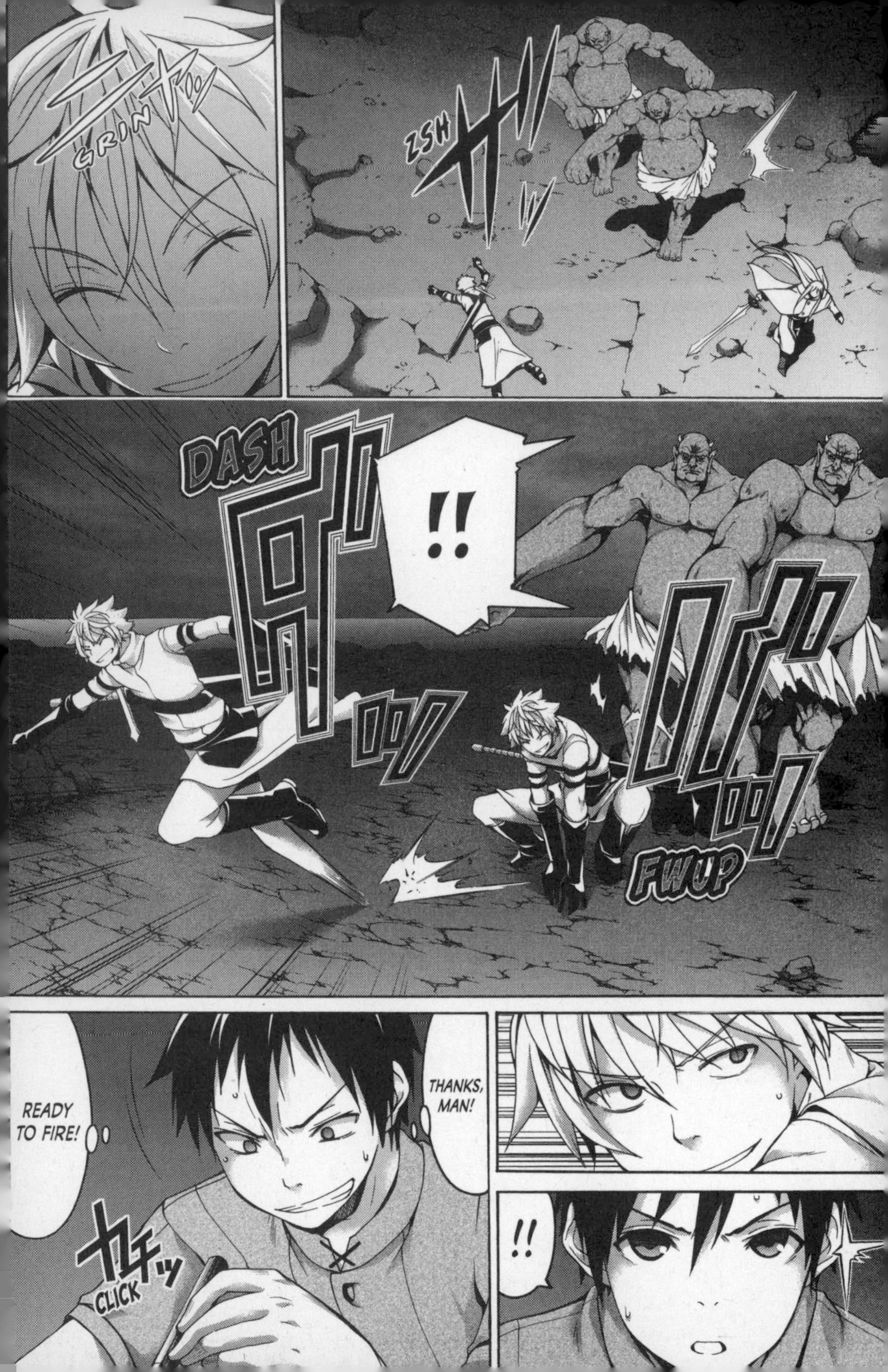
ZSH
GRIN
!!
DASH
FWUP
!!
THANKS, MAN!
READY TO FIRE!
CLICK

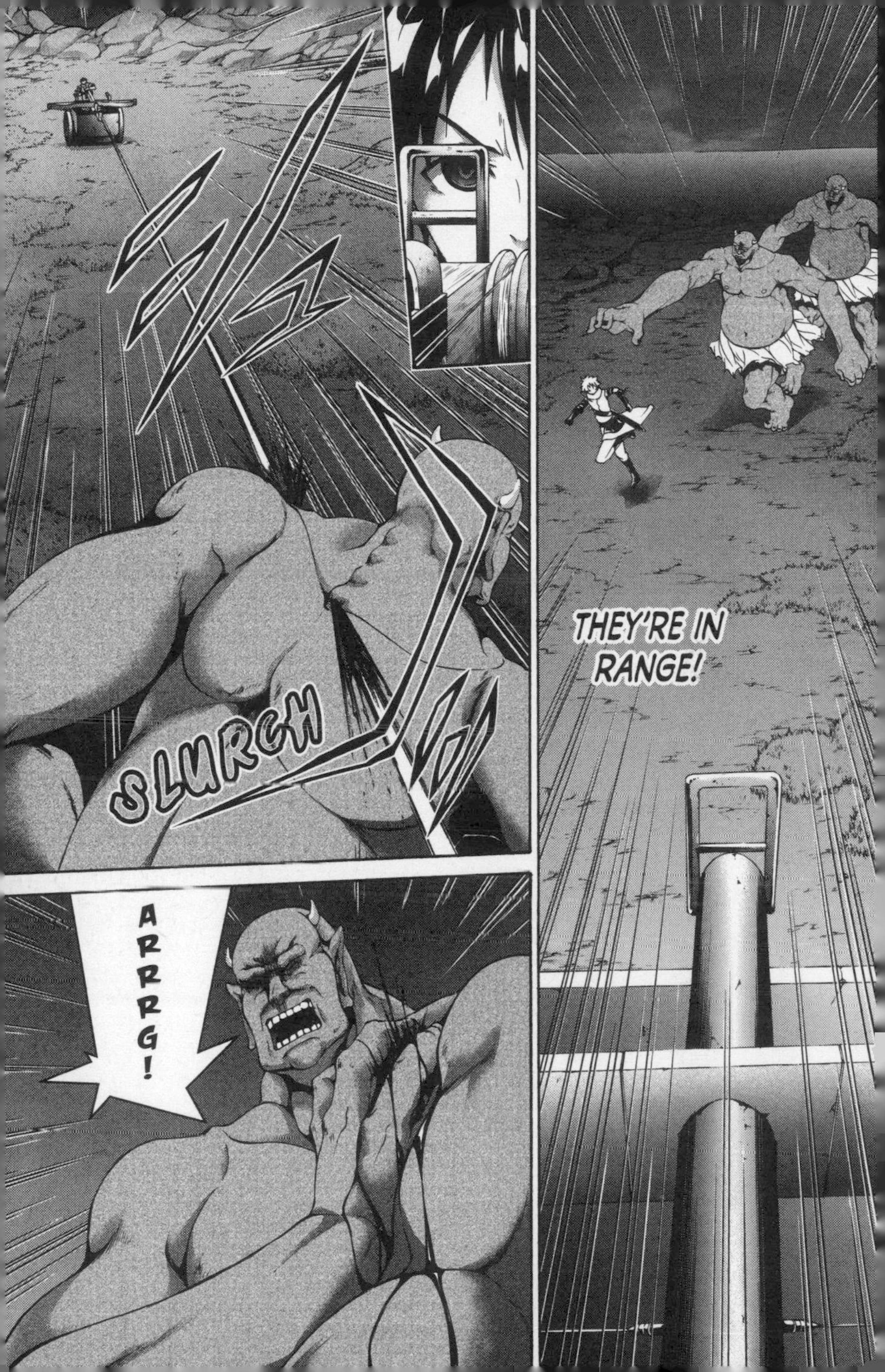
THEY'RE IN RANGE!
SLURCH
ARRRG!

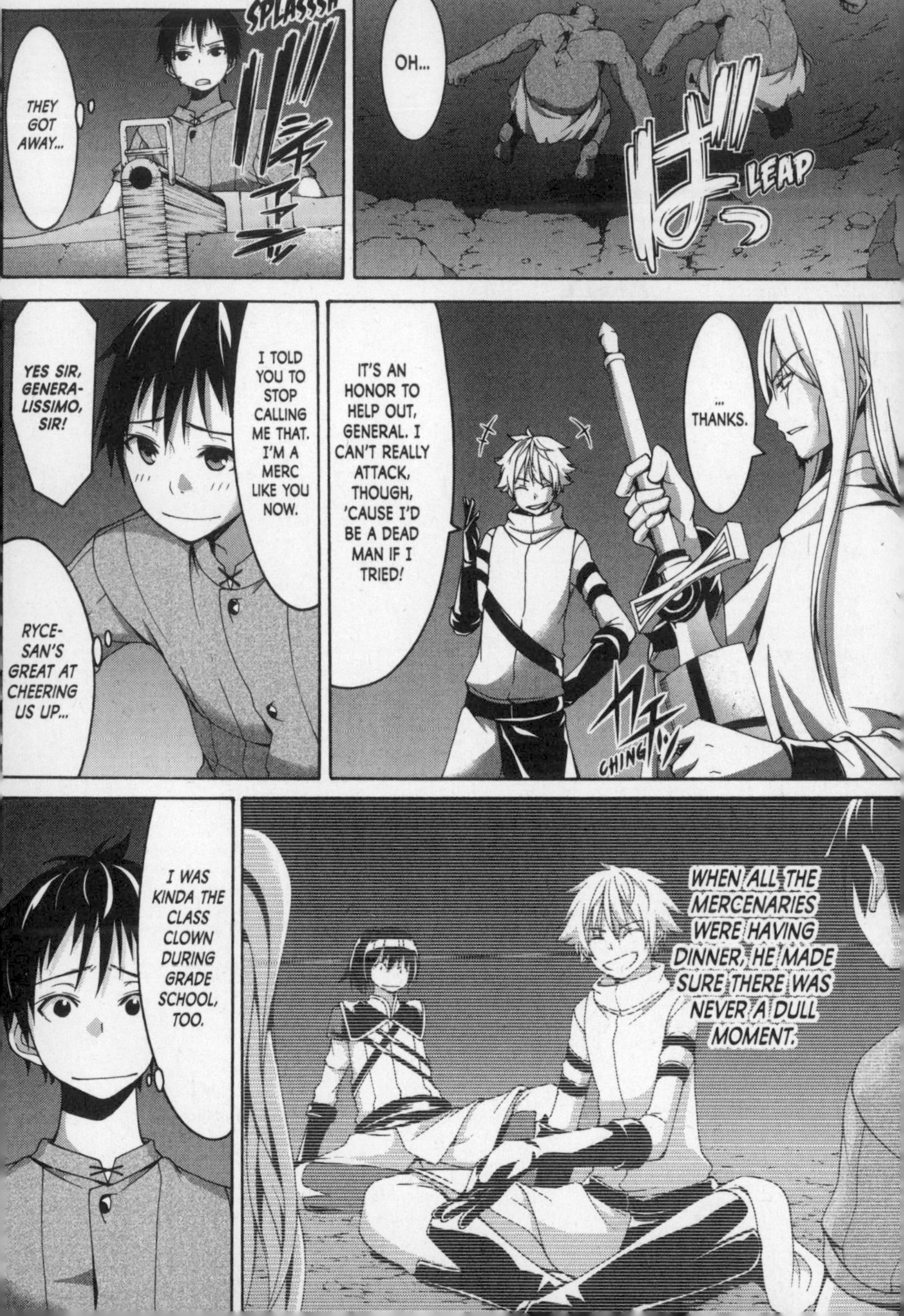
OH...
LEAP
SPLASSSH
THEY GOT AWAY...
... THANKS.
IT'S AN HONOR TO HELP OUT, GENERAL. I CAN'T REALLY ATTACK, THOUGH, 'CAUSE I'D BE A DEAD MAN IF I TRIED!
CHING
I TOLD YOU TO STOP CALLING ME THAT. I'M A MERC LIKE YOU NOW.
YES SIR, GENERA-LISSIMO, SIR!
RYCE-SAN'S GREAT AT CHEERING US UP...
WHEN ALL THE MERCENARIES WERE HAVING DINNER, HE MADE SURE THERE WAS NEVER A DULL MOMENT.
I WAS KINDA THE CLASS CLOWN DURING GRADE SCHOOL, TOO.

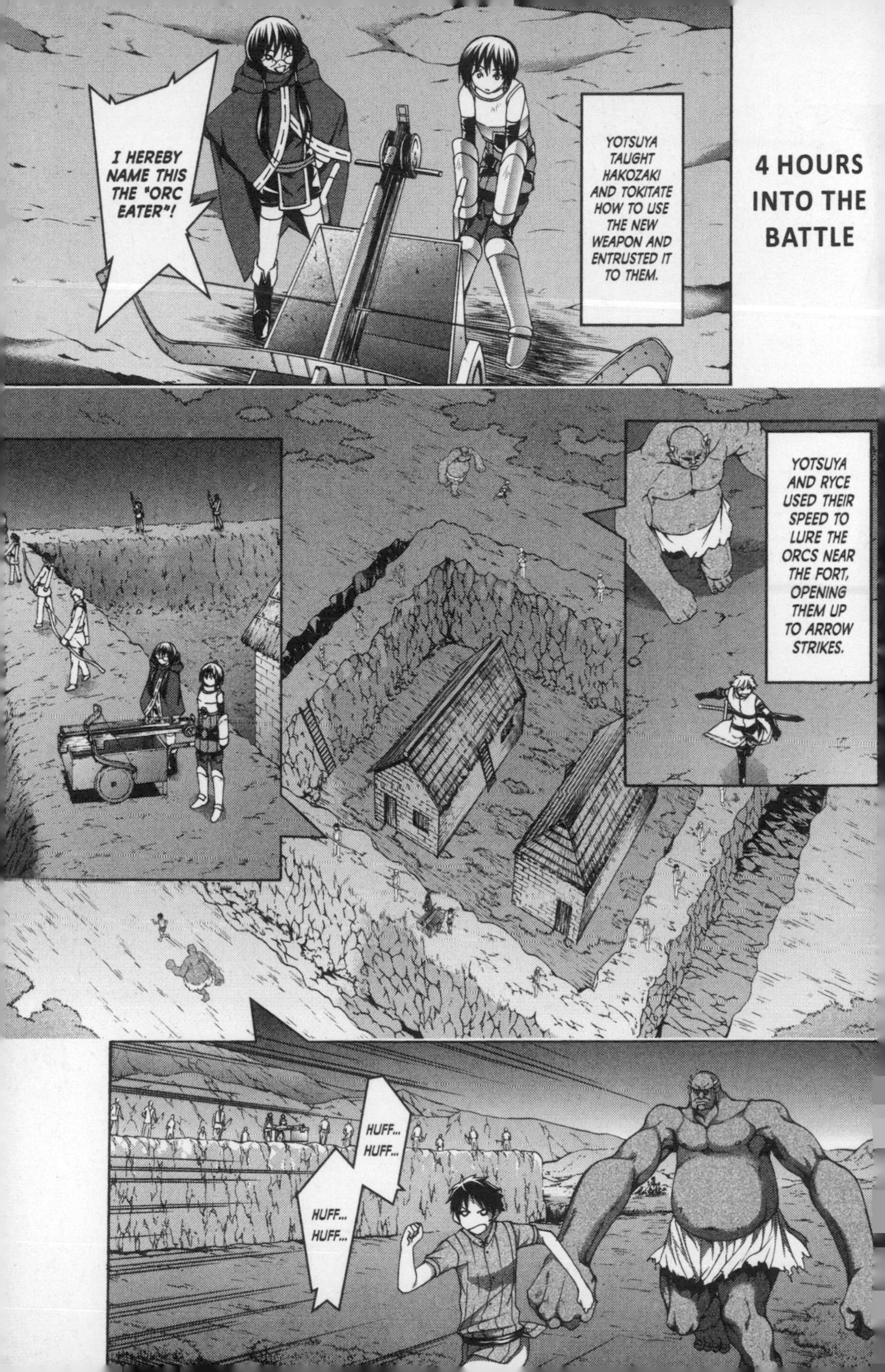
4 HOURS INTO THE BATTLE
YOTSUYA TAUGHT HAKOZAKI AND TOKITATE HOW TO USE THE NEW WEAPON AND ENTRUSTED IT TO THEM.
I HEREBY NAME THIS THE "ORC EATER"!
YOTSUYA AND RYCE USED THEIR SPEED TO LURE THE ORCS NEAR THE FORT, OPENING THEM UP TO ARROW STRIKES.
HUFF... HUFF...
HUFF... HUFF...

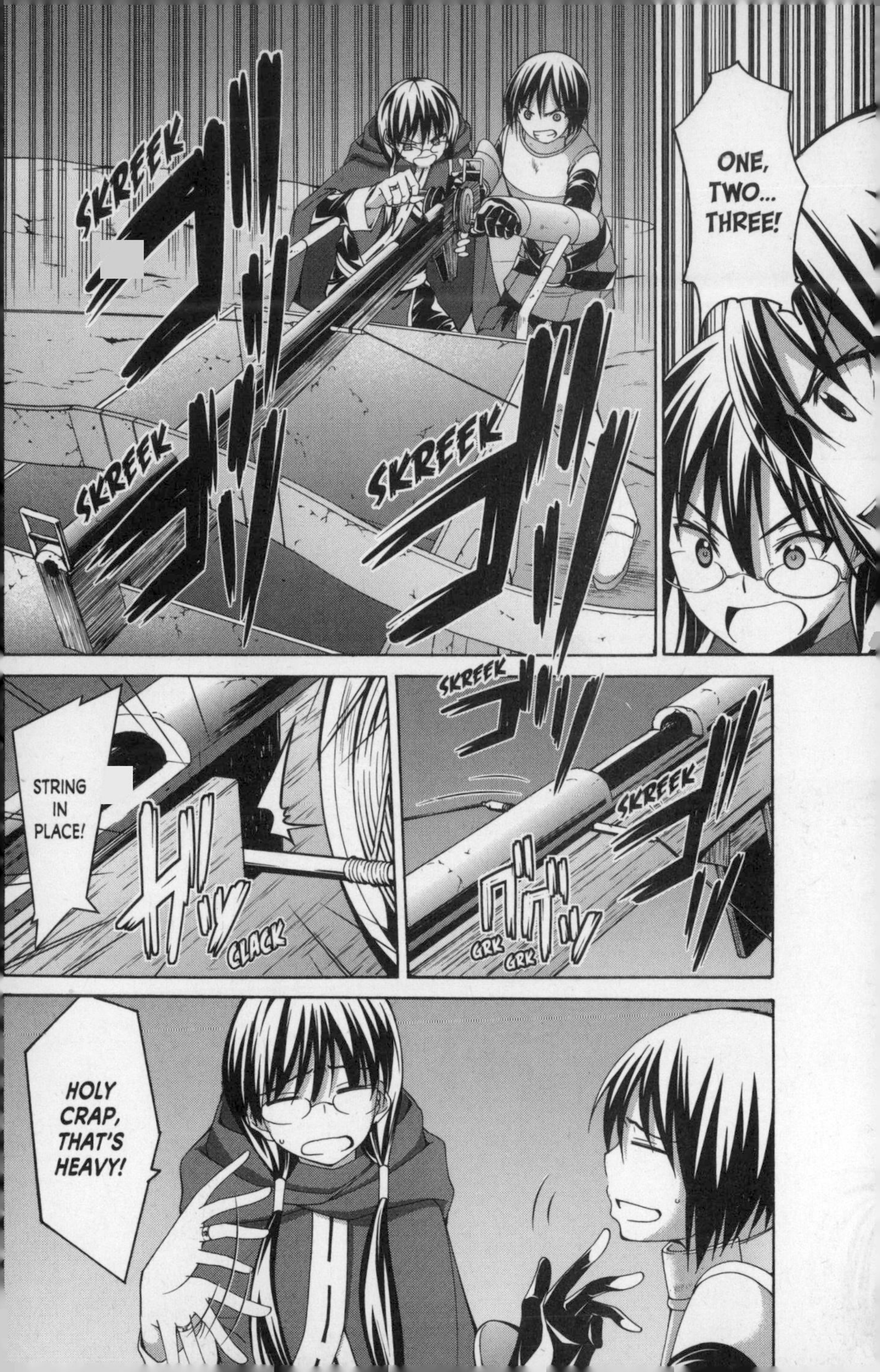
ONE, TWO... THREE!
SKREEK
SKREEK
SKREEK
SKREEK
SKREEK
GRK GRK
STRING IN PLACE!
CLACK
HOLY CRAP, THAT'S HEAVY!

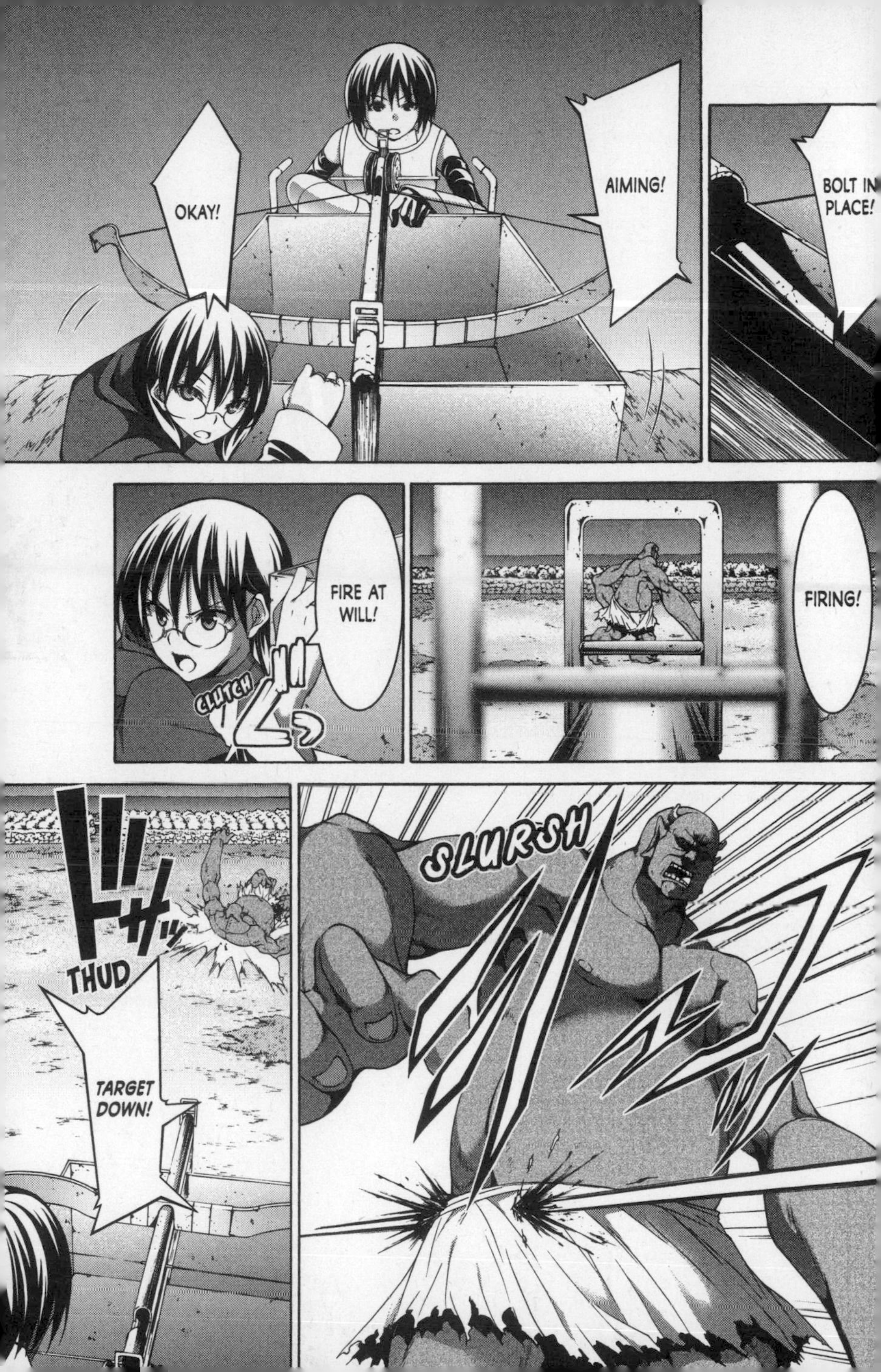
BOLT IN PLACE!
AIMING!
OKAY!
FIRING!
FIRE AT WILL!
CLUTCH
SLURSH
THUD
TARGET DOWN!

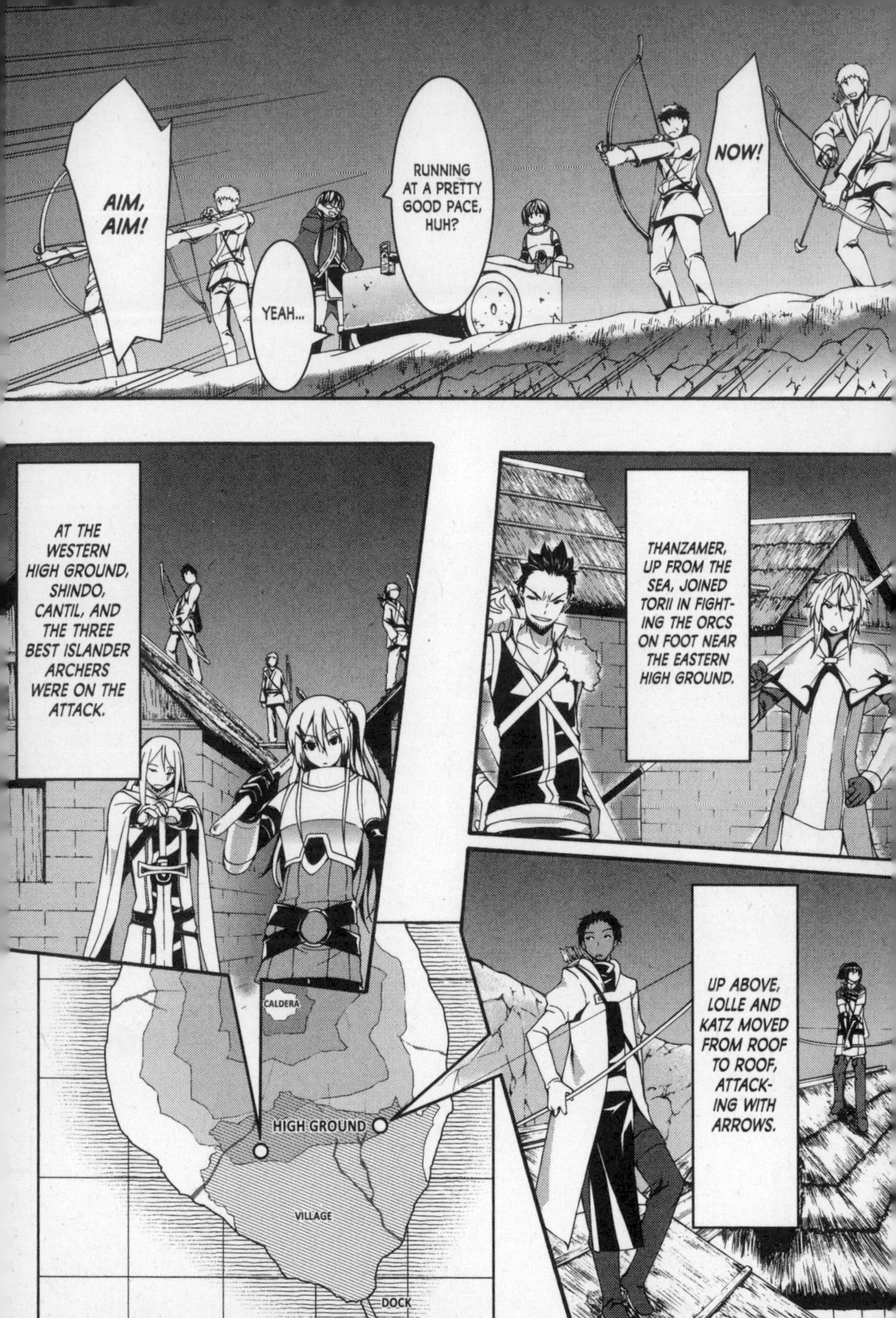
NOW!
RUNNING AT A PRETTY GOOD PACE, HUH?
YEAH...
AIM, AIM!
THANZAMER, UP FROM THE SEA, JOINED TORII IN FIGHTING THE ORCS ON FOOT NEAR THE EASTERN HIGH GROUND.
UP ABOVE, LOLLE AND KATZ MOVED FROM ROOF TO ROOF, ATTACKING WITH ARROWS.
AT THE WESTERN HIGH GROUND, SHINDO, CANTIL, AND THE THREE BEST ISLANDER ARCHERS WERE ON THE ATTACK.
CALDERA
HIGH GROUND
VILLAGE
DOCK

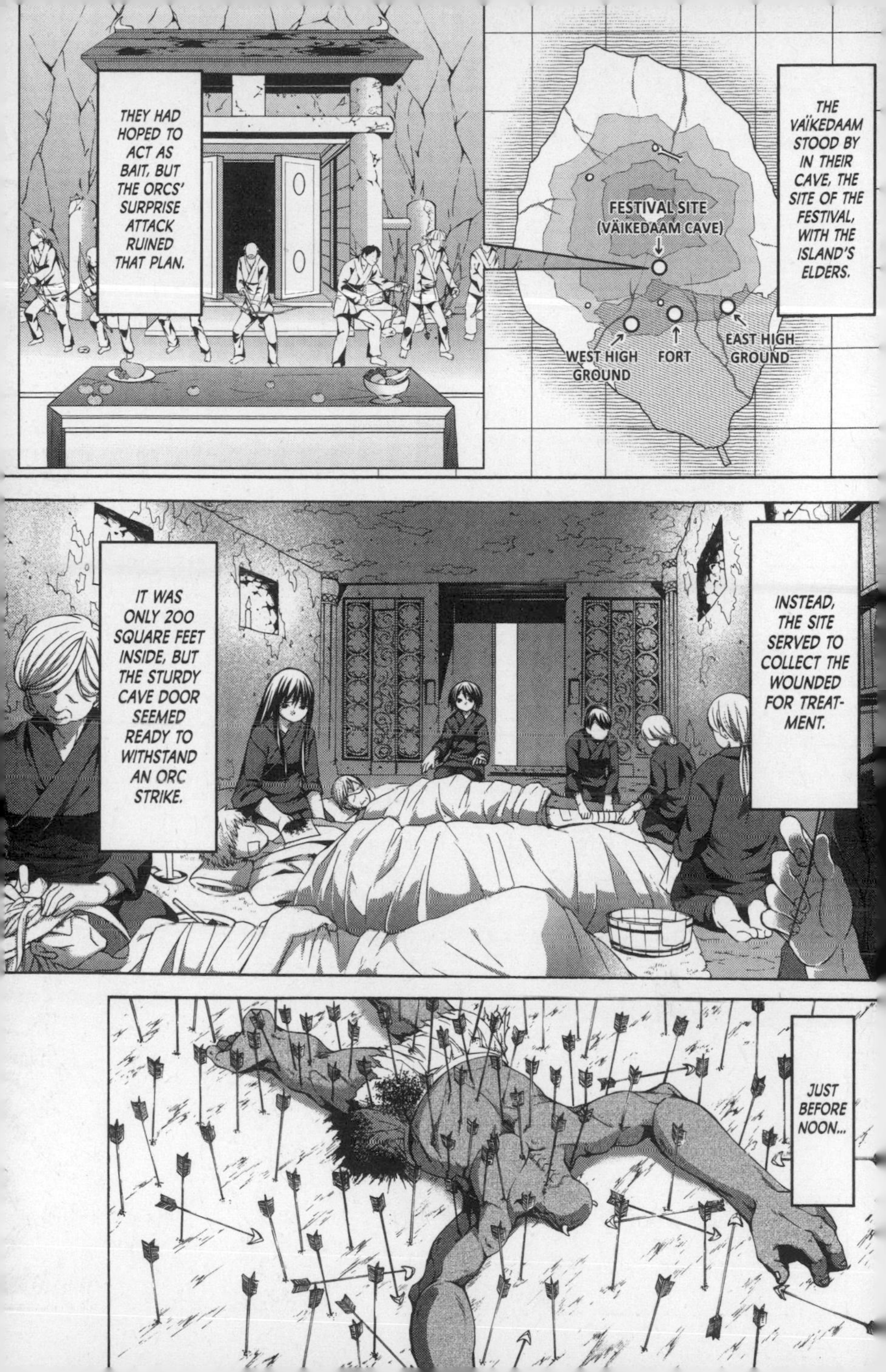
THE VAÏKEDAAM STOOD BY IN THEIR CAVE, THE SITE OF THE FESTIVAL, WITH THE ISLAND'S ELDERS.
FESTIVAL SITE (VÄIKEDAAM CAVE)
EAST HIGH GROUND
FORT
WEST HIGH GROUND
THEY HAD HOPED TO ACT AS BAIT, BUT THE ORCS' SURPRISE ATTACK RUINED THAT PLAN.
INSTEAD, THE SITE SERVED TO COLLECT THE WOUNDED FOR TREAT-MENT.
IT WAS ONLY 200 SQUARE FEET INSIDE, BUT THE STURDY CAVE DOOR SEEMED READY TO WITHSTAND AN ORC STRIKE.
JUST BEFORE NOON...

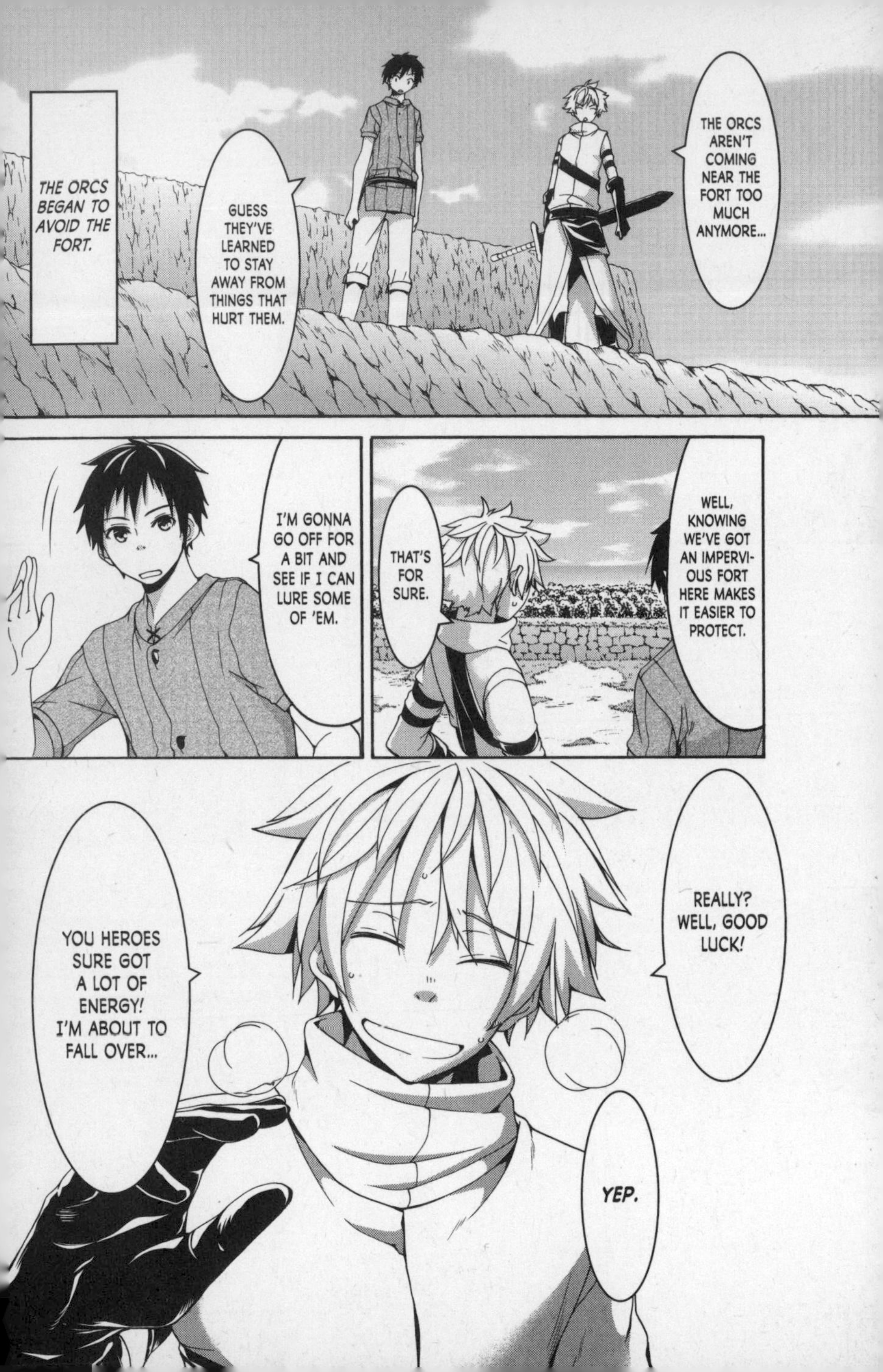
THE ORCS AREN'T COMING NEAR THE FORT TOO MUCH ANYMORE...
GUESS THEY'VE LEARNED TO STAY AWAY FROM THINGS THAT HURT THEM.
THE ORCS BEGAN TO AVOID THE FORT.
WELL, KNOWING WE'VE GOT AN IMPERVI-OUS FORT HERE MAKES IT EASIER TO PROTECT.
THAT'S FOR SURE.
I'M GONNA GO OFF FOR A BIT AND SEE IF I CAN LURE SOME OF 'EM.
REALLY? WELL, GOOD LUCK!
YOU HEROES SURE GOT A LOT OF ENERGY! I'M ABOUT TO FALL OVER...
YEP.

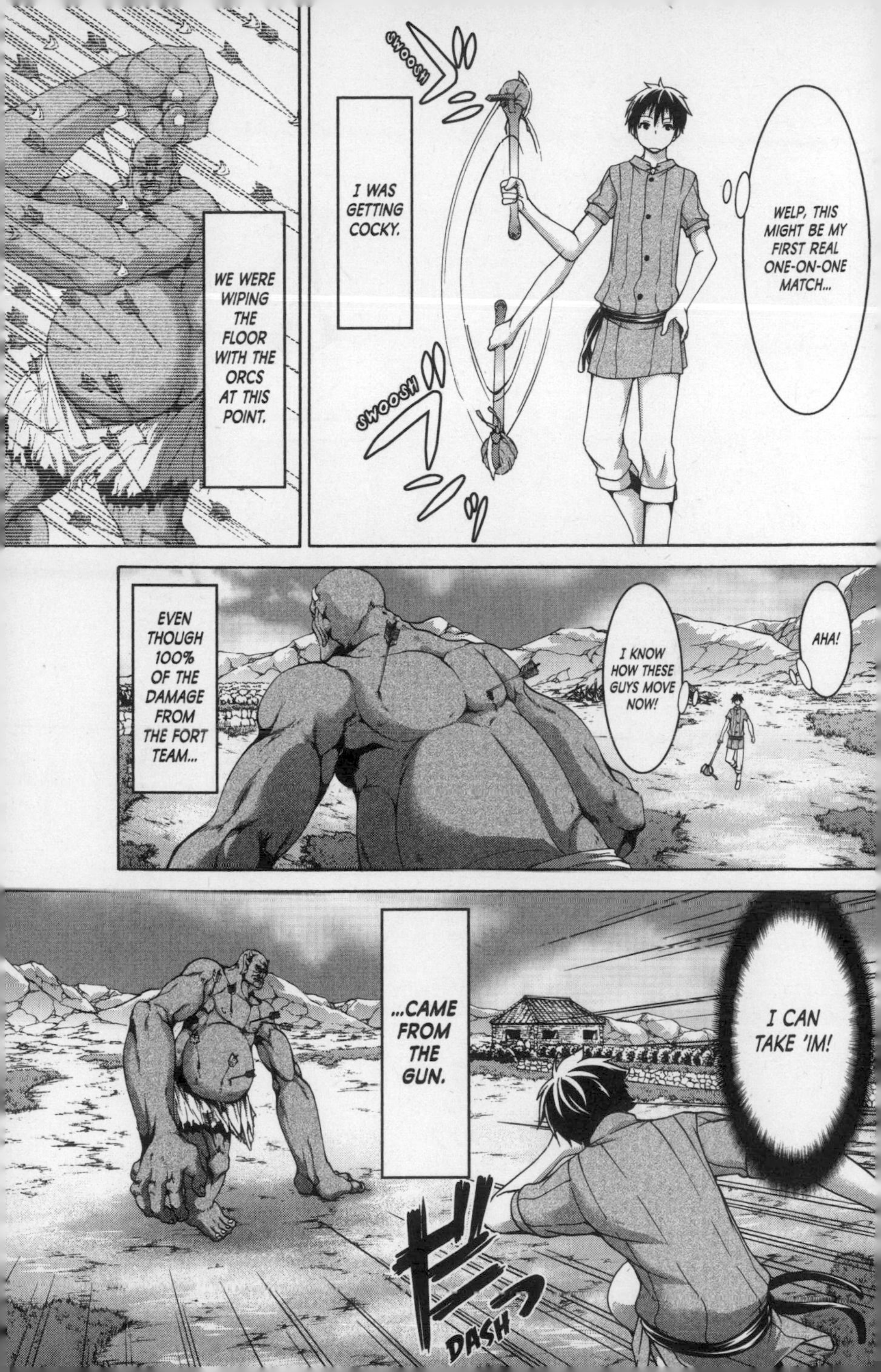
WELP, THIS MIGHT BE MY FIRST REAL ONE-ON-ONE MATCH...
SWOOSH
I WAS GETTING COCKY.
SWOOSH
WE WERE WIPING THE FLOOR WITH THE ORCS AT THIS POINT.
AHA!
I KNOW HOW THESE GUYS MOVE NOW!
EVEN THOUGH 100% OF THE DAMAGE FROM THE FORT TEAM...
I CAN TAKE 'IM!
...CAME FROM THE GUN.
DASH

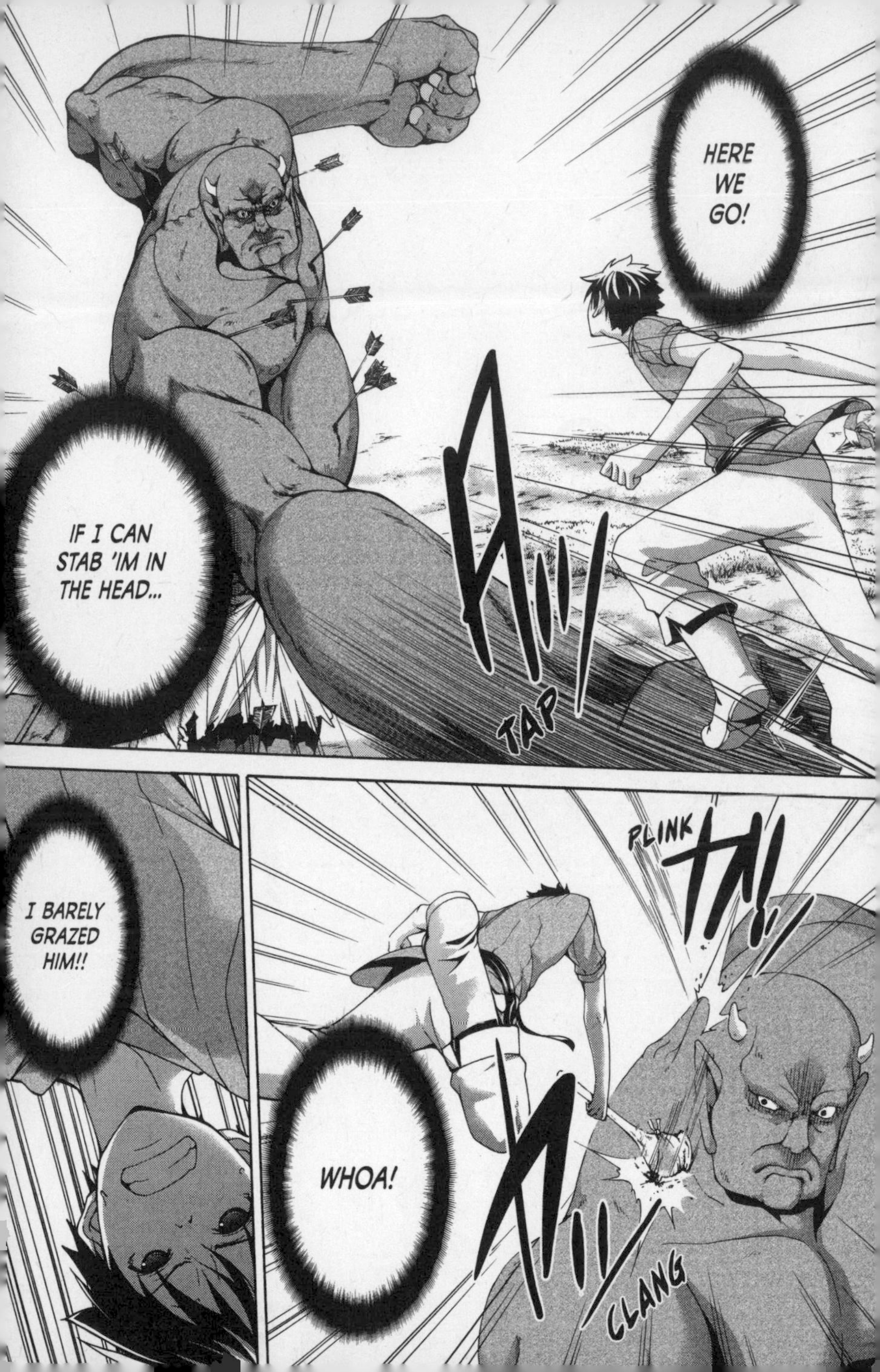
HERE WE GO!
IF I CAN STAB 'IM IN THE HEAD...
TAP
PLINK
WHOA!
CLANG
I BARELY GRAZED HIM!!

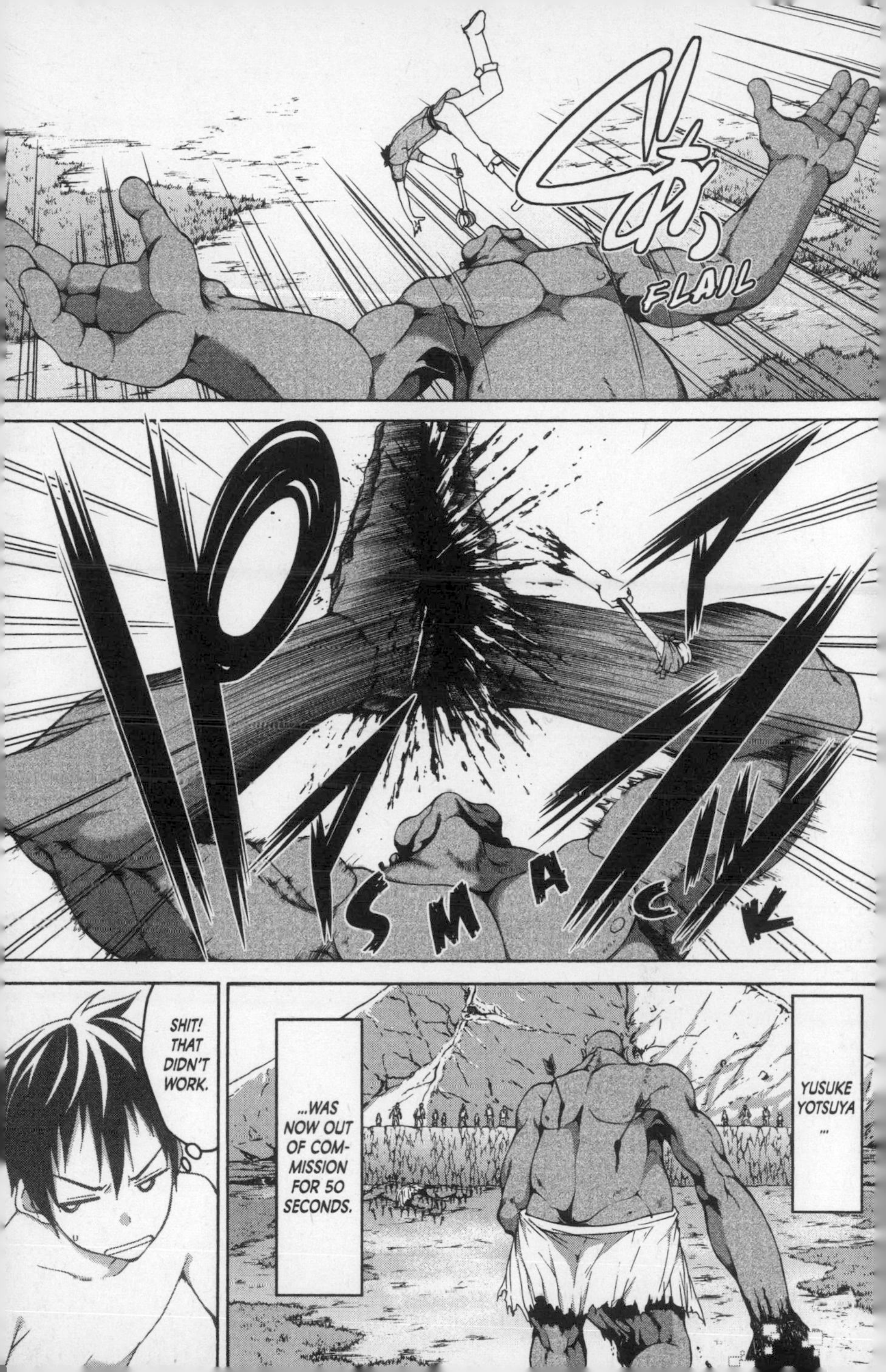
FLAIL
SMACK
YUSUKE YOTSUYA ...
...WAS NOW OUT OF COM-MISSION FOR 50 SECONDS.
SHIT! THAT DIDN'T WORK.

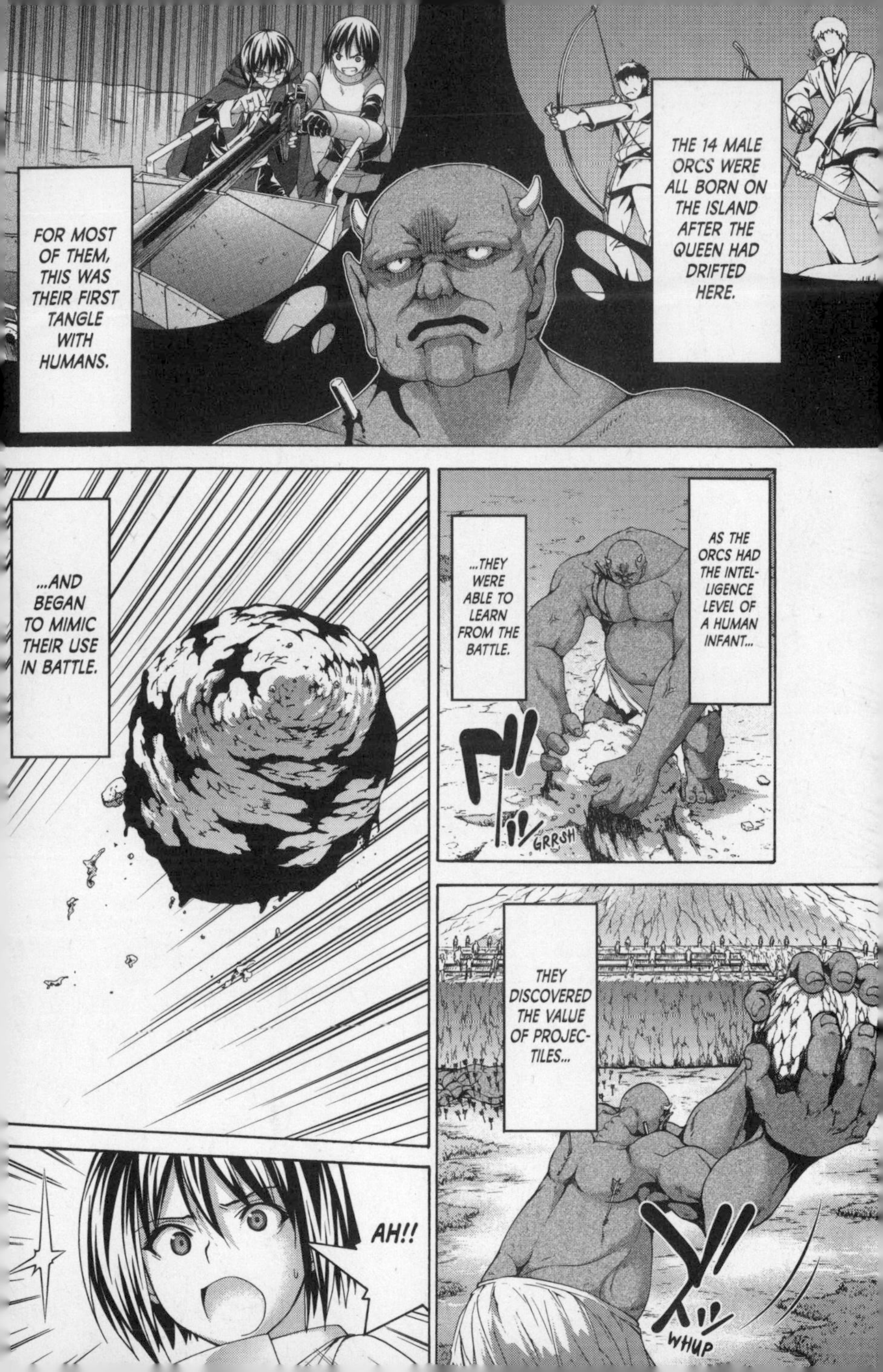
THE 14 MALE ORCS WERE ALL BORN ON THE ISLAND AFTER THE QUEEN HAD DRIFTED HERE.
FOR MOST OF THEM, THIS WAS THEIR FIRST TANGLE WITH HUMANS.
AS THE ORCS HAD THE INTEL-LIGENCE LEVEL OF A HUMAN INFANT...
...THEY WERE ABLE TO LEARN FROM THE BATTLE.
GRRSH
THEY DISCOVERED THE VALUE OF PROJEC-TILES...
WHUP
...AND BEGAN TO MIMIC THEIR USE IN BATTLE.
AH!!

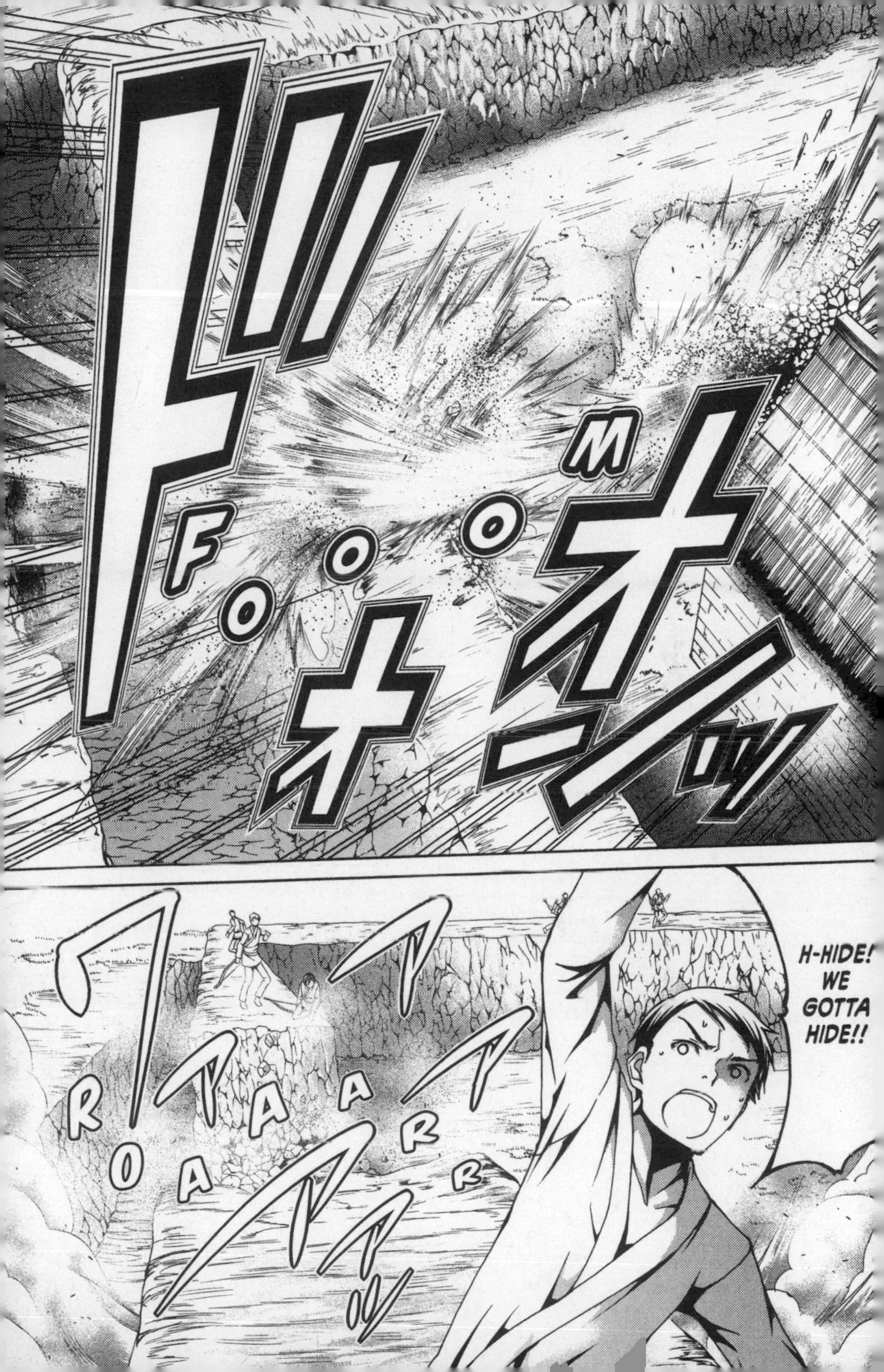
FOOOM
ROAARR
H-HIDE! WE GOTTA HIDE!!

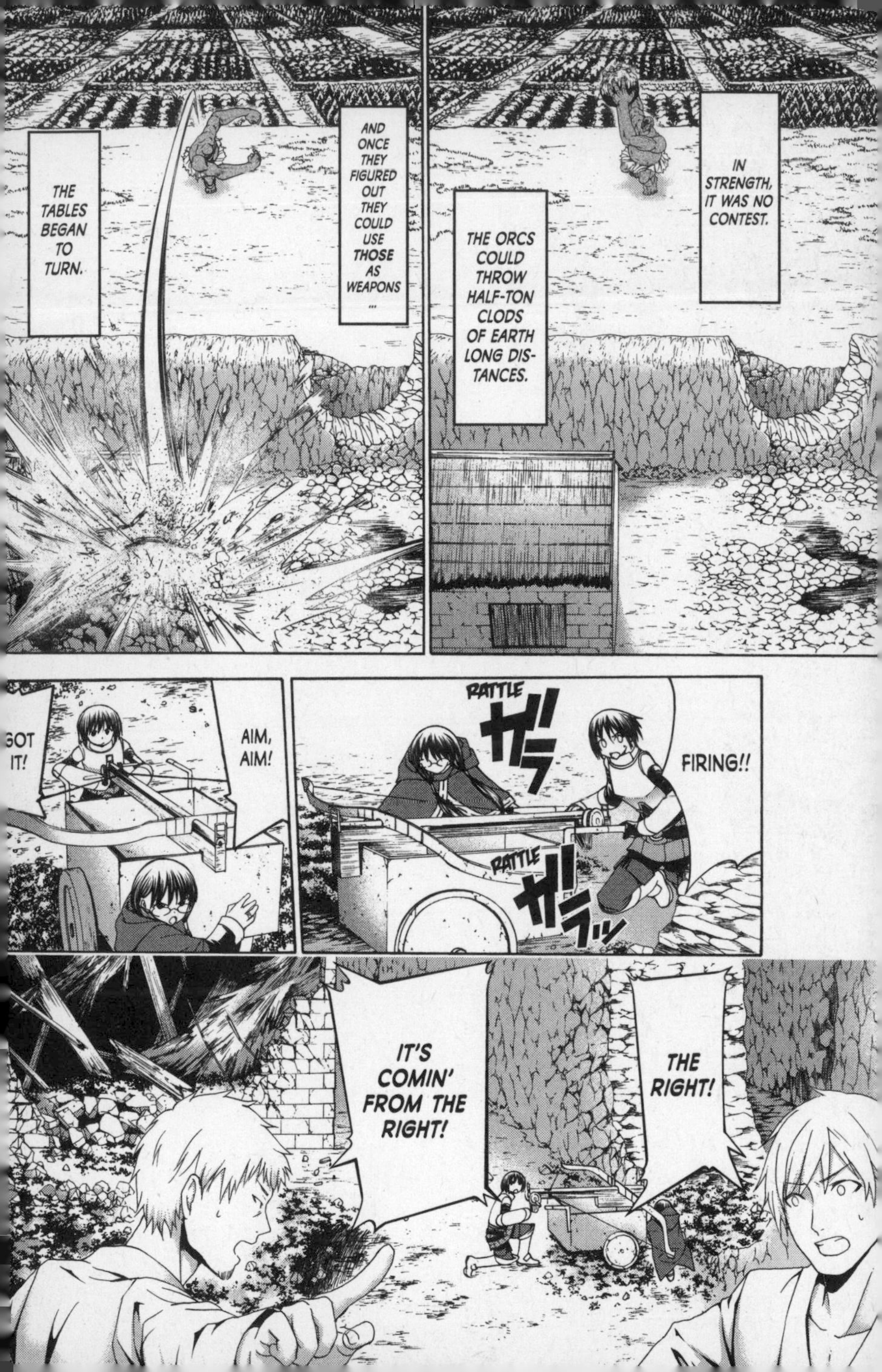
IN STRENGTH, IT WAS NO CONTEST.
THE ORCS COULD THROW HALF-TON CLODS OF EARTH LONG DISTANCES.
AND ONCE THEY FIGURED OUT THEY COULD USE THOSE AS WEAPONS ...
THE TABLES BEGAN TO TURN.
RATTLE
FIRING!!
RATTLE
AIM, AIM!
GOT IT!
THE RIGHT!
IT'S COMIN' FROM THE RIGHT!

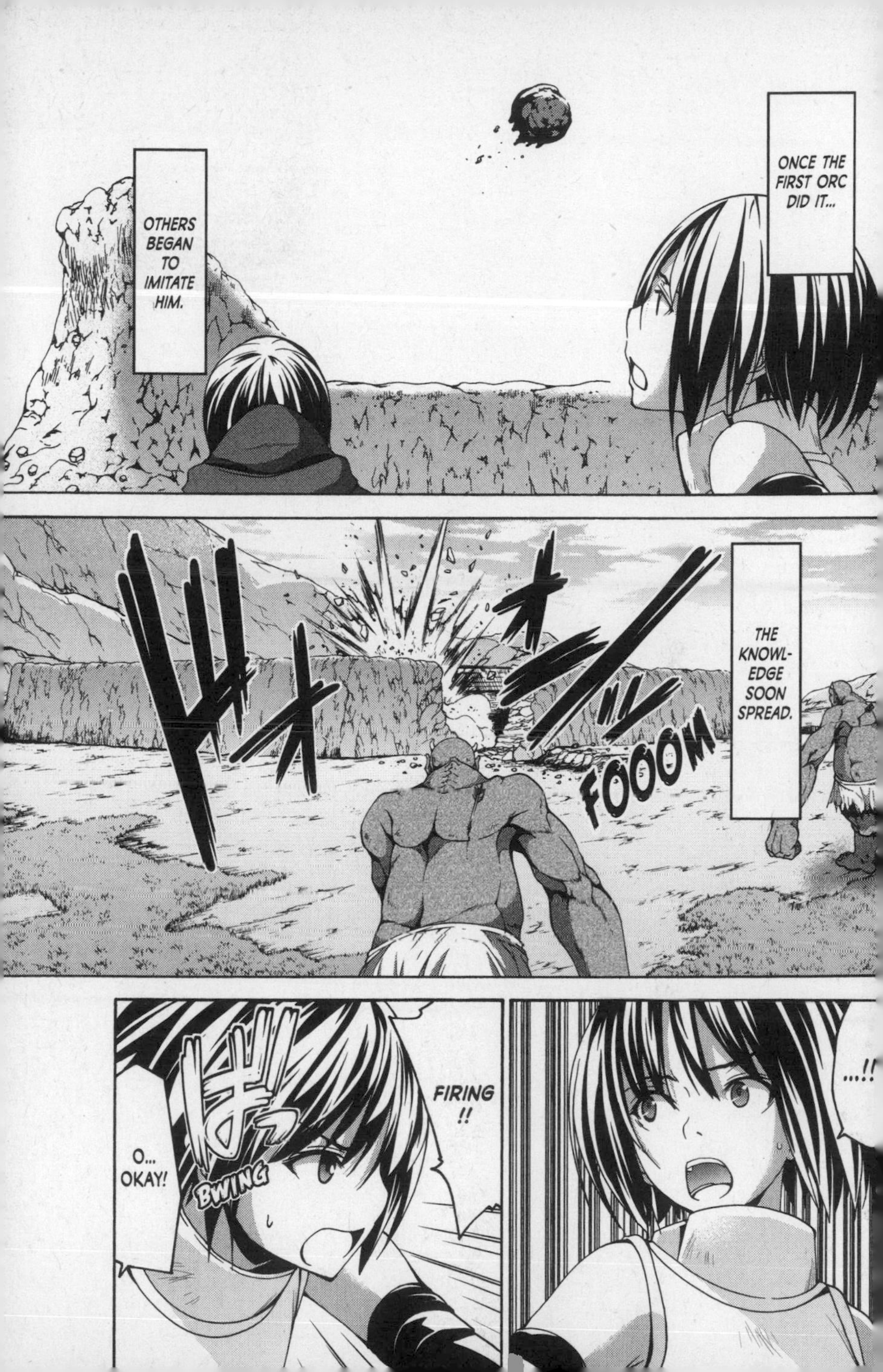
ONCE THE FIRST ORC DID IT...
OTHERS BEGAN TO IMITATE HIM.
THE KNOWL-EDGE SOON SPREAD.
FOOOM
...!!
FIRING !!
O... OKAY!
BWING

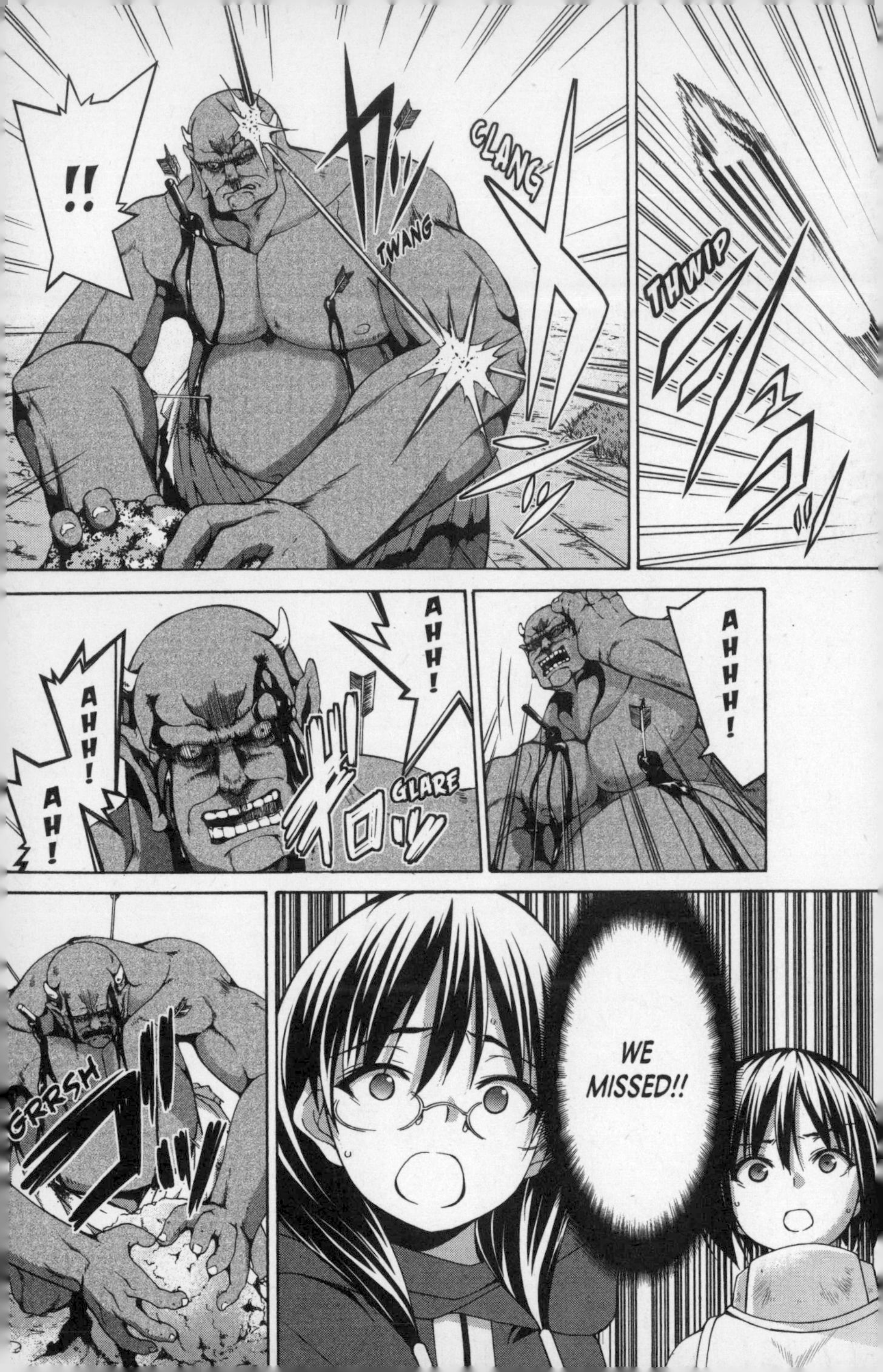
THWIP
CLANG
TWANG
!!
AHHHH!
AHH!
GLARE
AHH!
AH!
WE MISSED!!
GRRSH

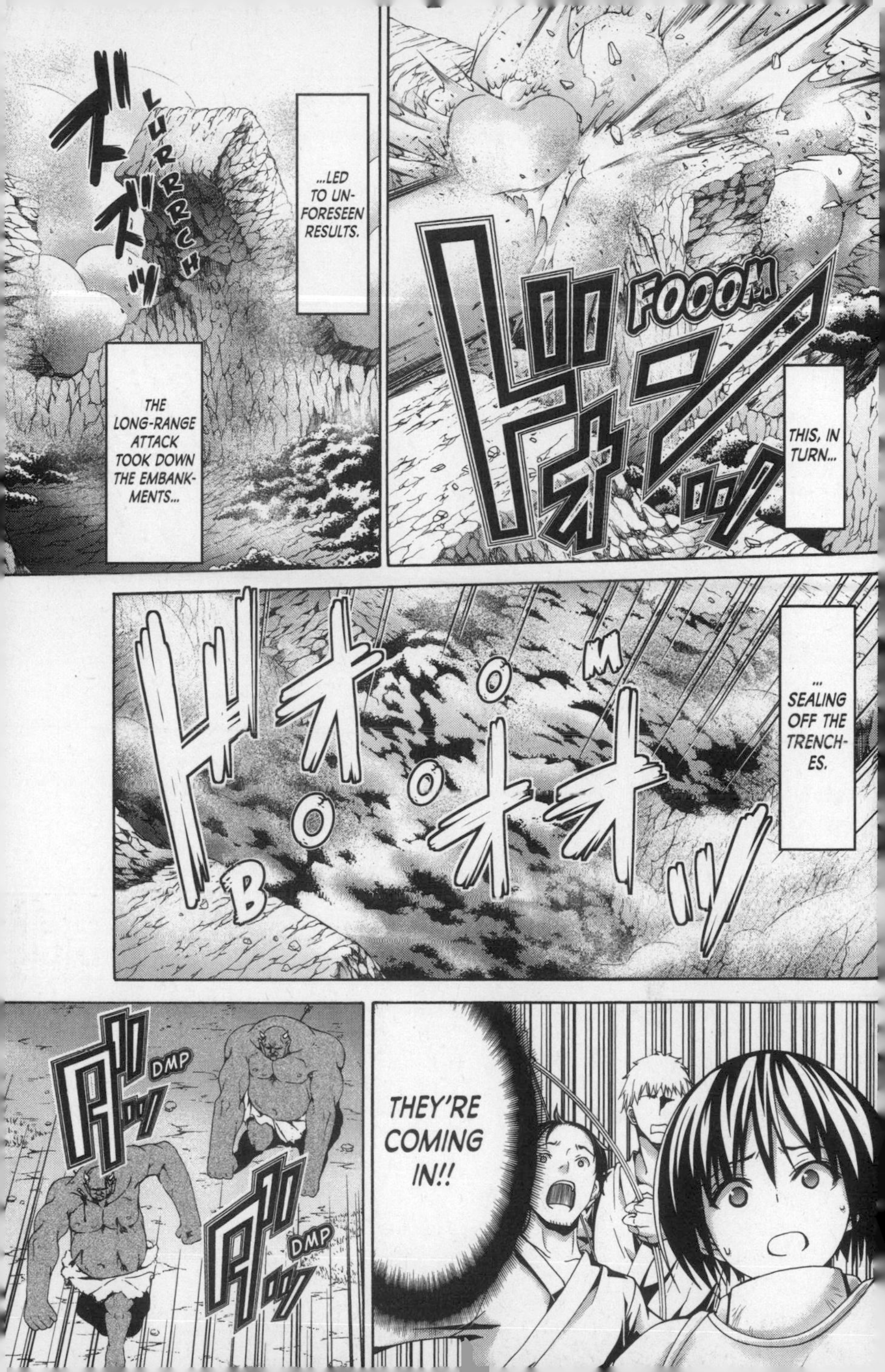
FOOOM
THIS, IN TURN...
...LED TO UN-FORESEEN RESULTS.
LURRRCH
THE LONG-RANGE ATTACK TOOK DOWN THE EMBANK-MENTS...
... SEALING OFF THE TRENCH-ES.
BOOOM
THEY'RE COMING IN!!
DMP
DMP

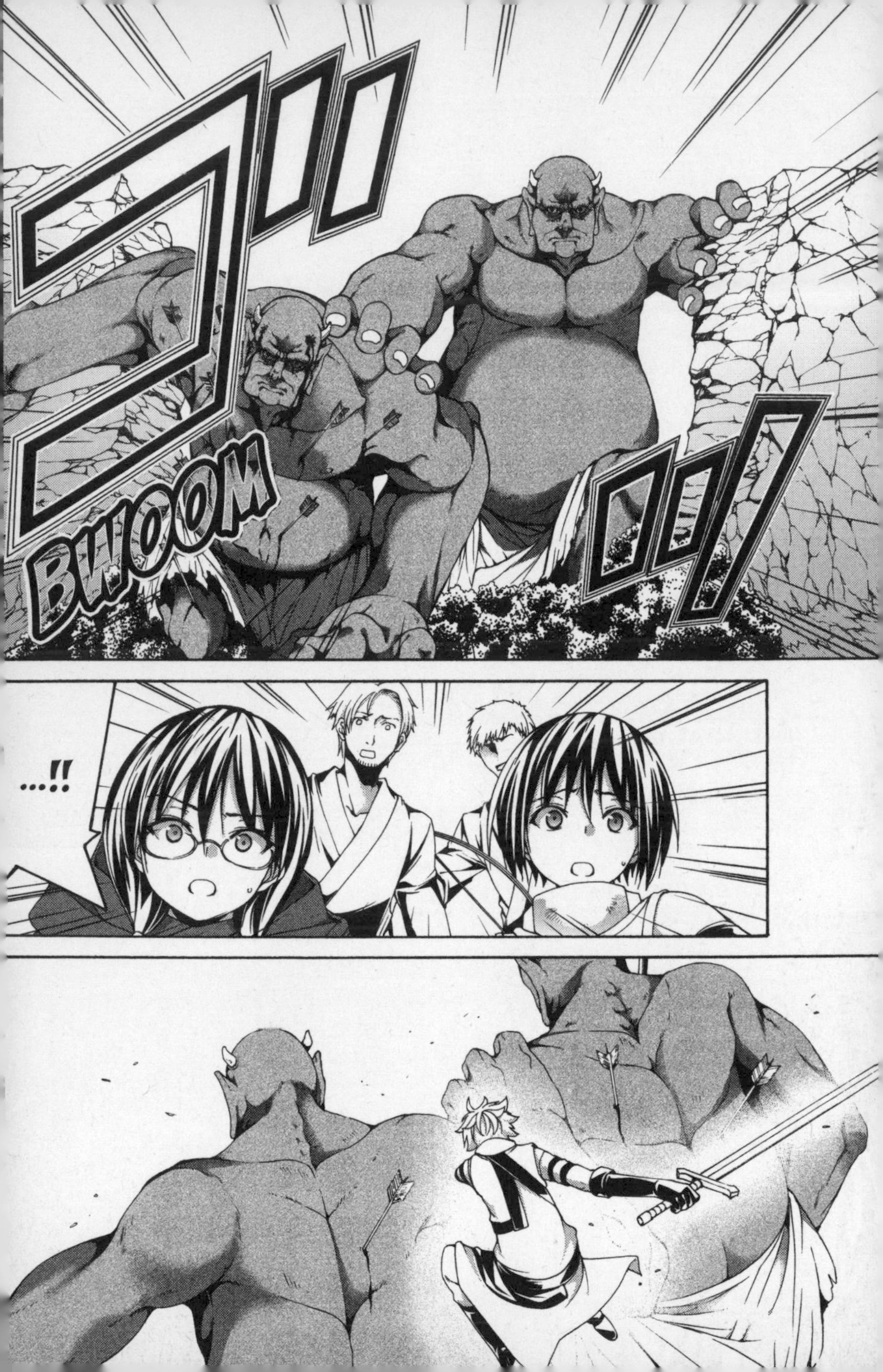
BWOOM
...!!

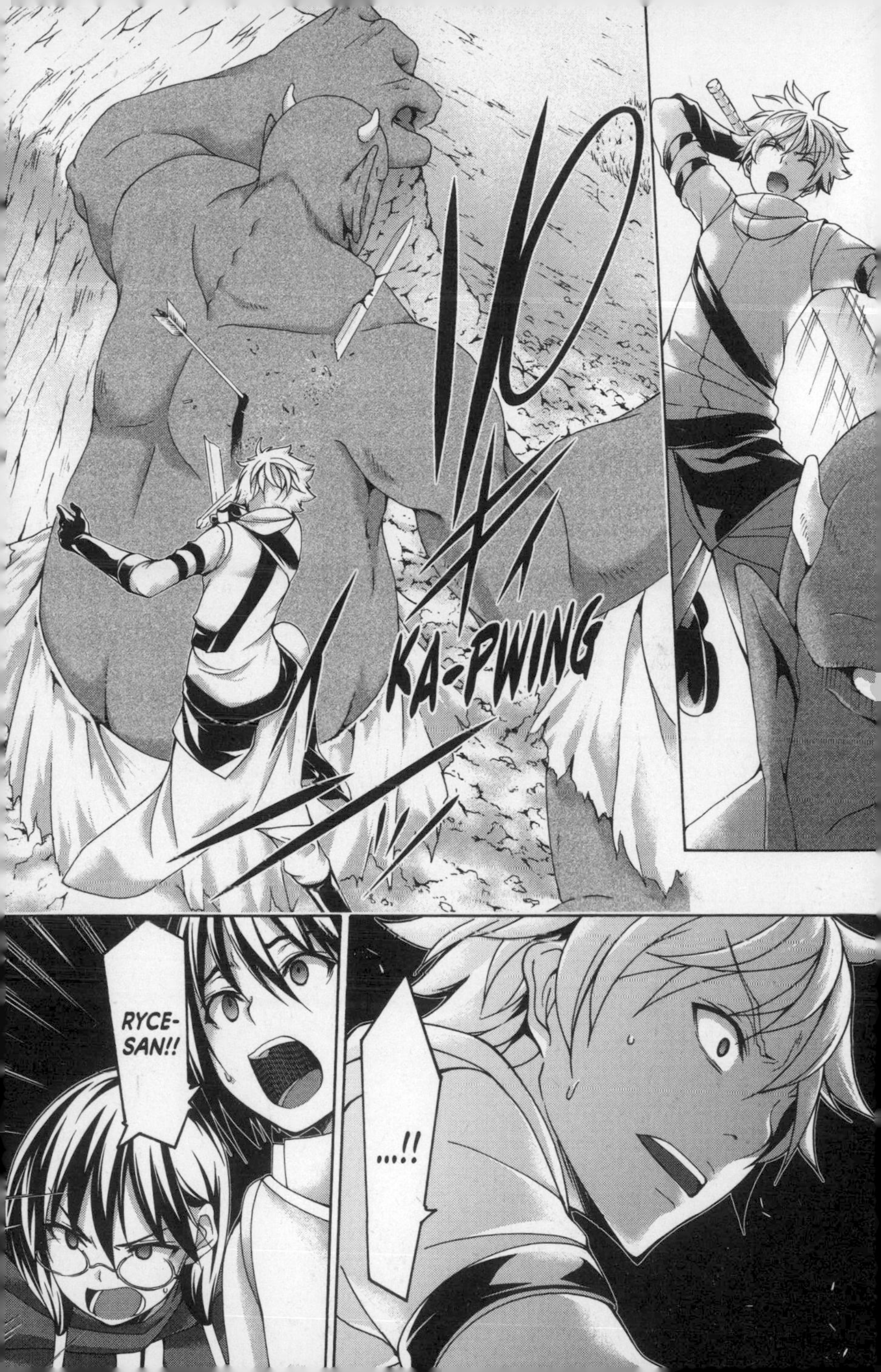
KA-PWING
RYCE-SAN!!
...!!

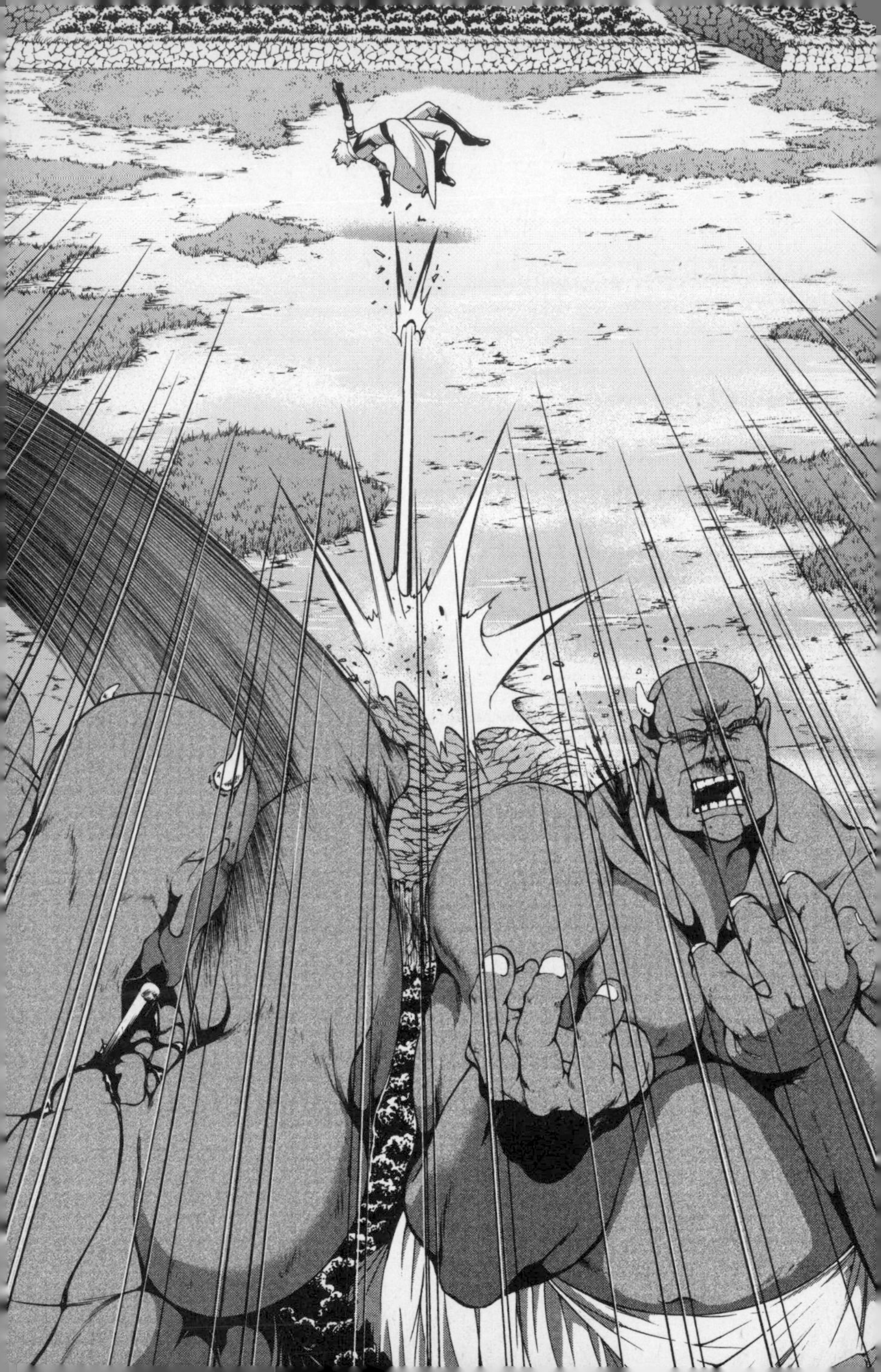

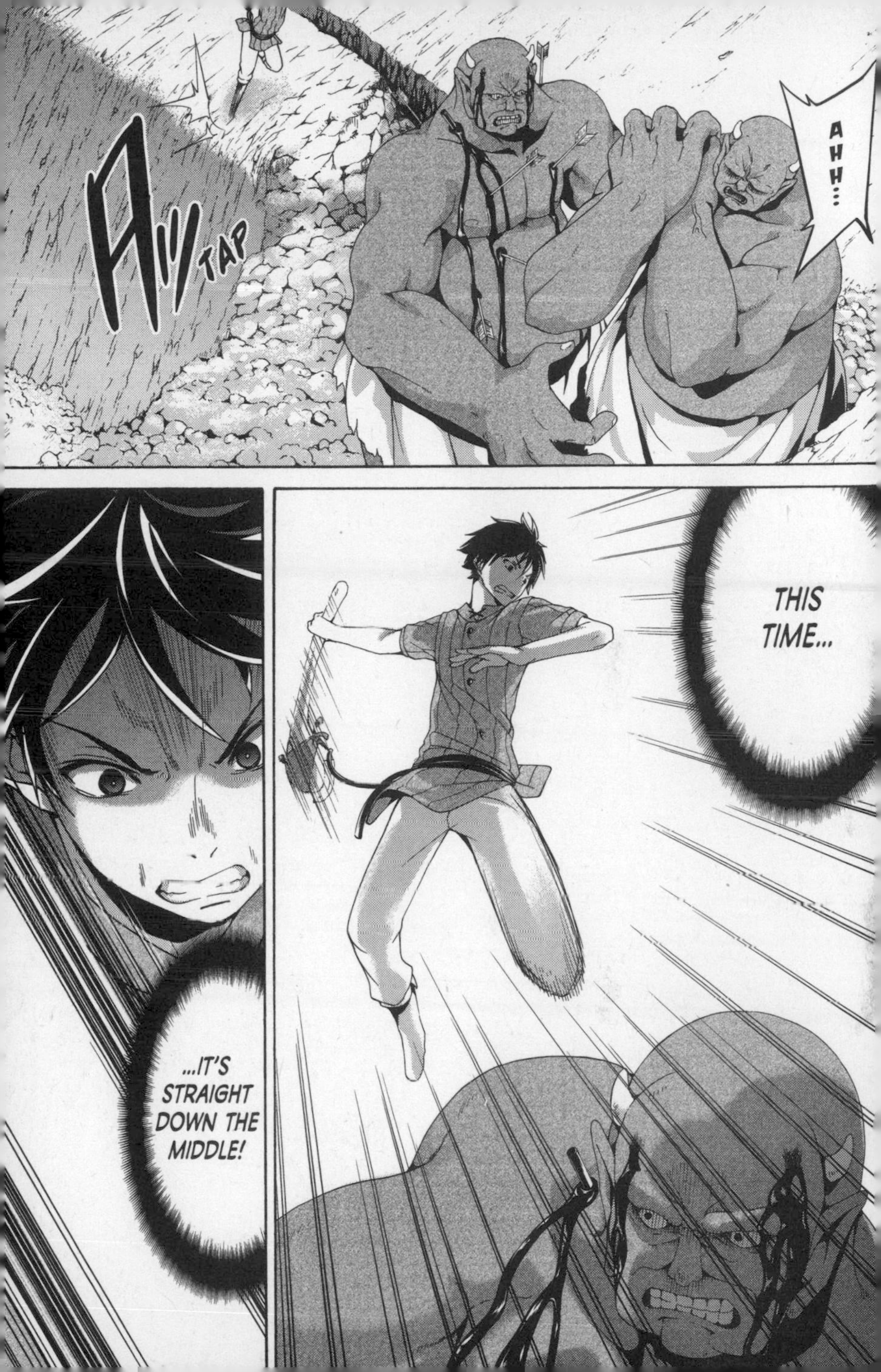
AHH...
TAP
THIS TIME...
...IT'S STRAIGHT DOWN THE MIDDLE!

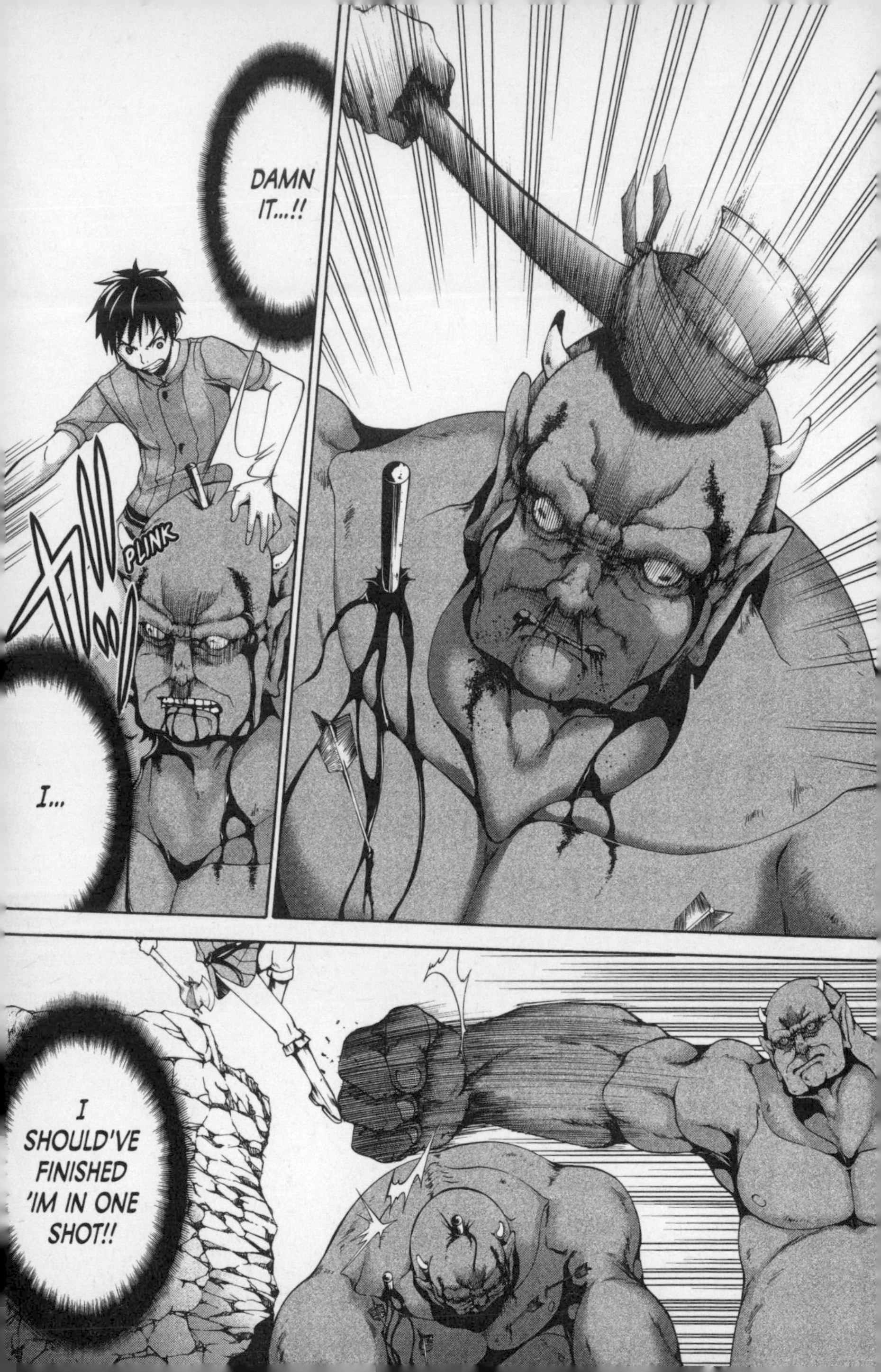
DAMN IT...!!
PLINK
I...
I SHOULD'VE FINISHED 'IM IN ONE SHOT!!

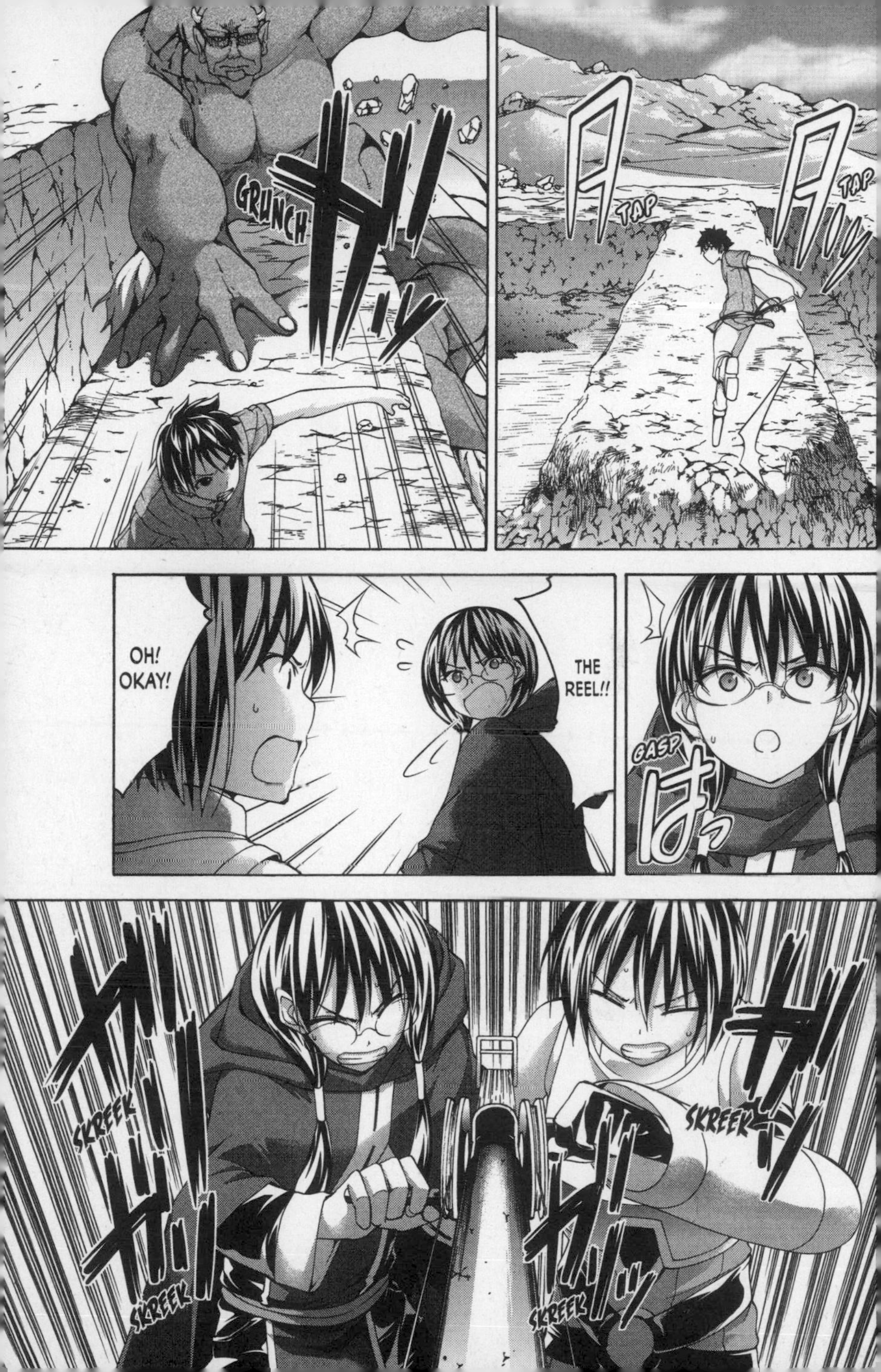
TAP
TAP
GRUNCH
GASP
はっ
THE REEL!!
OH! OKAY!
SKREEK
SKREEK
SKREEK
SKREEK

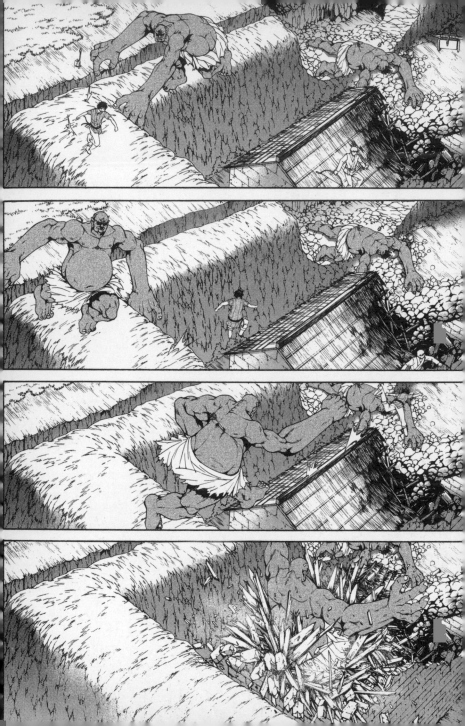

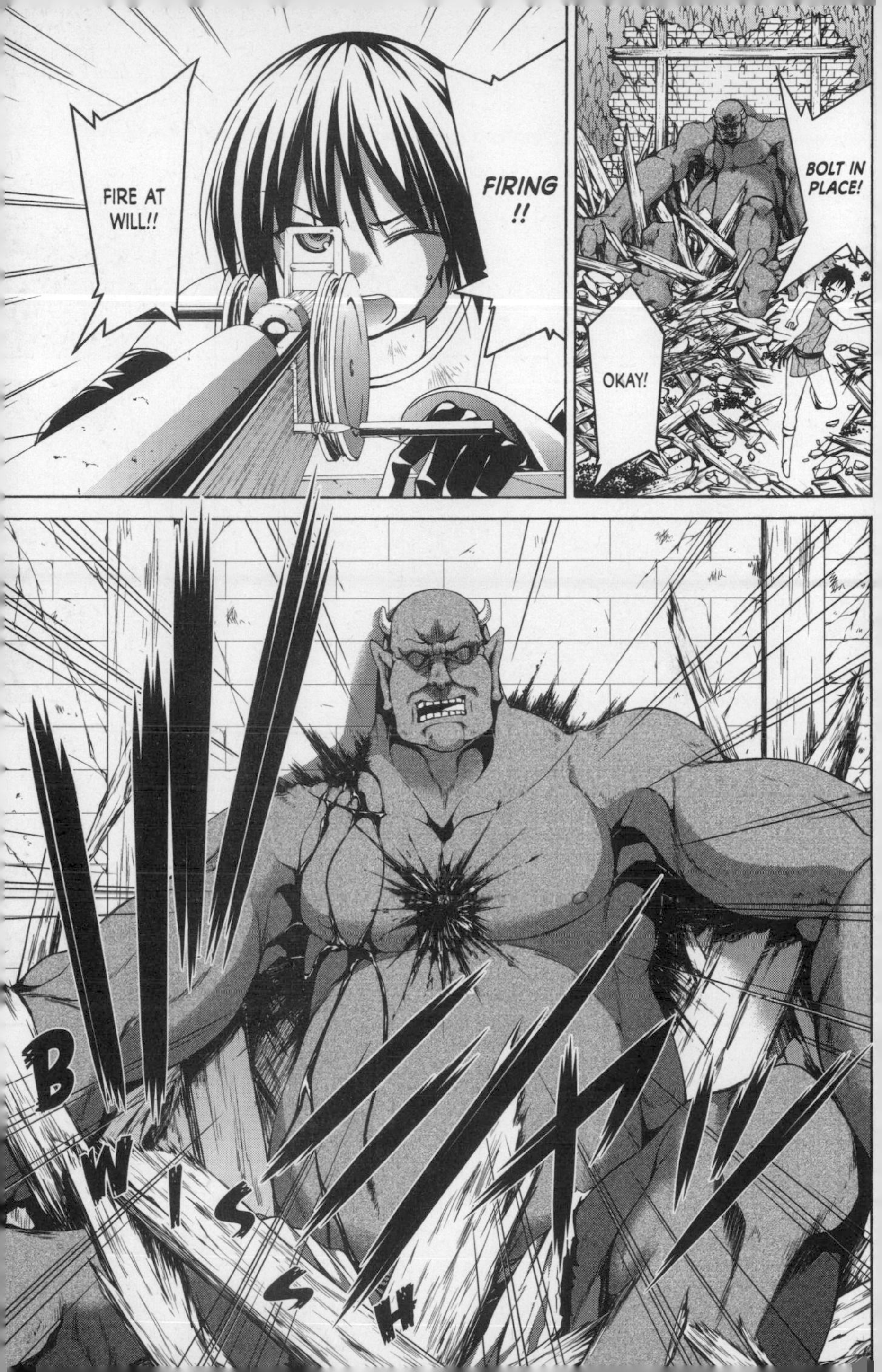
BOLT IN PLACE!
OKAY!
FIRING!!
FIRE AT WILL!!
BWISSH

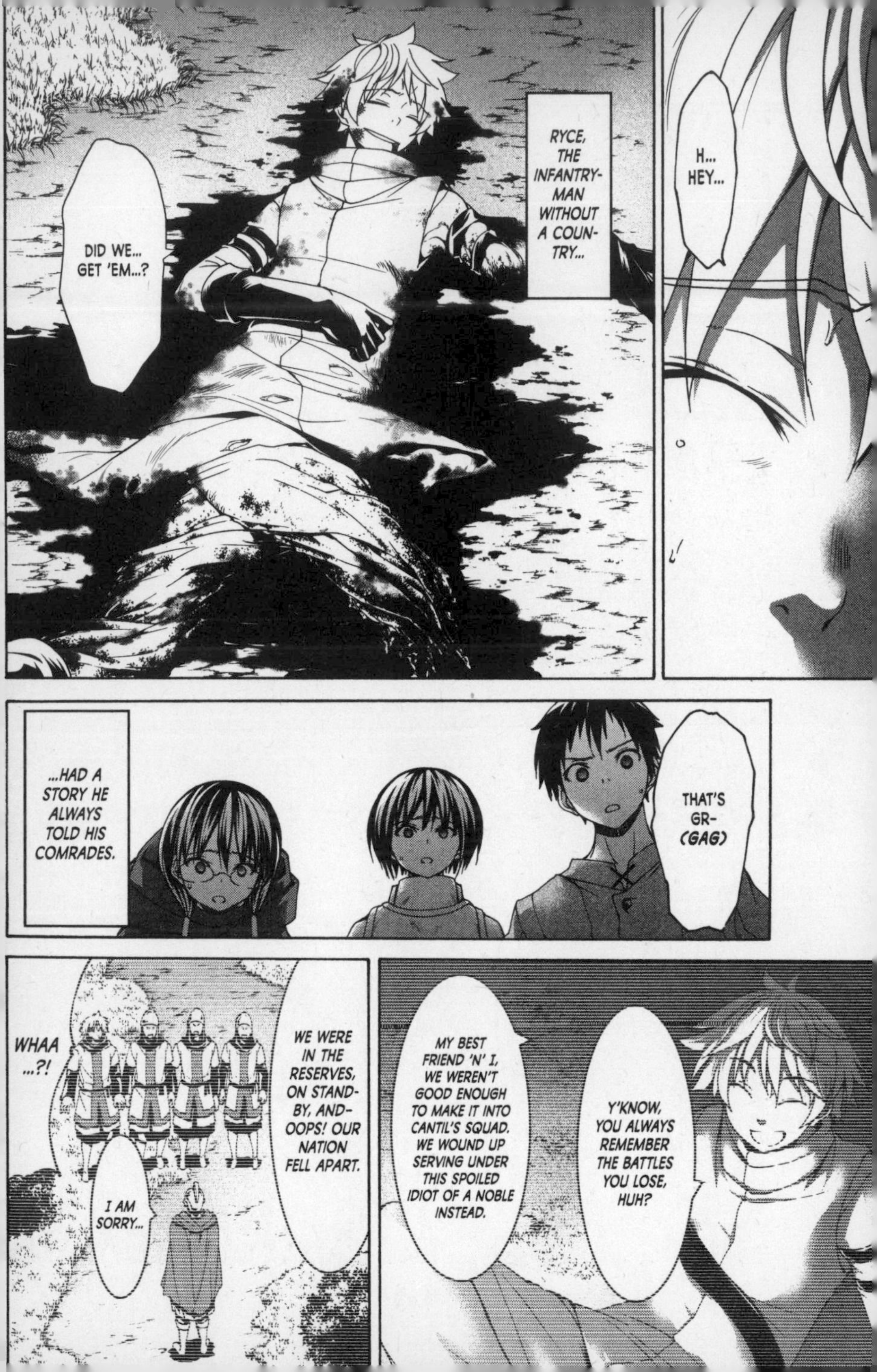
H... HEY...
RYCE, THE INFANTRY-MAN WITHOUT A COUN-TRY...
DID WE... GET 'EM...?
THAT'S GR- (GAG)
...HAD A STORY HE ALWAYS TOLD HIS COMRADES.
Y'KNOW, YOU ALWAYS REMEMBER THE BATTLES YOU LOSE, HUH?
MY BEST FRIEND 'N' I, WE WEREN'T GOOD ENOUGH TO MAKE IT INTO CANTIL'S SQUAD. WE WOUND UP SERVING UNDER THIS SPOILED IDIOT OF A NOBLE INSTEAD.
WE WERE IN THE RESERVES, ON STAND-BY, AND- OOPS! OUR NATION FELL APART.
WHAA ...?!
I AM SORRY...

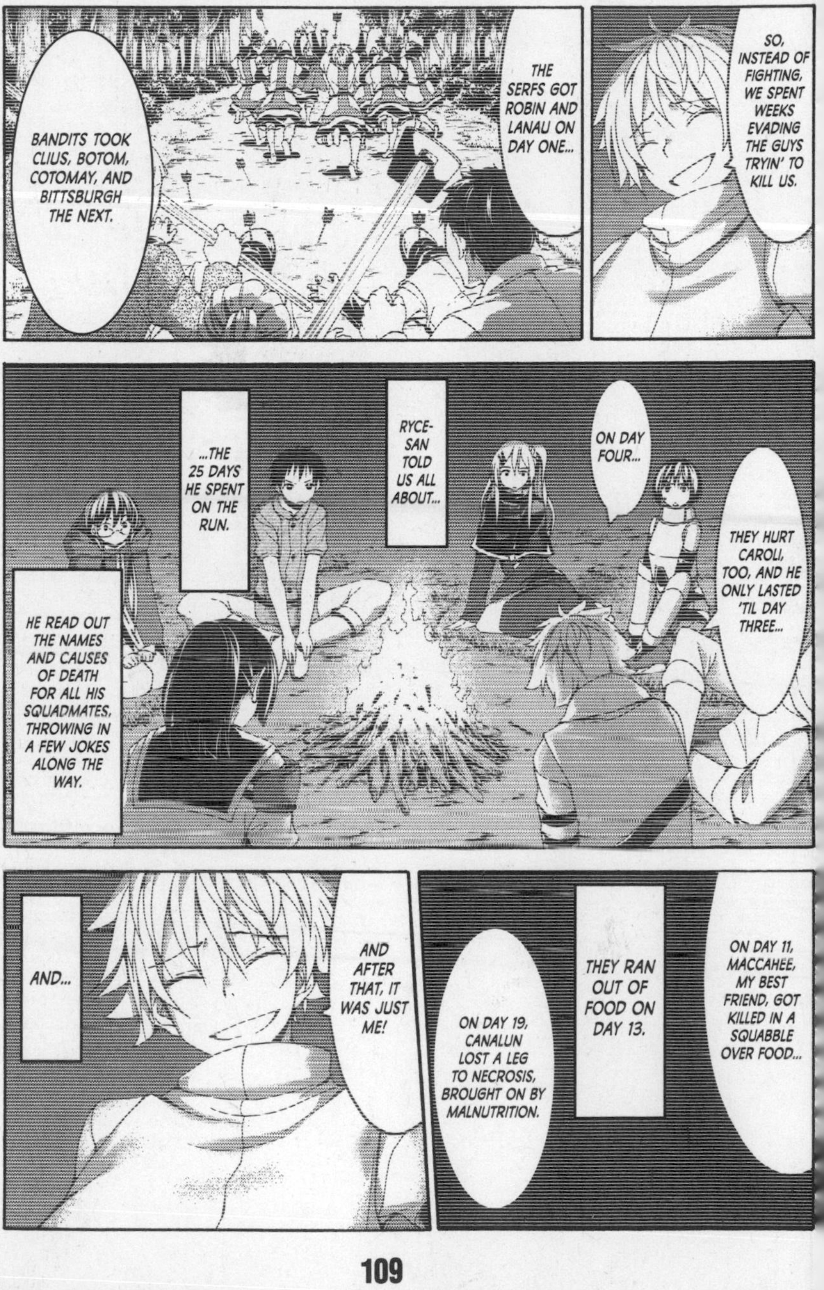
SO, INSTEAD OF FIGHTING, WE SPENT WEEKS EVADING THE GUYS TRYIN' TO KILL US.
THE SERFS GOT ROBIN AND LANAU ON DAY ONE...
BANDITS TOOK CLIUS, BOTOM, COTOMAY, AND BITTSBURGH THE NEXT.
ON DAY FOUR...
THEY HURT CAROLI, TOO, AND HE ONLY LASTED 'TIL DAY THREE...
RYCE-SAN TOLD US ALL ABOUT...
...THE 25 DAYS HE SPENT ON THE RUN.
HE READ OUT THE NAMES AND CAUSES OF DEATH FOR ALL HIS SQUADMATES, THROWING IN A FEW JOKES ALONG THE WAY.
ON DAY 11, MACCAHEE, MY BEST FRIEND, GOT KILLED IN A SQUABBLE OVER FOOD...
THEY RAN OUT OF FOOD ON DAY 13.
ON DAY 19, CANALUN LOST A LEG TO NECROSIS, BROUGHT ON BY MALNUTRITION.
AND AFTER THAT, IT WAS JUST ME!
AND...

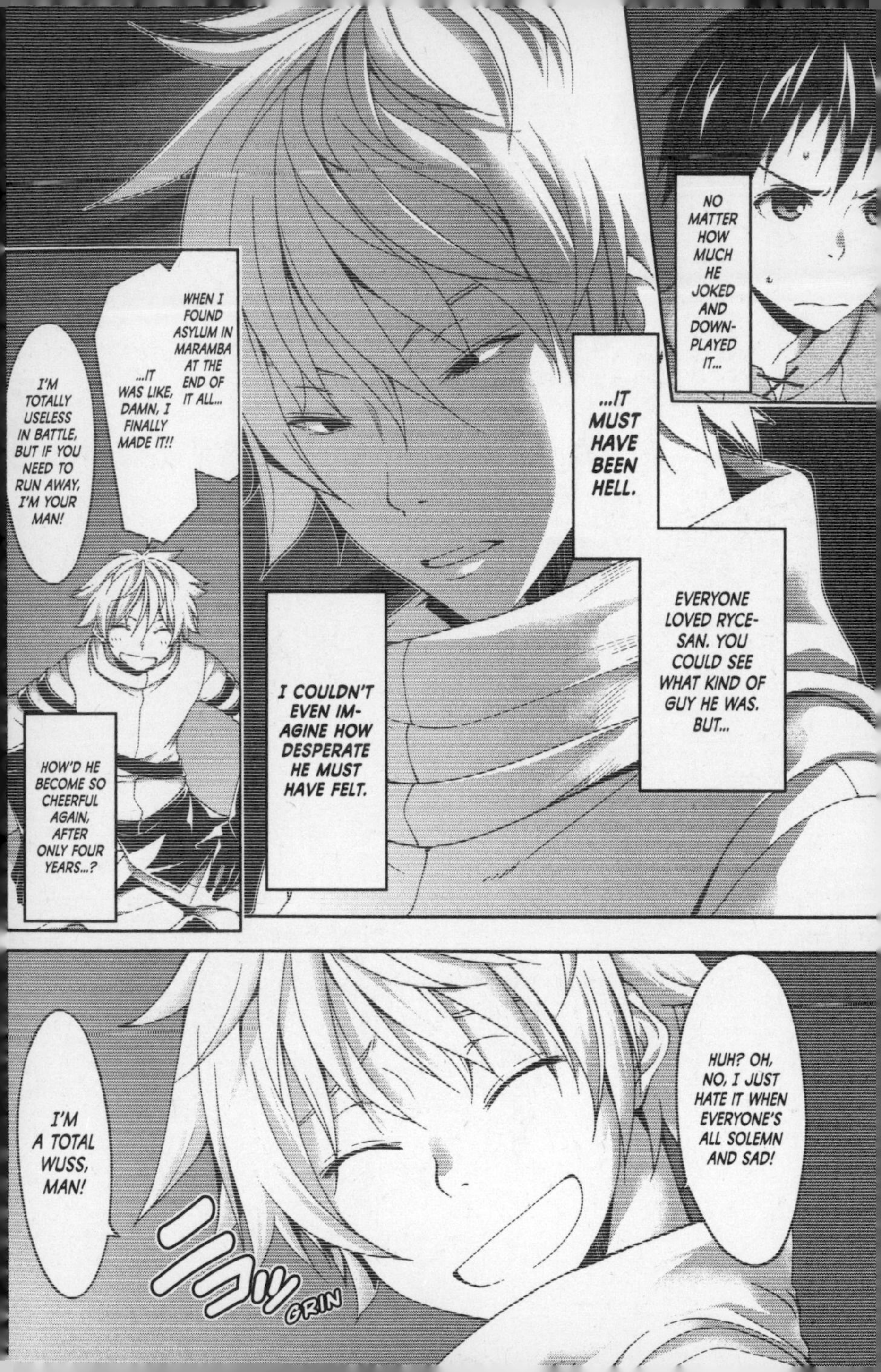
NO MATTER HOW MUCH HE JOKED AND DOWN-PLAYED IT...
...IT MUST HAVE BEEN HELL.
EVERYONE LOVED RYCE-SAN. YOU COULD SEE WHAT KIND OF GUY HE WAS. BUT...
I COULDN'T EVEN IM-AGINE HOW DESPERATE HE MUST HAVE FELT.
WHEN I FOUND ASYLUM IN MARAMBA AT THE END OF IT ALL...
...IT WAS LIKE, DAMN, I FINALLY MADE IT!!
I'M TOTALLY USELESS IN BATTLE, BUT IF YOU NEED TO RUN AWAY, I'M YOUR MAN!
HOW'D HE BECOME SO CHEERFUL AGAIN, AFTER ONLY FOUR YEARS...?
HUH? OH, NO, I JUST HATE IT WHEN EVERYONE'S ALL SOLEMN AND SAD!
I'M A TOTAL WUSS, MAN!
ニコッ
GRIN

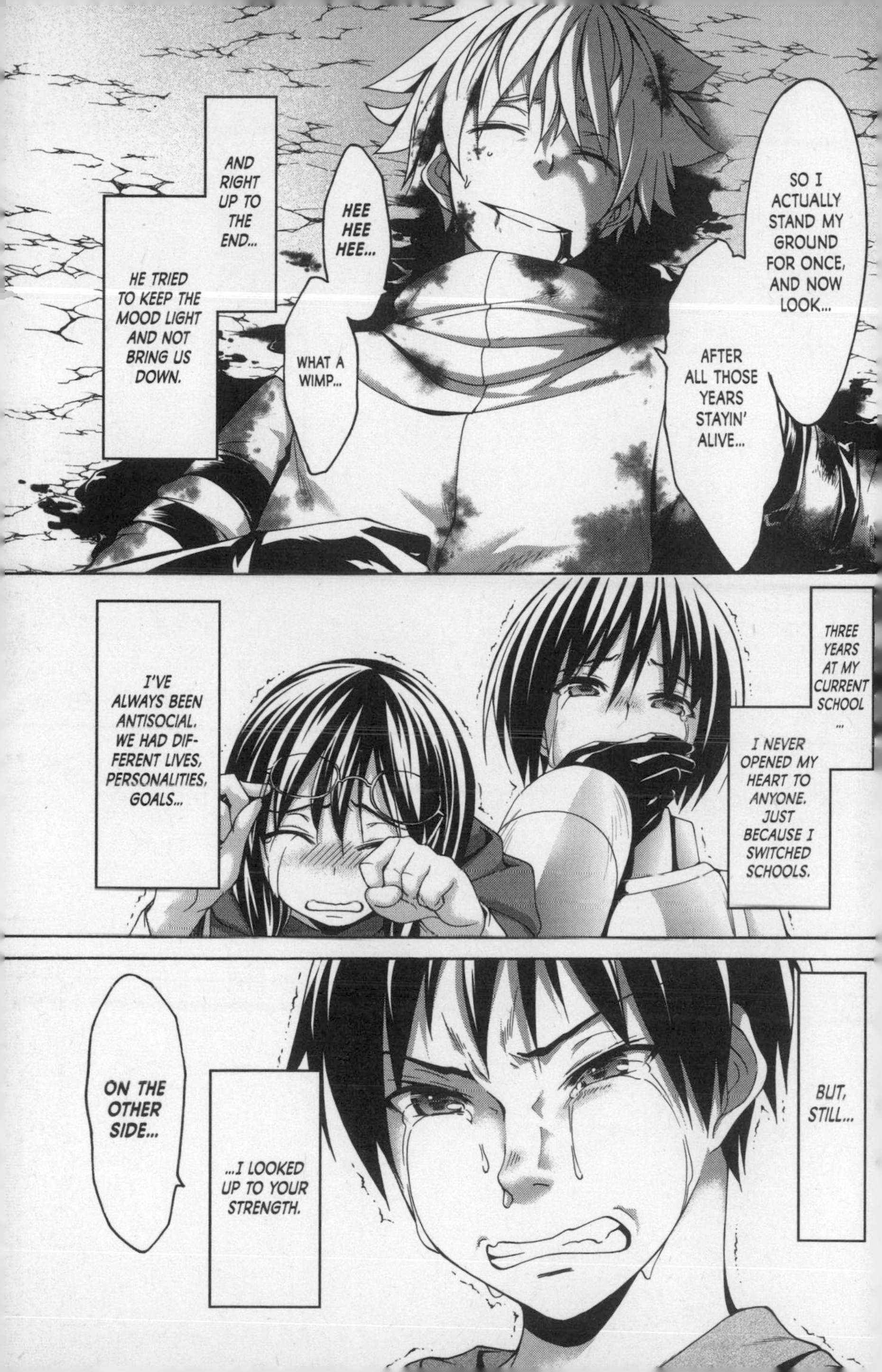
SO I ACTUALLY STAND MY GROUND FOR ONCE, AND NOW LOOK...
AFTER ALL THOSE YEARS STAYIN' ALIVE...
HEE HEE HEE...
WHAT A WIMP...
AND RIGHT UP TO THE END...
HE TRIED TO KEEP THE MOOD LIGHT AND NOT BRING US DOWN.
THREE YEARS AT MY CURRENT SCHOOL ...
I NEVER OPENED MY HEART TO ANYONE. JUST BECAUSE I SWITCHED SCHOOLS.
I'VE ALWAYS BEEN ANTISOCIAL. WE HAD DIF-FERENT LIVES, PERSONALITIES, GOALS...
BUT, STILL...
...I LOOKED UP TO YOUR STRENGTH.
ON THE OTHER SIDE...

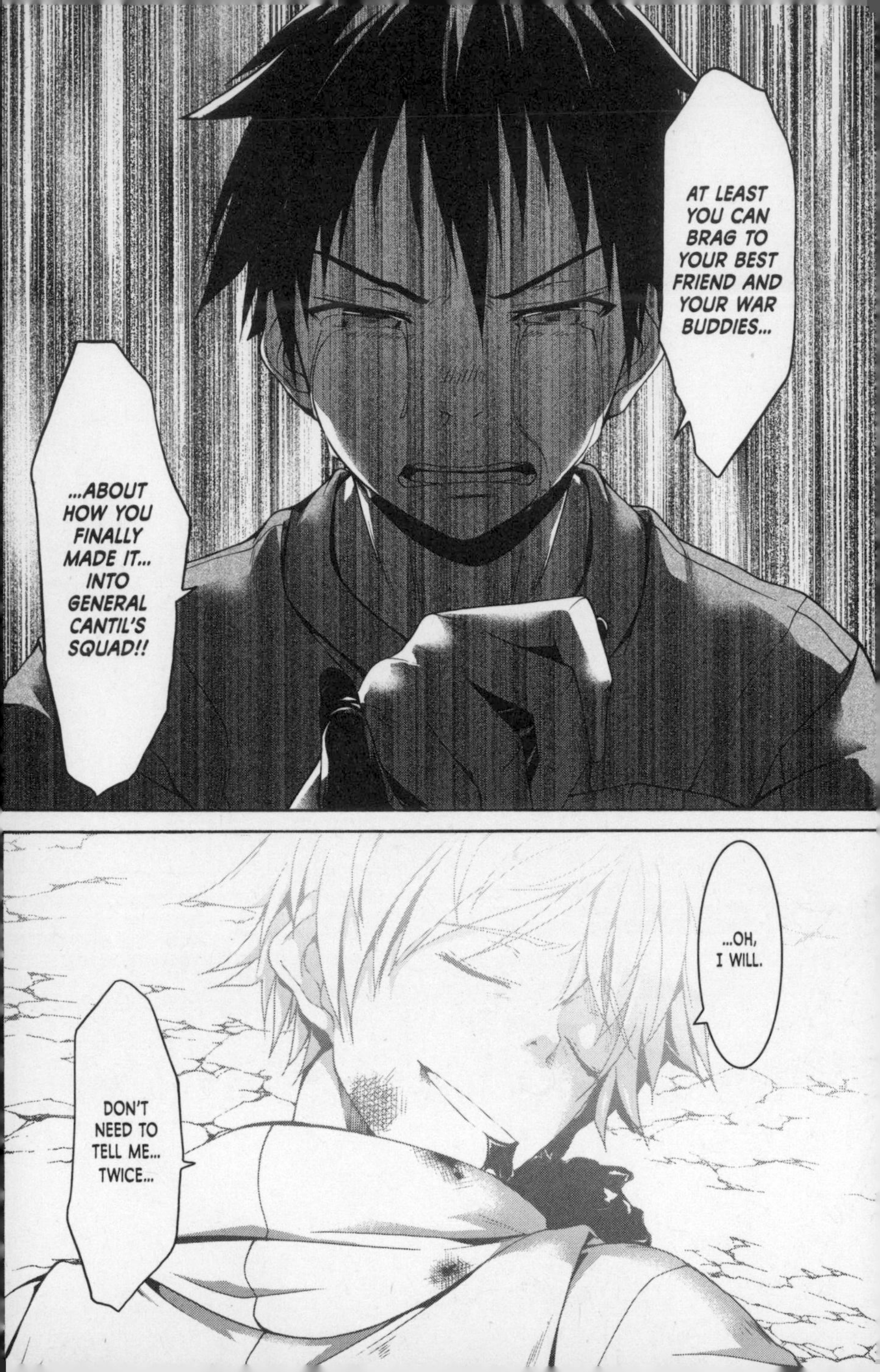
AT LEAST YOU CAN BRAG TO YOUR BEST FRIEND AND YOUR WAR BUDDIES...
...ABOUT HOW YOU FINALLY MADE IT... INTO GENERAL CANTIL'S SQUAD!!
...OH, I WILL.
DON'T NEED TO TELL ME... TWICE...

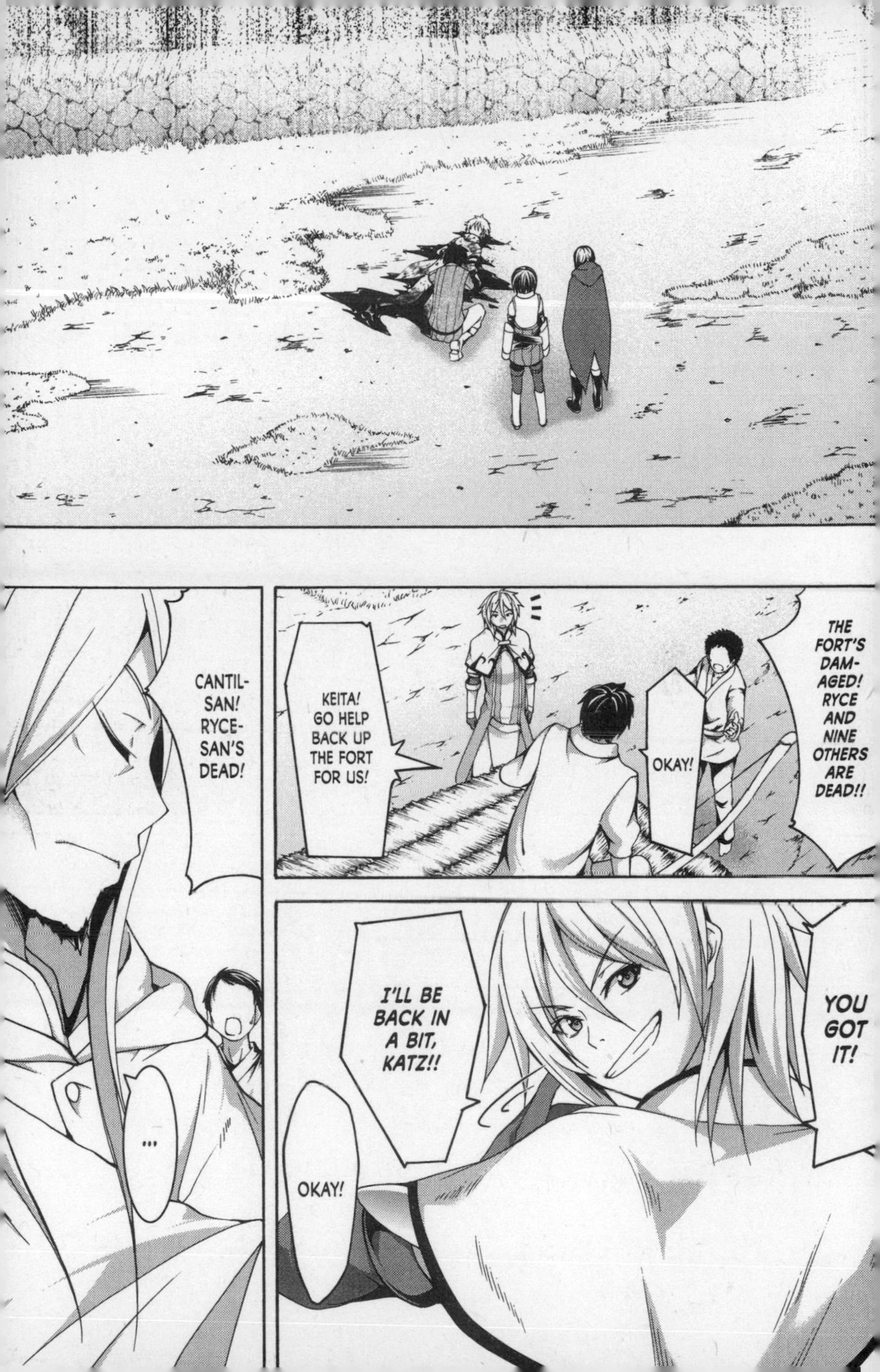
THE FORT'S DAM-AGED! RYCE AND NINE OTHERS ARE DEAD!!
KEITA! GO HELP BACK UP THE FORT FOR US!
OKAY!
YOU GOT IT!
I'LL BE BACK IN A BIT, KATZ!!
OKAY!
CANTIL-SAN! RYCE-SAN'S DEAD!
...

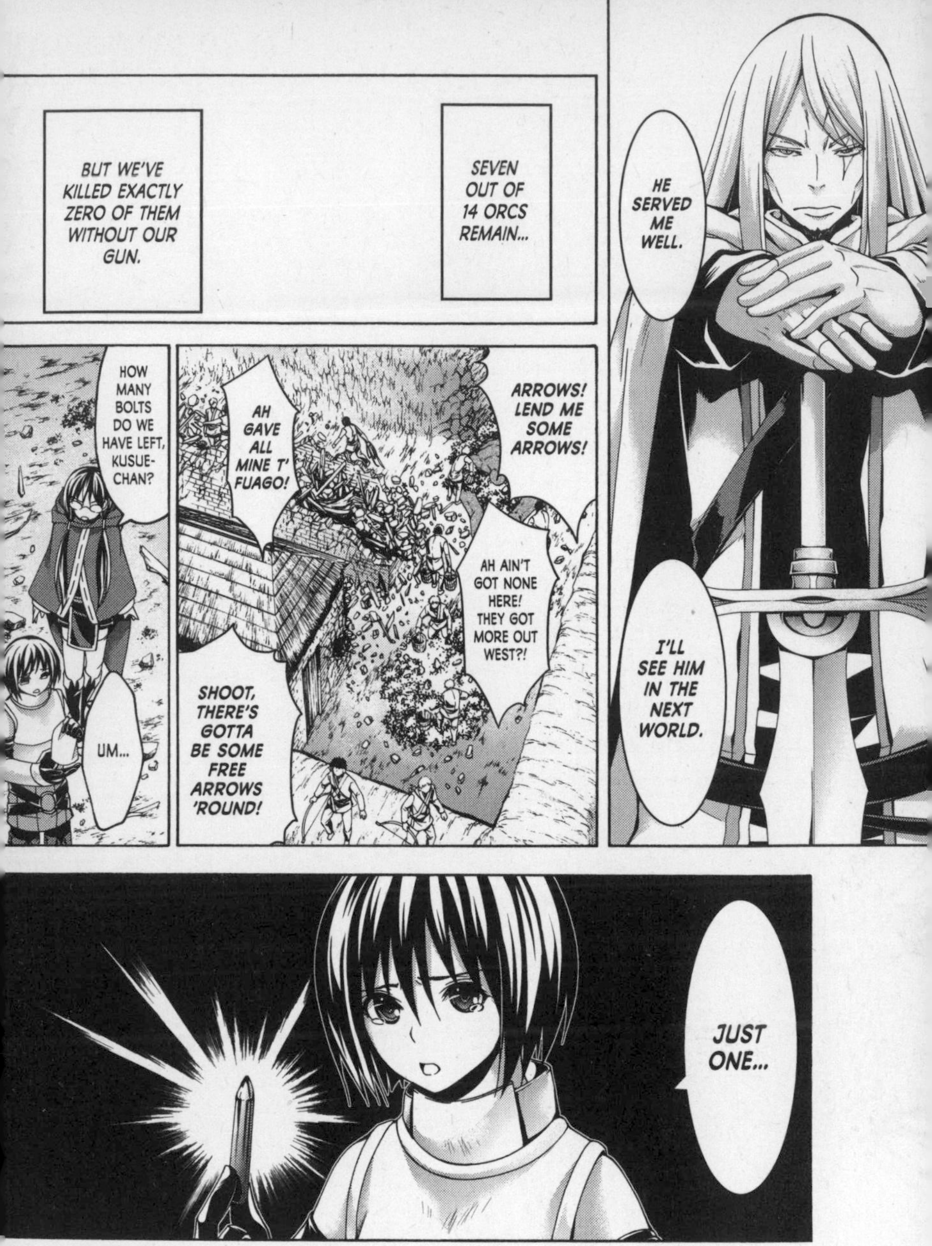
HE SERVED ME WELL.
I'LL SEE HIM IN THE NEXT WORLD.
SEVEN OUT OF 14 ORCS REMAIN...
BUT WE'VE KILLED EXACTLY ZERO OF THEM WITHOUT OUR GUN.
ARROWS! LEND ME SOME ARROWS!
AH GAVE ALL MINE T' FUAGO!
AH AIN'T GOT NONE HERE! THEY GOT MORE OUT WEST?!
SHOOT, THERE'S GOTTA BE SOME FREE ARROWS 'ROUND!
HOW MANY BOLTS DO WE HAVE LEFT, KUSUE-CHAN?
UM...
JUST ONE...

REMAINING QUEST TIME: 1 DAY AND 12 HOURS

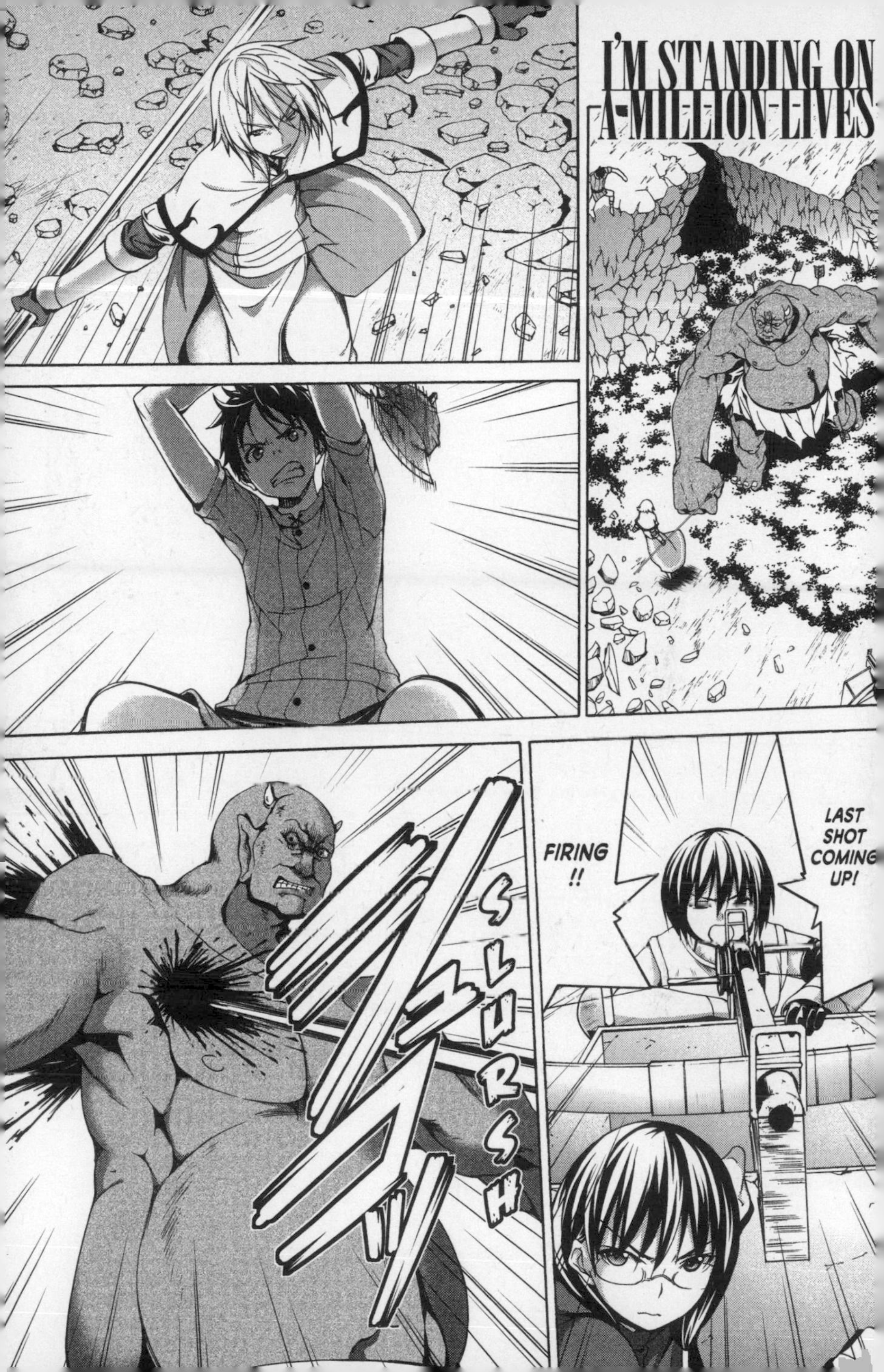
I'M STANDING ON
A MILLION LIVES
LAST SHOT COMING UP!
FIRING !!
SLURSH

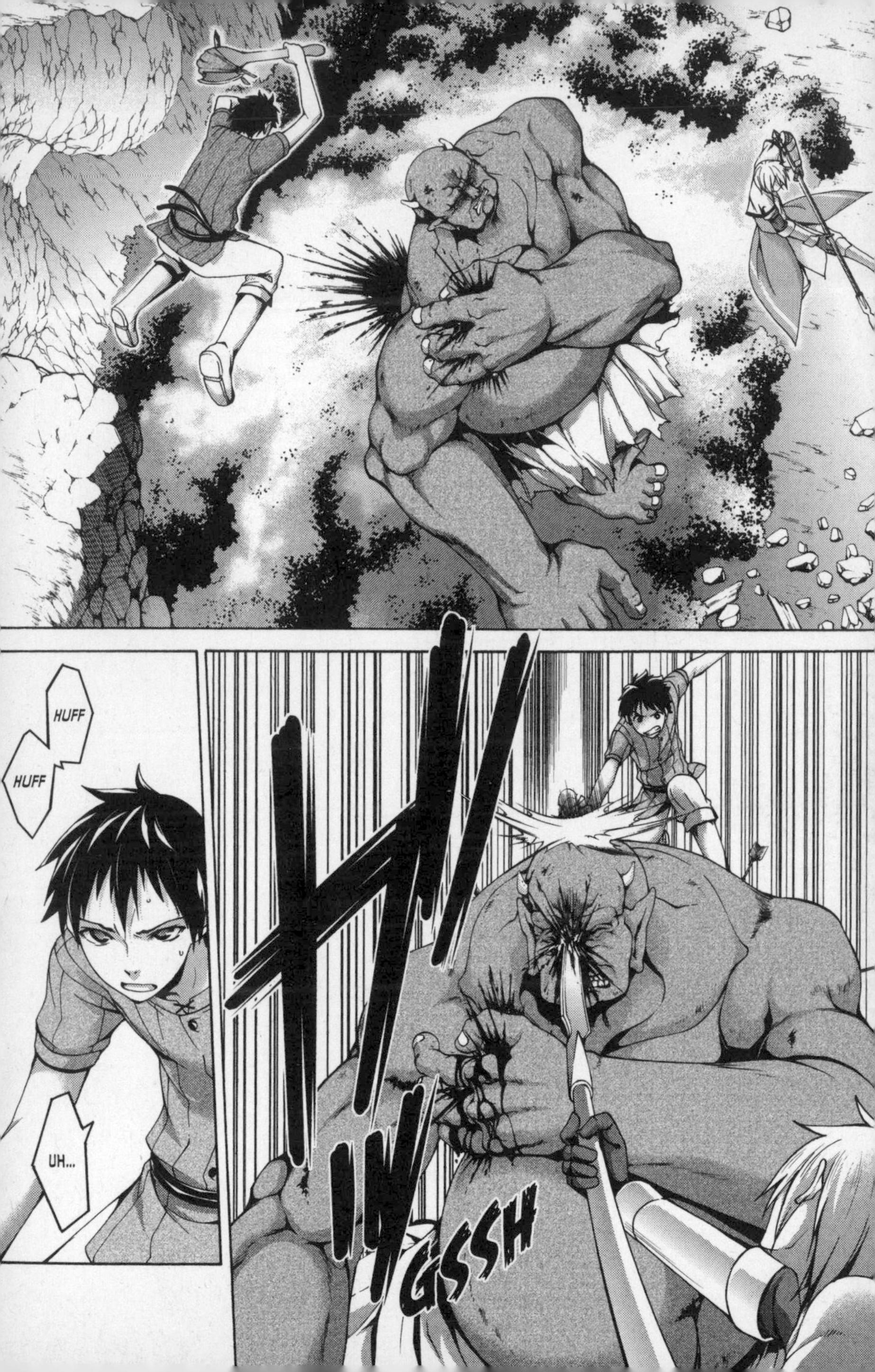
GSSH
HUFF
HUFF
UH...

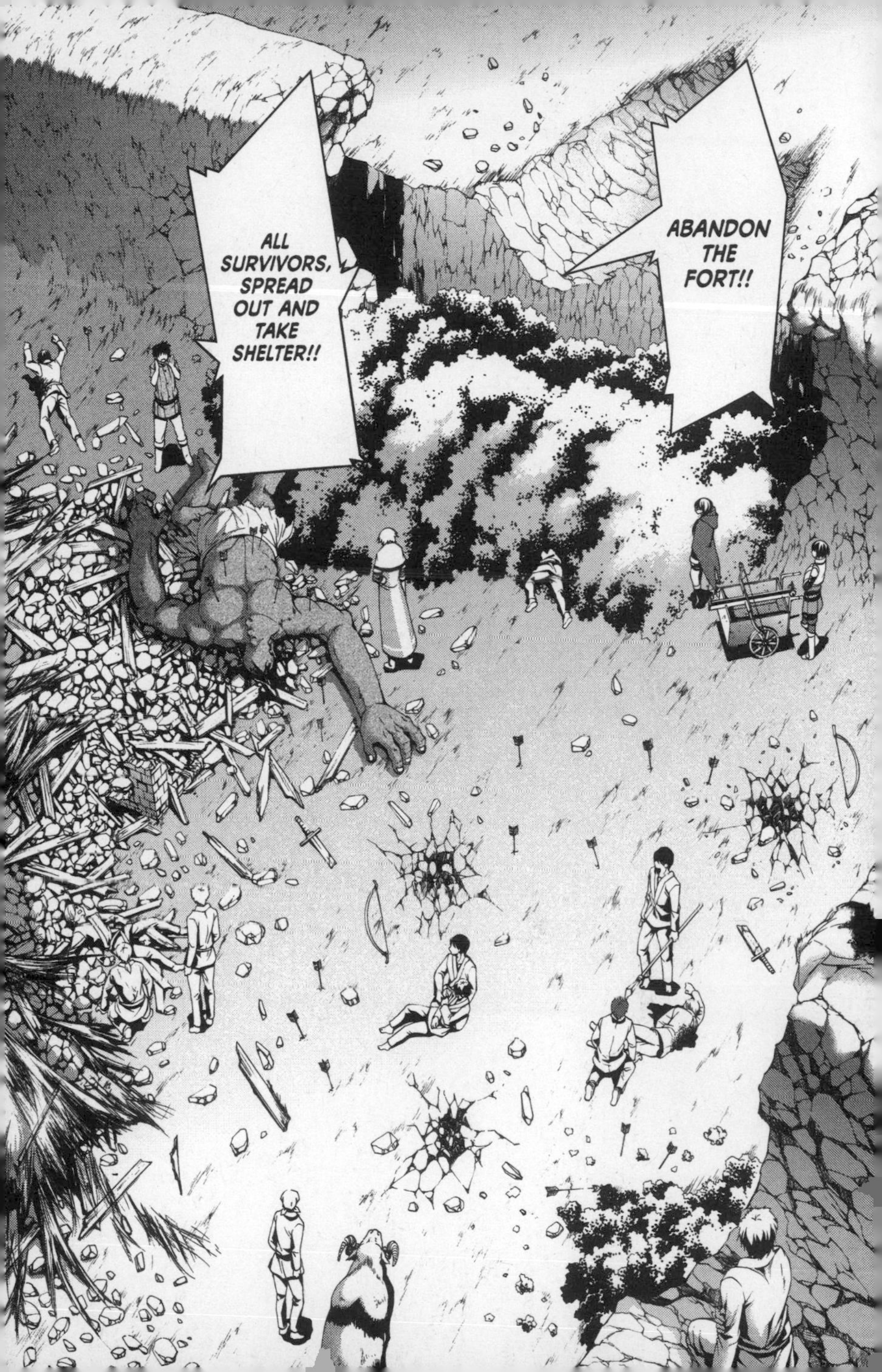
ABANDON THE FORT!!
ALL SURVIVORS, SPREAD OUT AND TAKE SHELTER!!

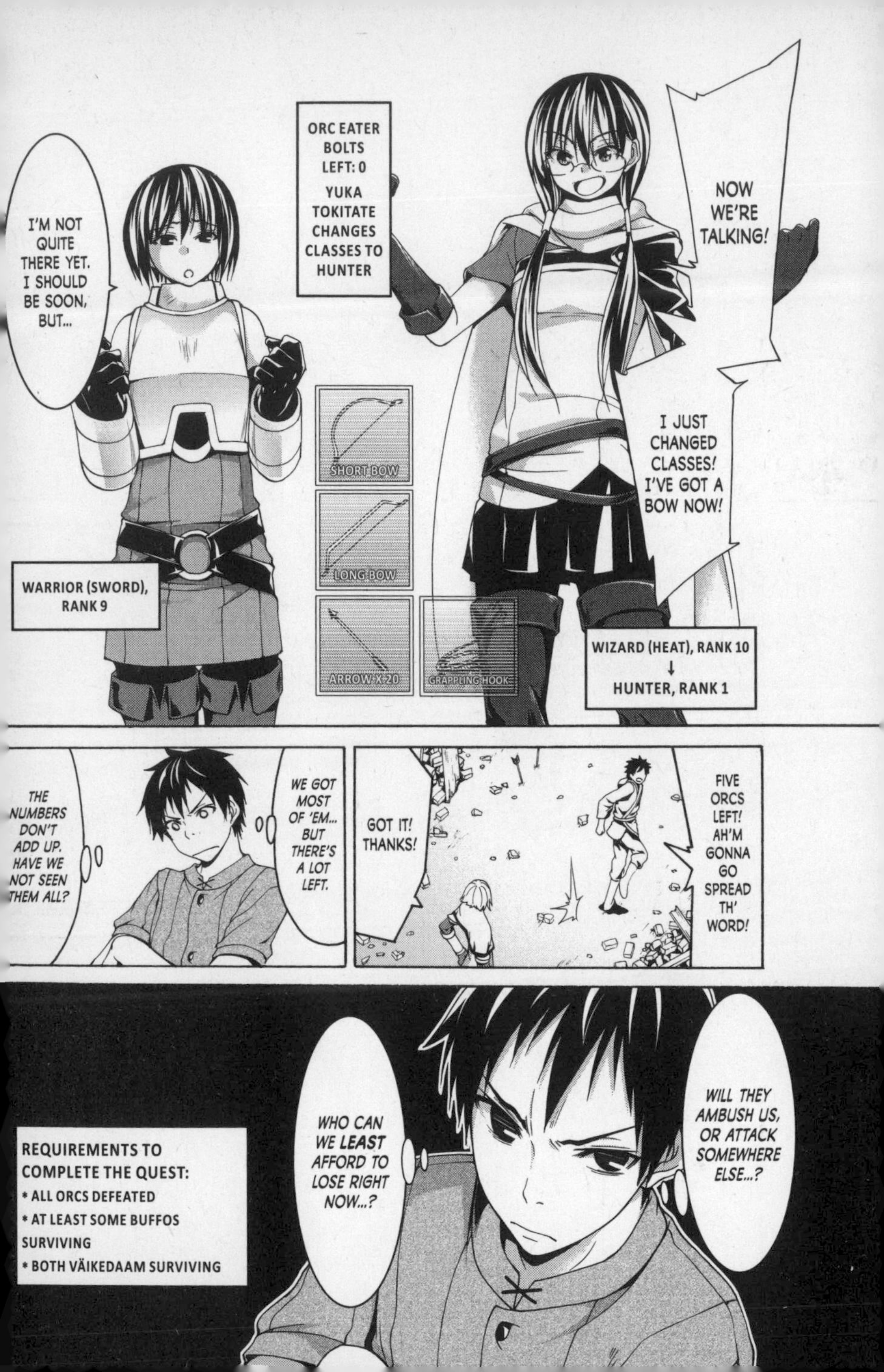
NOW WE'RE TALKING!
ORC EATER BOLTS LEFT: 0
YUKA TOKITATE CHANGES CLASSES TO HUNTER
I'M NOT QUITE THERE YET. I SHOULD BE SOON, BUT...
I JUST CHANGED CLASSES! I'VE GOT A BOW NOW!
SHORT BOW
LONG BOW
WIZARD (HEAT), RANK 10 ↓ HUNTER, RANK 1
GRAPPLING HOOK
ARROW X 20
WARRIOR (SWORD), RANK 9
FIVE ORCS LEFT! AH'M GONNA GO SPREAD TH' WORD!
GOT IT! THANKS!
WE GOT MOST OF 'EM... BUT THERE'S A LOT LEFT.
THE NUMBERS DON'T ADD UP. HAVE WE NOT SEEN THEM ALL?
WILL THEY AMBUSH US, OR ATTACK SOMEWHERE ELSE...?
WHO CAN WE LEAST AFFORD TO LOSE RIGHT NOW...?
REQUIREMENTS TO COMPLETE THE QUEST:
* ALL ORCS DEFEATED
* AT LEAST SOME BUFFOS SURVIVING
* BOTH VÄIKEDAAM SURVIVING

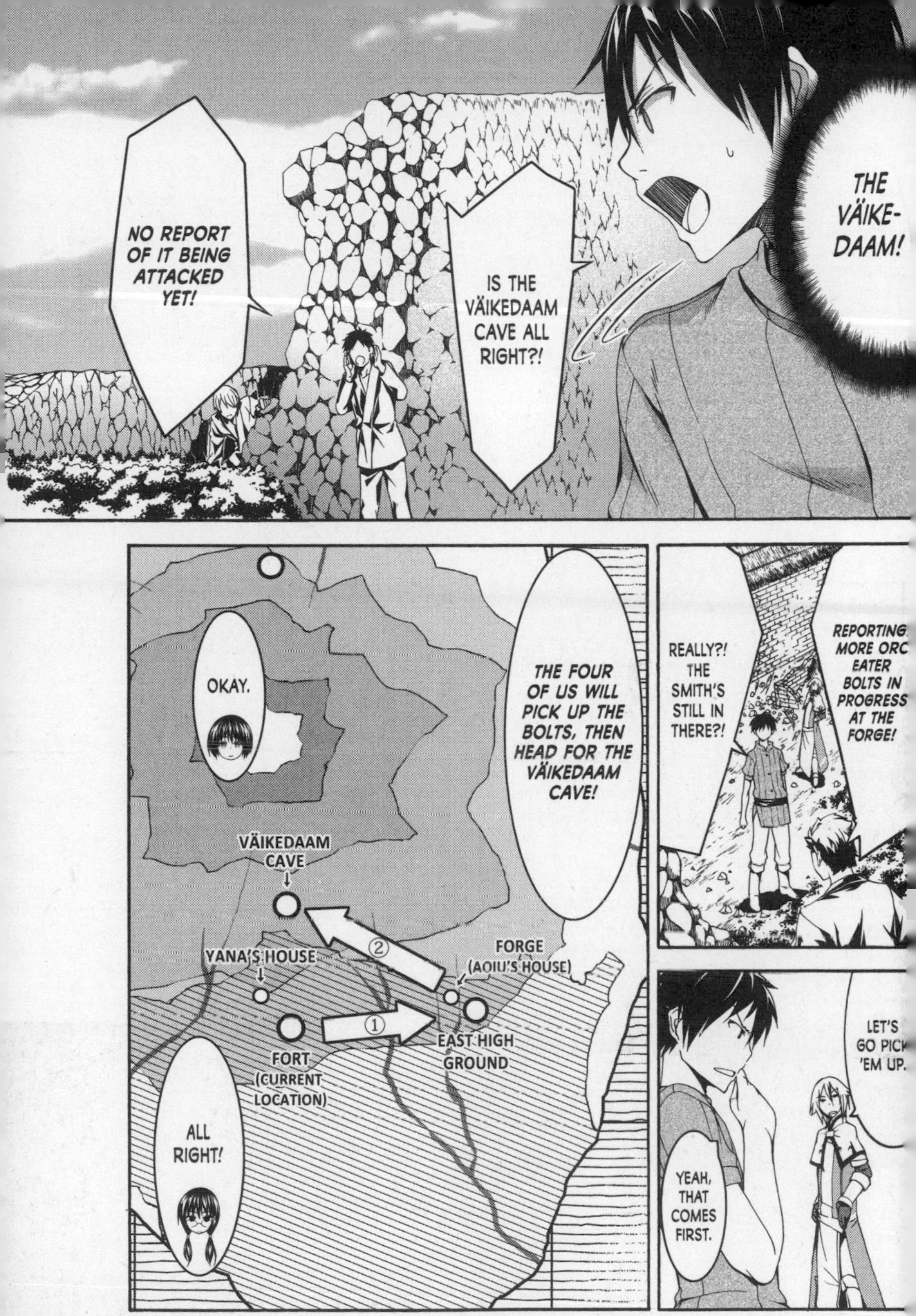
THE VÄIKE-DAAM!
IS THE VÄIKEDAAM CAVE ALL RIGHT?!
NO REPORT OF IT BEING ATTACKED YET!
REPORTING: MORE ORC EATER BOLTS IN PROGRESS AT THE FORGE!
REALLY?! THE SMITH'S STILL IN THERE?!
LET'S GO PICK 'EM UP.
YEAH, THAT COMES FIRST.
THE FOUR OF US WILL PICK UP THE BOLTS, THEN HEAD FOR THE VÄIKEDAAM CAVE!
OKAY.
VÄIKEDAAM CAVE
FORGE (AOIU'S HOUSE)
YANA'S HOUSE
②
①
EAST HIGH GROUND
FORT (CURRENT LOCATION)
ALL RIGHT!

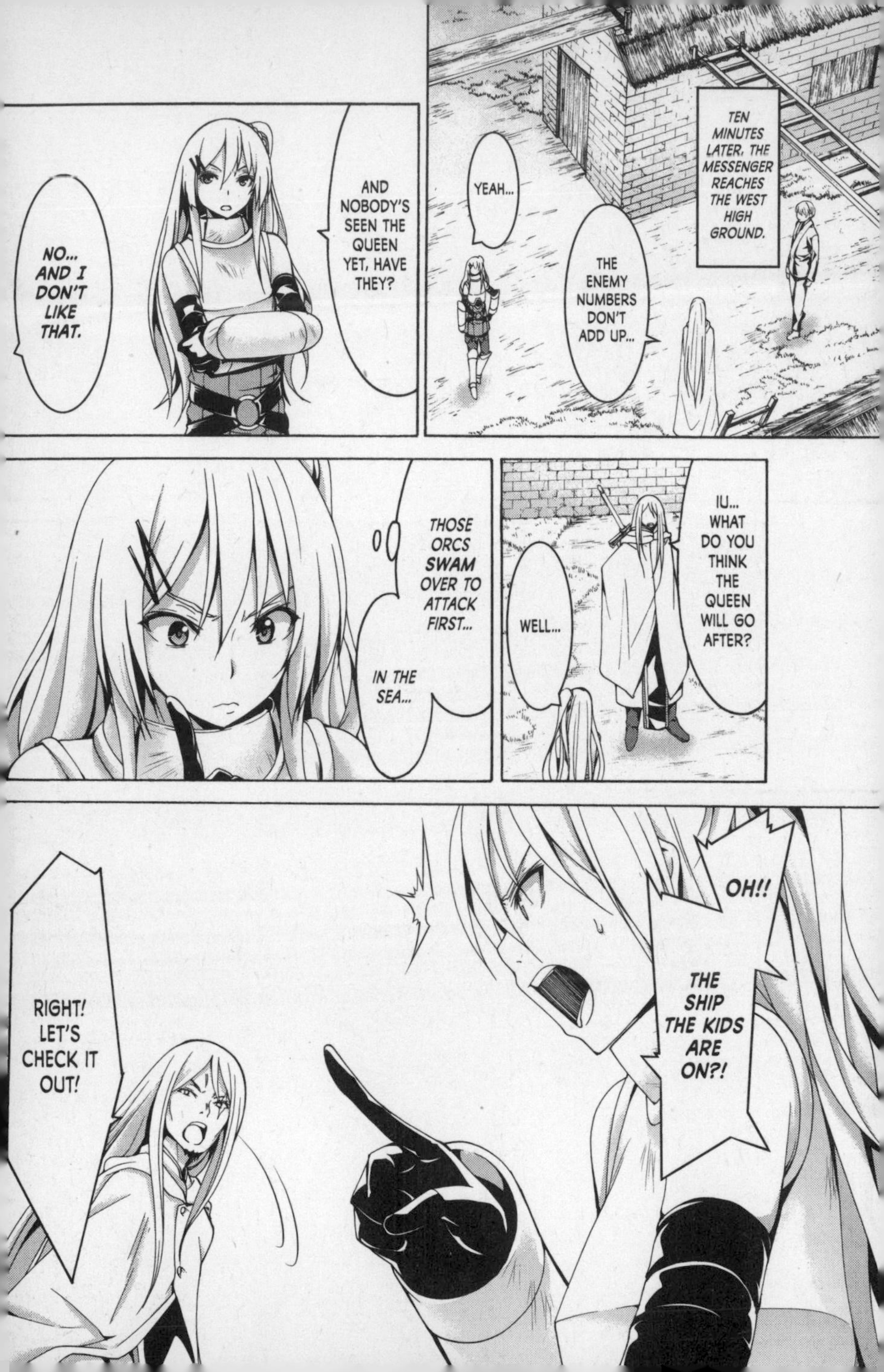
TEN MINUTES LATER, THE MESSENGER REACHES THE WEST HIGH GROUND.
THE ENEMY NUMBERS DON'T ADD UP...
YEAH...
AND NOBODY'S SEEN THE QUEEN YET, HAVE THEY?
NO... AND I DON'T LIKE THAT.
IU... WHAT DO YOU THINK THE QUEEN WILL GO AFTER?
WELL...
THOSE ORCS SWAM OVER TO ATTACK FIRST...
IN THE SEA...
OH!!
THE SHIP THE KIDS ARE ON?!
RIGHT! LET'S CHECK IT OUT!

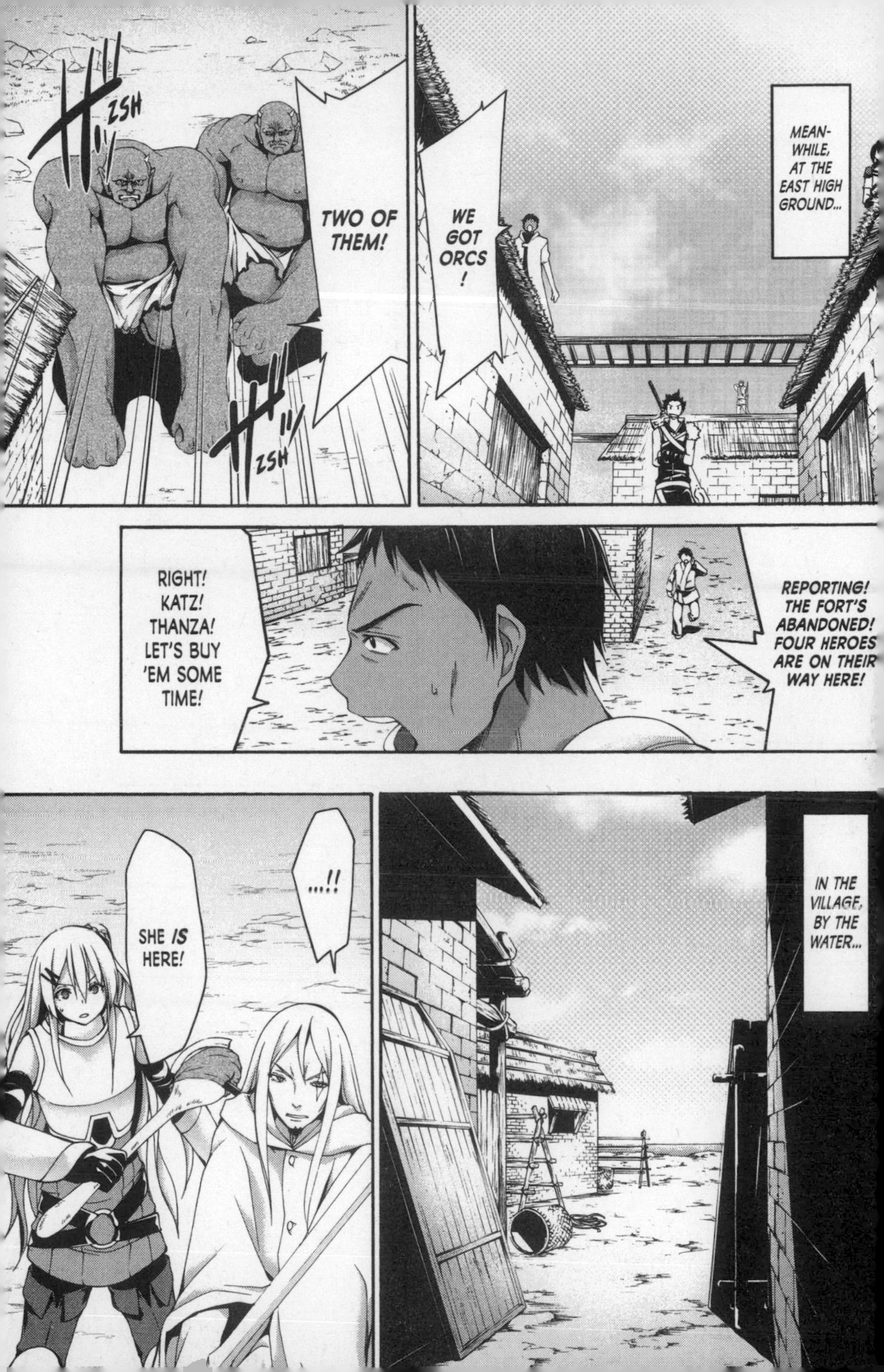
MEAN-WHILE, AT THE EAST HIGH GROUND...
WE GOT ORCS!
TWO OF THEM!
ZSH
ZSH
REPORTING! THE FORT'S ABANDONED! FOUR HEROES ARE ON THEIR WAY HERE!
RIGHT! KATZ! THANZA! LET'S BUY 'EM SOME TIME!
IN THE VILLAGE, BY THE WATER...
...!!
SHE *IS* HERE!

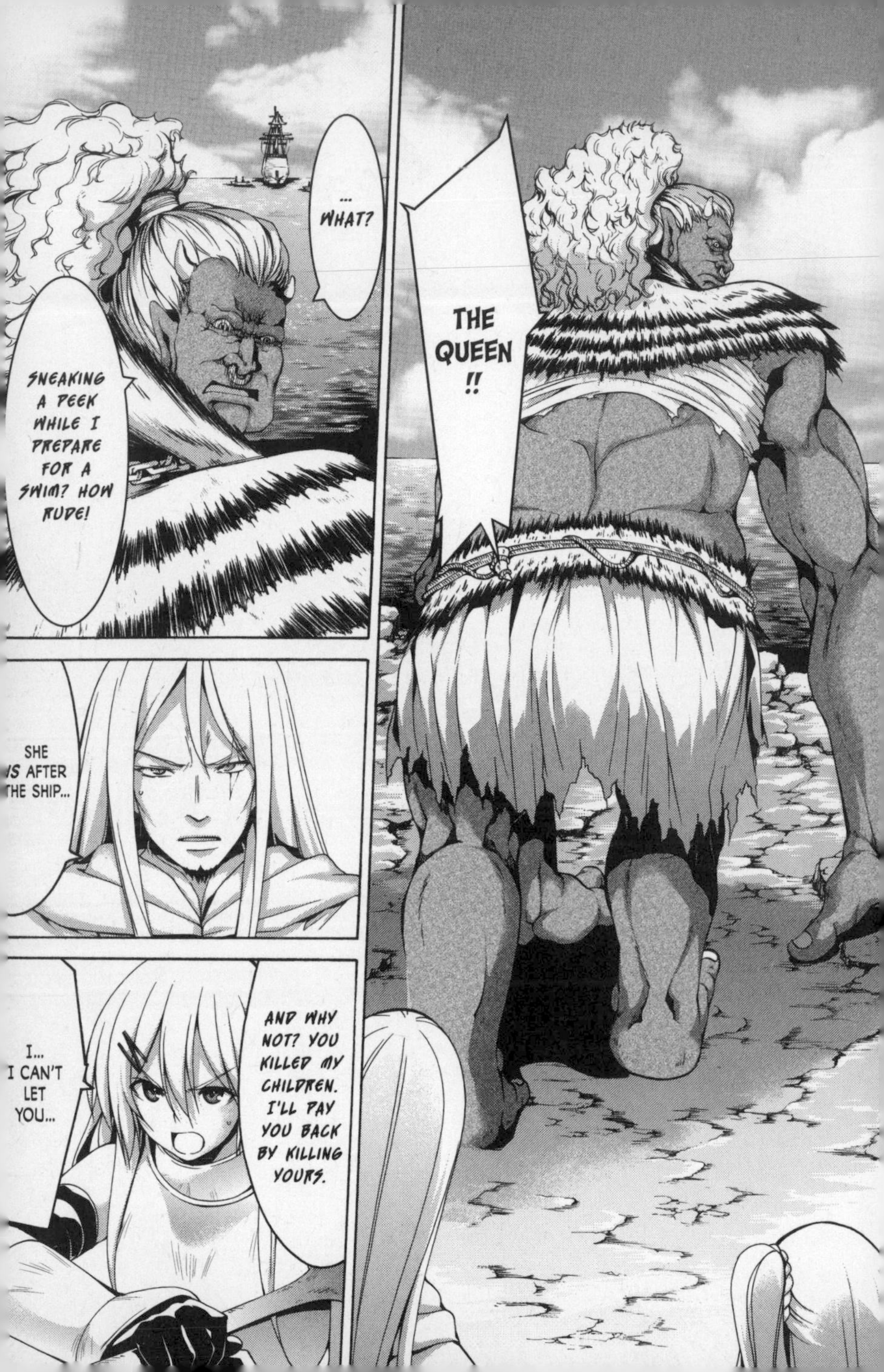
THE QUEEN!!
...WHAT?
SNEAKING A PEEK WHILE I PREPARE FOR A SWIM? HOW RUDE!
SHE IS AFTER THE SHIP...
AND WHY NOT? YOU KILLED MY CHILDREN. I'LL PAY YOU BACK BY KILLING YOURS.
I... I CAN'T LET YOU...

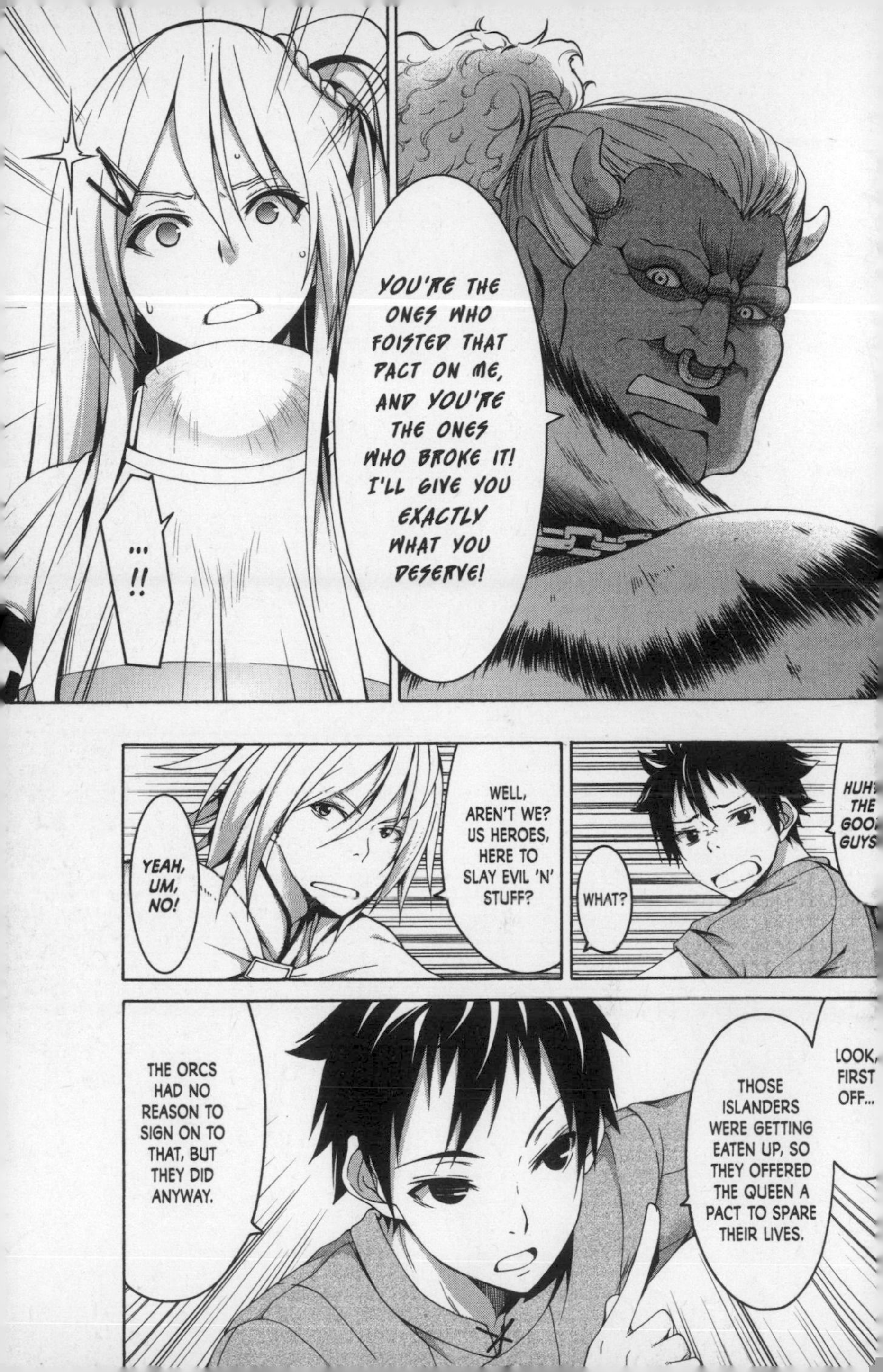
YOU'RE THE ONES WHO FOISTED THAT PACT ON ME, AND YOU'RE THE ONES WHO BROKE IT! I'LL GIVE YOU EXACTLY WHAT YOU DESERVE!
... !!
HUH THE GOO GUYS
WHAT?
WELL, AREN'T WE? US HEROES, HERE TO SLAY EVIL 'N' STUFF?
YEAH, UM, NO!
LOOK, FIRST OFF...
THOSE ISLANDERS WERE GETTING EATEN UP, SO THEY OFFERED THE QUEEN A PACT TO SPARE THEIR LIVES.
THE ORCS HAD NO REASON TO SIGN ON TO THAT, BUT THEY DID ANYWAY.

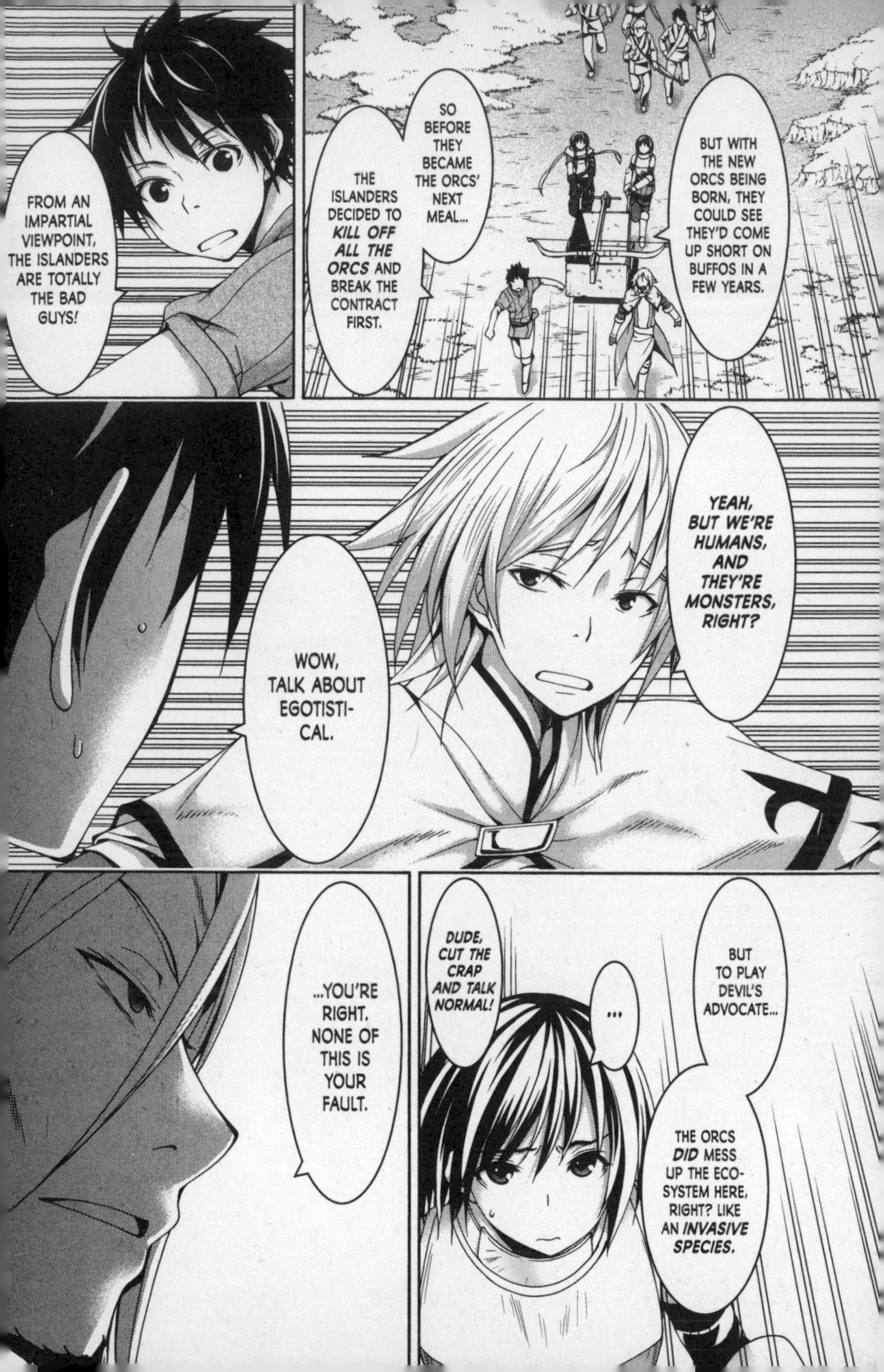
BUT WITH THE NEW ORCS BEING BORN, THEY COULD SEE THEY'D COME UP SHORT ON BUFFOS IN A FEW YEARS.
SO BEFORE THEY BECAME THE ORCS' NEXT MEAL...
THE ISLANDERS DECIDED TO *KILL OFF ALL THE ORCS* AND BREAK THE CONTRACT FIRST.
FROM AN IMPARTIAL VIEWPOINT, THE ISLANDERS ARE TOTALLY THE BAD GUYS!
YEAH, BUT WE'RE HUMANS, AND THEY'RE MONSTERS, RIGHT?
WOW, TALK ABOUT EGOTISTI-CAL.
BUT TO PLAY DEVIL'S ADVOCATE...
THE ORCS *DID* MESS UP THE ECO-SYSTEM HERE, RIGHT? LIKE AN *INVASIVE SPECIES.*
...
DUDE, CUT THE CRAP AND TALK NORMAL!
...YOU'RE RIGHT. NONE OF THIS IS YOUR FAULT.

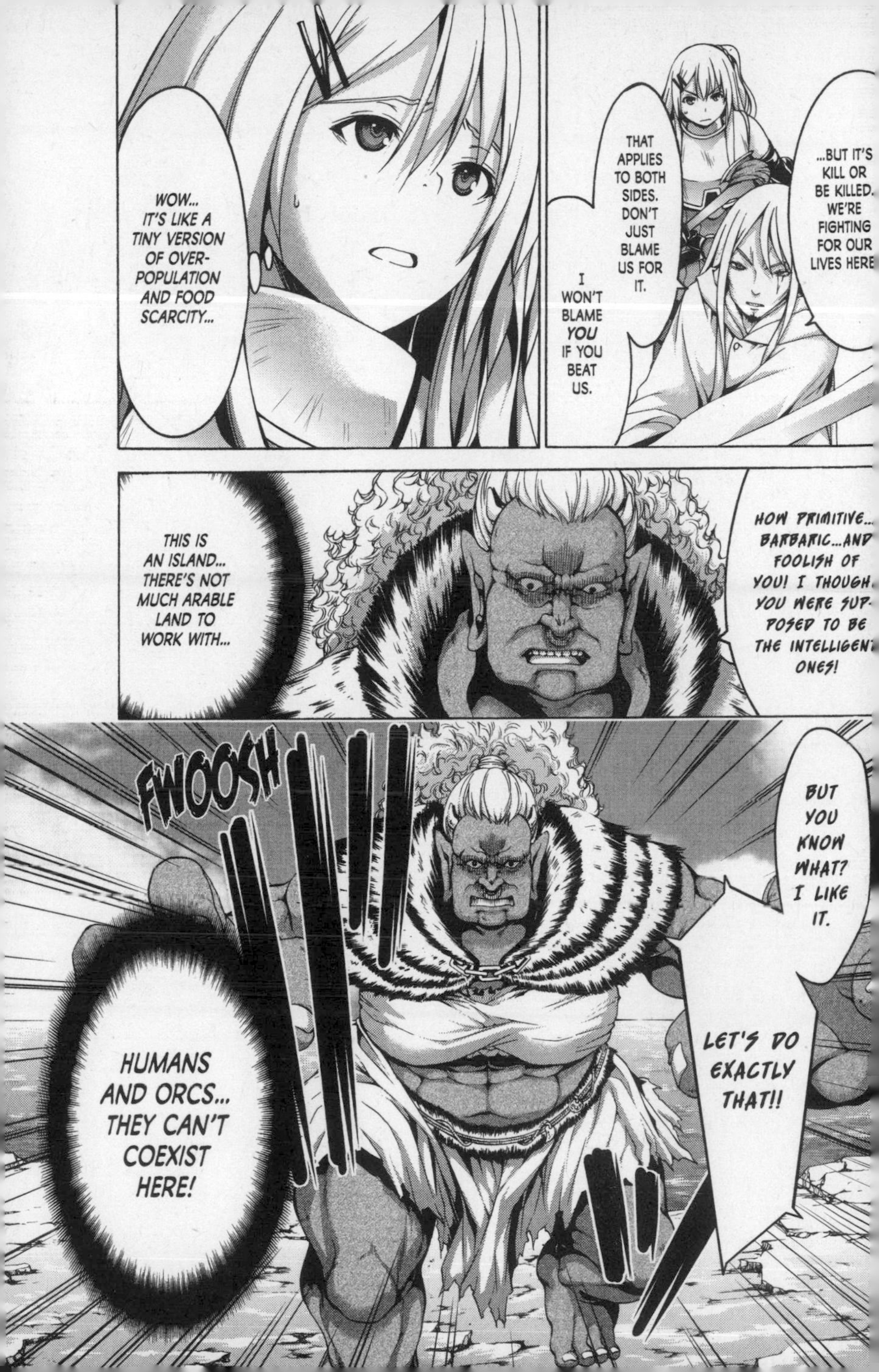
...BUT IT'S KILL OR BE KILLED. WE'RE FIGHTING FOR OUR LIVES HERE
THAT APPLIES TO BOTH SIDES. DON'T JUST BLAME US FOR IT.
I WON'T BLAME *YOU* IF YOU BEAT US.
WOW... IT'S LIKE A TINY VERSION OF OVER-POPULATION AND FOOD SCARCITY...
HOW PRIMITIVE... BARBARIC...AND FOOLISH OF YOU! I THOUGH YOU WERE SUP-POSED TO BE THE INTELLIGEN ONES!
THIS IS AN ISLAND... THERE'S NOT MUCH ARABLE LAND TO WORK WITH...
BUT YOU KNOW WHAT? I LIKE IT.
FWOOSH
LET'S DO EXACTLY THAT!!
HUMANS AND ORCS... THEY CAN'T COEXIST HERE!

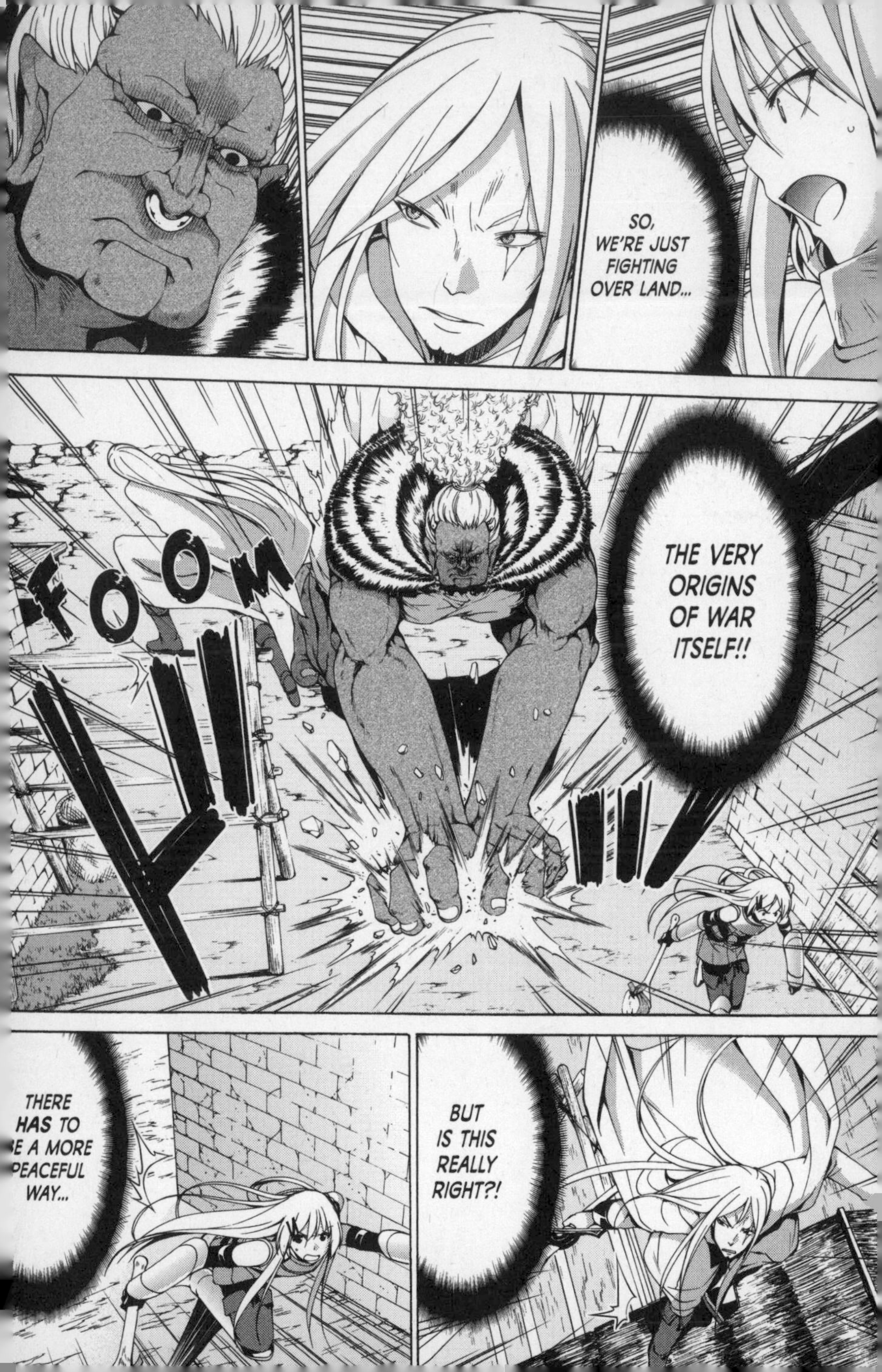
SO, WE'RE JUST FIGHTING OVER LAND...
THE VERY ORIGINS OF WAR ITSELF!!
FOOM
BUT IS THIS REALLY RIGHT?!
THERE HAS TO E A MORE EACEFUL WAY...

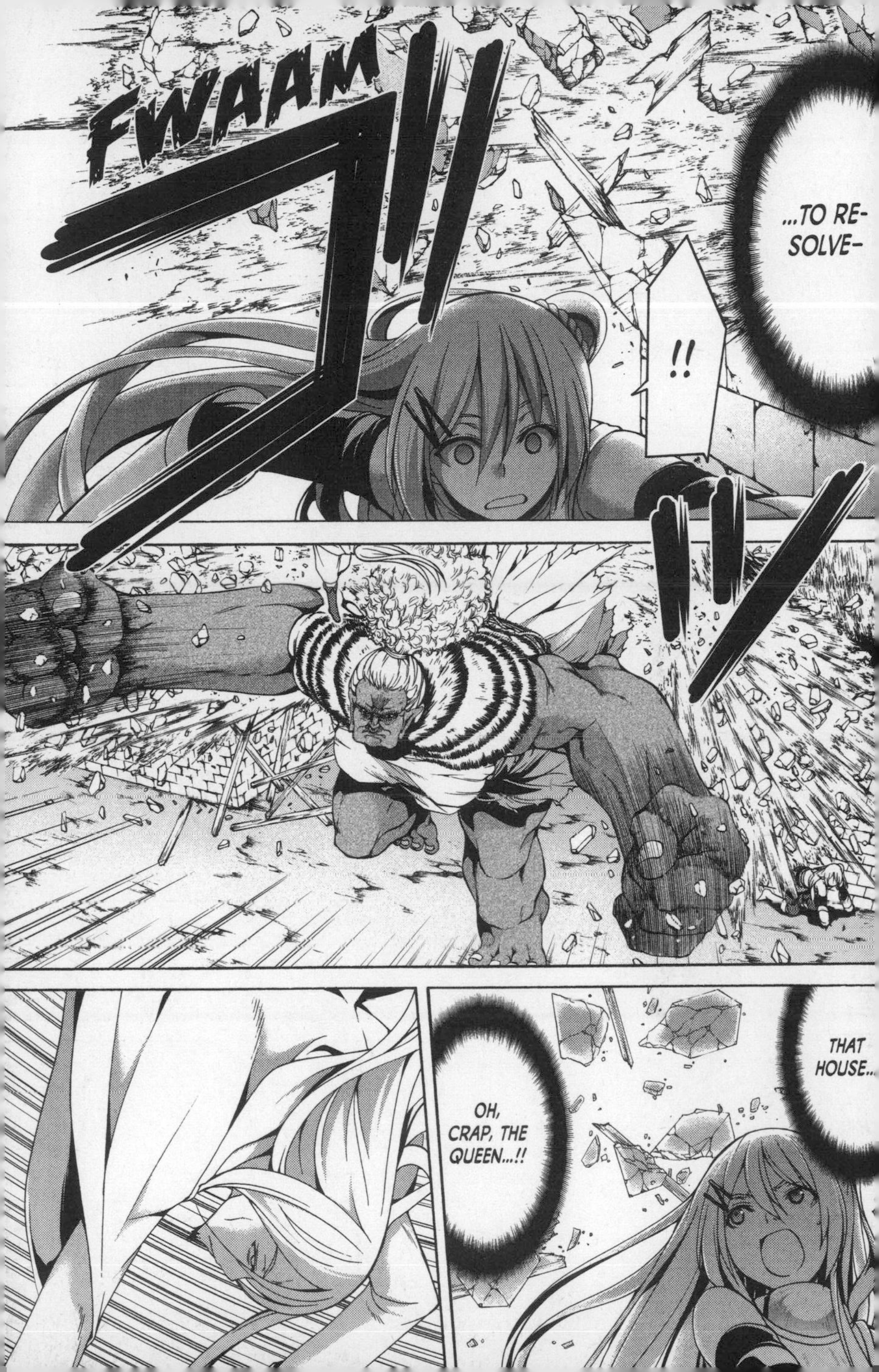
...TO RE-
SOLVE-
!!
FWAAM
THAT HOUSE...
OH, CRAP, THE QUEEN...!!

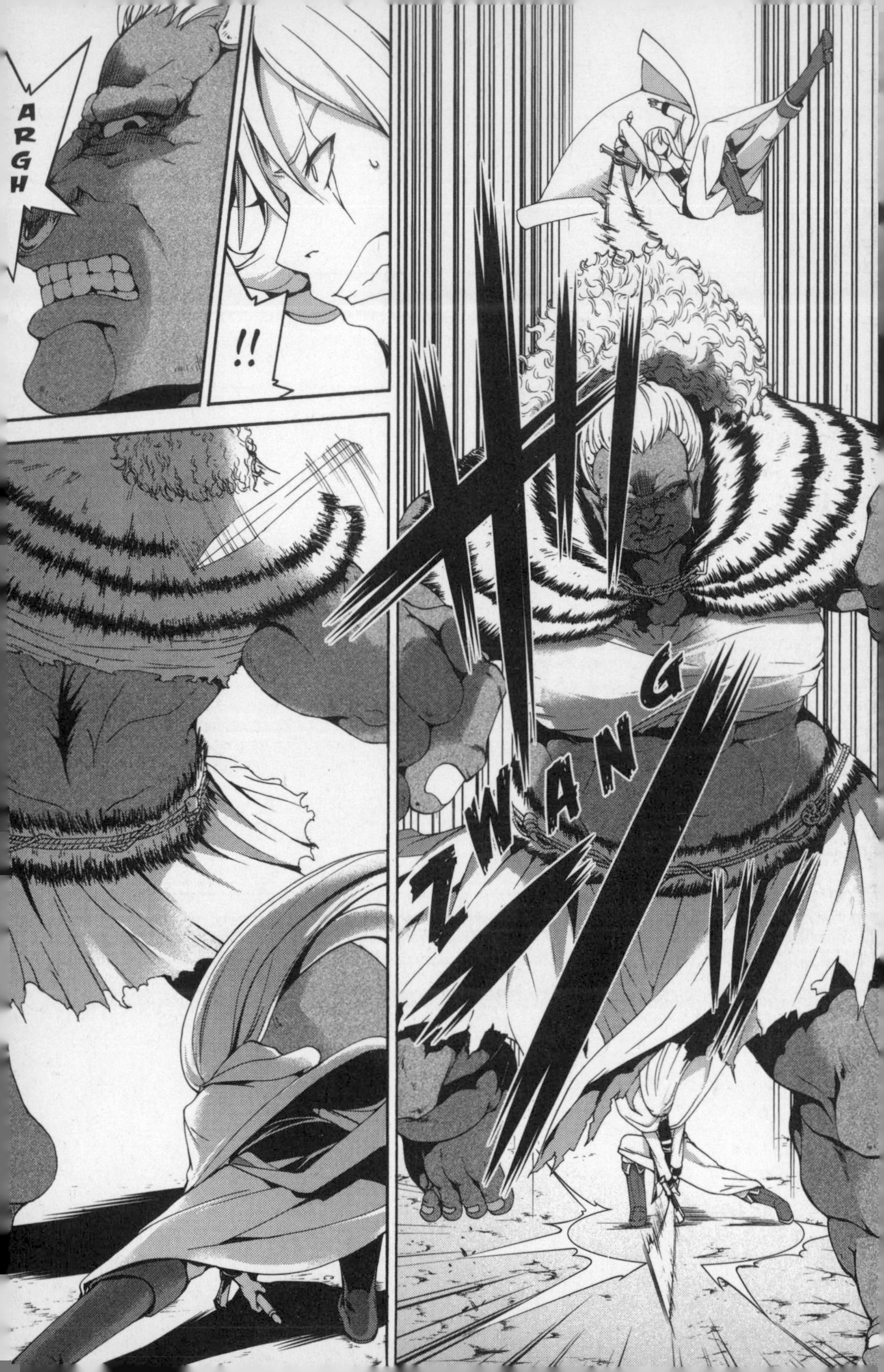
ZWANG
!!
ARGH

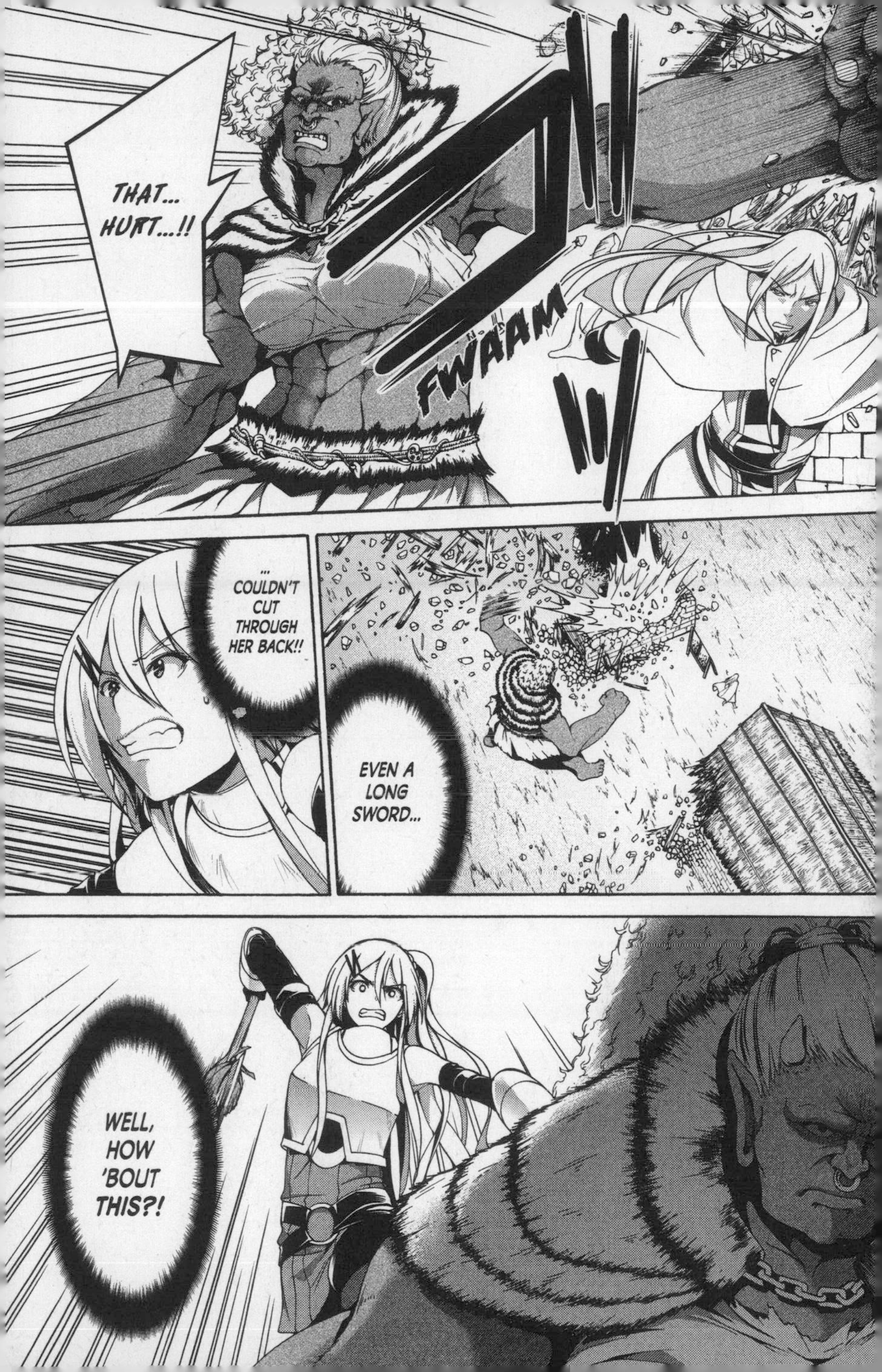
FWAAM
THAT... HURT...!!
EVEN A LONG SWORD...
... COULDN'T CUT THROUGH HER BACK!!
WELL, HOW 'BOUT THIS?!

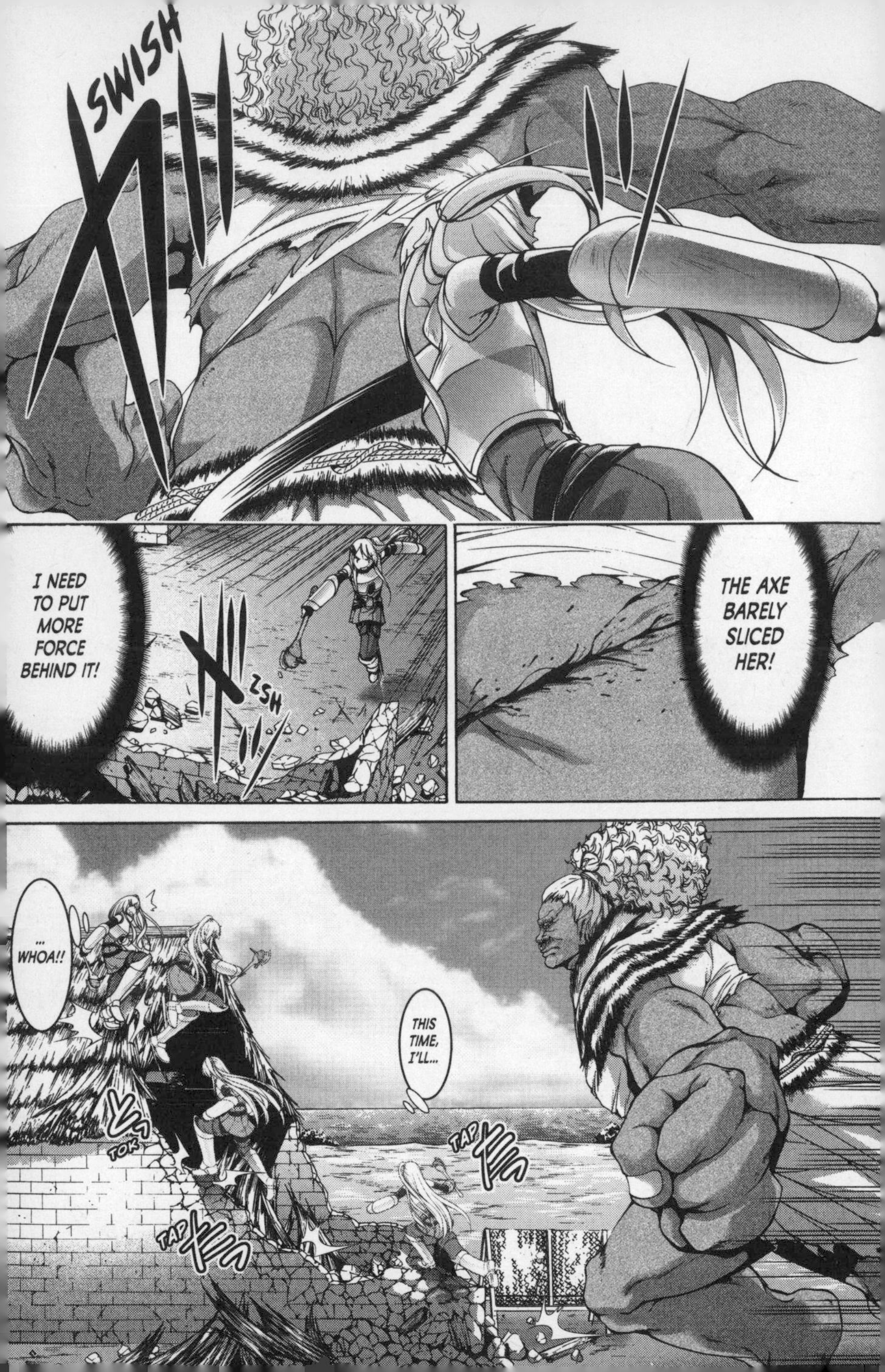
SWISH
THE AXE BARELY SLICED HER!
I NEED TO PUT MORE FORCE BEHIND IT!
ZSH
THIS TIME, I'LL...
TAP
...WHOA!!
TOK
TAP

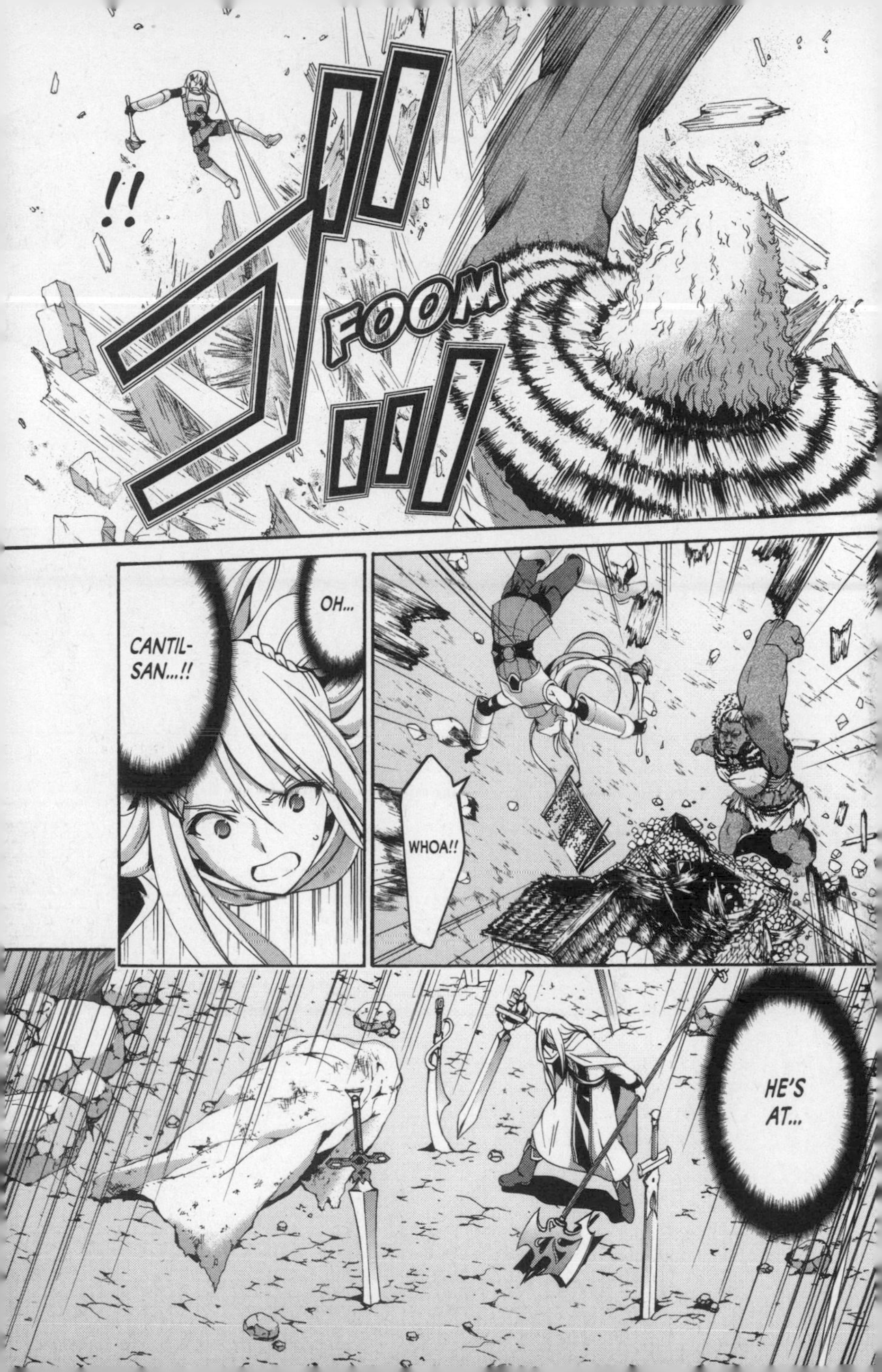
FOOM
!!
WHOA!!
OH...
CANTIL-SAN...!!
HE'S AT...

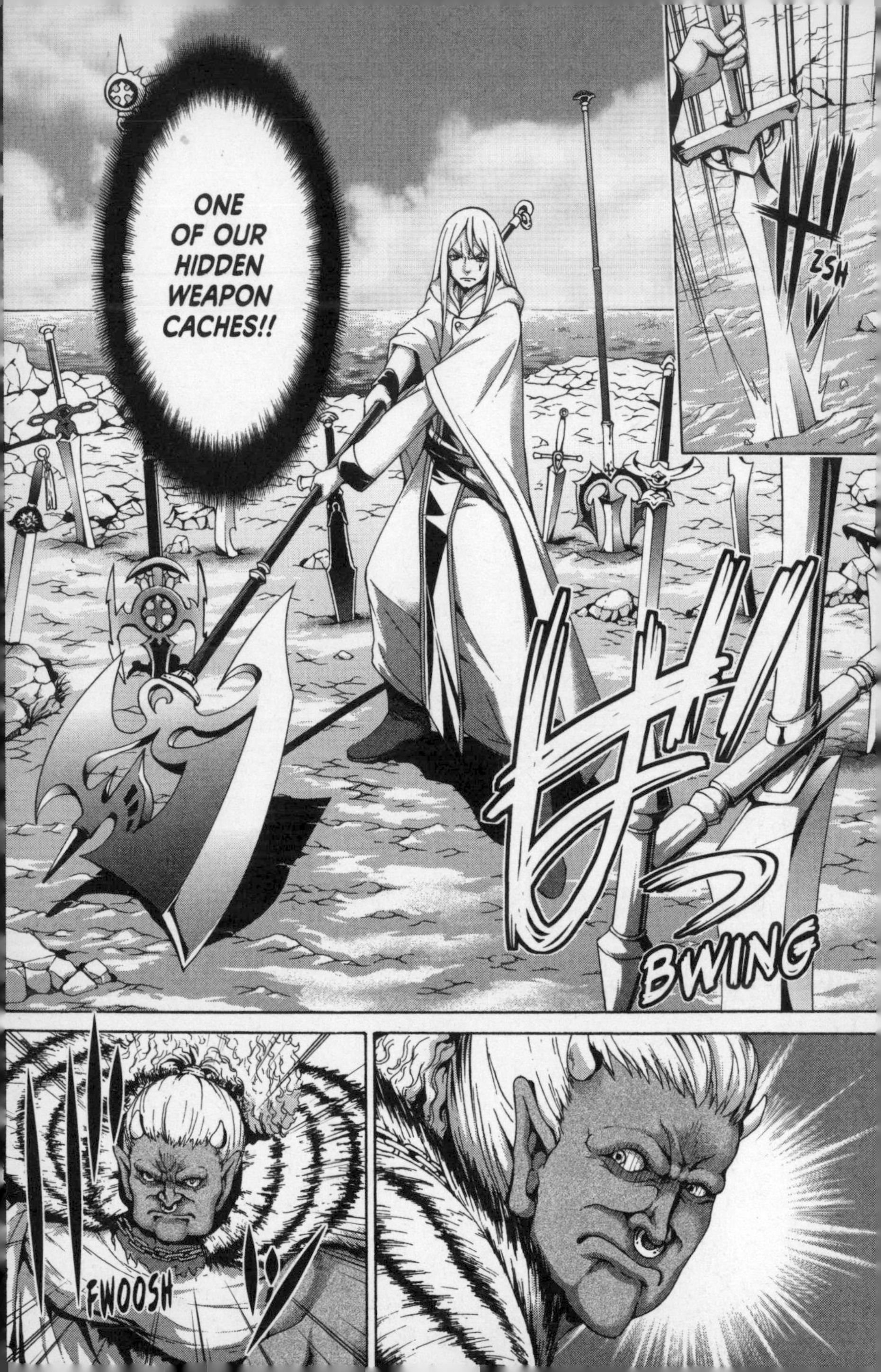
ZSH
ONE OF OUR HIDDEN WEAPON CACHES!!
BWING
FWOOSH

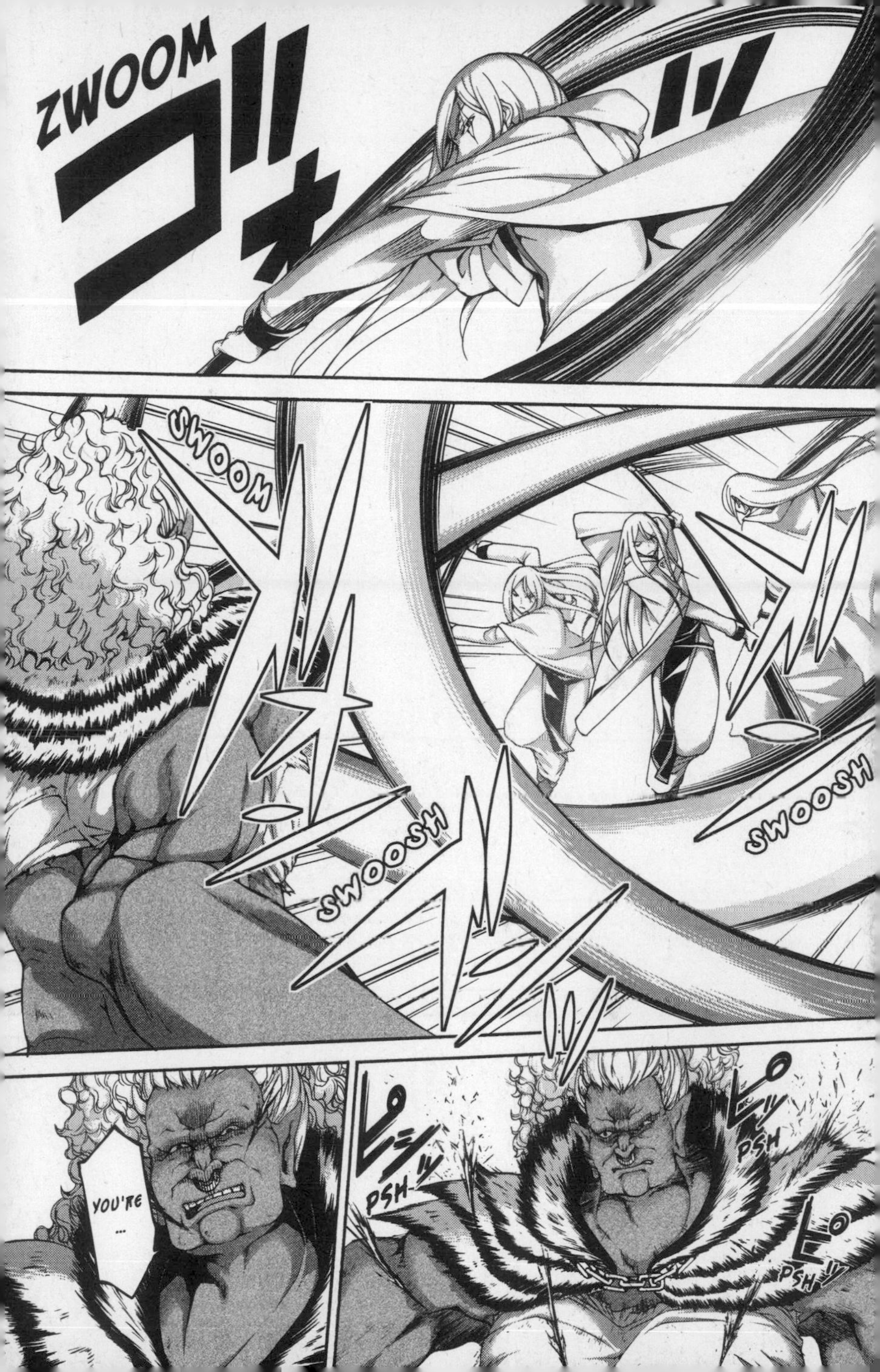
ZWOOM
ゴォッ!!
SWOOSH
SWOOM
SWOOSH
ピッ
PSH
ピシッ!!
PSH-!!
ピッ
PSH!!
YOU'RE ...

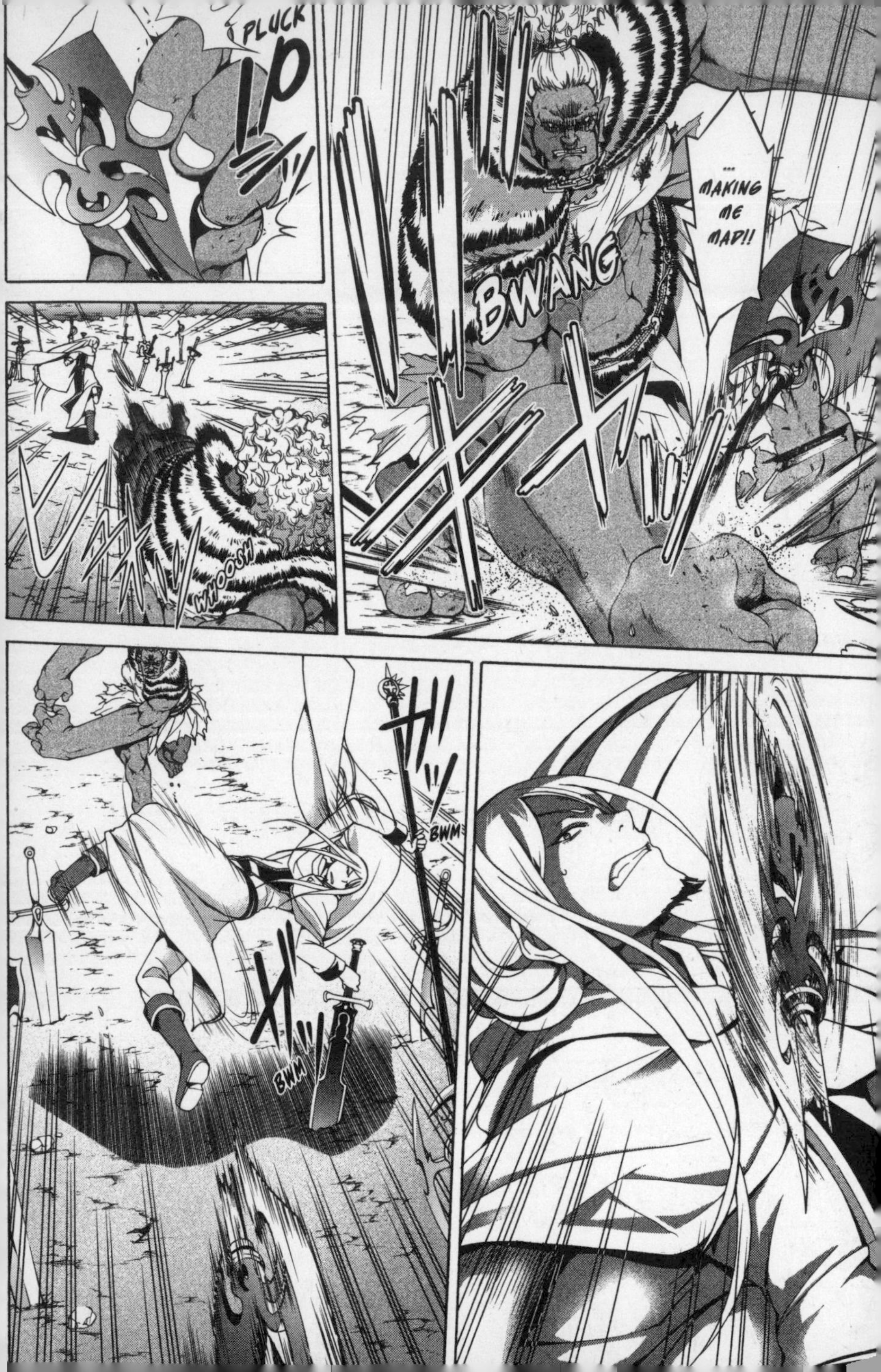
...MAKING ME MAD!!
BWANG
PLUCK
WHOOSH
BWM
BWM

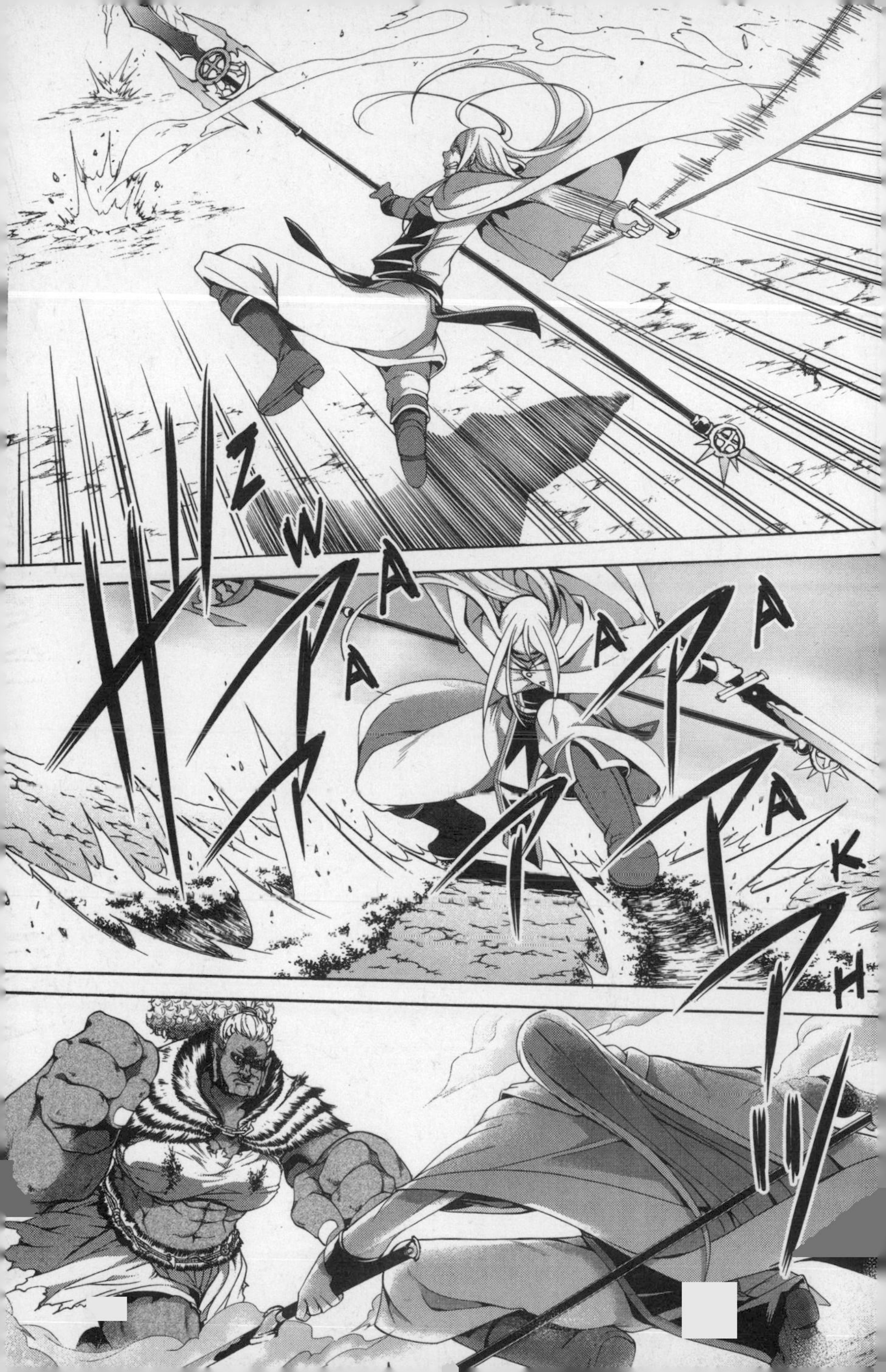
ZWAAAAAKH

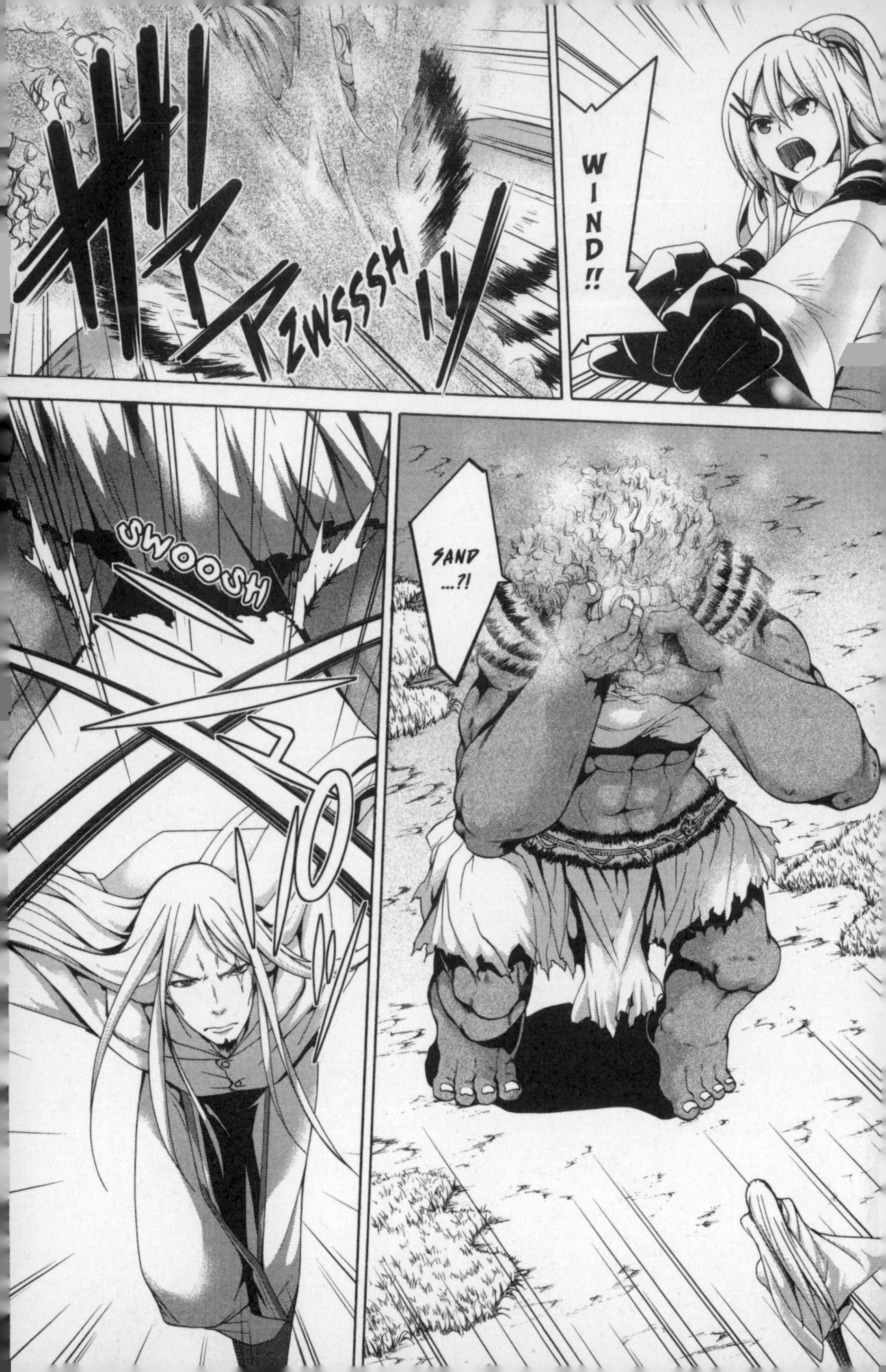
WIND!!
ZWSSSH
SAND ...?!
SWOOSH

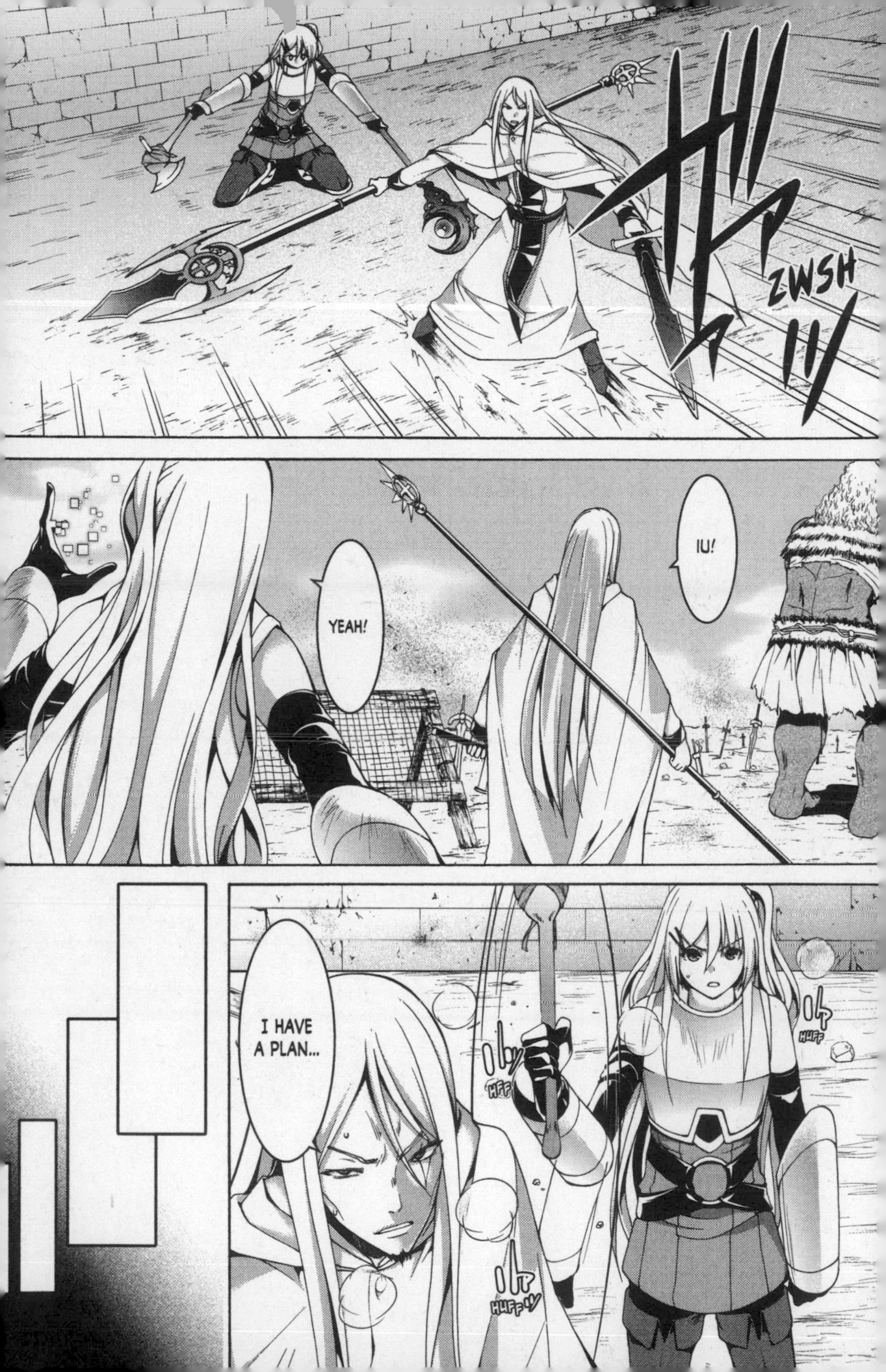
ZWSH
IU!
YEAH!
HUFF
HFF
I HAVE A PLAN...
HUFF

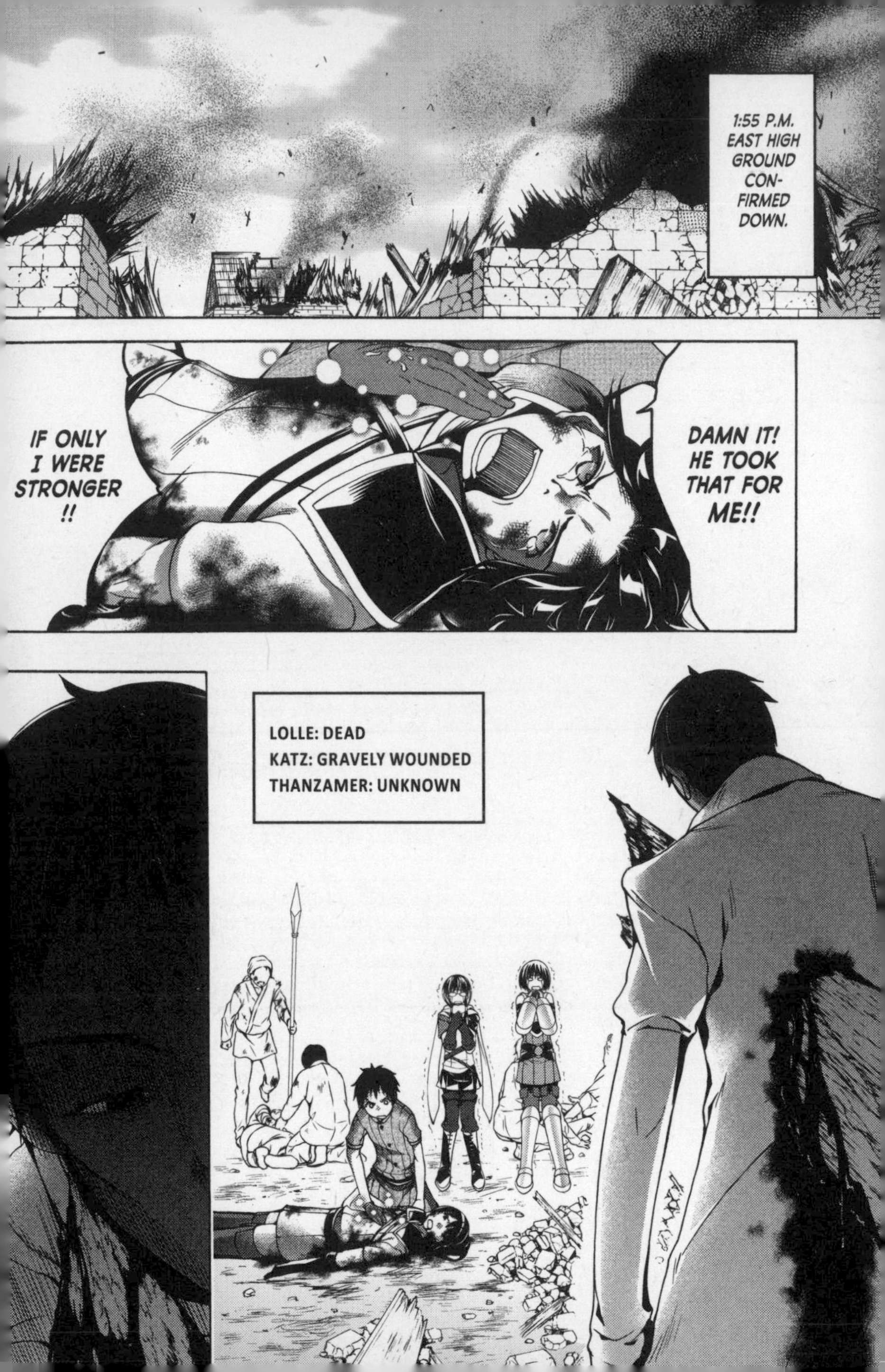
1:55 P.M. EAST HIGH GROUND CON-FIRMED DOWN.
DAMN IT! HE TOOK THAT FOR ME!!
IF ONLY I WERE STRONGER !!
LOLLE: DEAD
KATZ: GRAVELY WOUNDED
THANZAMER: UNKNOWN

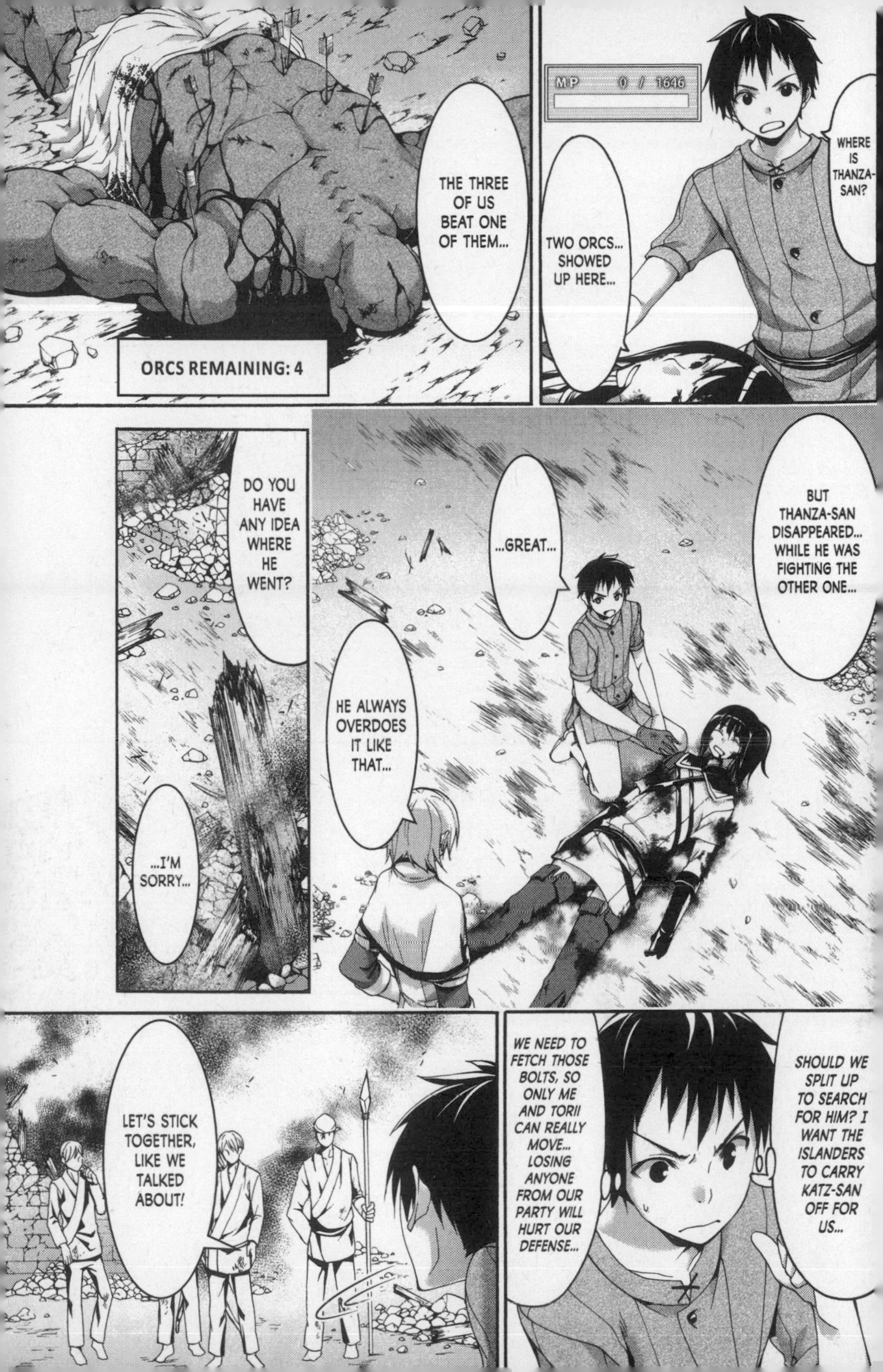
WHERE IS THANZA-SAN?
MP 0 / 1646
TWO ORCS... SHOWED UP HERE...
THE THREE OF US BEAT ONE OF THEM...
ORCS REMAINING: 4
BUT THANZA-SAN DISAPPEARED... WHILE HE WAS FIGHTING THE OTHER ONE...
...GREAT...
HE ALWAYS OVERDOES IT LIKE THAT...
DO YOU HAVE ANY IDEA WHERE HE WENT?
...I'M SORRY...
SHOULD WE SPLIT UP TO SEARCH FOR HIM? I WANT THE ISLANDERS TO CARRY KATZ-SAN OFF FOR US...
WE NEED TO FETCH THOSE BOLTS, SO ONLY ME AND TORII CAN REALLY MOVE... LOSING ANYONE FROM OUR PARTY WILL HURT OUR DEFENSE...
LET'S STICK TOGETHER, LIKE WE TALKED ABOUT!

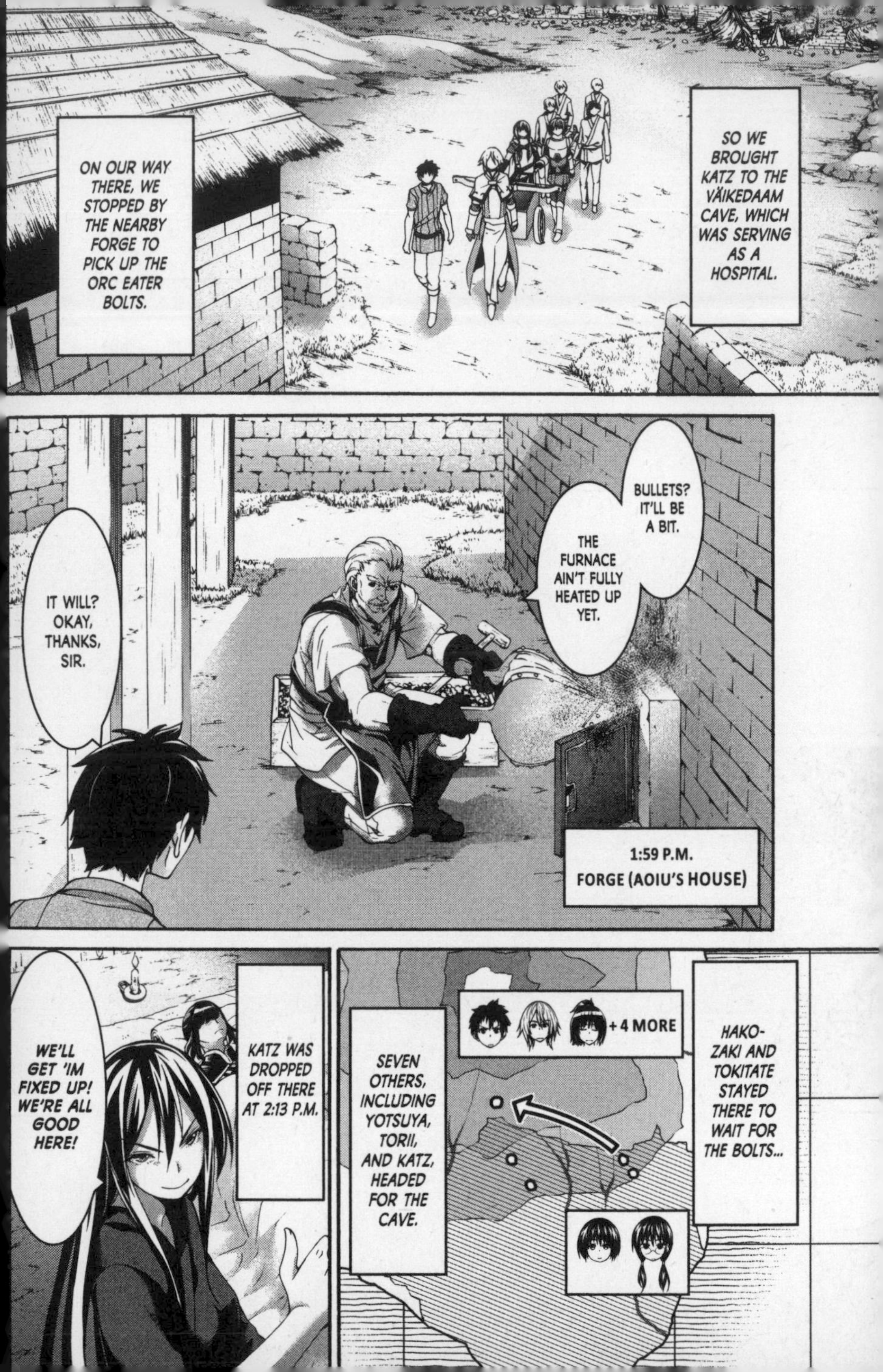
SO WE BROUGHT KATZ TO THE VÄIKEDAAM CAVE, WHICH WAS SERVING AS A HOSPITAL.
ON OUR WAY THERE, WE STOPPED BY THE NEARBY FORGE TO PICK UP THE ORC EATER BOLTS.
BULLETS? IT'LL BE A BIT.
THE FURNACE AIN'T FULLY HEATED UP YET.
1:59 P.M.
FORGE (AOIU'S HOUSE)
IT WILL? OKAY, THANKS, SIR.
HAKO-ZAKI AND TOKITATE STAYED THERE TO WAIT FOR THE BOLTS...
+4 MORE
SEVEN OTHERS, INCLUDING YOTSUYA, TORII, AND KATZ, HEADED FOR THE CAVE.
KATZ WAS DROPPED OFF THERE AT 2:13 P.M.
WE'LL GET 'IM FIXED UP! WE'RE ALL GOOD HERE!

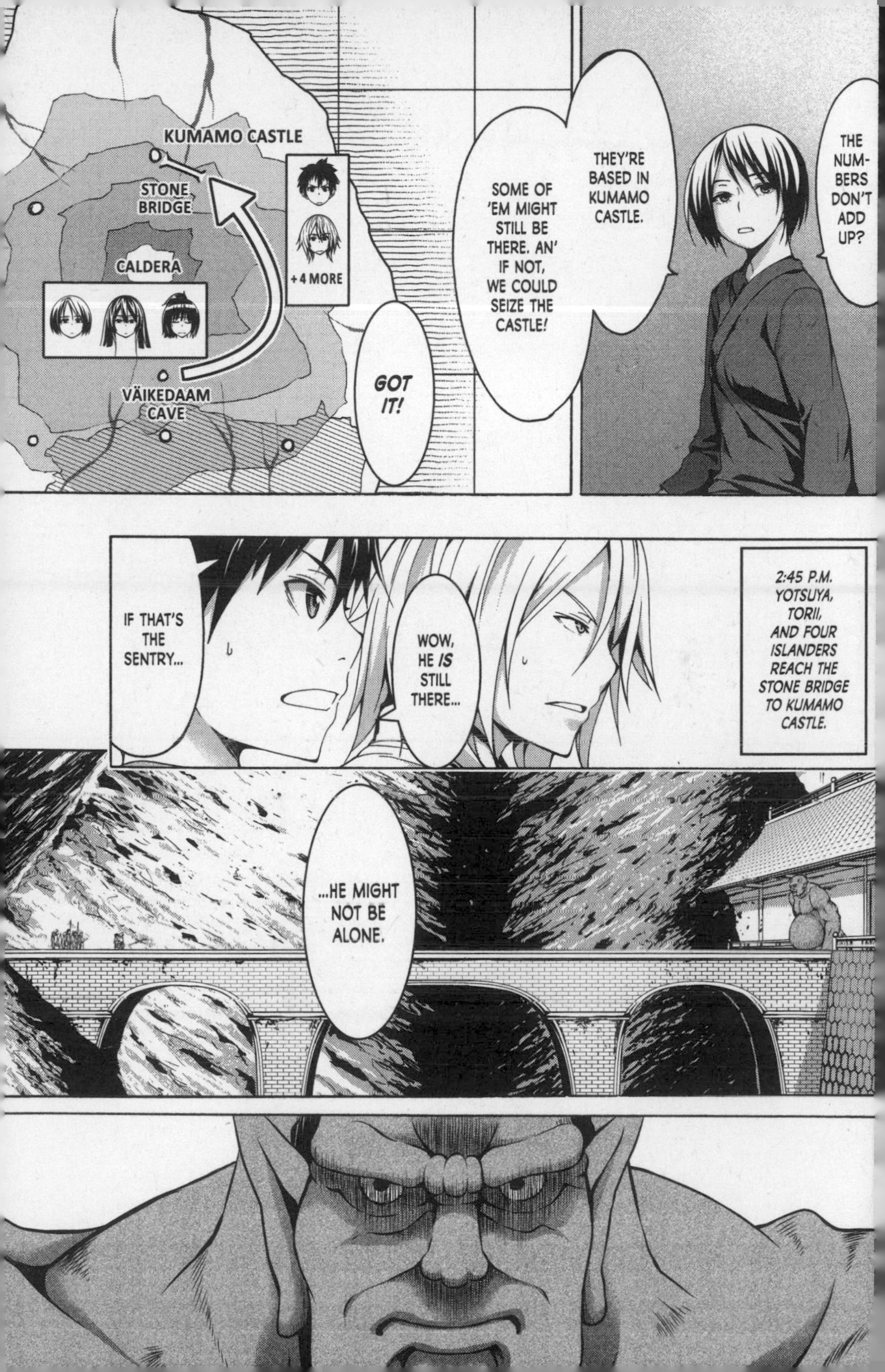
THE NUMBERS DON'T ADD UP?
THEY'RE BASED IN KUMAMO CASTLE.
SOME OF 'EM MIGHT STILL BE THERE. AN' IF NOT, WE COULD SEIZE THE CASTLE!
GOT IT!
KUMAMO CASTLE
STONE BRIDGE
+4 MORE
CALDERA
VÄIKEDAAM CAVE
2:45 P.M. YOTSUYA, TORII, AND FOUR ISLANDERS REACH THE STONE BRIDGE TO KUMAMO CASTLE.
WOW, HE *IS* STILL THERE...
IF THAT'S THE SENTRY...
...HE MIGHT NOT BE ALONE.

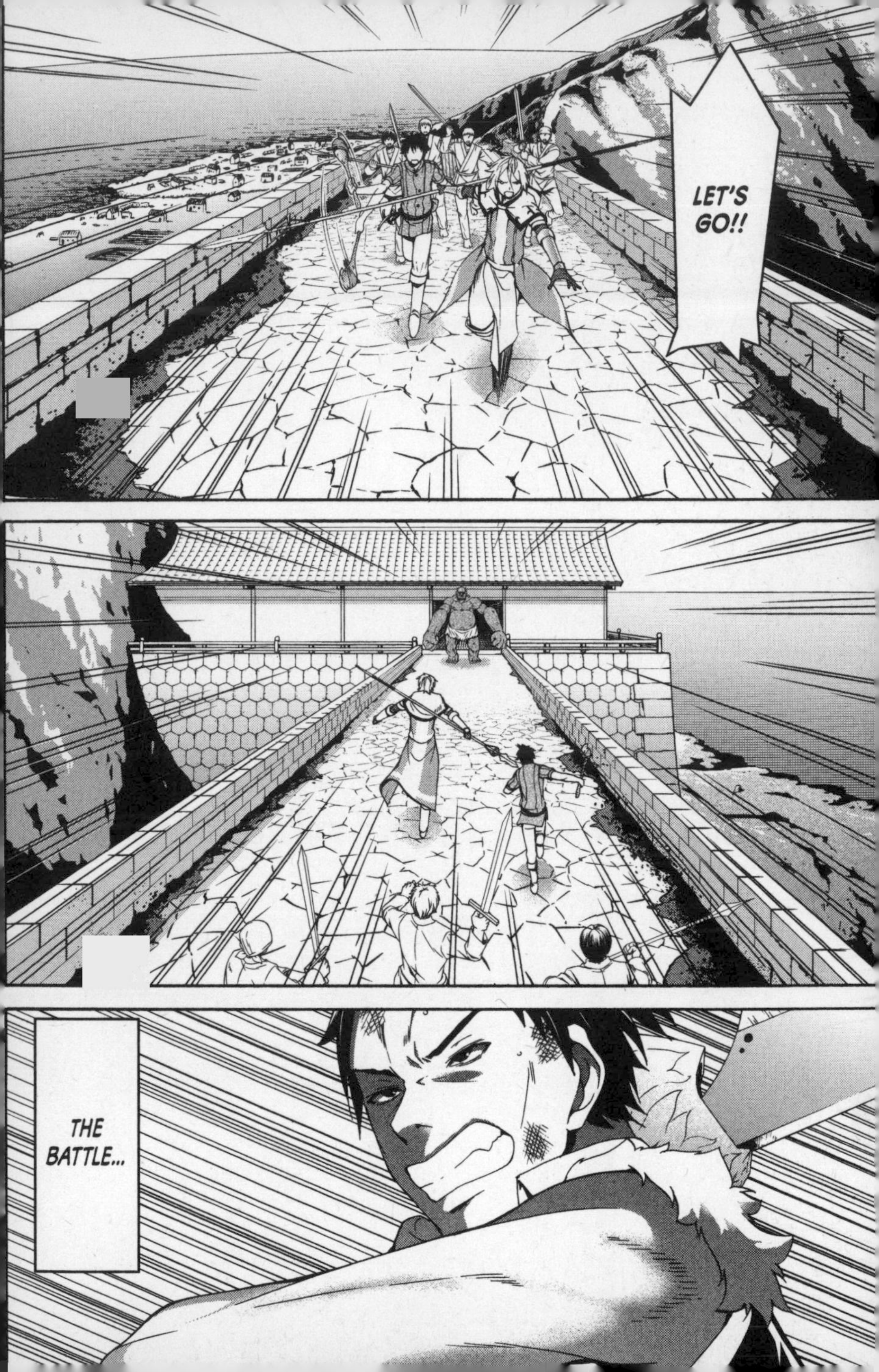
LET'S GO!!
THE BATTLE...

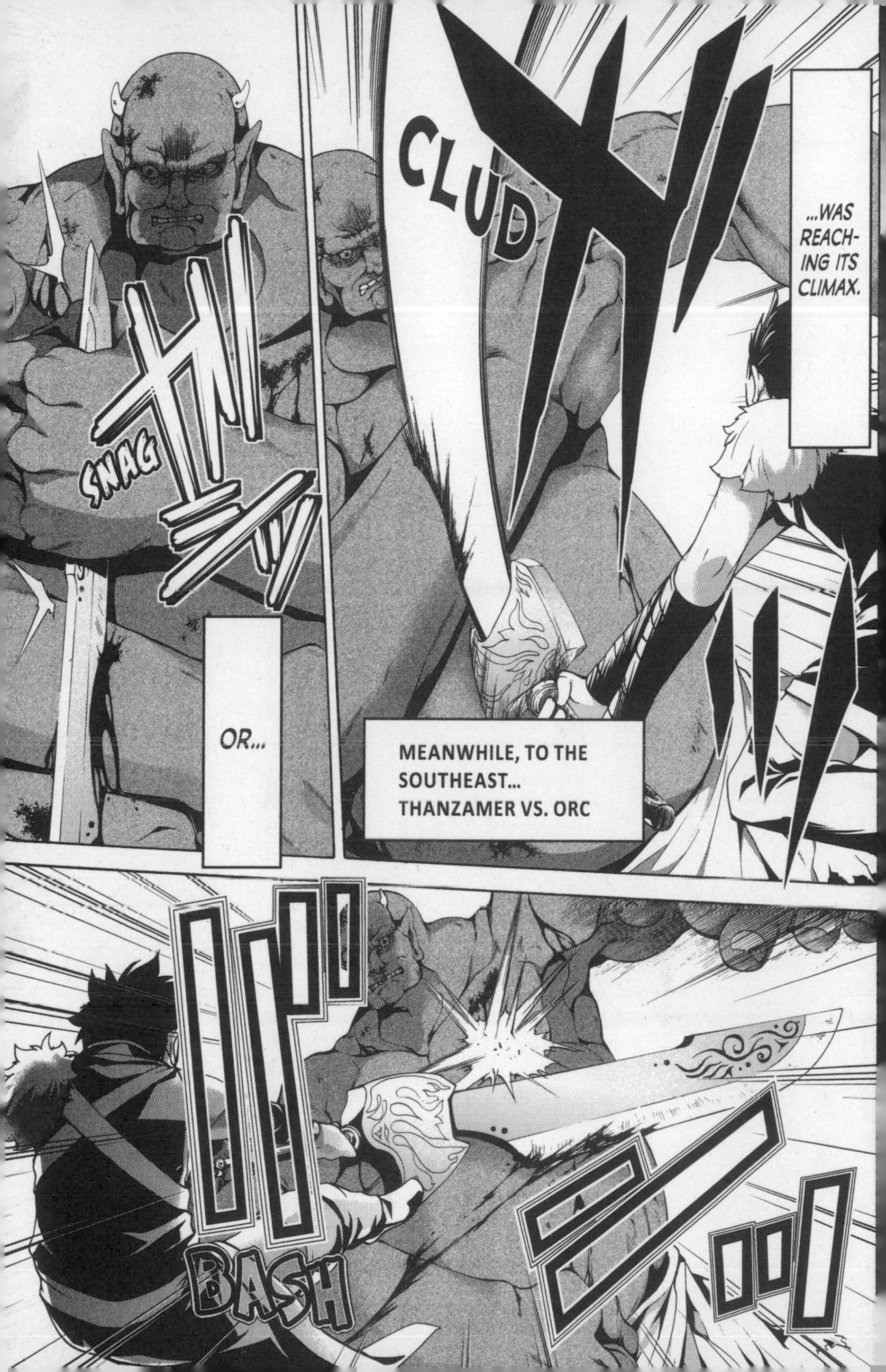
...WAS REACHING ITS CLIMAX.
CLUD
MEANWHILE, TO THE SOUTHEAST...
THANZAMER VS. ORC
SNAG
OR...
BASH

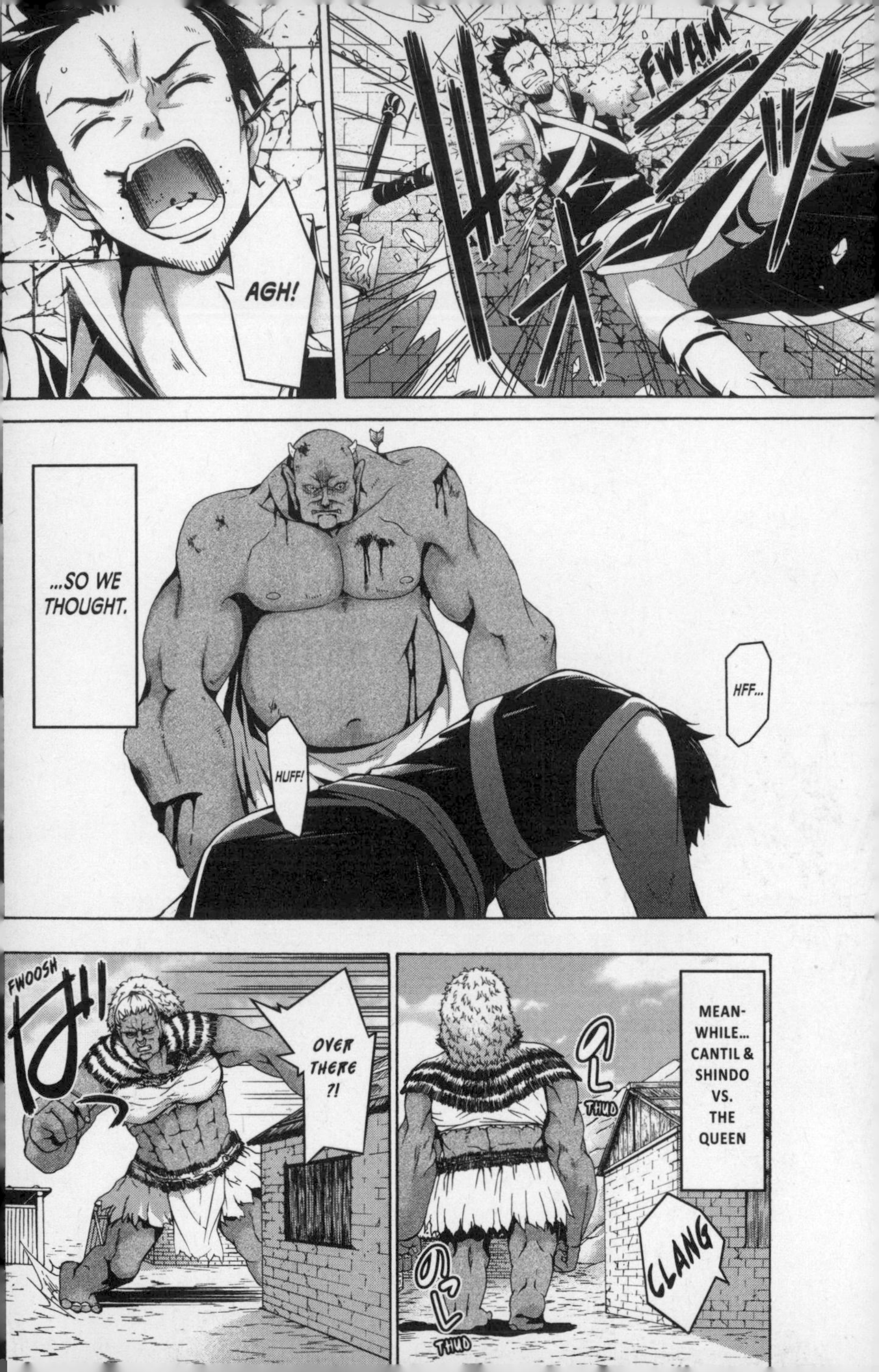
FWAM
AGH!
...SO WE THOUGHT.
HFF...
HUFF!
MEAN-WHILE... CANTIL & SHINDO VS. THE QUEEN
THUD
CLANG
THUD
FWOOSH
OVER THERE ?!

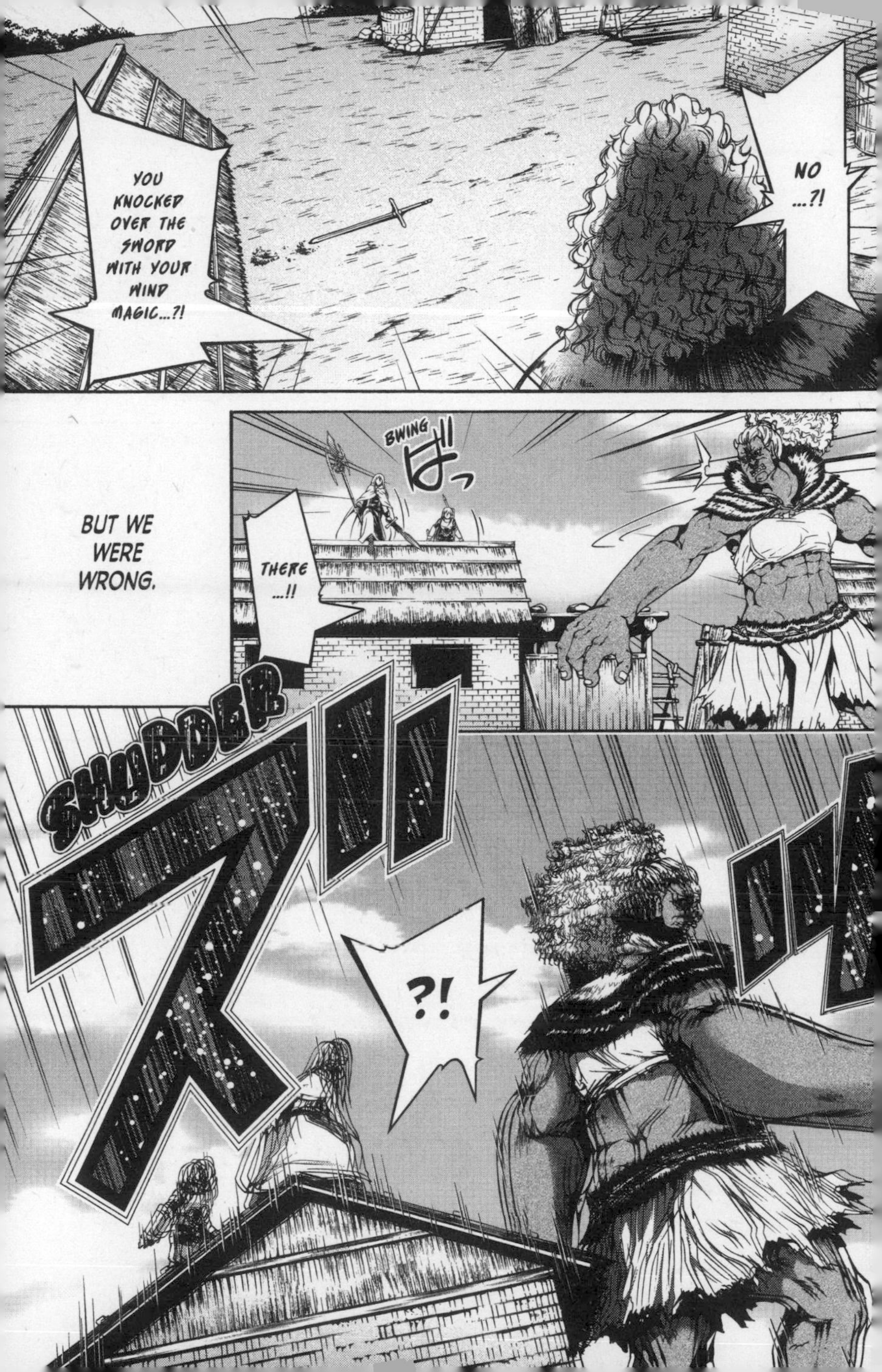
NO ...?!
YOU KNOCKED OVER THE SWORD WITH YOUR WIND MAGIC...?!
BWING
ばっ
THERE ...!!
BUT WE WERE WRONG.
SHUDDER
?!

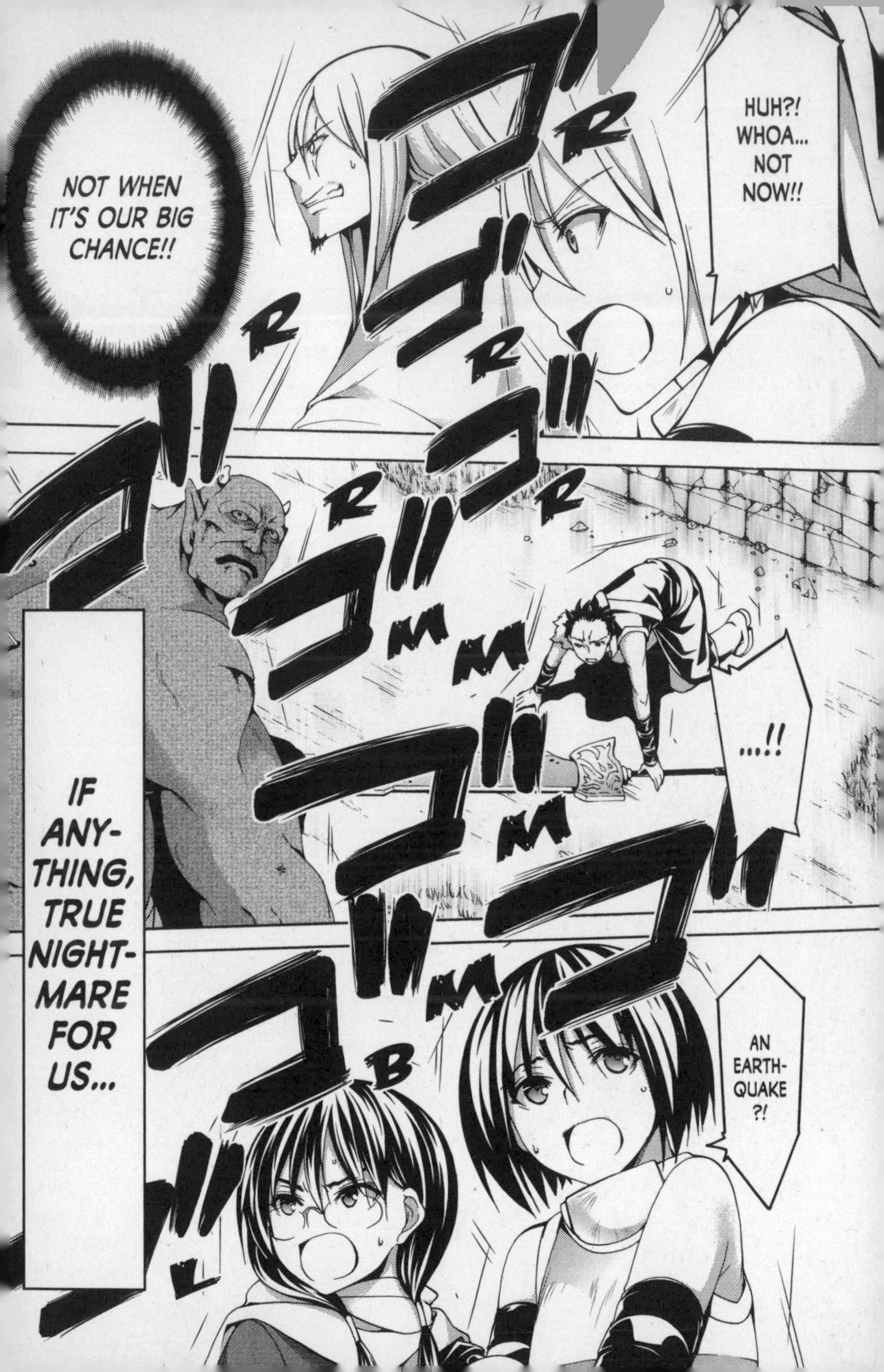
HUH?! WHOA... NOT NOW!!
NOT WHEN IT'S OUR BIG CHANCE!!
...!!
AN EARTH-QUAKE?!
IF ANY-THING, TRUE NIGHT-MARE FOR US...

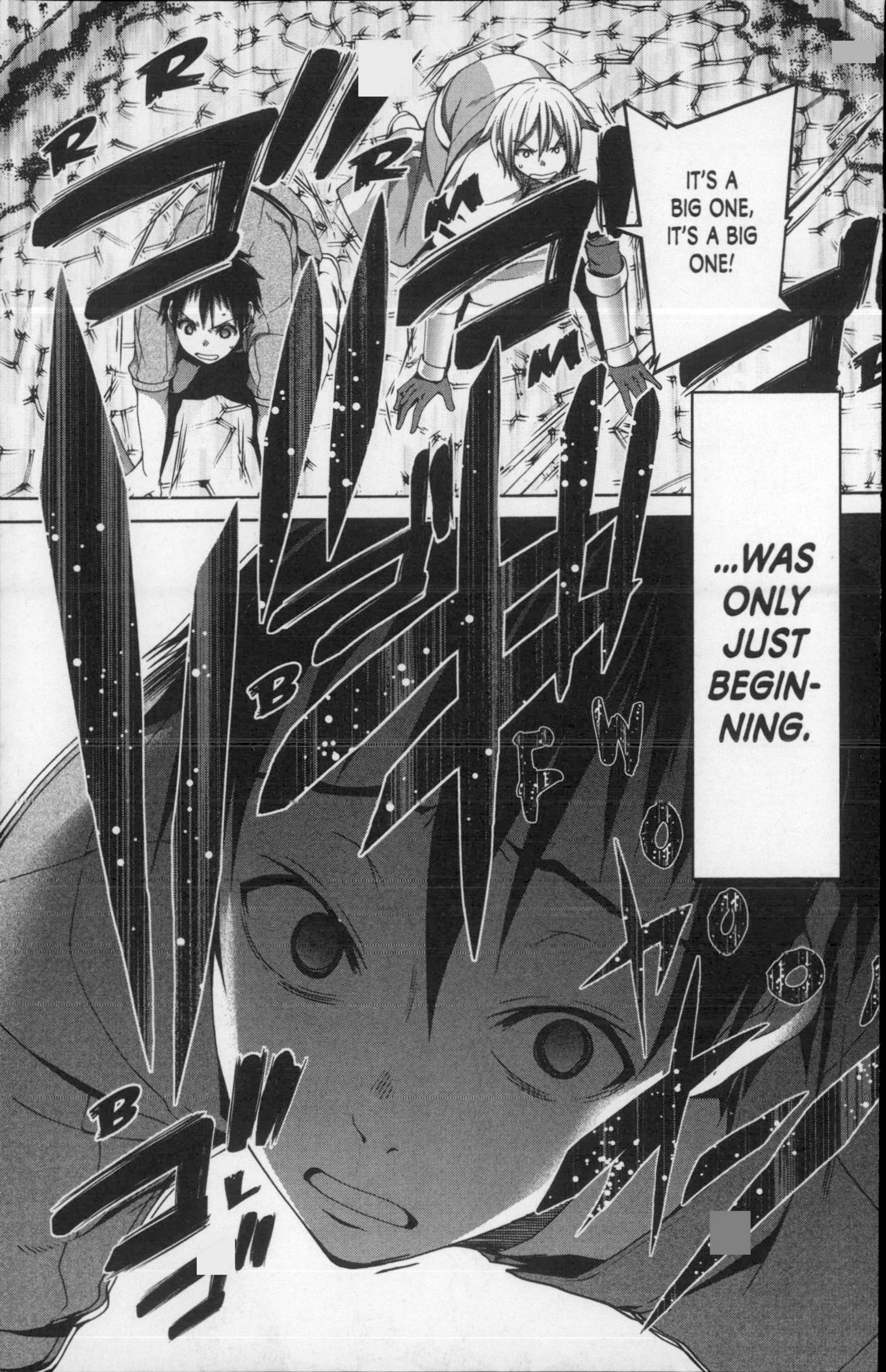
IT'S A BIG ONE, IT'S A BIG ONE!
...WAS ONLY JUST BEGINNING.

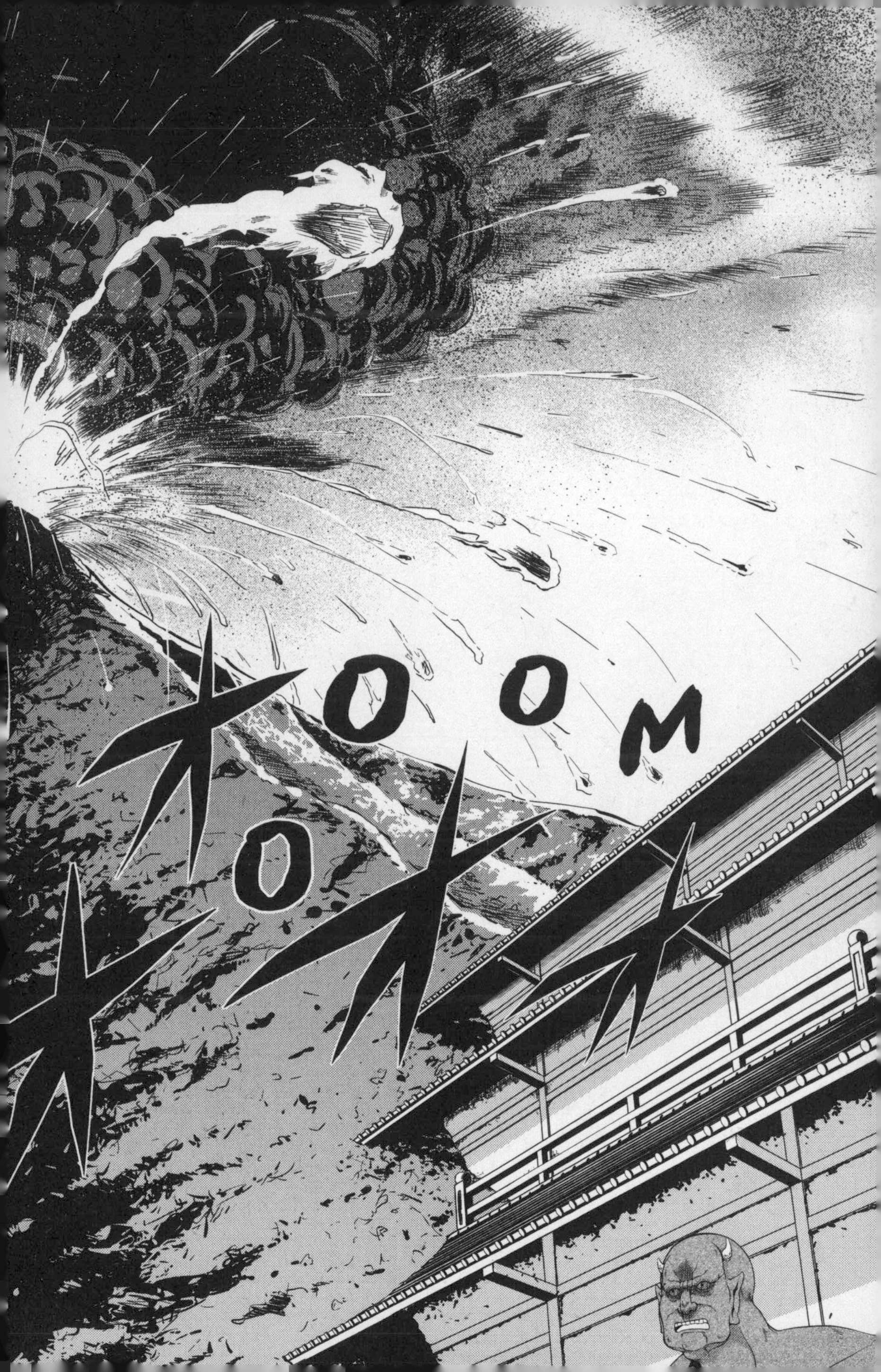

BOOOM

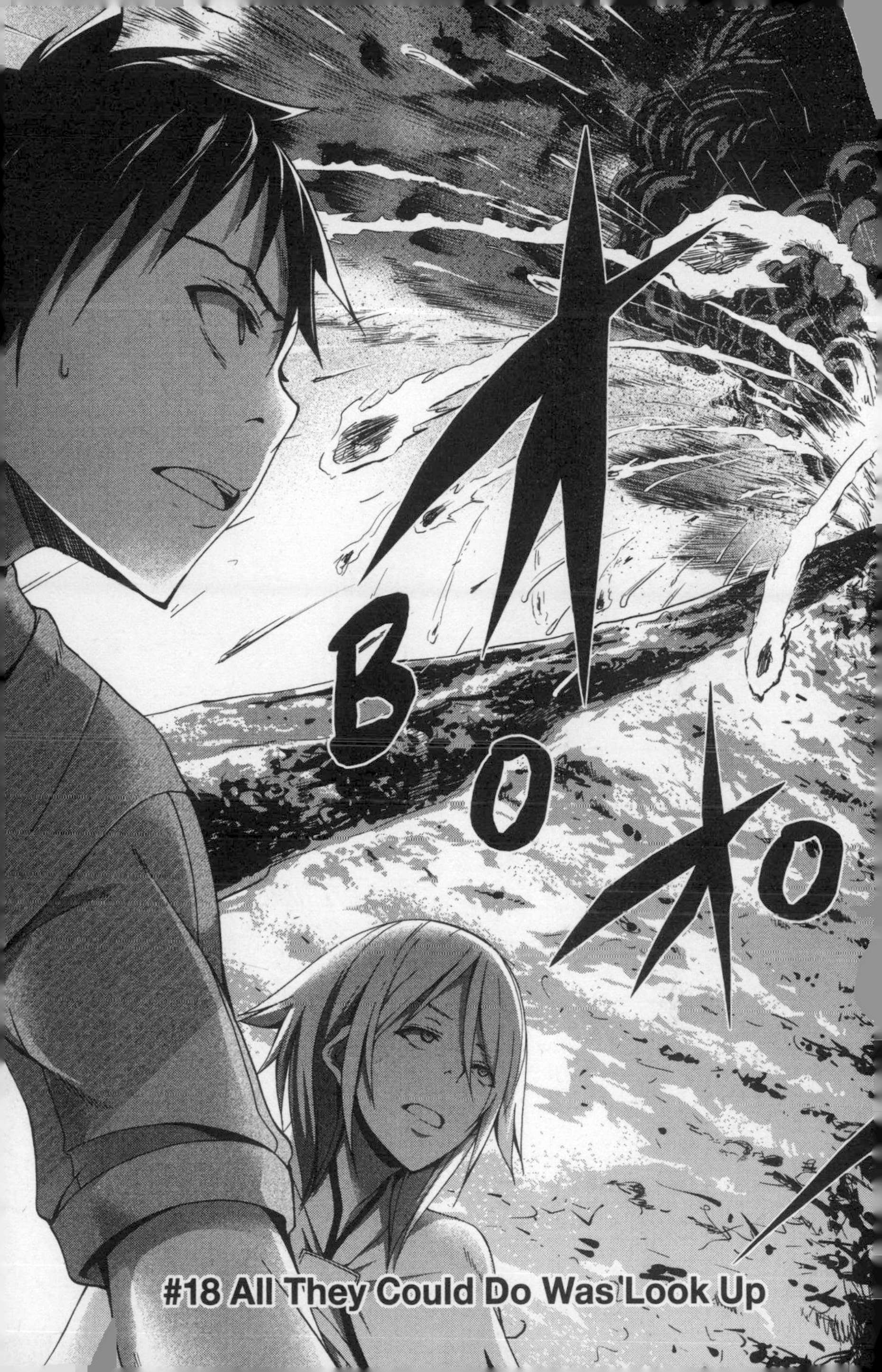
BOOO
#18 All They Could Do Was Look Up

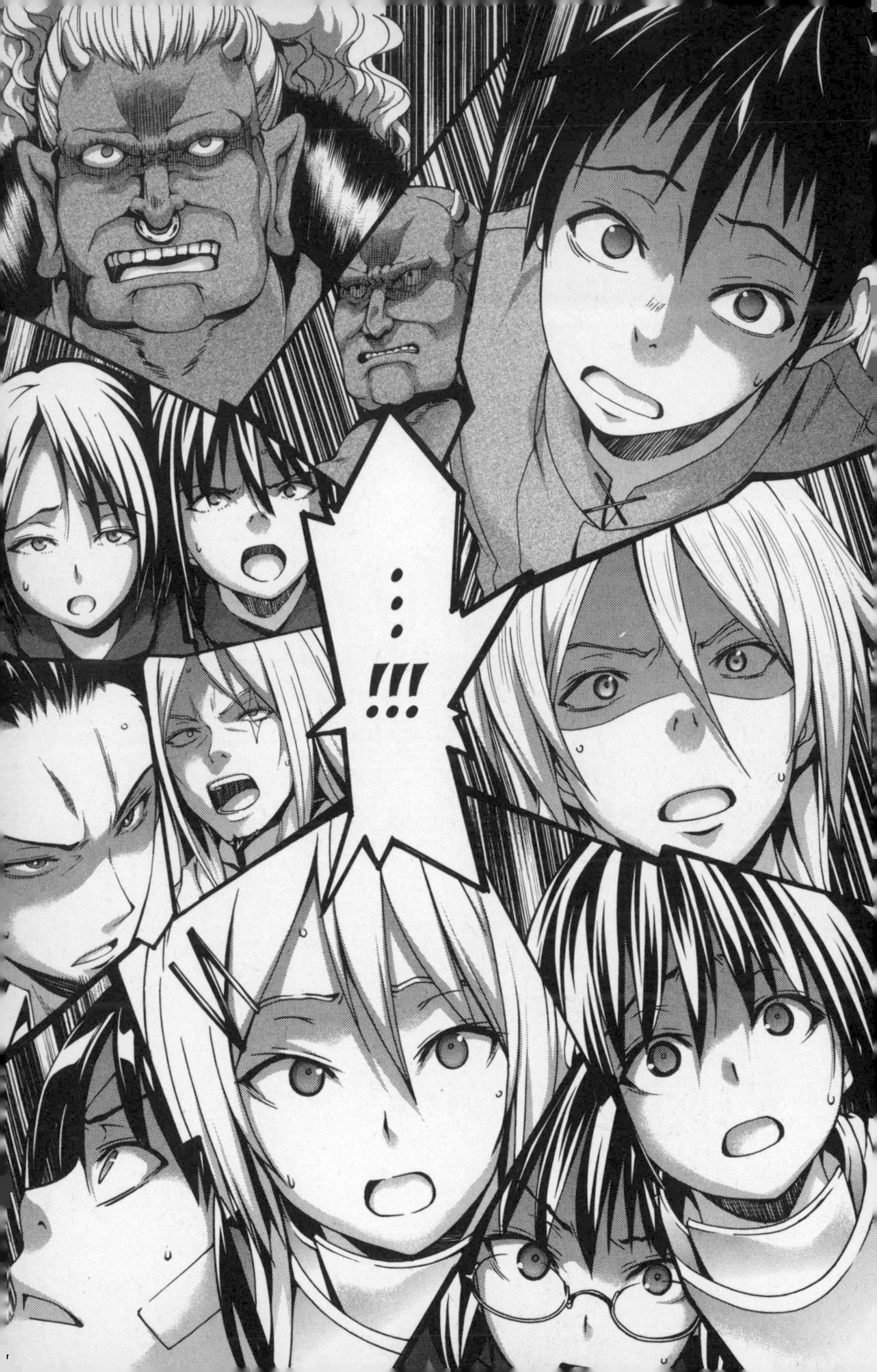
...!!!

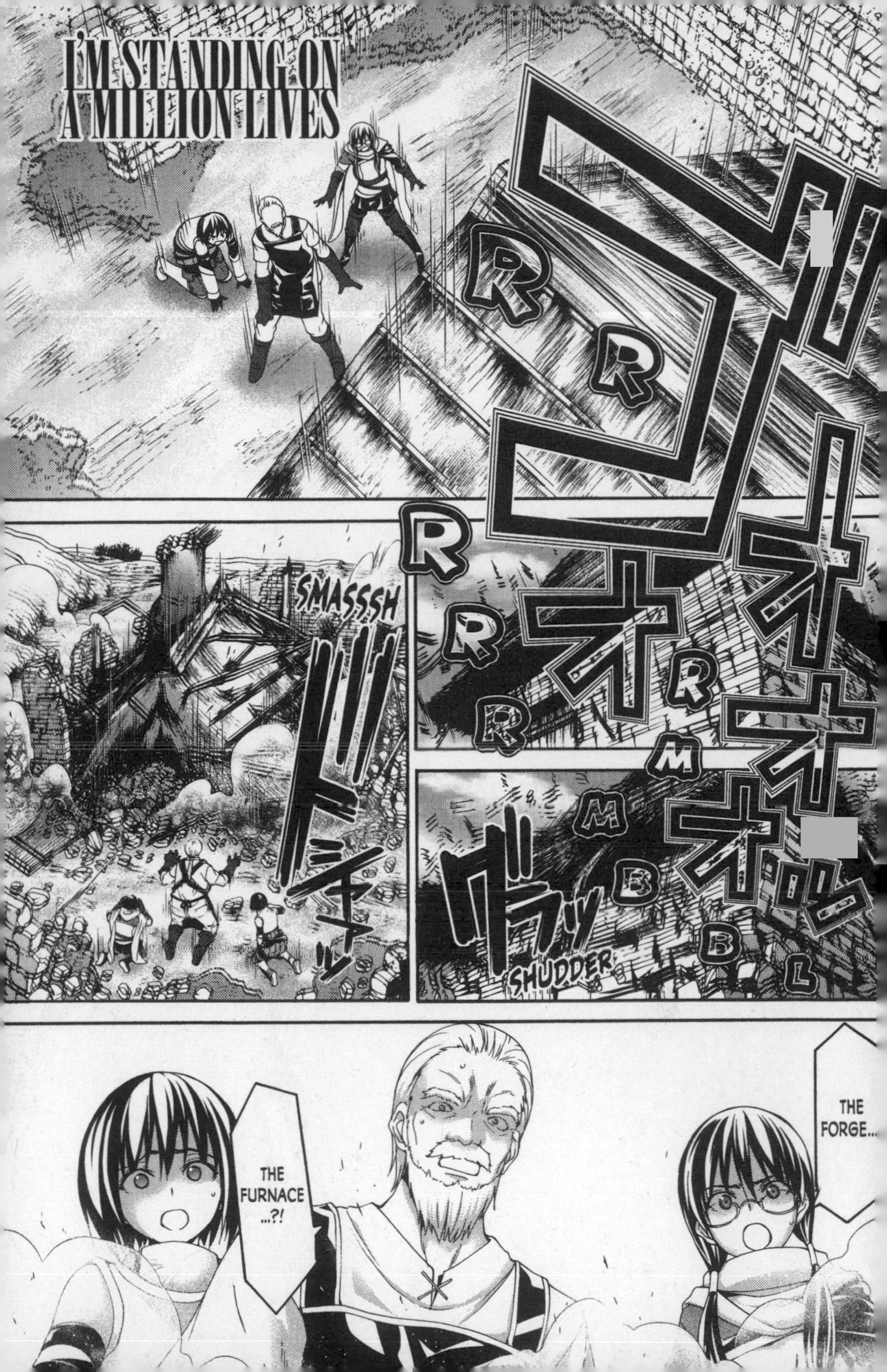
I'M STANDING ON A MILLION LIVES
R R
R R R R M M B B L
SHUDDER
SMASSSH
THE FORGE...
THE FURNACE ...?!

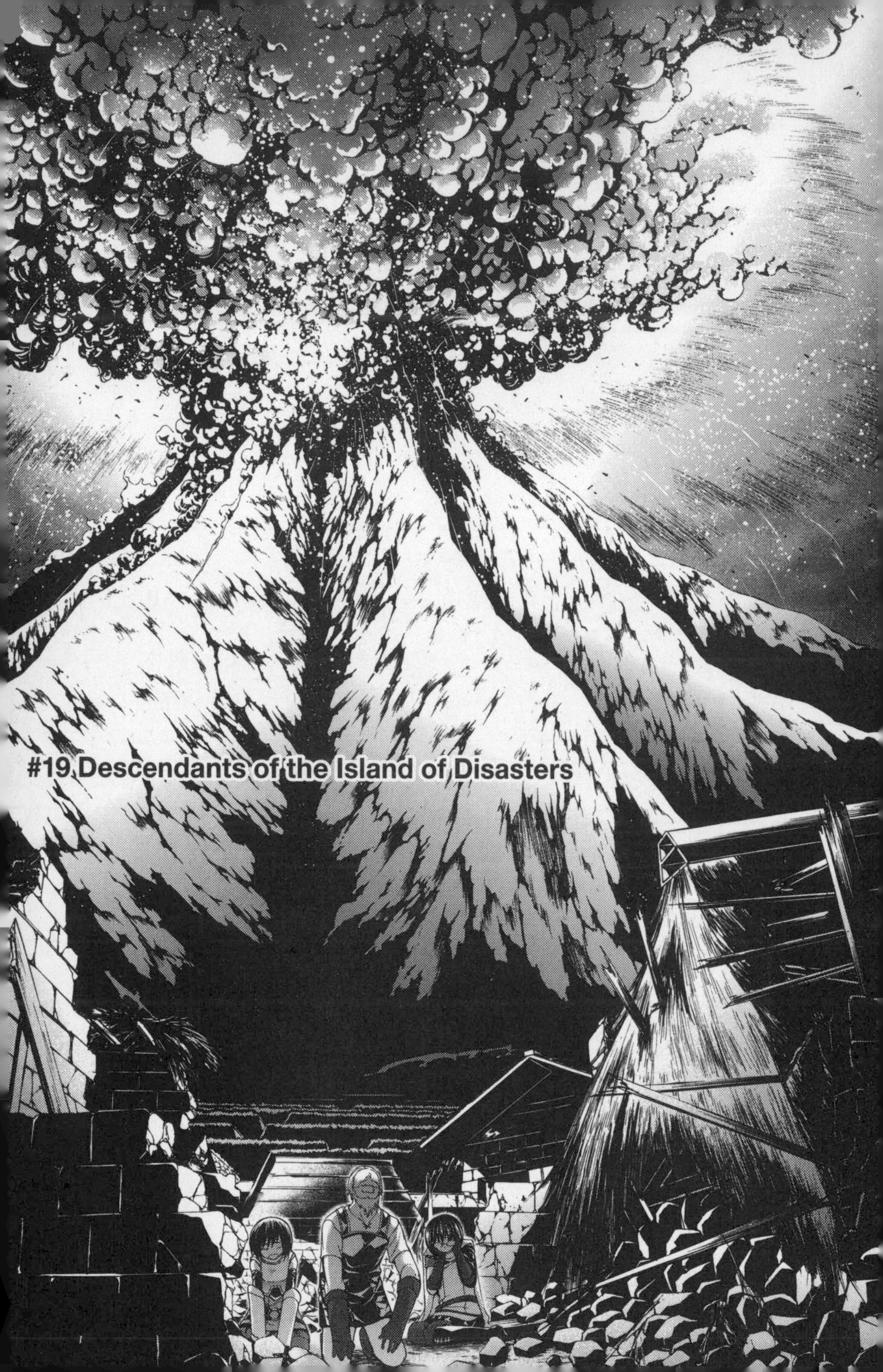
#19 Descendants of the Island of Disasters

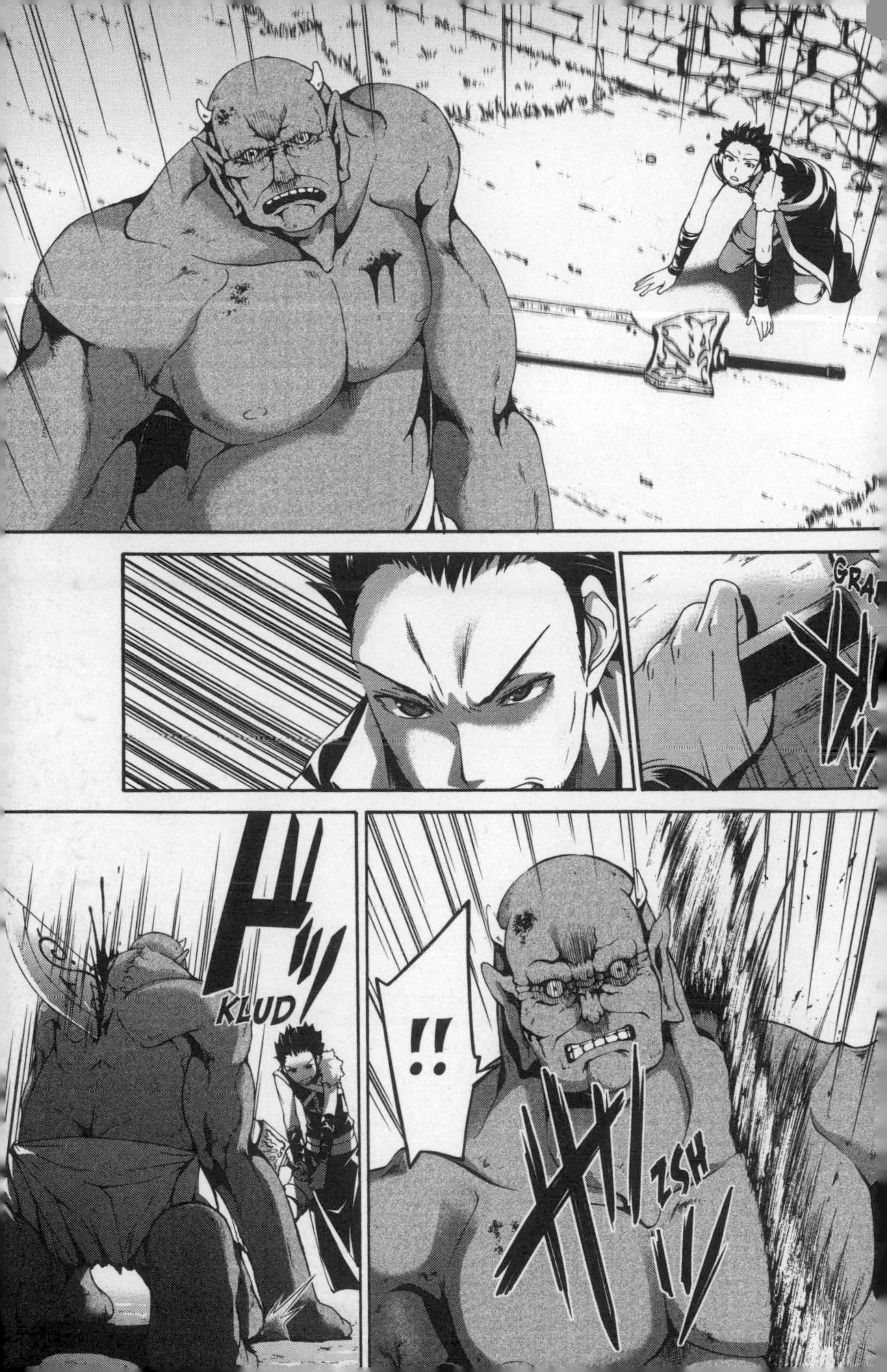
GRA
!!
ZSH
KLUD

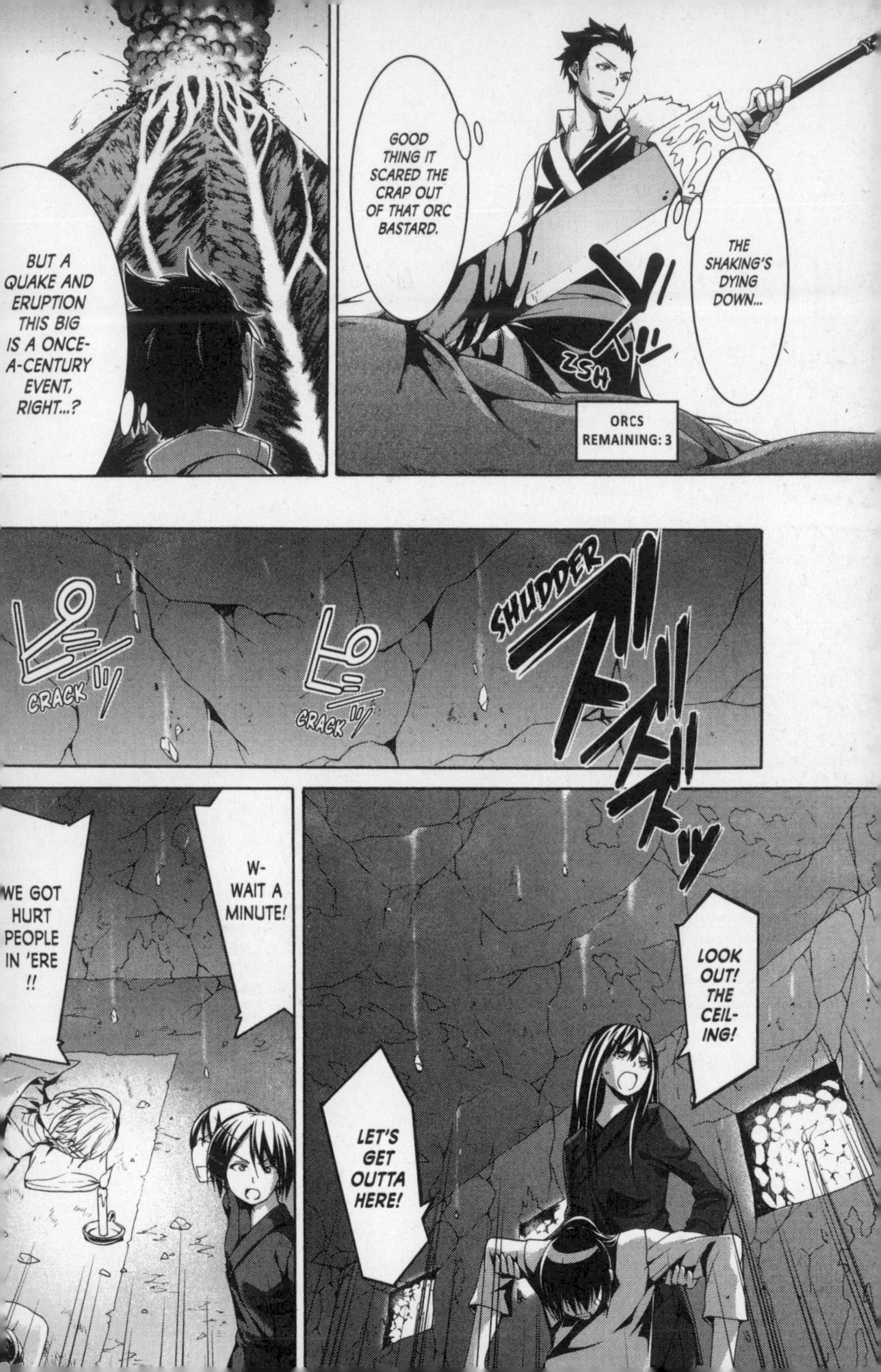
THE SHAKING'S DYING DOWN...
GOOD THING IT SCARED THE CRAP OUT OF THAT ORC BASTARD.
ZSH
ORCS REMAINING: 3
BUT A QUAKE AND ERUPTION THIS BIG IS A ONCE-A-CENTURY EVENT, RIGHT...?
SHUDDER
CRACK
CRACK
LOOK OUT! THE CEIL-ING!
LET'S GET OUTTA HERE!
W-WAIT A MINUTE!
WE GOT HURT PEOPLE IN 'ERE !!

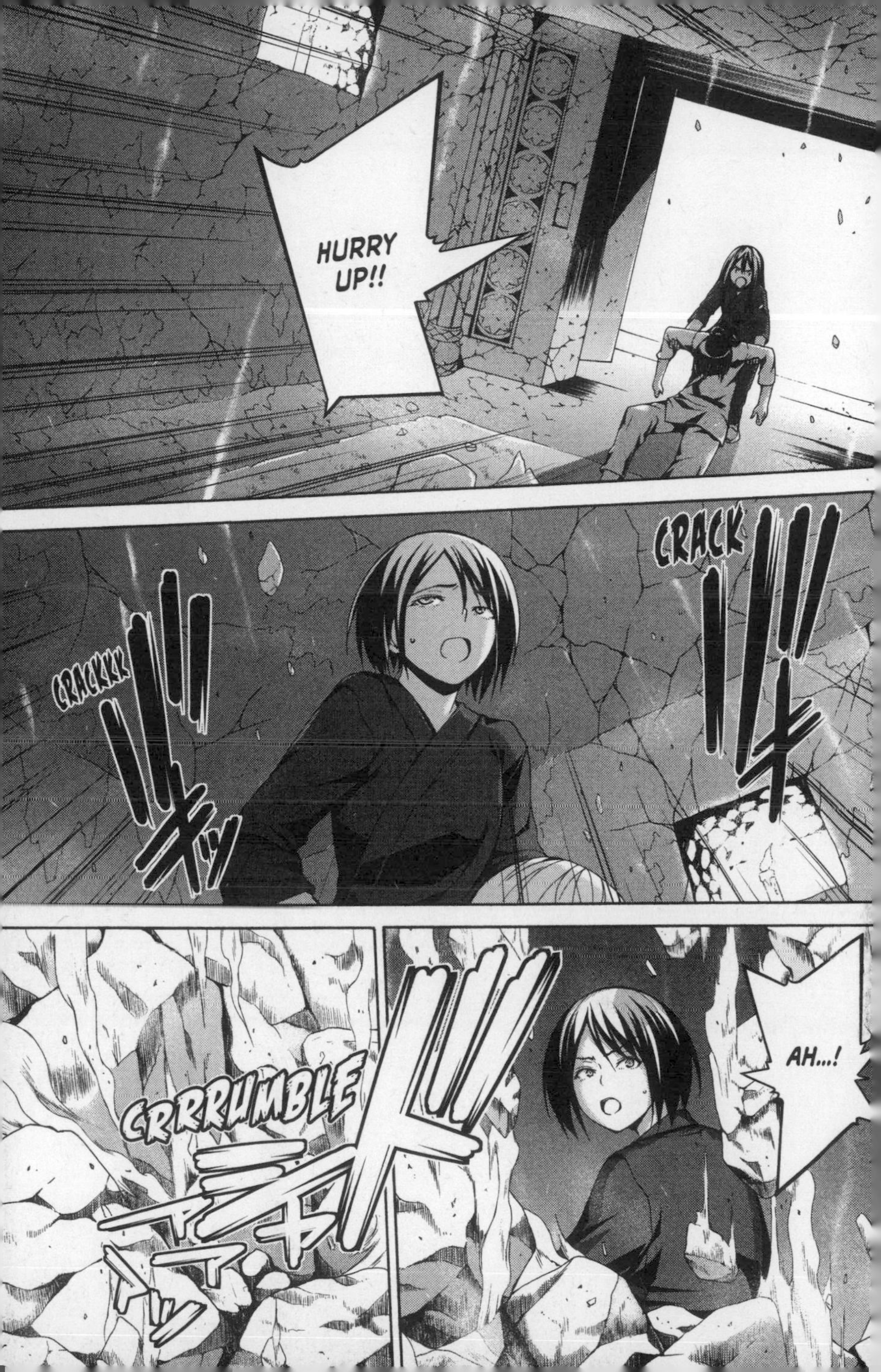
HURRY UP!!
CRACK
CRACKKK
AH...!
CRRRUMBLE

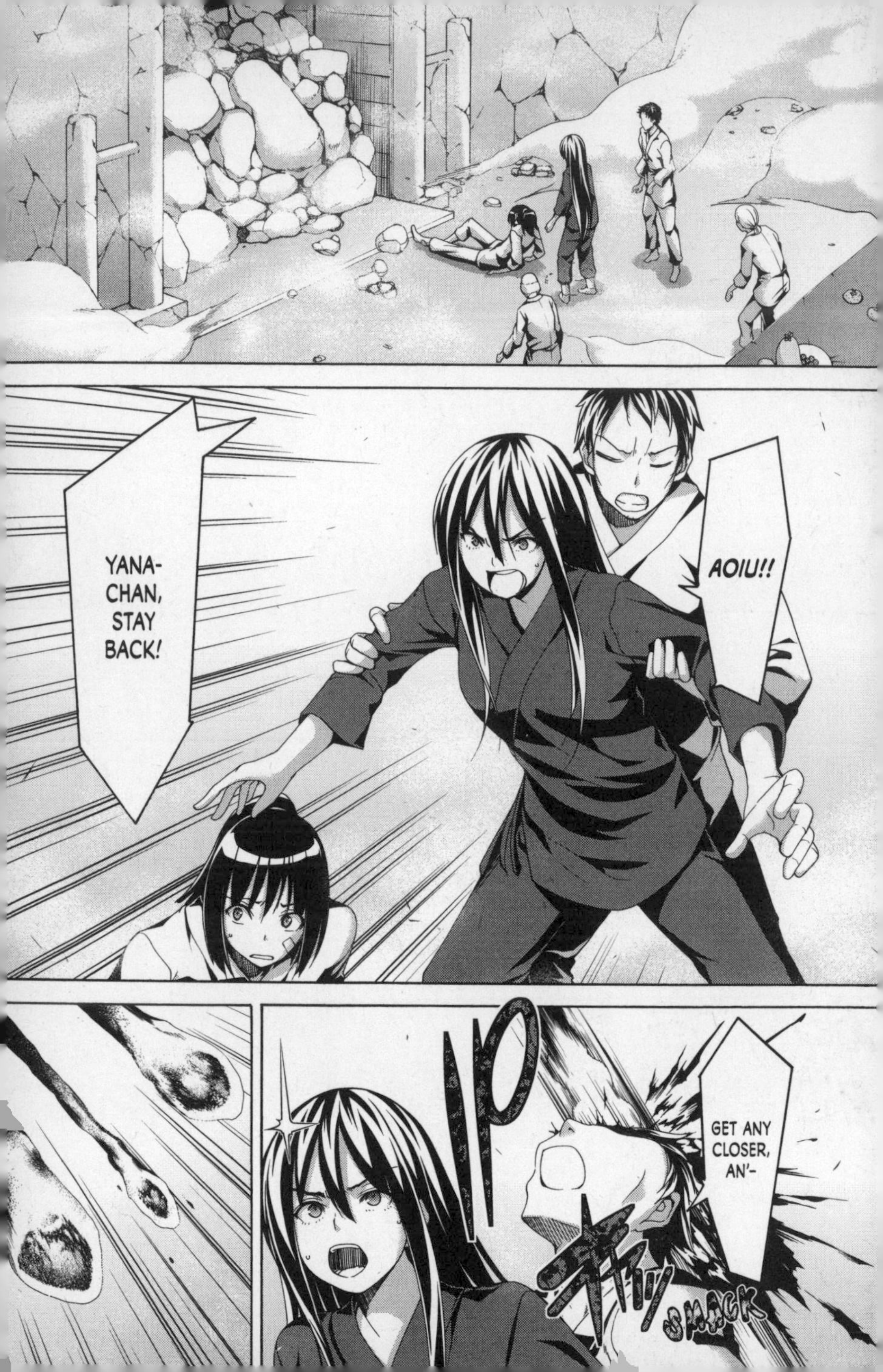
AOIU!!
YANA-CHAN, STAY BACK!
GET ANY CLOSER, AN'-
SMACK

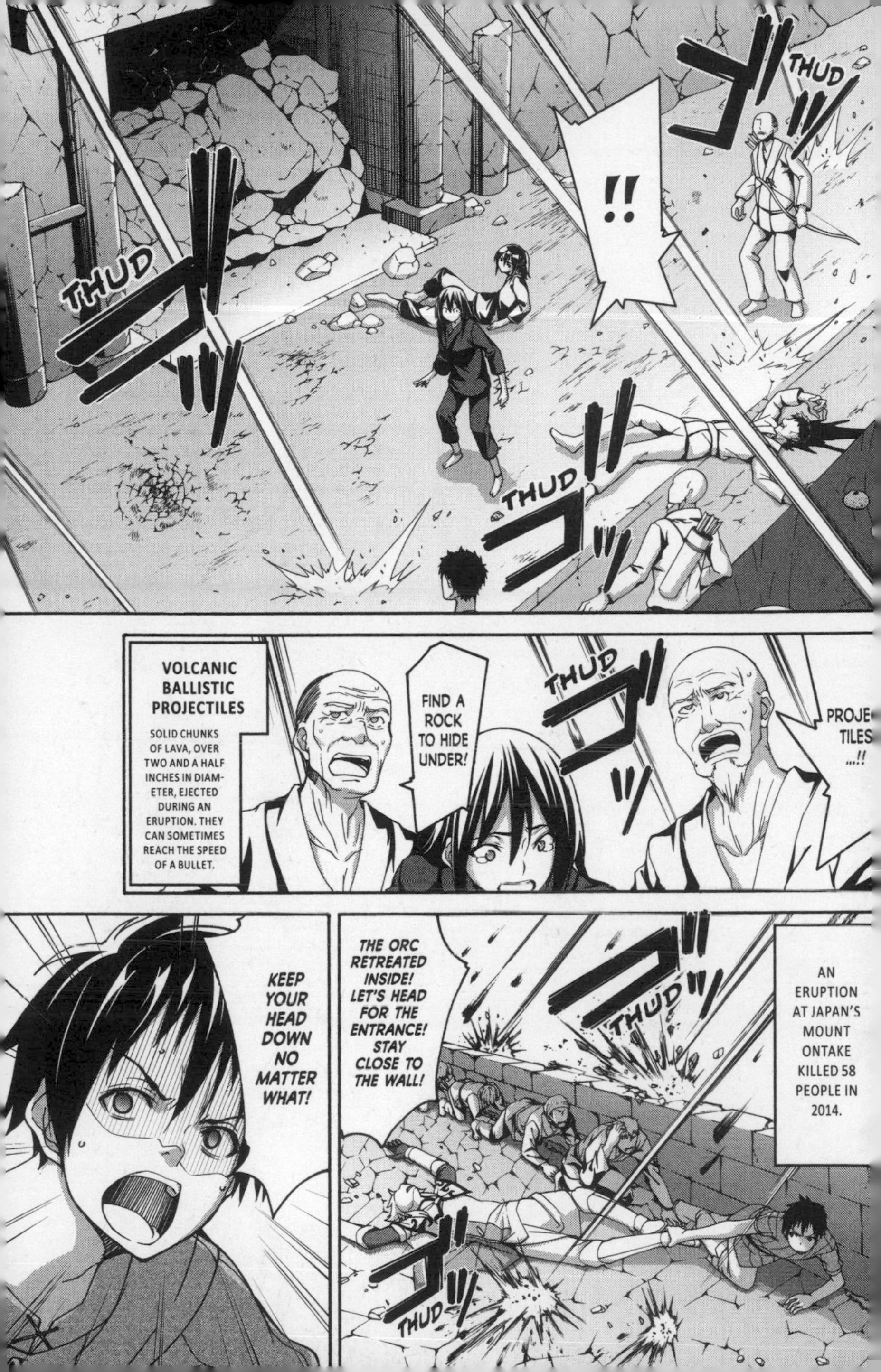
THUD
!!
THUD
THUD
PROJECTILES ...!!
THUD
FIND A ROCK TO HIDE UNDER!
VOLCANIC BALLISTIC PROJECTILES
SOLID CHUNKS OF LAVA, OVER TWO AND A HALF INCHES IN DIAMETER, EJECTED DURING AN ERUPTION. THEY CAN SOMETIMES REACH THE SPEED OF A BULLET.
AN ERUPTION AT JAPAN'S MOUNT ONTAKE KILLED 58 PEOPLE IN 2014.
THUD
THE ORC RETREATED INSIDE! LET'S HEAD FOR THE ENTRANCE! STAY CLOSE TO THE WALL!
THUD
KEEP YOUR HEAD DOWN NO MATTER WHAT!

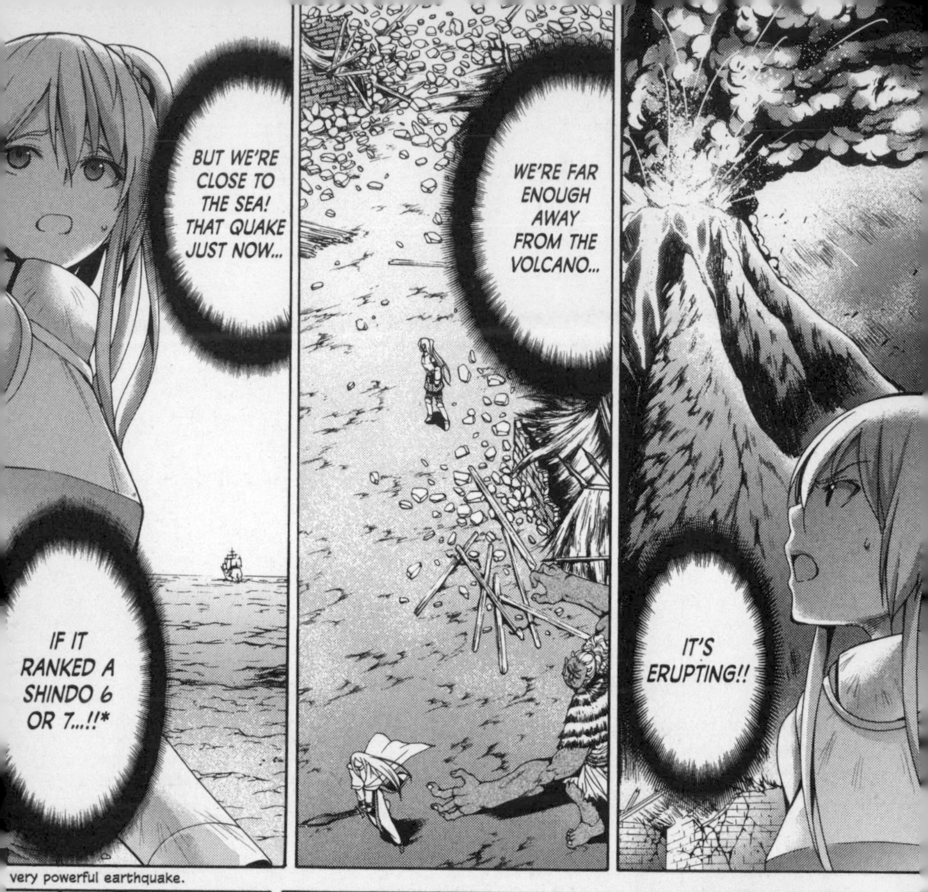
IT'S ERUPTING!!
WE'RE FAR ENOUGH AWAY FROM THE VOLCANO...
BUT WE'RE CLOSE TO THE SEA! THAT QUAKE JUST NOW...
IF IT RANKED A SHINDO 6 OR 7...!!*

very powerful earthquake.

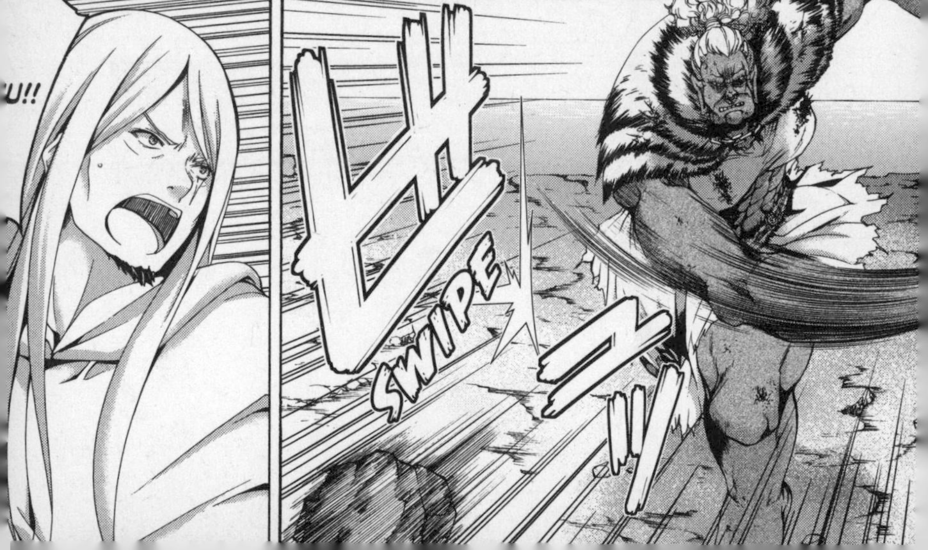
SWIPE
U!!

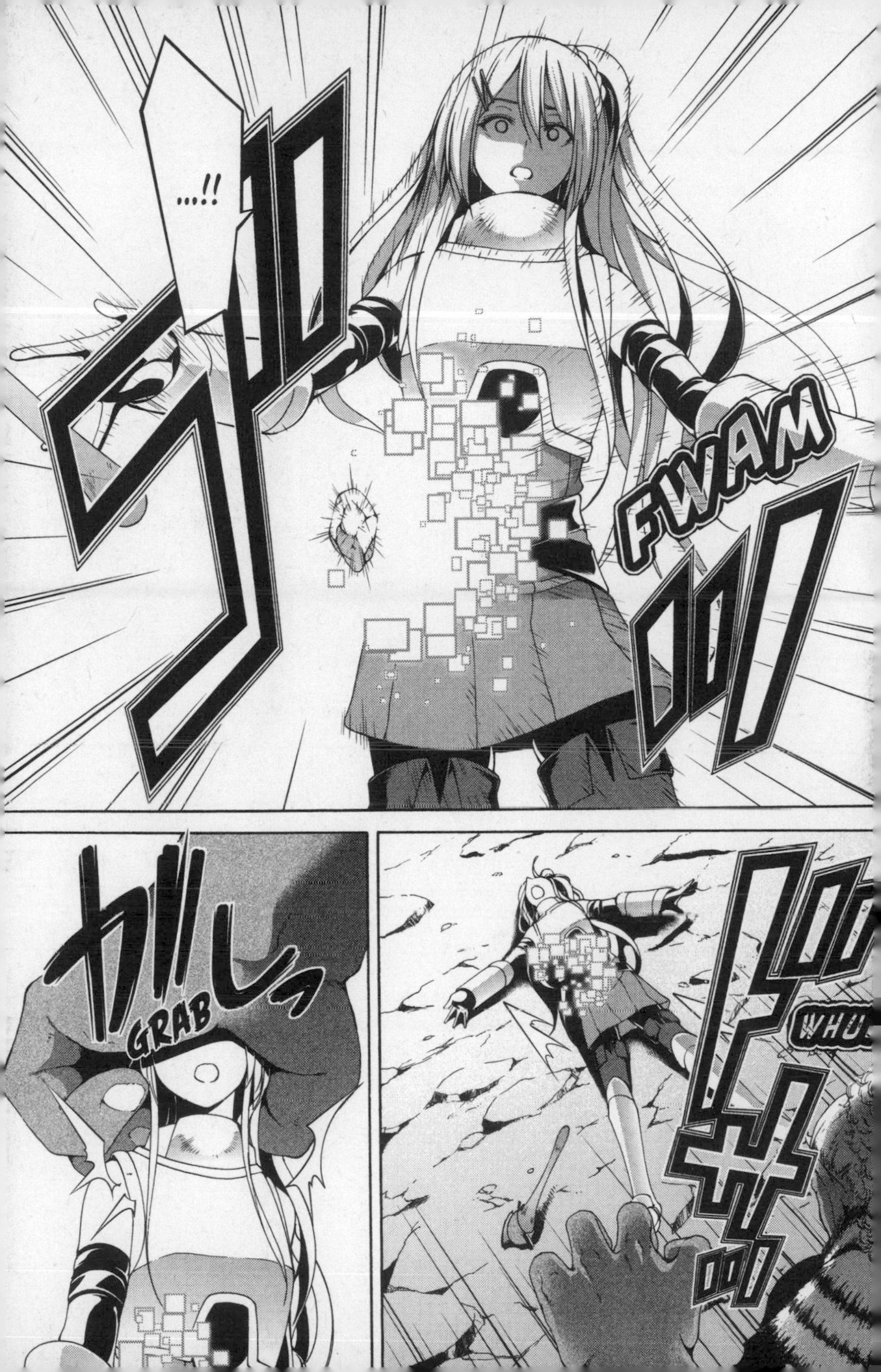
...!!
FWAM
WHU
GRAB

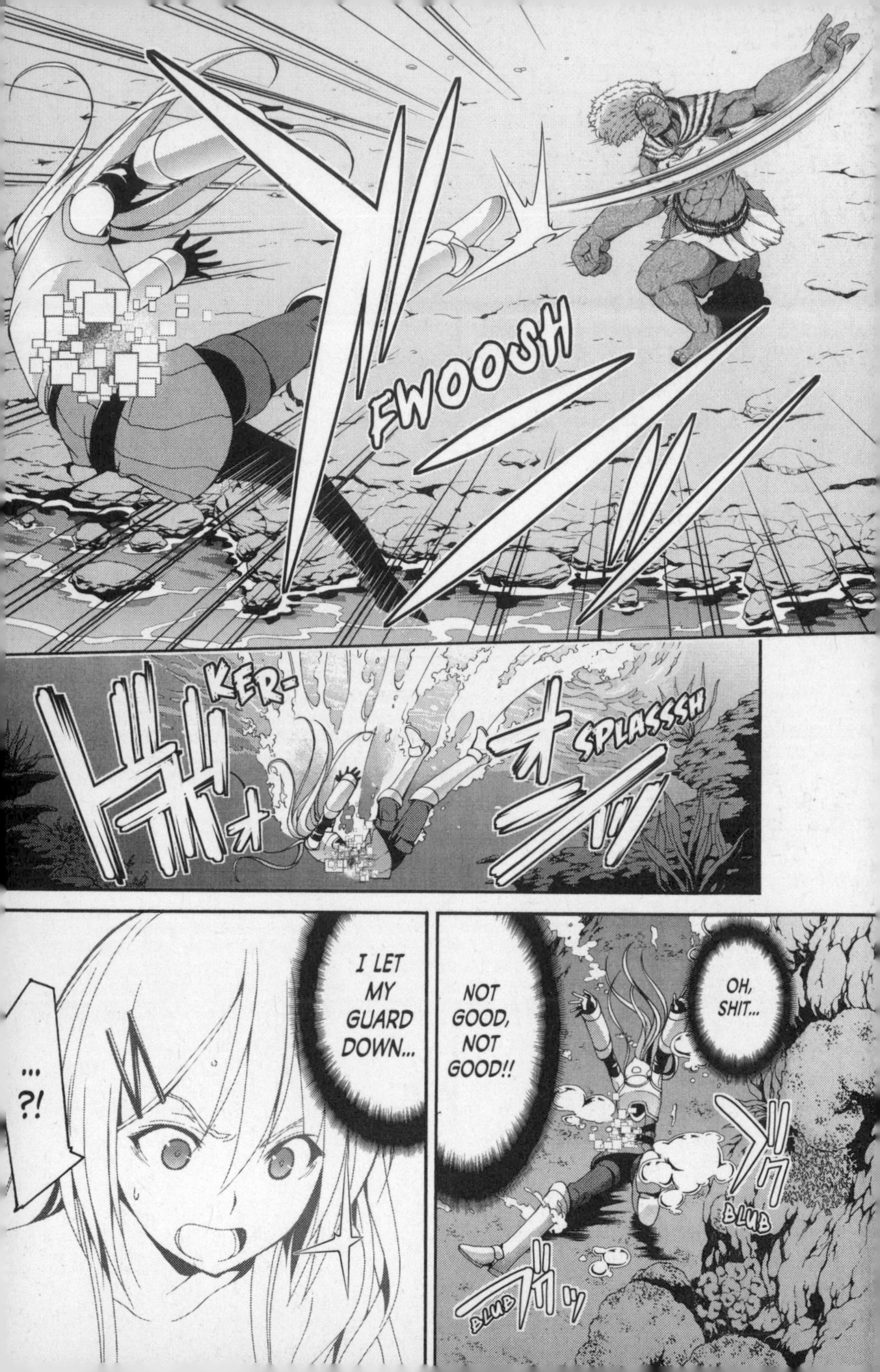
FWOOSH
KER-
SPLASSSH
OH, SHIT...
NOT GOOD, NOT GOOD!!
BLUB
BLUB
I LET MY GUARD DOWN...
...?!

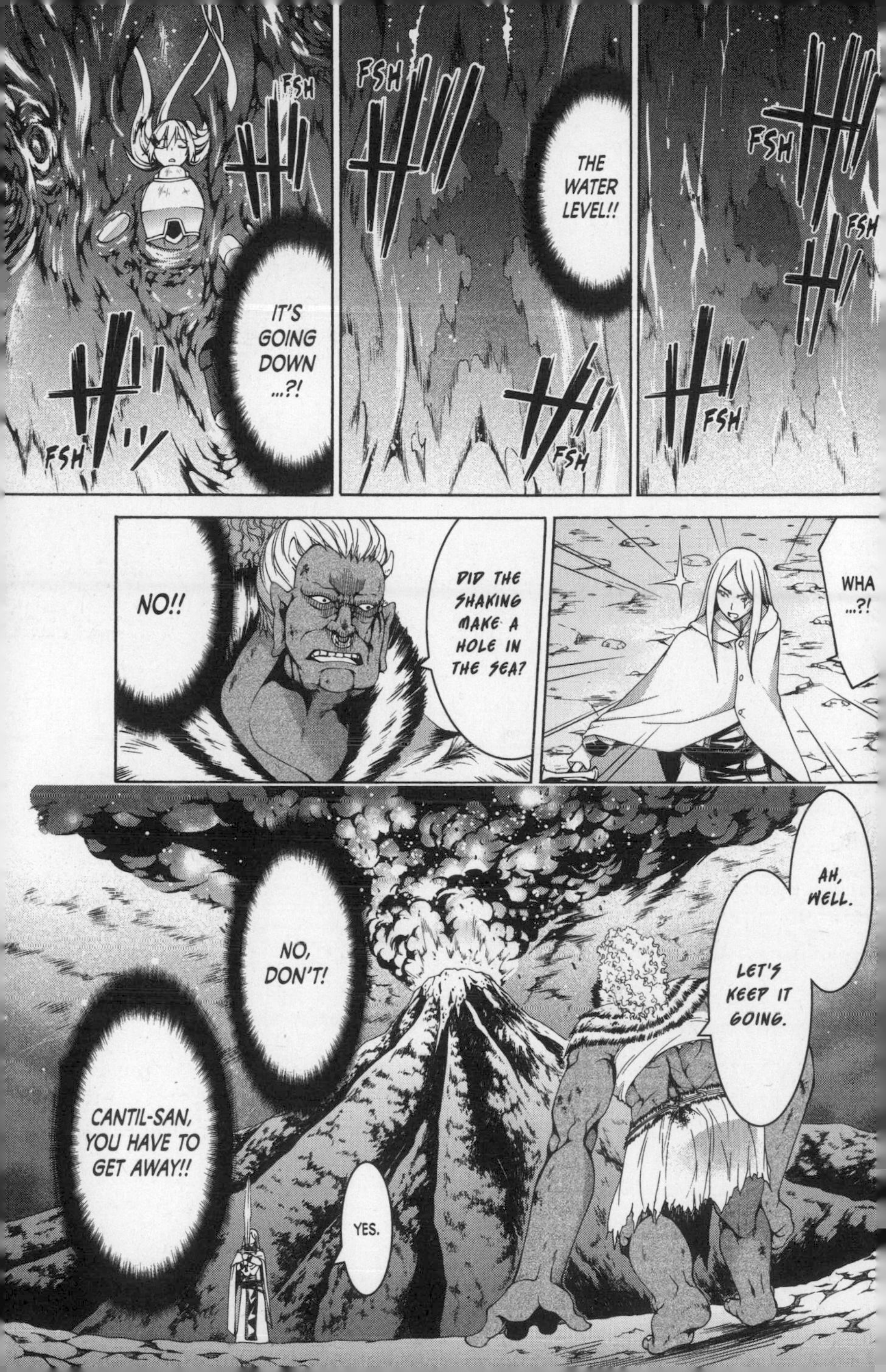
FSH
FSH
FSH
THE WATER LEVEL!!
FSH
FSH
FSH
IT'S GOING DOWN ...?!
FSH
WHA ...?!
DID THE SHAKING MAKE A HOLE IN THE SEA?
NO!!
AH, WELL.
LET'S KEEP IT GOING.
NO, DON'T!
CANTIL-SAN, YOU HAVE TO GET AWAY!!
YES.

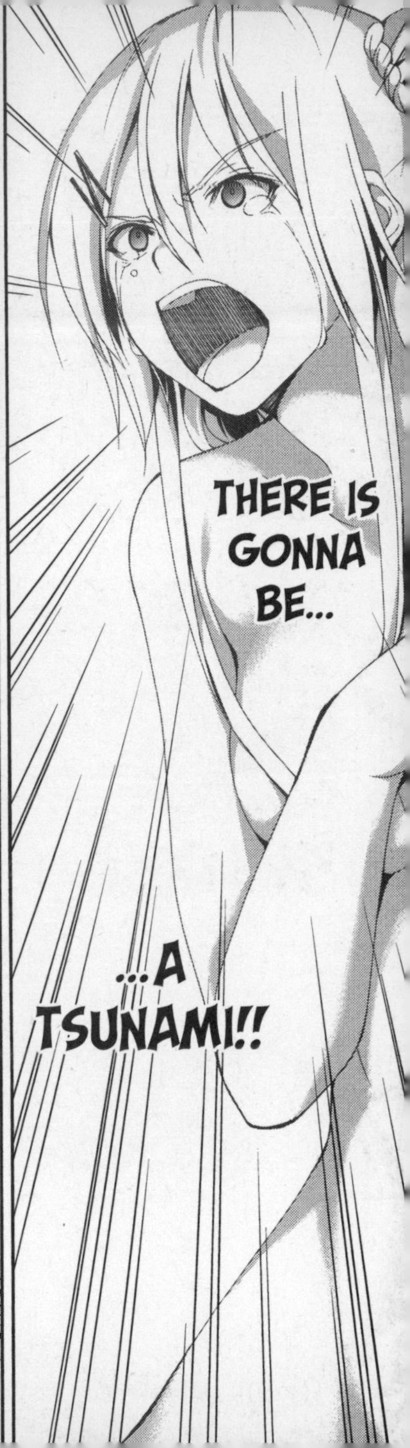
THERE IS GONNA BE...
...A TSUNAMI!!
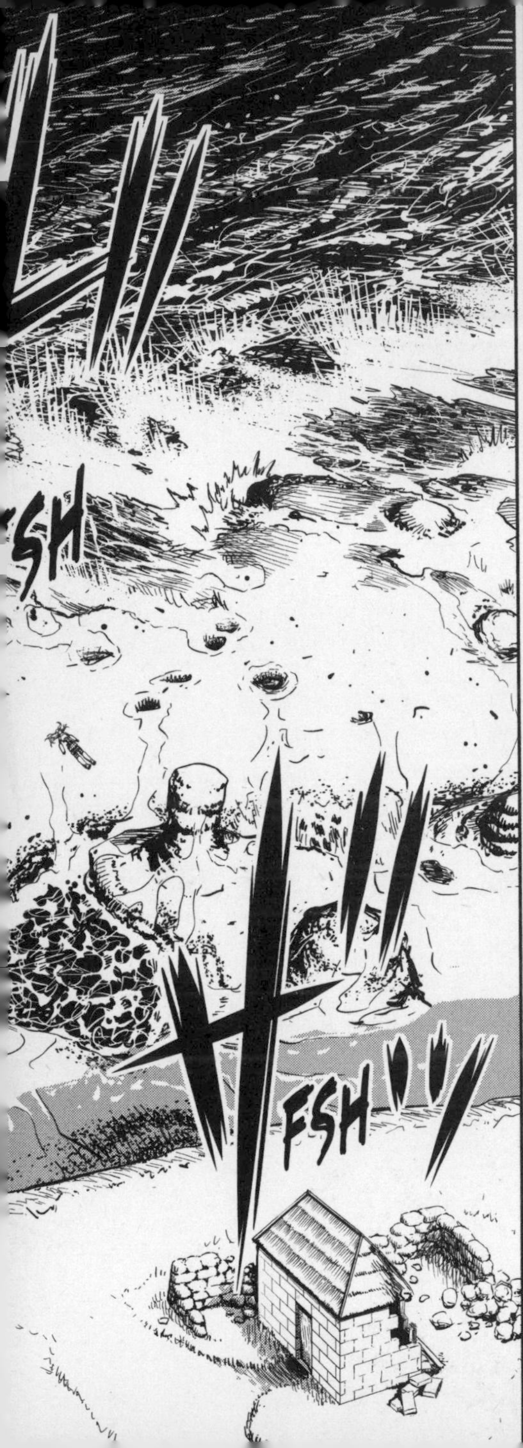
FSH
FSH

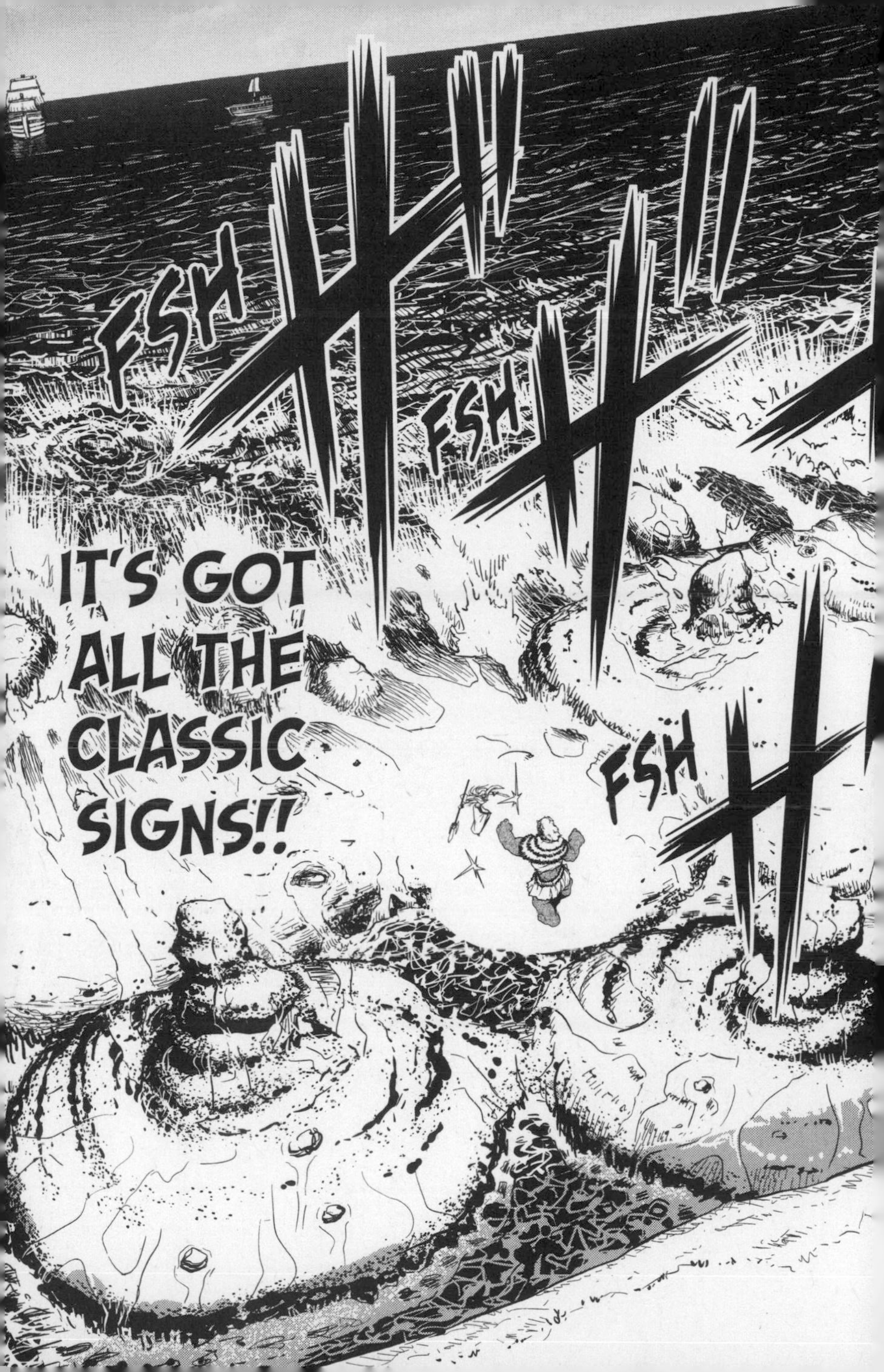
FSH
FSH
IT'S GOT ALL THE CLASSIC SIGNS!!
FSH

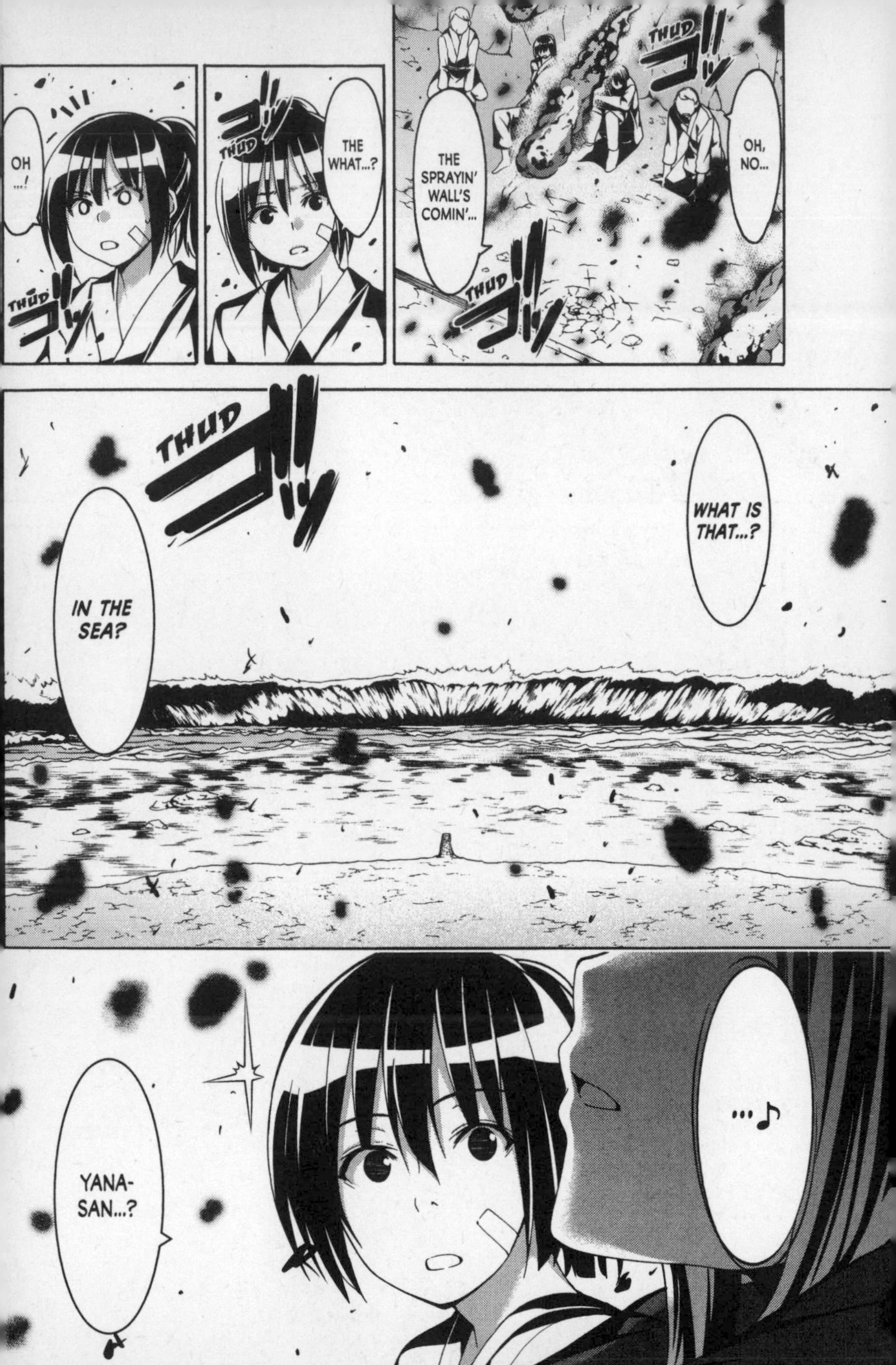
THUD
OH, NO...
THE SPRAYIN' WALL'S COMIN'...
THUD
THE WHAT...?
THUD
OH ...!
THUD
WHAT IS THAT...?
THUD
IN THE SEA?
...♪
YANA-SAN...?

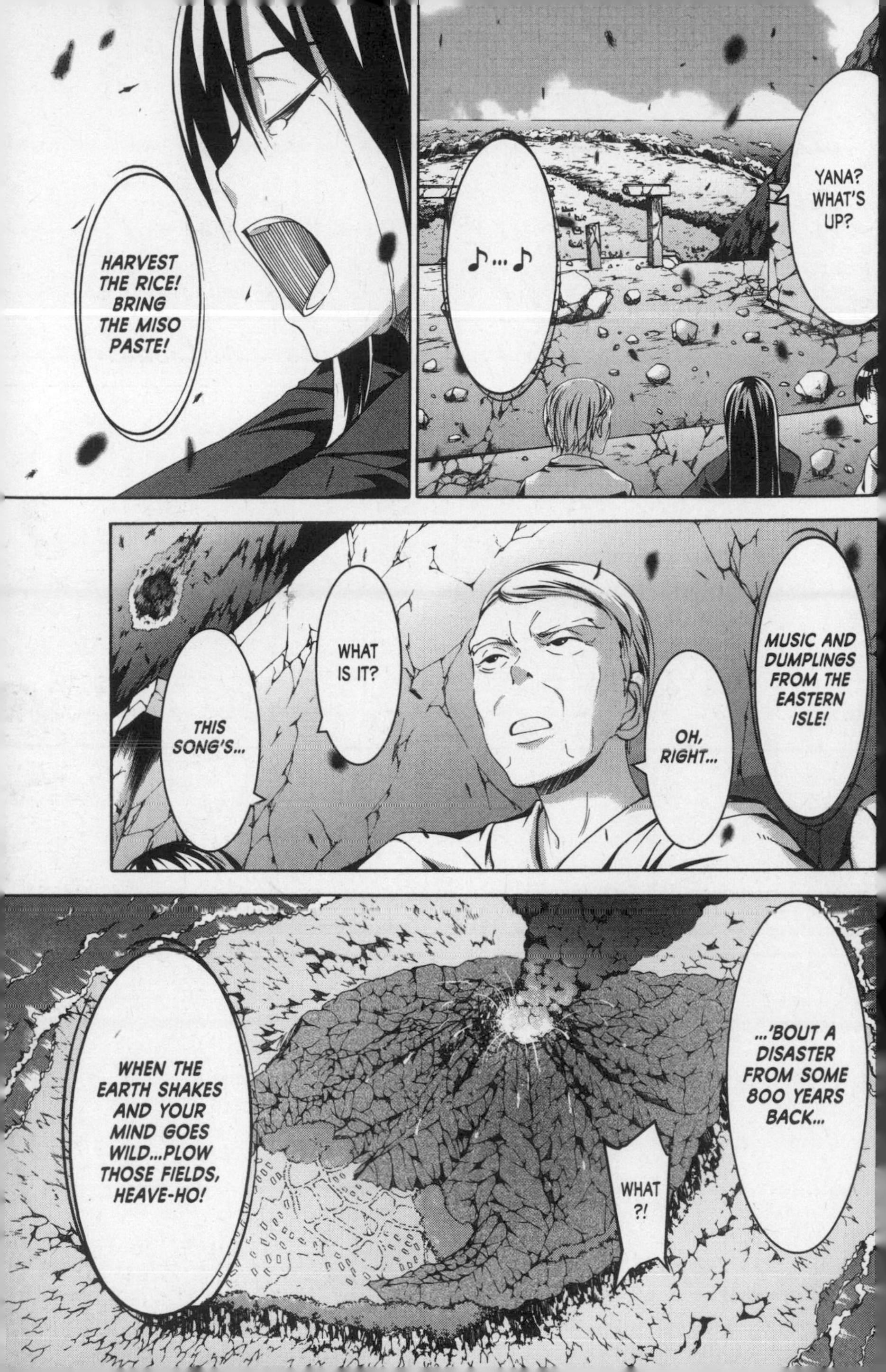
YANA? WHAT'S UP?
♪...♪
HARVEST THE RICE! BRING THE MISO PASTE!
MUSIC AND DUMPLINGS FROM THE EASTERN ISLE!
OH, RIGHT...
WHAT IS IT?
THIS SONG'S...
...'BOUT A DISASTER FROM SOME 800 YEARS BACK...
WHAT ?!
WHEN THE EARTH SHAKES AND YOUR MIND GOES WILD...PLOW THOSE FIELDS, HEAVE-HO!

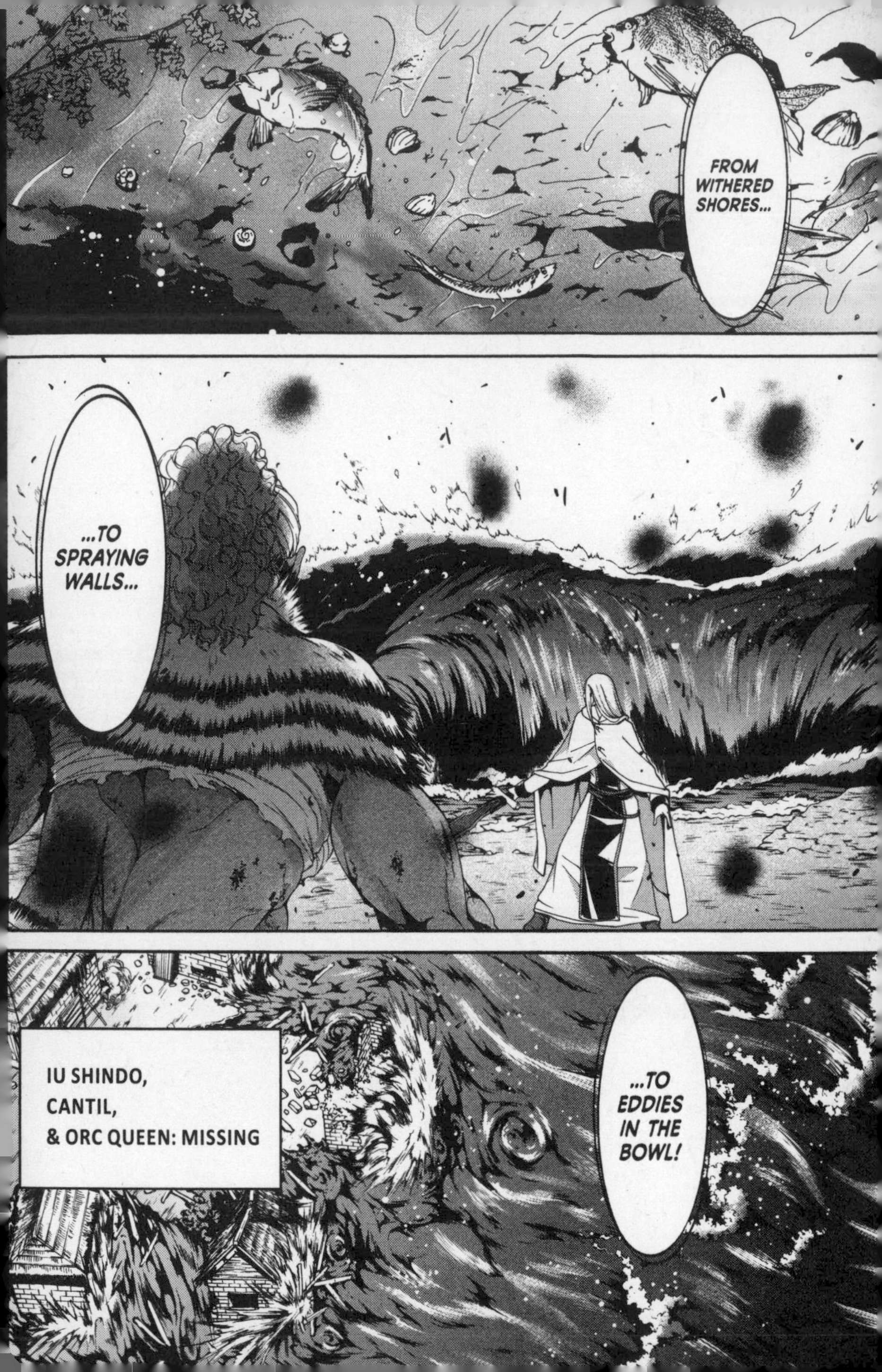
FROM WITHERED SHORES...
...TO SPRAYING WALLS...
...TO EDDIES IN THE BOWL!
IU SHINDO, CANTIL, & ORC QUEEN: MISSING

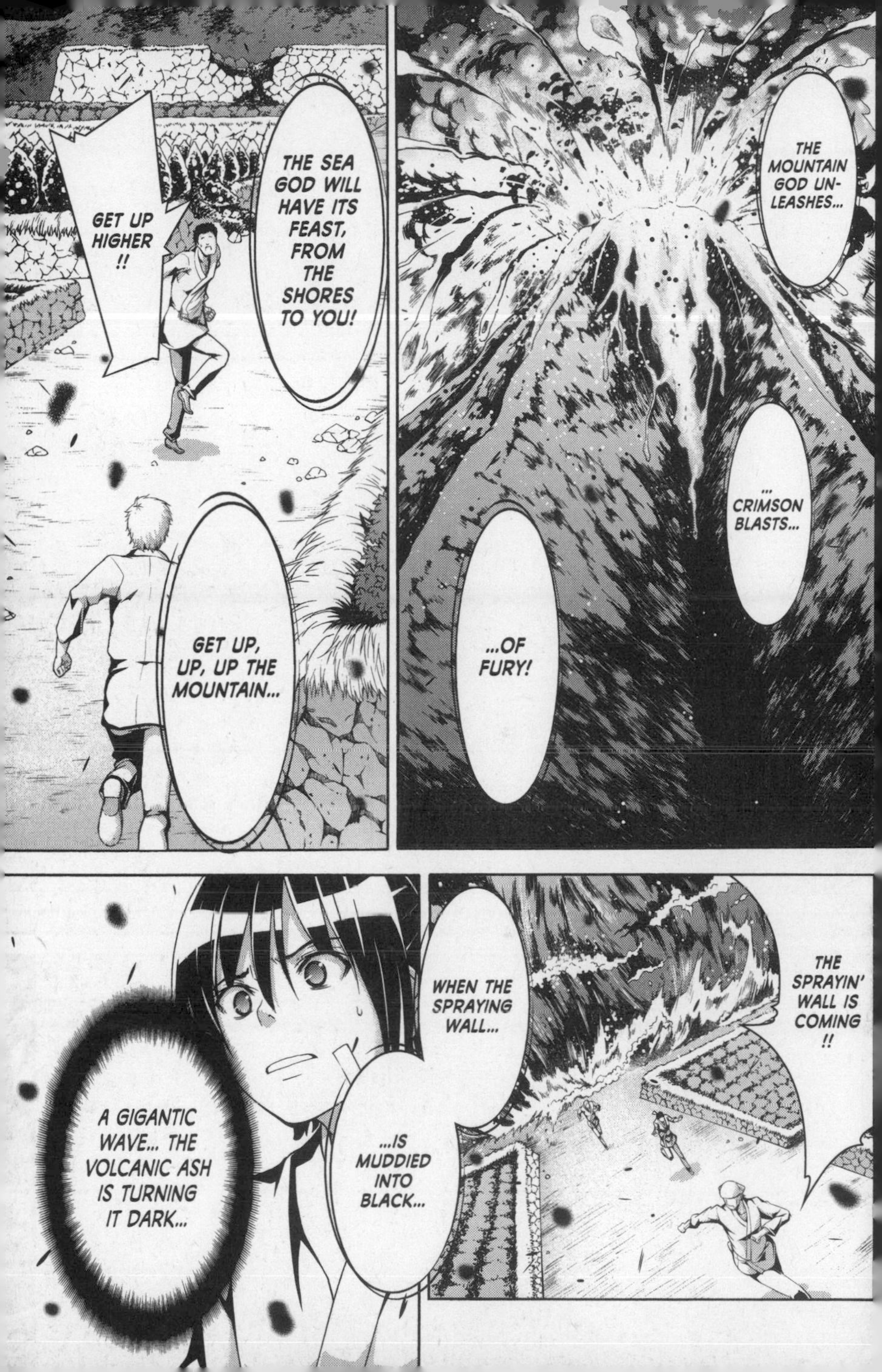
THE MOUNTAIN GOD UN-LEASHES...
...CRIMSON BLASTS...
...OF FURY!
THE SEA GOD WILL HAVE ITS FEAST, FROM THE SHORES TO YOU!
GET UP HIGHER!!
GET UP, UP, UP THE MOUNTAIN...
THE SPRAYIN' WALL IS COMING!!
WHEN THE SPRAYING WALL...
...IS MUDDIED INTO BLACK...
A GIGANTIC WAVE... THE VOLCANIC ASH IS TURNING IT DARK...

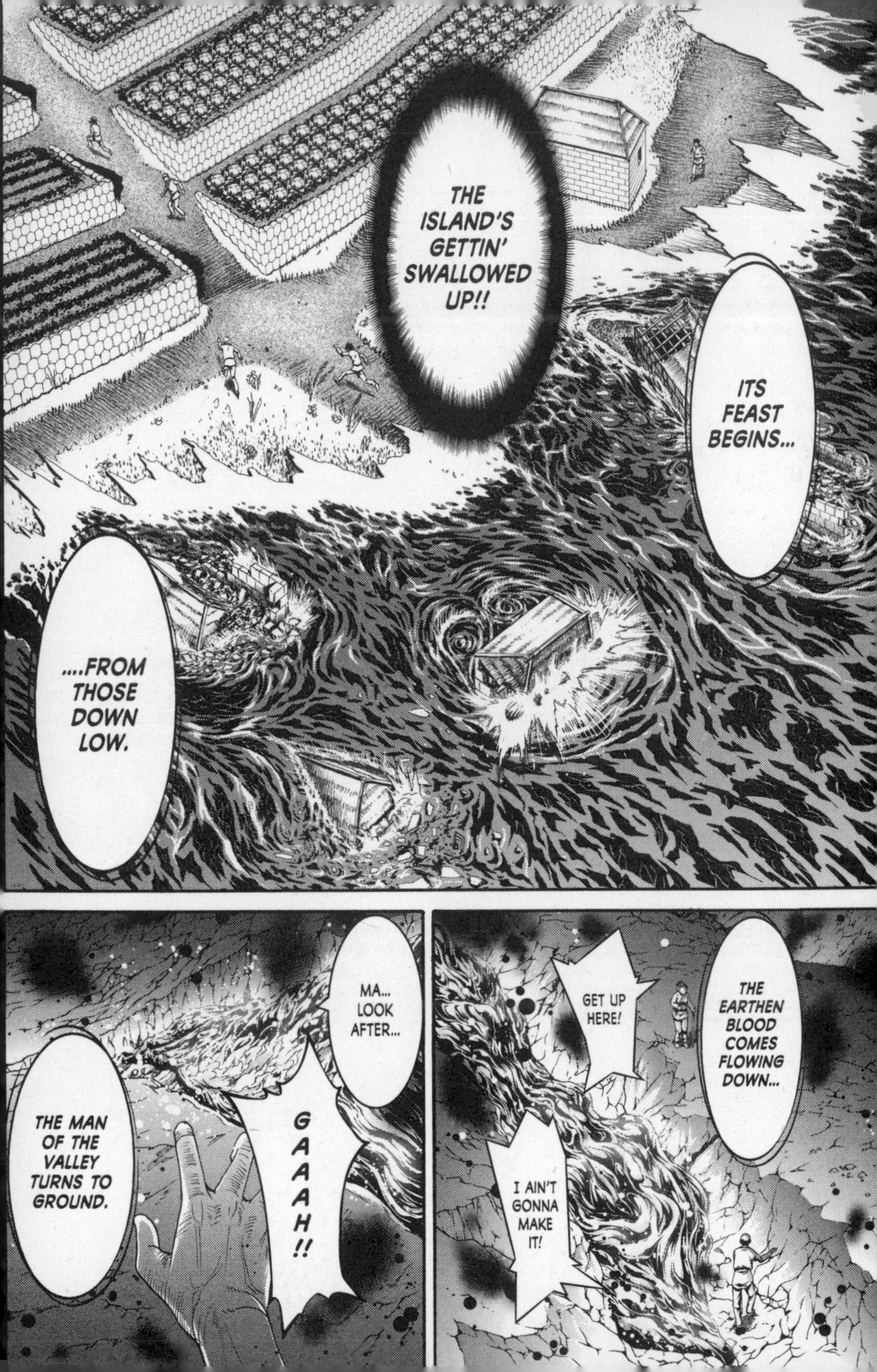
THE ISLAND'S GETTIN' SWALLOWED UP!!
ITS FEAST BEGINS...
....FROM THOSE DOWN LOW.
THE EARTHEN BLOOD COMES FLOWING DOWN...
GET UP HERE!
I AIN'T GONNA MAKE IT!
MA... LOOK AFTER...
GAAAAH!!
THE MAN OF THE VALLEY TURNS TO GROUND.

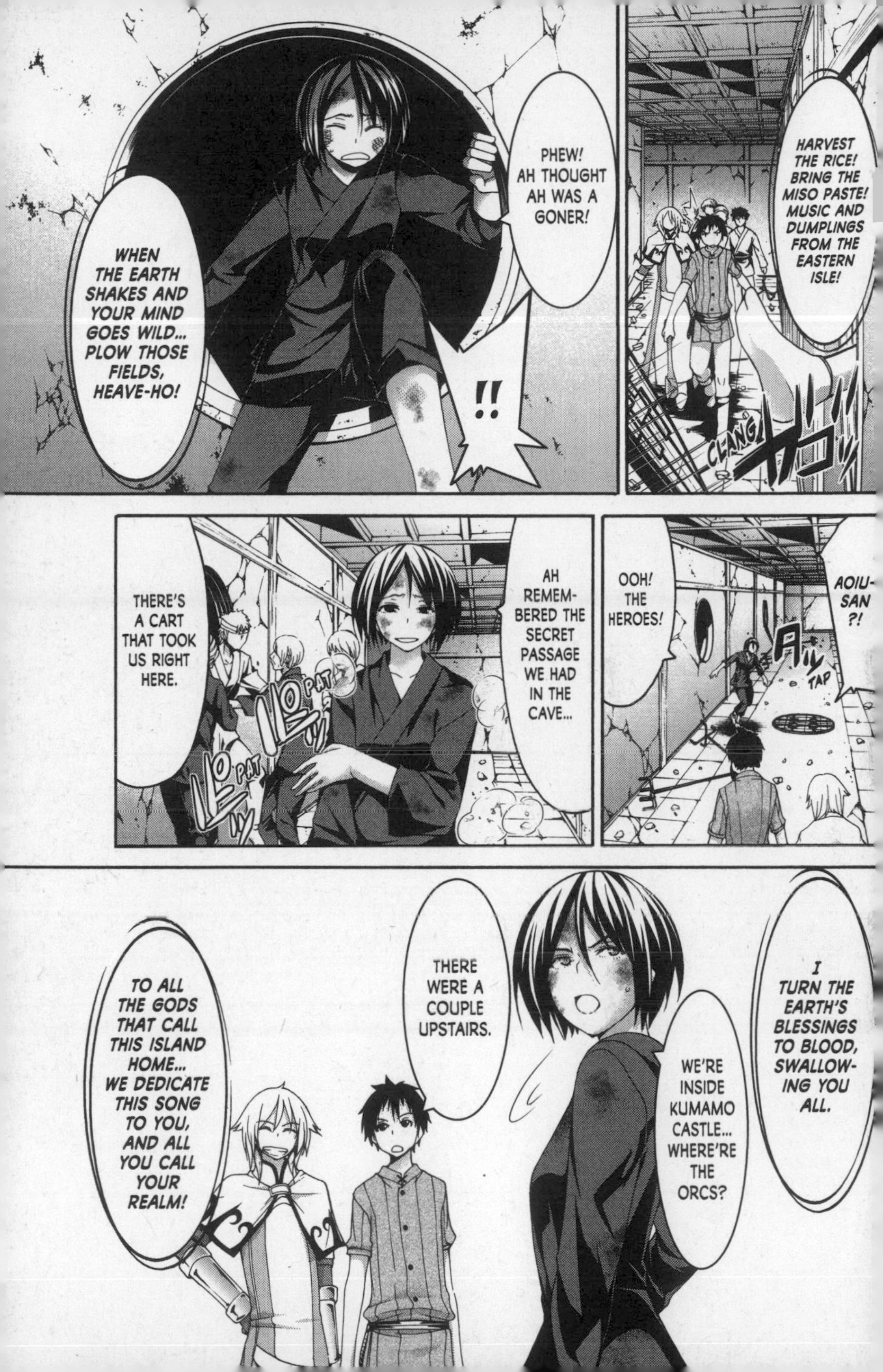
HARVEST THE RICE! BRING THE MISO PASTE! MUSIC AND DUMPLINGS FROM THE EASTERN ISLE!
CLANG
PHEW! AH THOUGHT AH WAS A GONER!
WHEN THE EARTH SHAKES AND YOUR MIND GOES WILD... PLOW THOSE FIELDS, HEAVE-HO!
!!
AOIU-SAN?!
OOH! THE HEROES!
TAP
AH REMEMBERED THE SECRET PASSAGE WE HAD IN THE CAVE...
PAT
THERE'S A CART THAT TOOK US RIGHT HERE.
PAT
I TURN THE EARTH'S BLESSINGS TO BLOOD, SWALLOWING YOU ALL.
WE'RE INSIDE KUMAMO CASTLE... WHERE'RE THE ORCS?
THERE WERE A COUPLE UPSTAIRS.
TO ALL THE GODS THAT CALL THIS ISLAND HOME... WE DEDICATE THIS SONG TO YOU, AND ALL YOU CALL YOUR REALM!

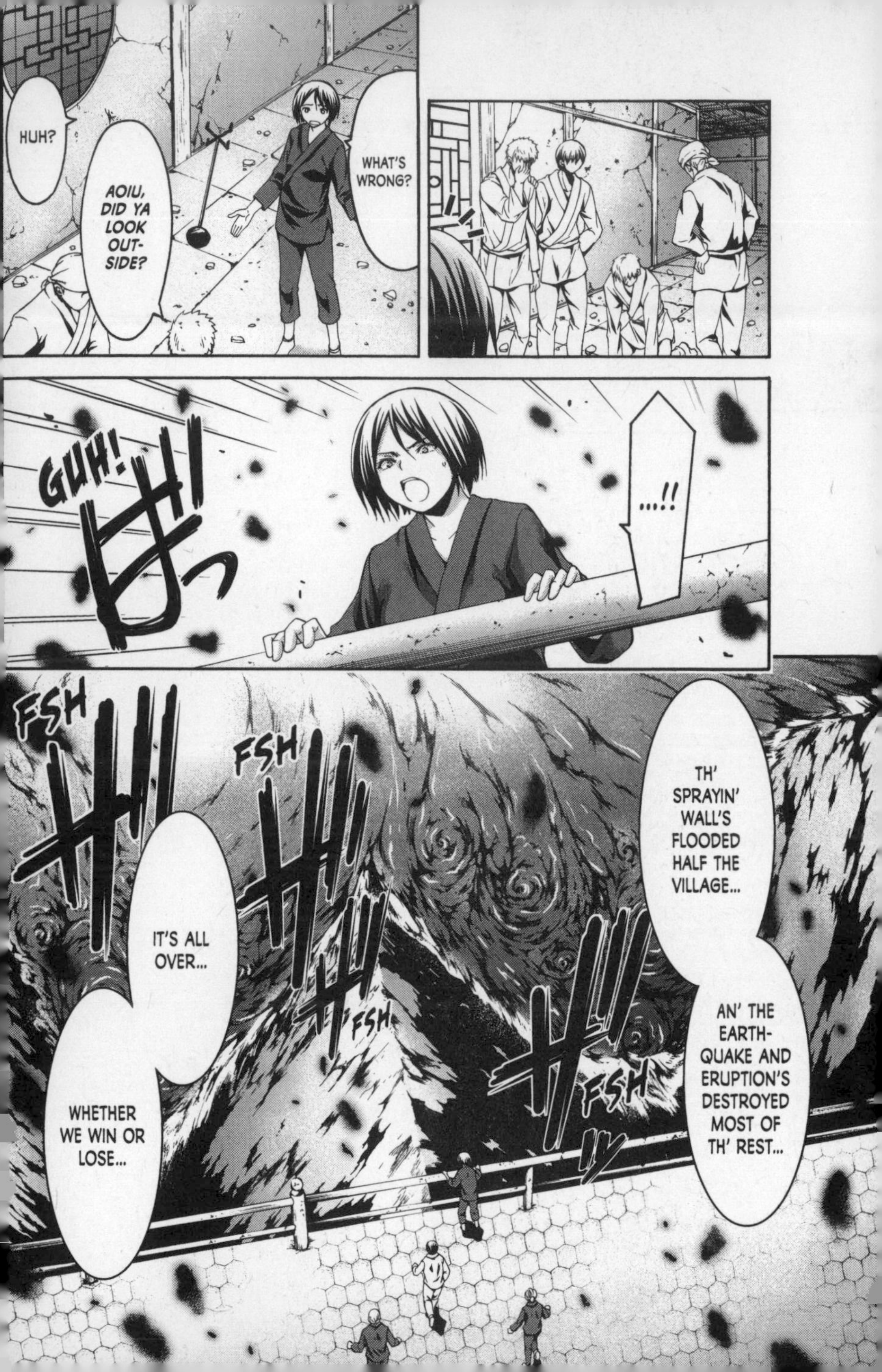
WHAT'S WRONG?
AOIU, DID YA LOOK OUT-SIDE?
HUH?
...!!
GUH!
TH' SPRAYIN' WALL'S FLOODED HALF THE VILLAGE...
FSH
FSH
AN' THE EARTH-QUAKE AND ERUPTION'S DESTROYED MOST OF TH' REST...
IT'S ALL OVER...
FSH
FSH
WHETHER WE WIN OR LOSE...

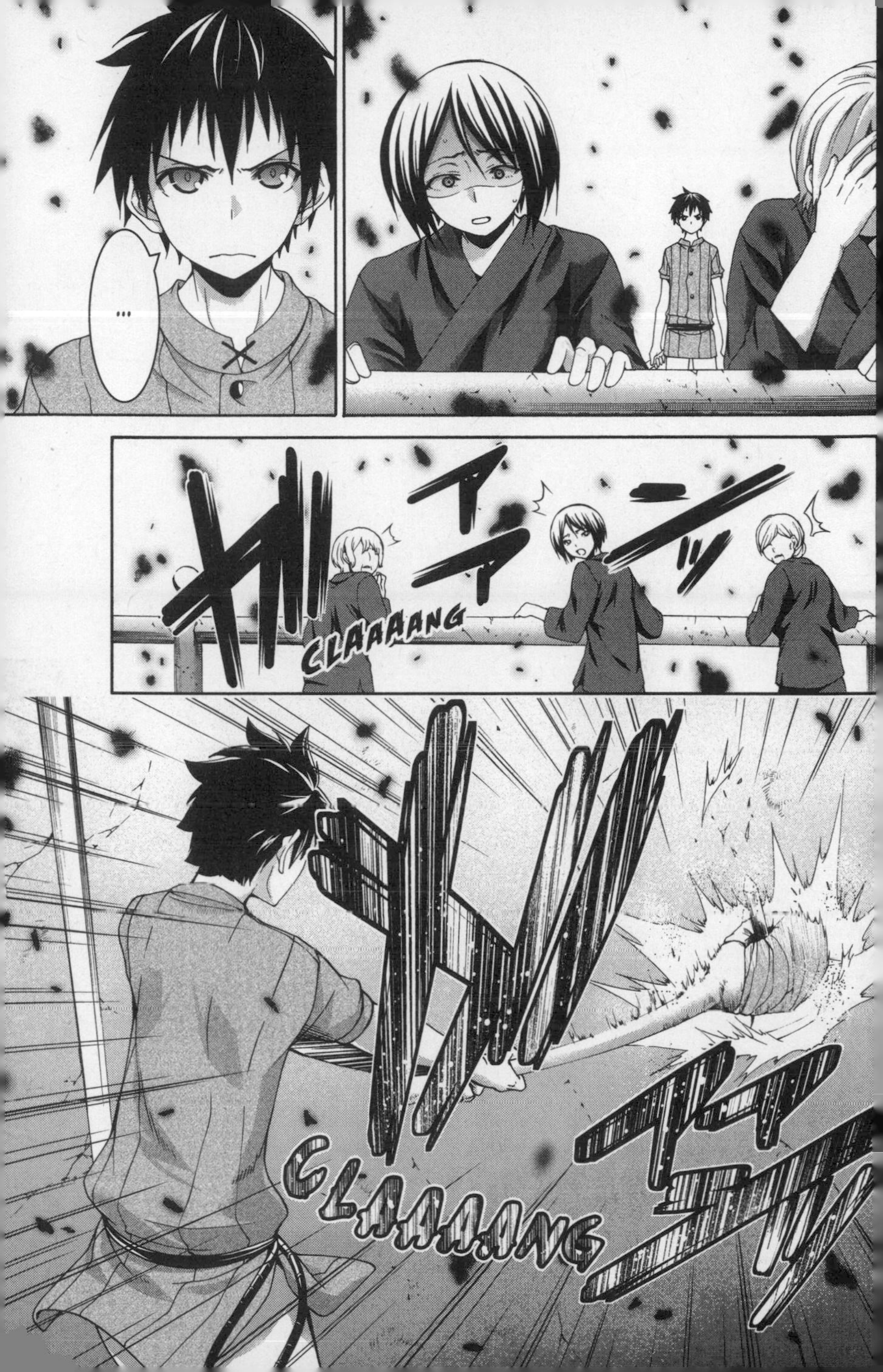
...
CLAAAANG
CLAAAANG

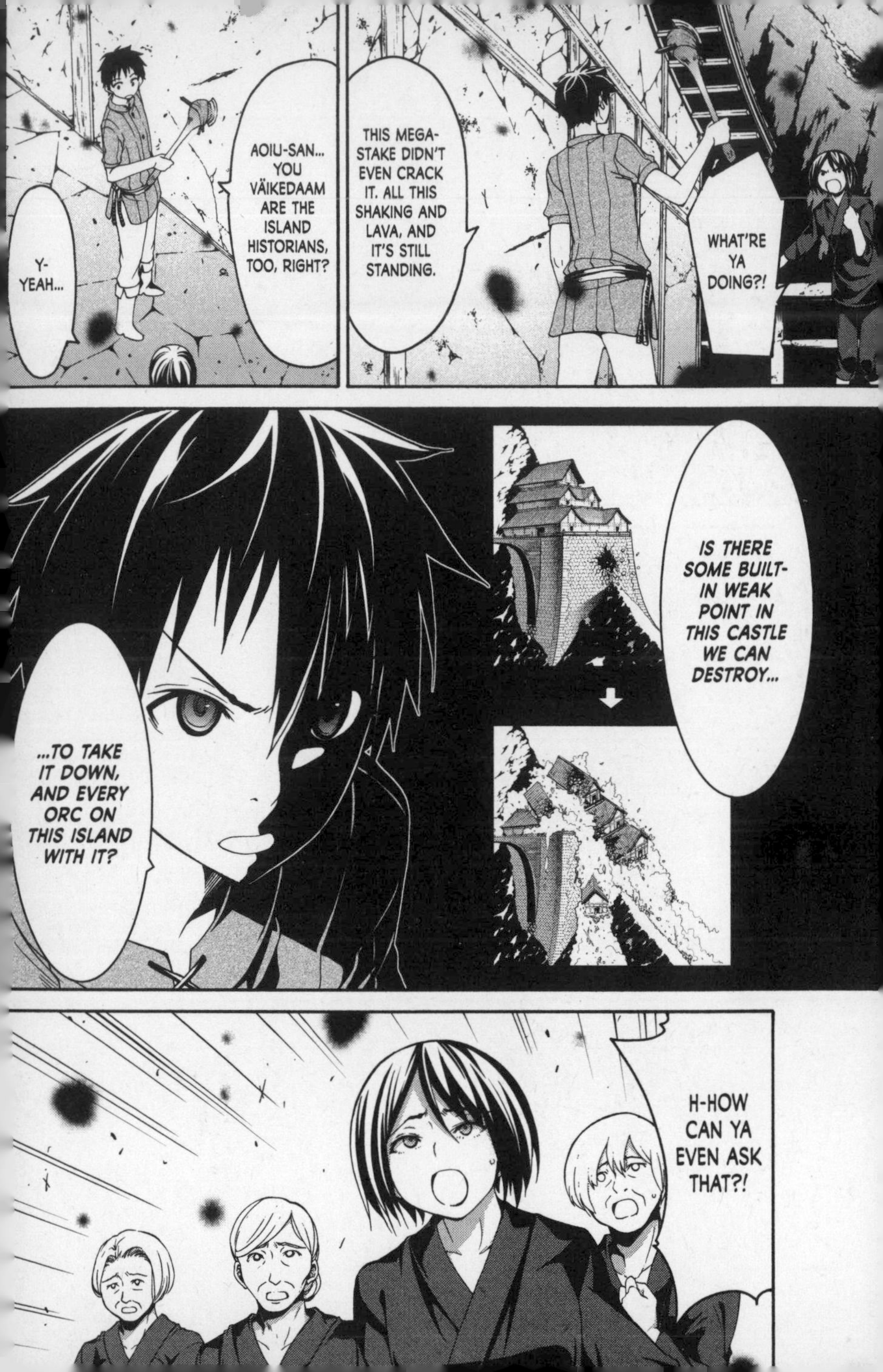
WHAT'RE YA DOING?!
THIS MEGA-STAKE DIDN'T EVEN CRACK IT. ALL THIS SHAKING AND LAVA, AND IT'S STILL STANDING.
AOIU-SAN... YOU VÄIKEDAAM ARE THE ISLAND HISTORIANS, TOO, RIGHT?
Y-YEAH...
IS THERE SOME BUILT-IN WEAK POINT IN THIS CASTLE WE CAN DESTROY...
...TO TAKE IT DOWN, AND EVERY ORC ON THIS ISLAND WITH IT?
H-HOW CAN YA EVEN ASK THAT?!

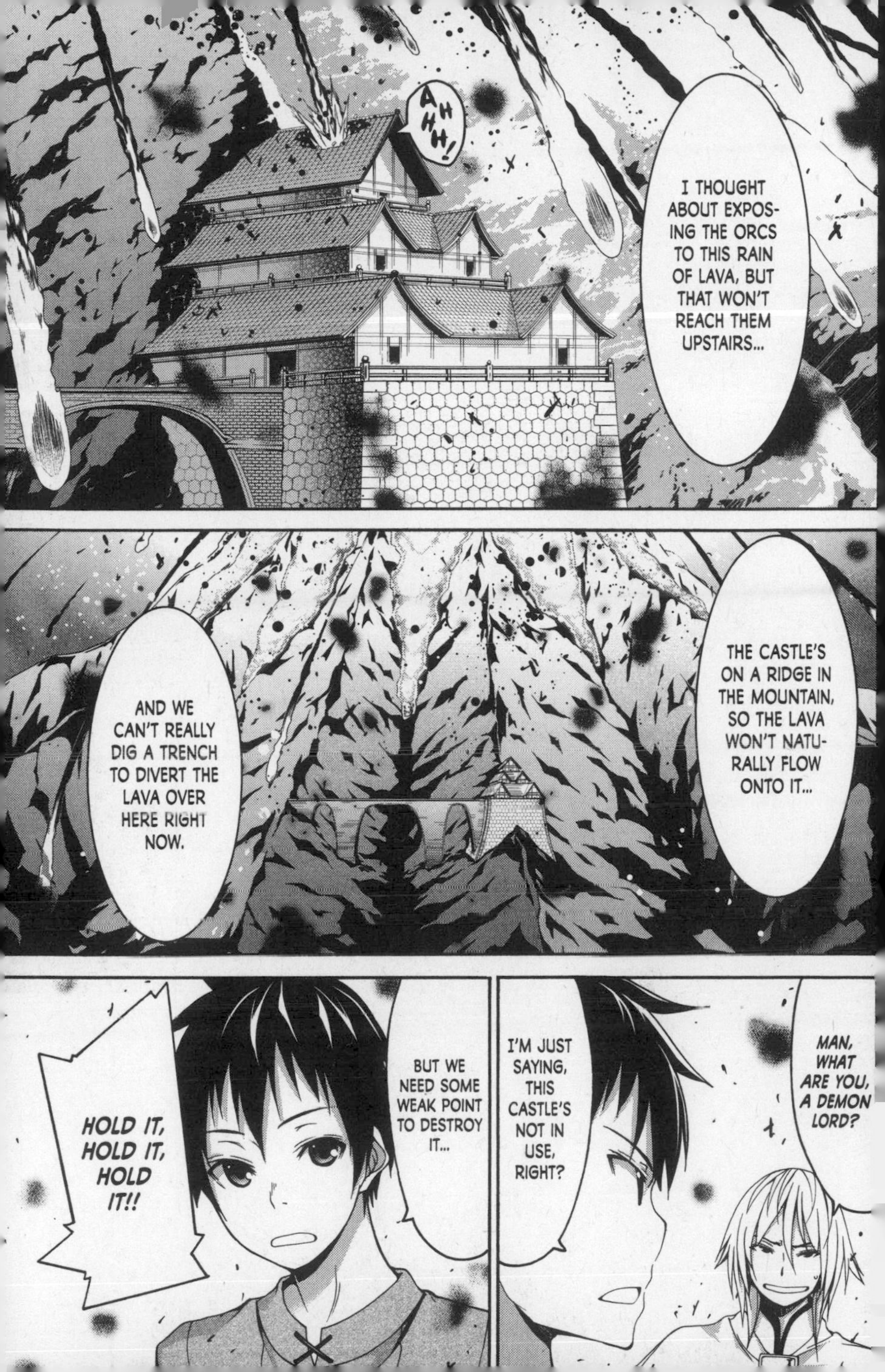
I THOUGHT ABOUT EXPOSING THE ORCS TO THIS RAIN OF LAVA, BUT THAT WON'T REACH THEM UPSTAIRS...
AHHH!
THE CASTLE'S ON A RIDGE IN THE MOUNTAIN, SO THE LAVA WON'T NATURALLY FLOW ONTO IT...
AND WE CAN'T REALLY DIG A TRENCH TO DIVERT THE LAVA OVER HERE RIGHT NOW.
MAN, WHAT ARE YOU, A DEMON LORD?
I'M JUST SAYING, THIS CASTLE'S NOT IN USE, RIGHT?
BUT WE NEED SOME WEAK POINT TO DESTROY IT...
HOLD IT, HOLD IT, HOLD IT!!

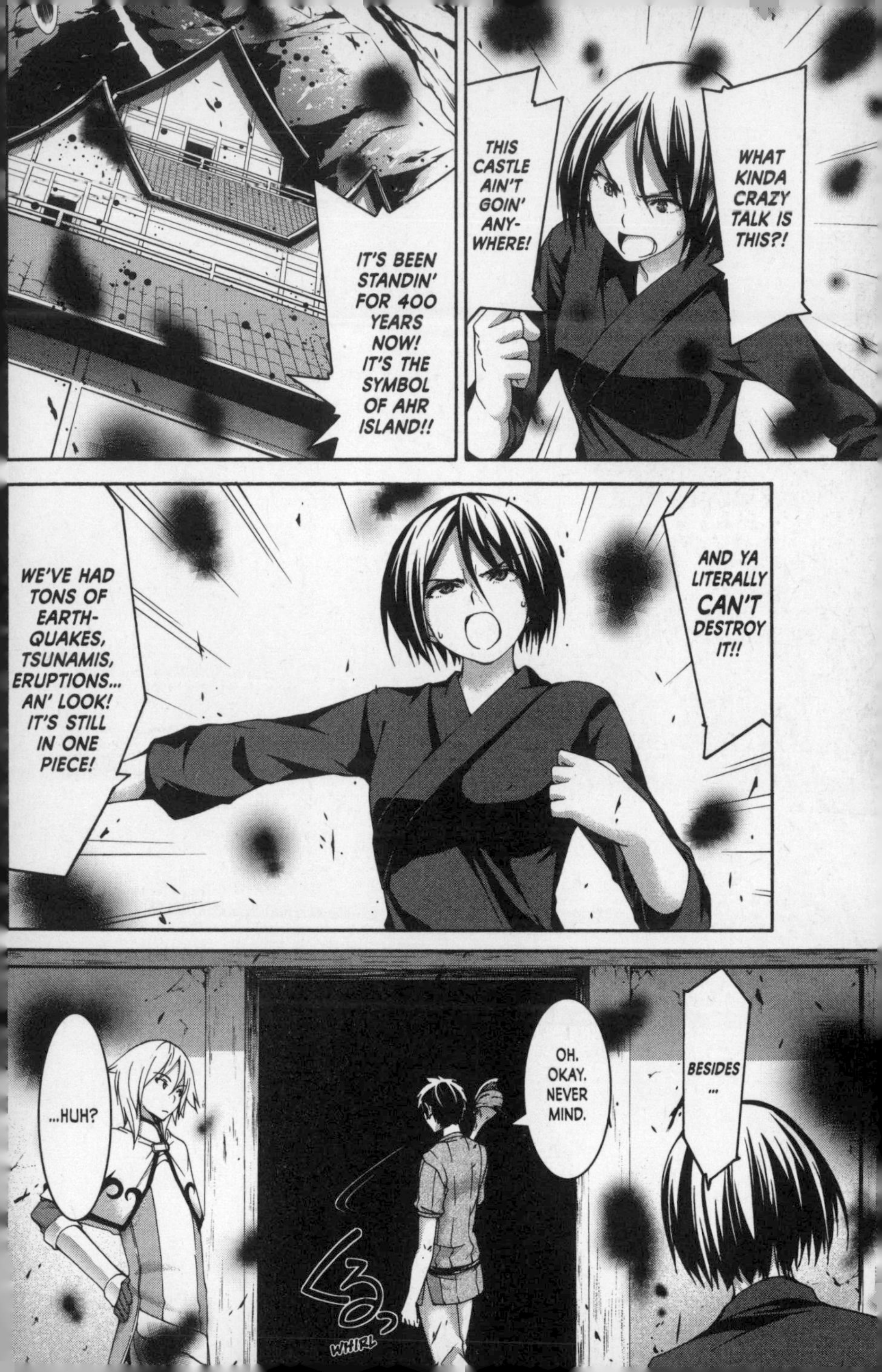
WHAT KINDA CRAZY TALK IS THIS?!
THIS CASTLE AIN'T GOIN' ANY-WHERE!
IT'S BEEN STANDIN' FOR 400 YEARS NOW! IT'S THE SYMBOL OF AHR ISLAND!!
AND YA LITERALLY CAN'T DESTROY IT!!
WE'VE HAD TONS OF EARTH-QUAKES, TSUNAMIS, ERUPTIONS... AN' LOOK! IT'S STILL IN ONE PIECE!
BESIDES...
OH. OKAY. NEVER MIND.
WHIRL
...HUH?

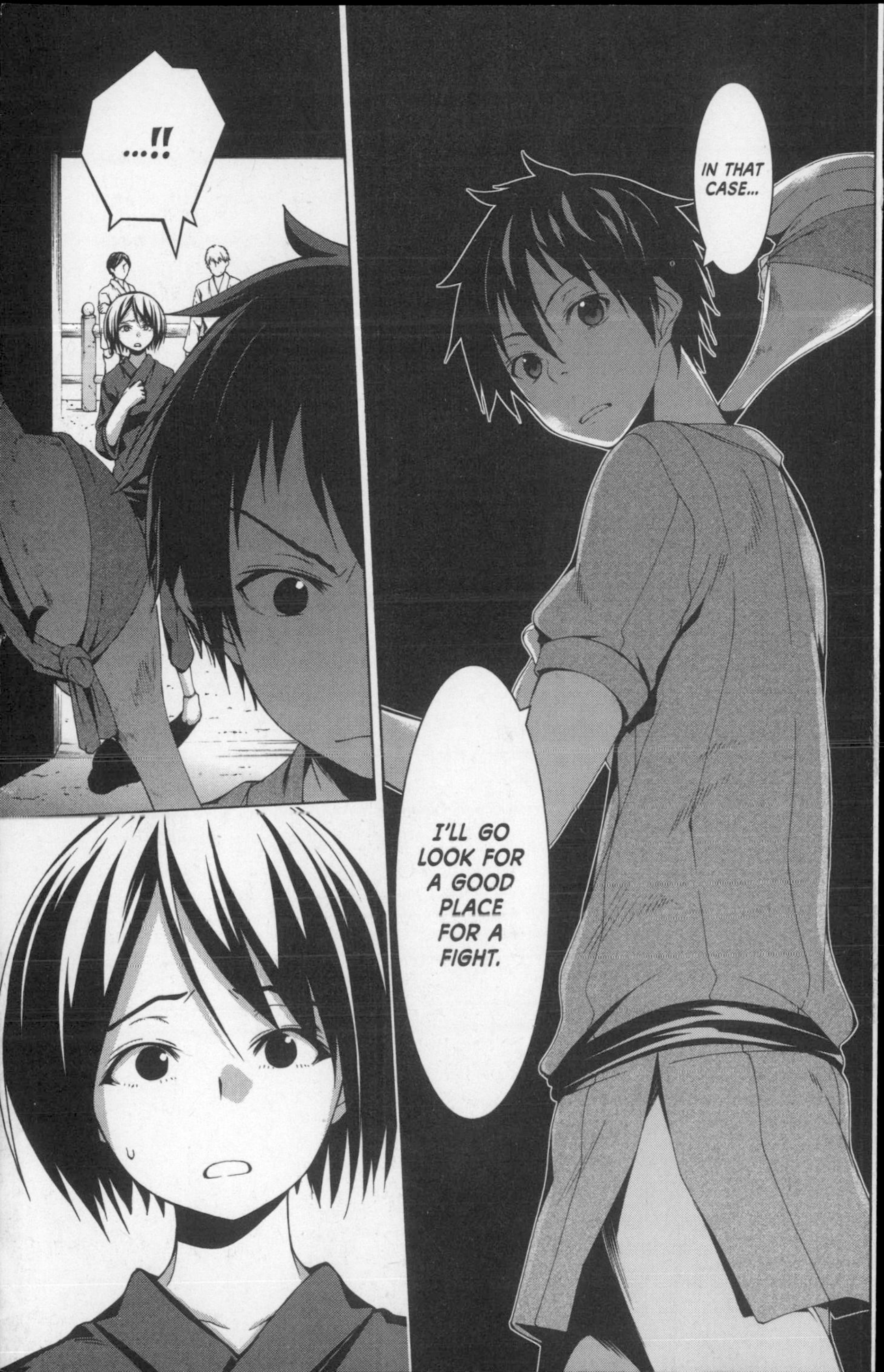
IN THAT CASE...
I'LL GO LOOK FOR A GOOD PLACE FOR A FIGHT.
...!!

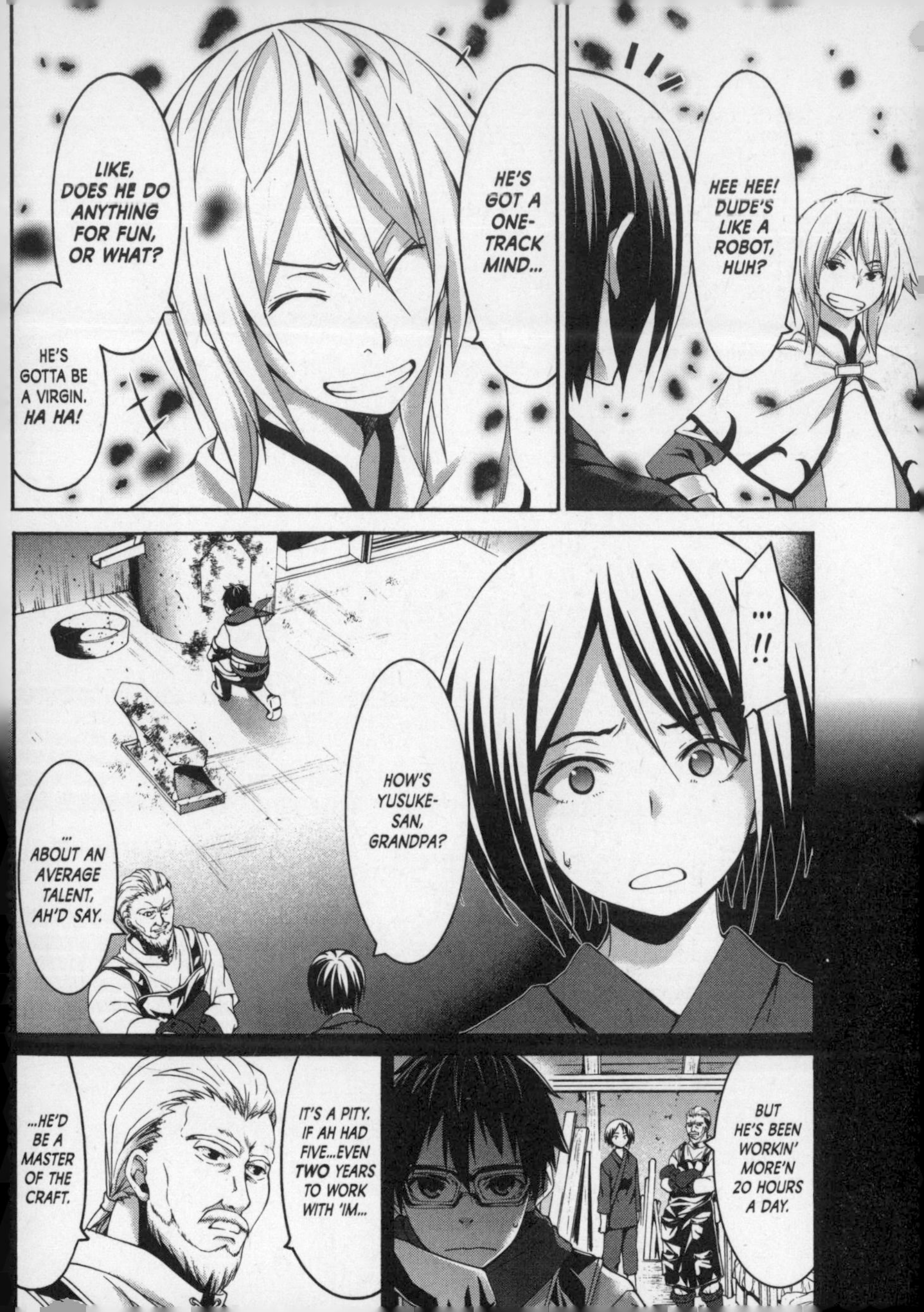
HEE HEE! DUDE'S LIKE A ROBOT, HUH?
HE'S GOT A ONE-TRACK MIND...
LIKE, DOES HE DO ANYTHING FOR FUN, OR WHAT?
HE'S GOTTA BE A VIRGIN. HA HA!
...!!
HOW'S YUSUKE-SAN, GRANDPA?
...ABOUT AN AVERAGE TALENT, AH'D SAY.
BUT HE'S BEEN WORKIN' MORE'N 20 HOURS A DAY.
IT'S A PITY. IF AH HAD FIVE...EVEN TWO YEARS TO WORK WITH 'IM...
...HE'D BE A MASTER OF THE CRAFT.

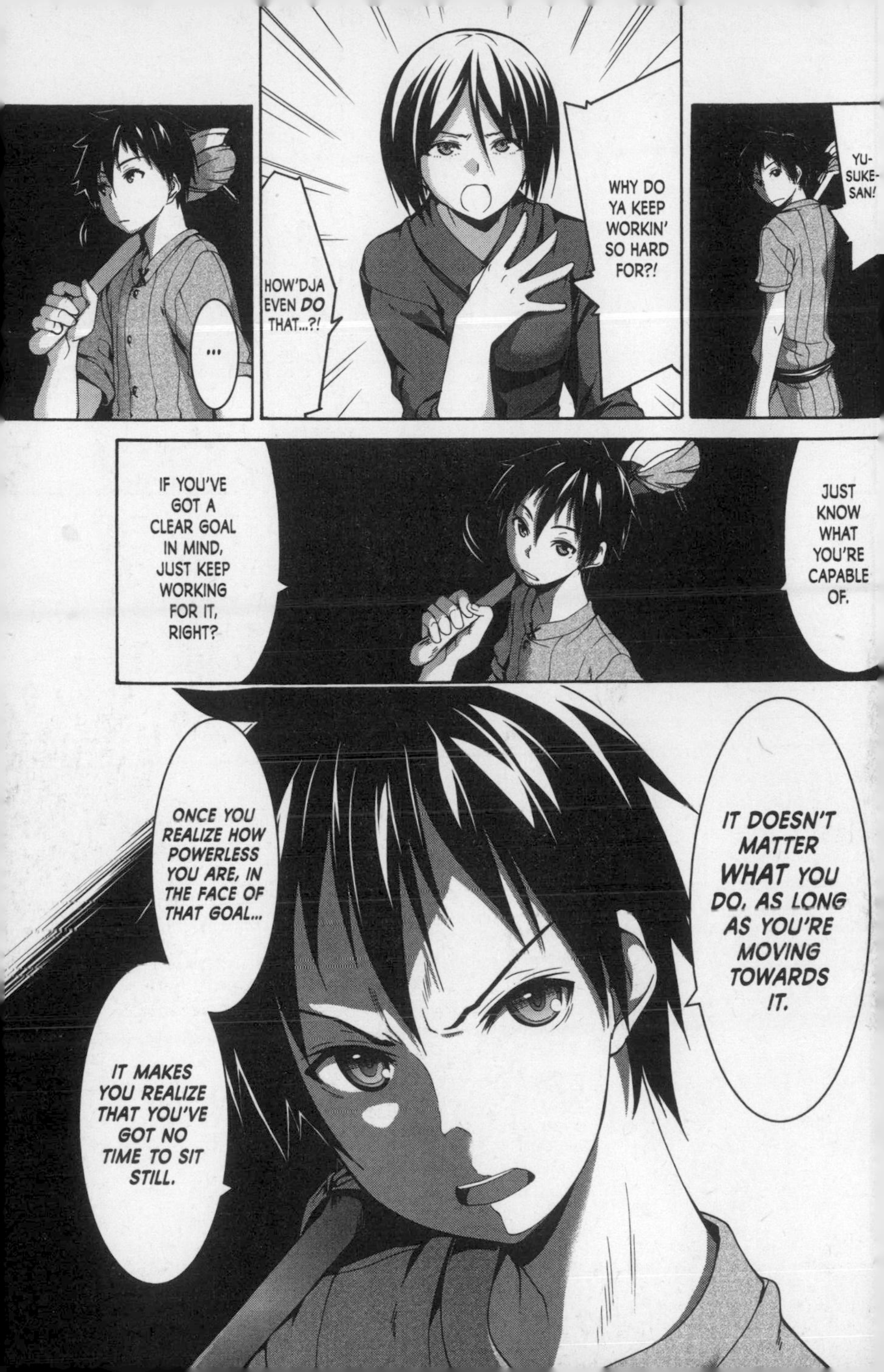
YU-SUKE-SAN!
WHY DO YA KEEP WORKIN' SO HARD FOR?!
HOW'DJA EVEN *DO* THAT...?!
...
JUST KNOW WHAT YOU'RE CAPABLE OF.
IF YOU'VE GOT A CLEAR GOAL IN MIND, JUST KEEP WORKING FOR IT, RIGHT?
IT DOESN'T MATTER WHAT YOU DO. AS LONG AS YOU'RE MOVING TOWARDS IT.
ONCE YOU REALIZE HOW POWERLESS YOU ARE, IN THE FACE OF THAT GOAL...
IT MAKES YOU REALIZE THAT YOU'VE GOT NO TIME TO SIT STILL.

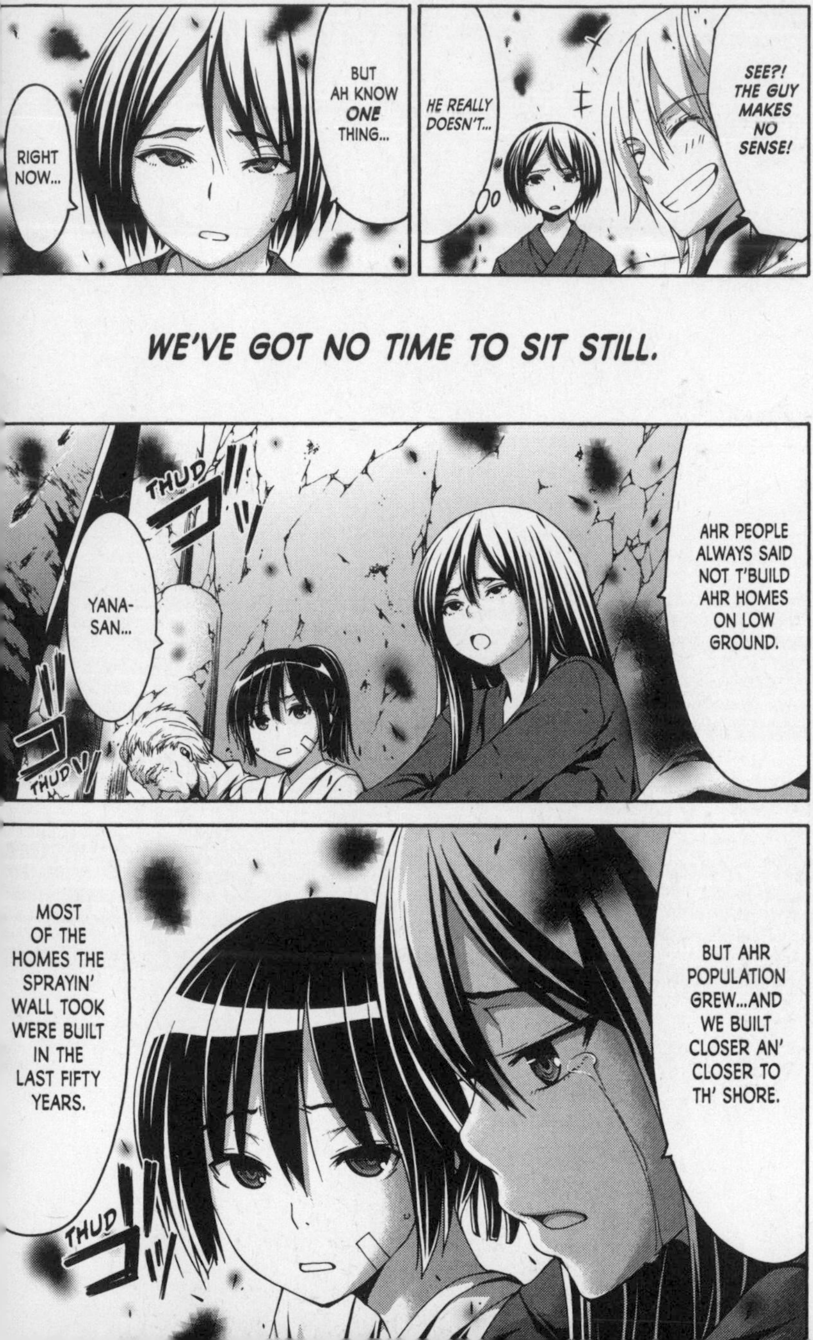
SEE?! THE GUY MAKES NO SENSE!
HE REALLY DOESN'T...
BUT AH KNOW ONE THING...
RIGHT NOW...
WE'VE GOT NO TIME TO SIT STILL.
AHR PEOPLE ALWAYS SAID NOT T'BUILD AHR HOMES ON LOW GROUND.
THUD
YANA-SAN...
THUD
BUT AHR POPULATION GREW...AND WE BUILT CLOSER AN' CLOSER TO TH' SHORE.
MOST OF THE HOMES THE SPRAYIN' WALL TOOK WERE BUILT IN THE LAST FIFTY YEARS.
THUD

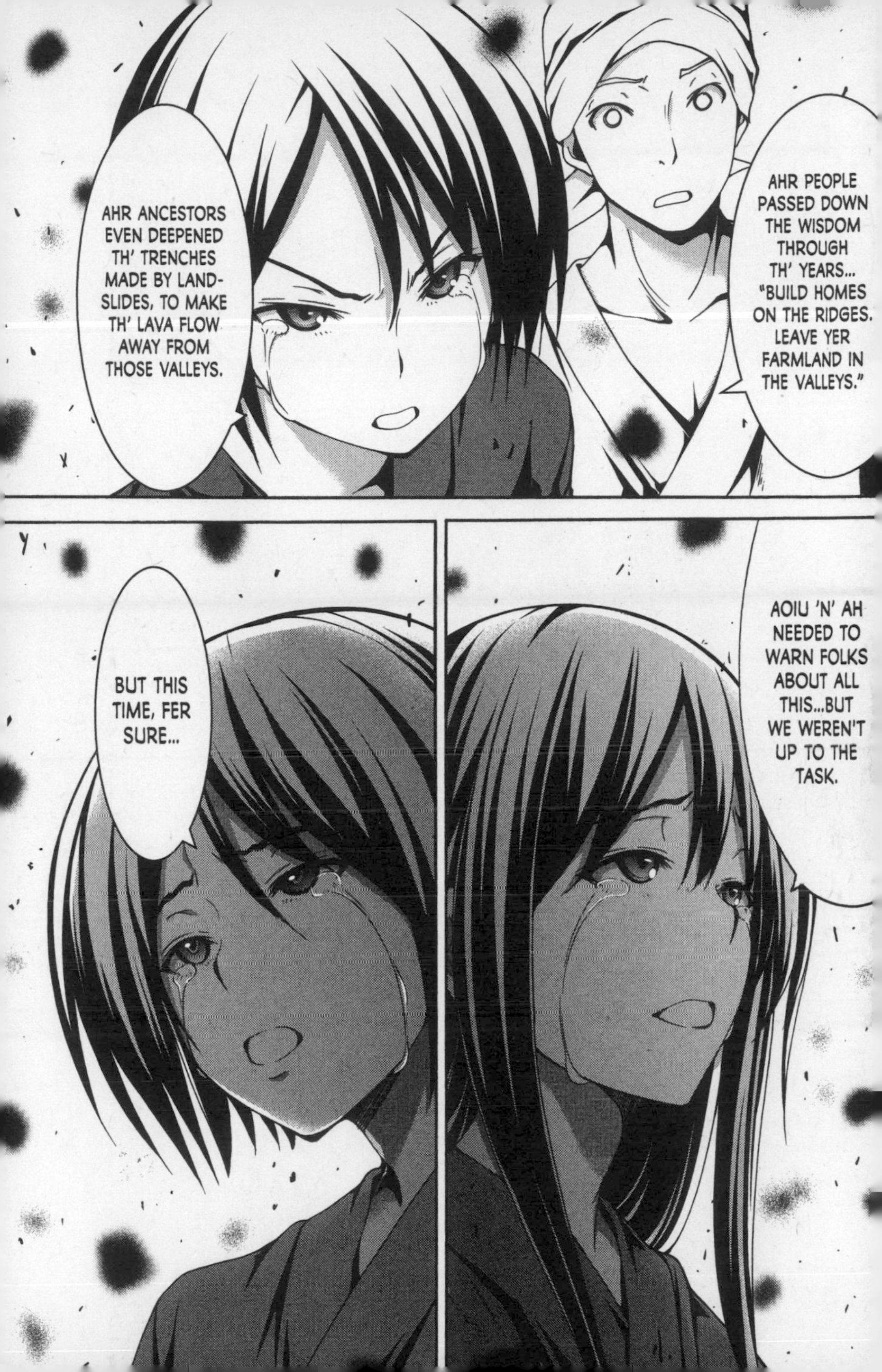
AHR PEOPLE PASSED DOWN THE WISDOM THROUGH TH' YEARS... "BUILD HOMES ON THE RIDGES. LEAVE YER FARMLAND IN THE VALLEYS."
AHR ANCESTORS EVEN DEEPENED TH' TRENCHES MADE BY LAND-SLIDES, TO MAKE TH' LAVA FLOW AWAY FROM THOSE VALLEYS.
AOIU 'N' AH NEEDED TO WARN FOLKS ABOUT ALL THIS...BUT WE WEREN'T UP TO THE TASK.
BUT THIS TIME, FER SURE...

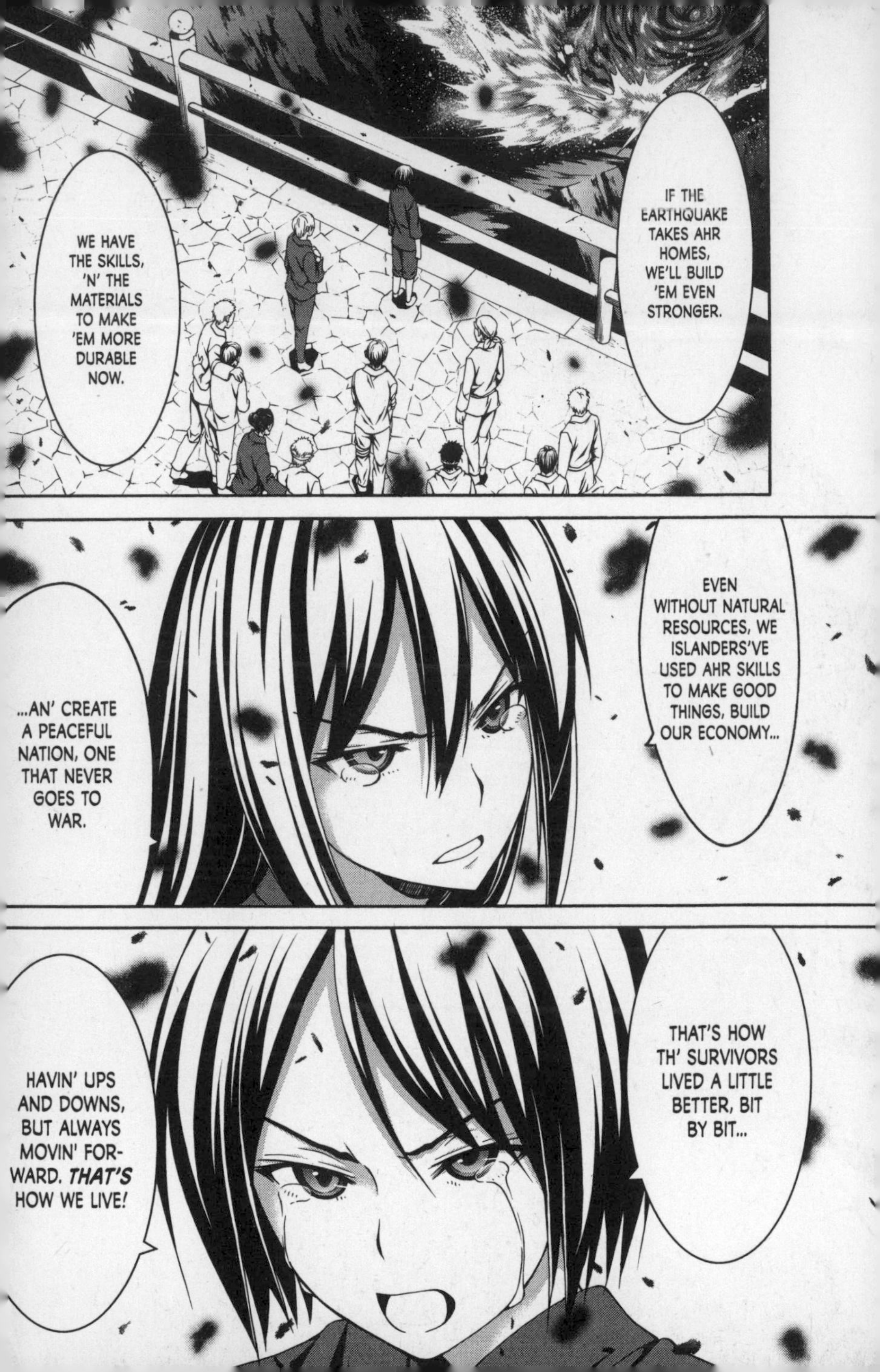
IF THE EARTHQUAKE TAKES AHR HOMES, WE'LL BUILD 'EM EVEN STRONGER.
WE HAVE THE SKILLS, 'N' THE MATERIALS TO MAKE 'EM MORE DURABLE NOW.
EVEN WITHOUT NATURAL RESOURCES, WE ISLANDERS'VE USED AHR SKILLS TO MAKE GOOD THINGS, BUILD OUR ECONOMY...
...AN' CREATE A PEACEFUL NATION, ONE THAT NEVER GOES TO WAR.
THAT'S HOW TH' SURVIVORS LIVED A LITTLE BETTER, BIT BY BIT...
HAVIN' UPS AND DOWNS, BUT ALWAYS MOVIN' FOR-WARD. *THAT'S* HOW WE LIVE!

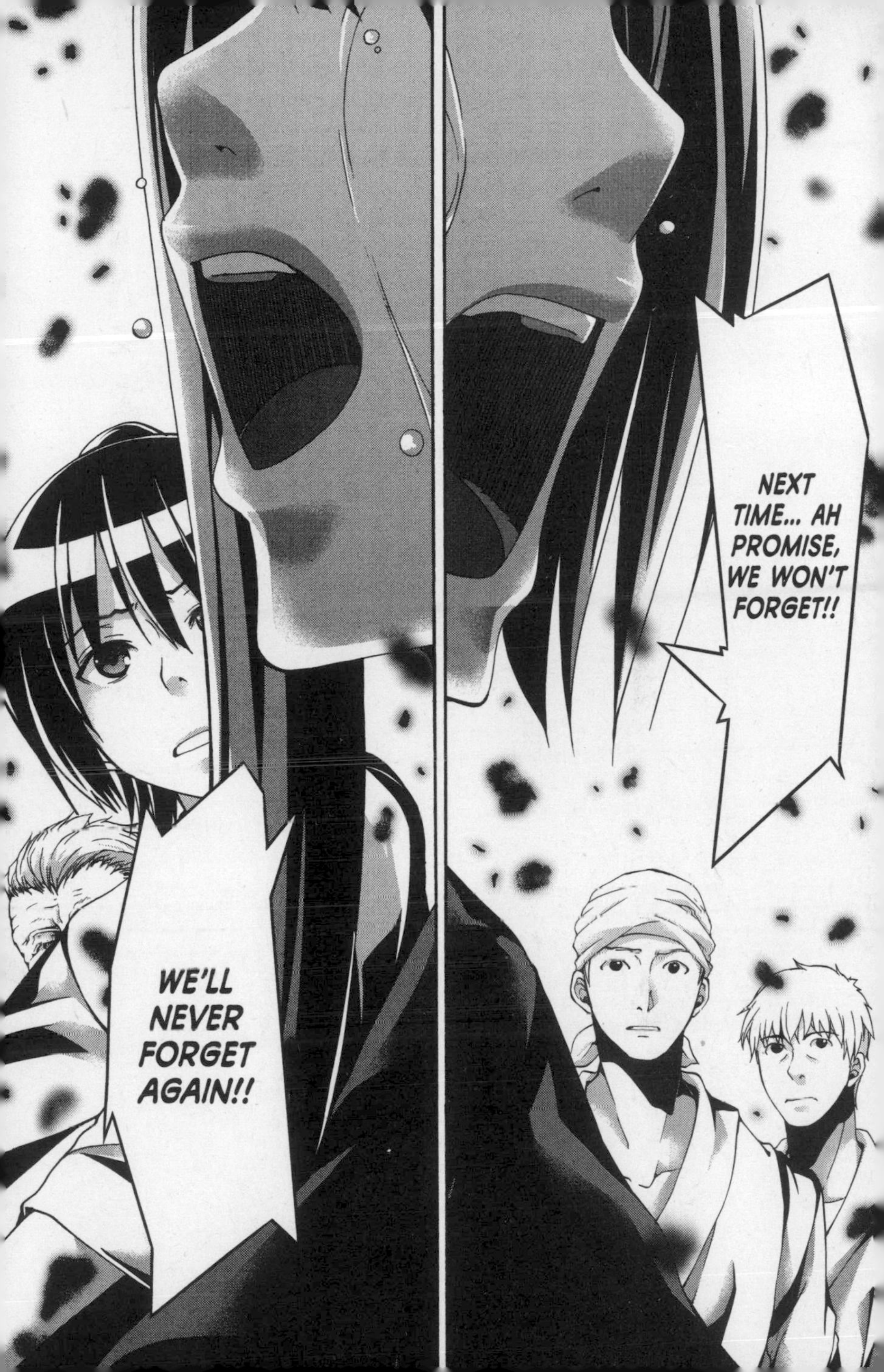
NEXT TIME... AH PROMISE, WE WON'T FORGET!!
WE'LL NEVER FORGET AGAIN!!

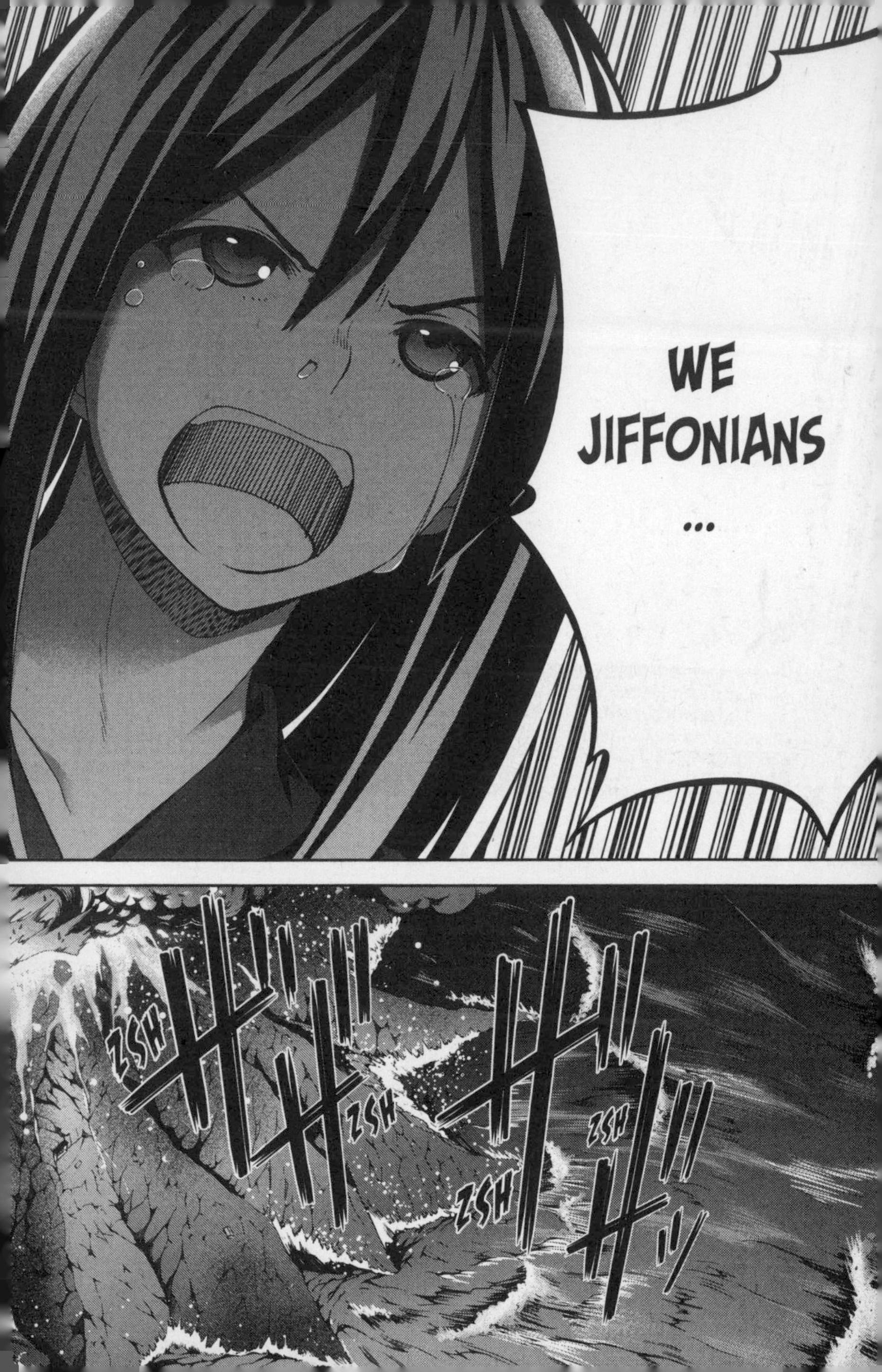
WE JIFFONIANS ...
ZSH
ZSH
ZSH
ZSH

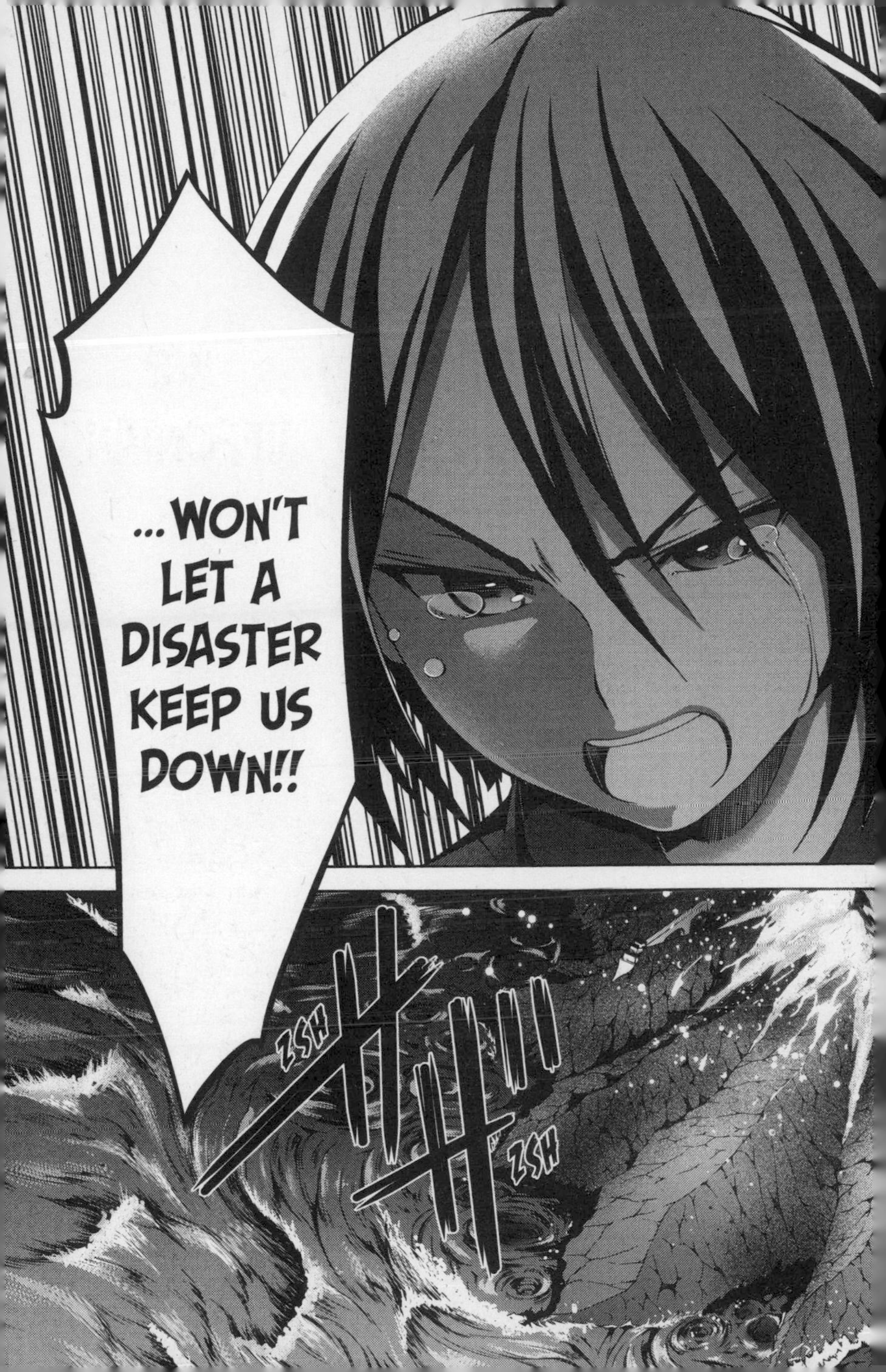
...WON'T LET A DISASTER KEEP US DOWN!!
ZSH
ZSH

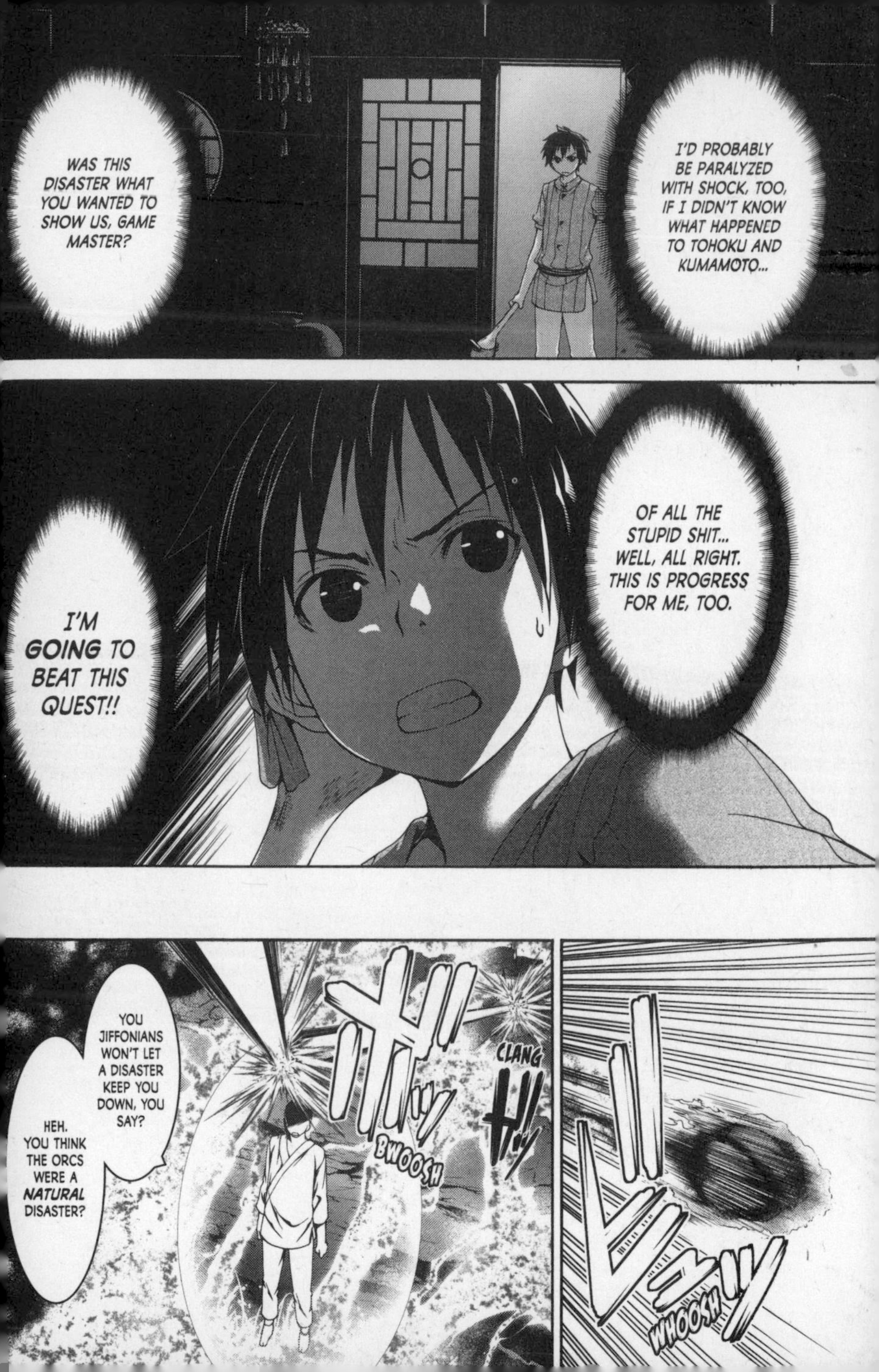
I'D PROBABLY BE PARALYZED WITH SHOCK, TOO, IF I DIDN'T KNOW WHAT HAPPENED TO TOHOKU AND KUMAMOTO...
WAS THIS DISASTER WHAT YOU WANTED TO SHOW US, GAME MASTER?
OF ALL THE STUPID SHIT... WELL, ALL RIGHT. THIS IS PROGRESS FOR ME, TOO.
I'M *GOING* TO BEAT THIS QUEST!!
WHOOSH
CLANG
BWOOSH
YOU JIFFONIANS WON'T LET A DISASTER KEEP YOU DOWN, YOU SAY?
HEH. YOU THINK THE ORCS WERE A *NATURAL* DISASTER?

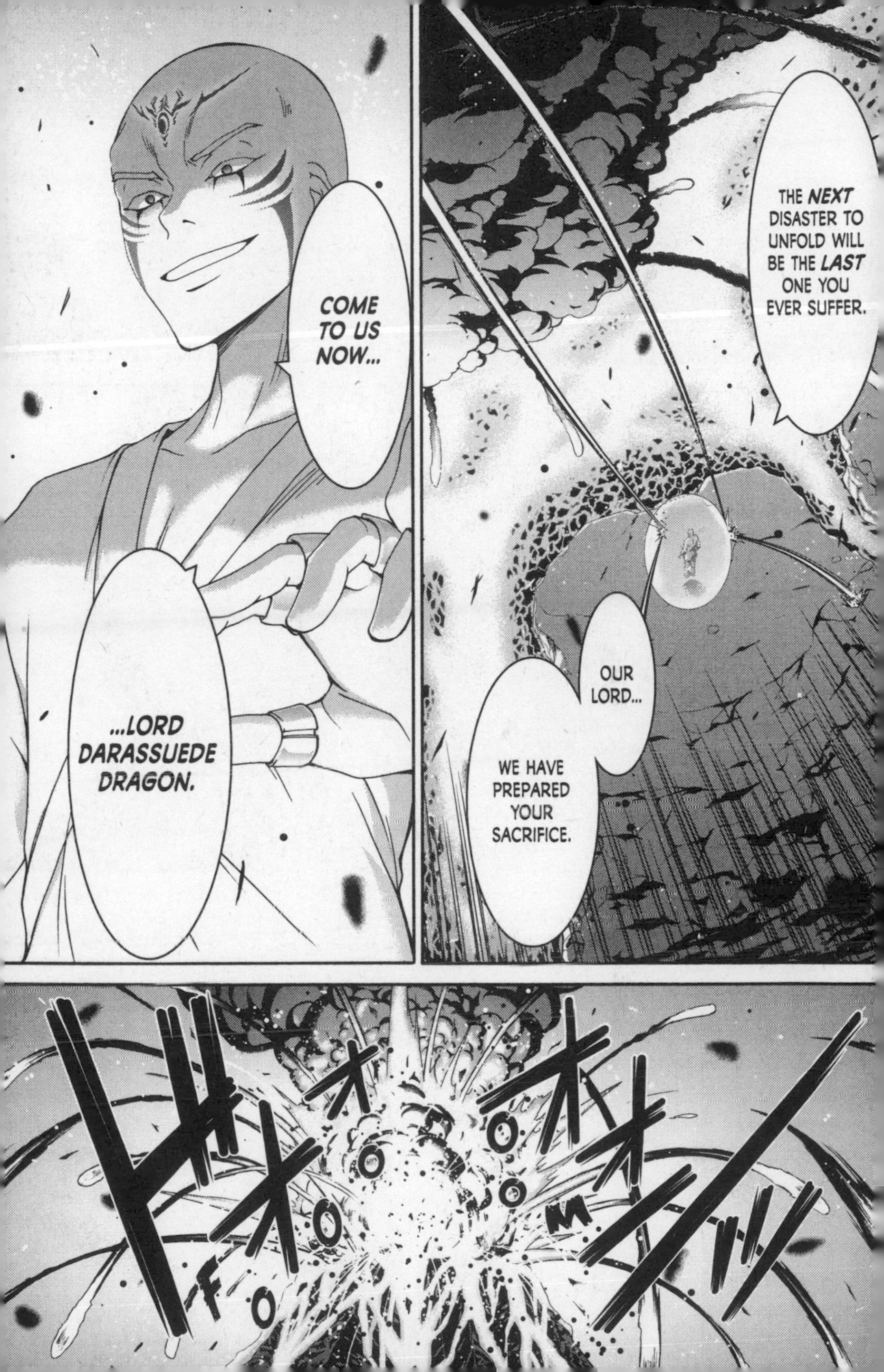
THE NEXT DISASTER TO UNFOLD WILL BE THE LAST ONE YOU EVER SUFFER.
OUR LORD...
WE HAVE PREPARED YOUR SACRIFICE.
COME TO US NOW...
...LORD DARASSUEDE DRAGON.

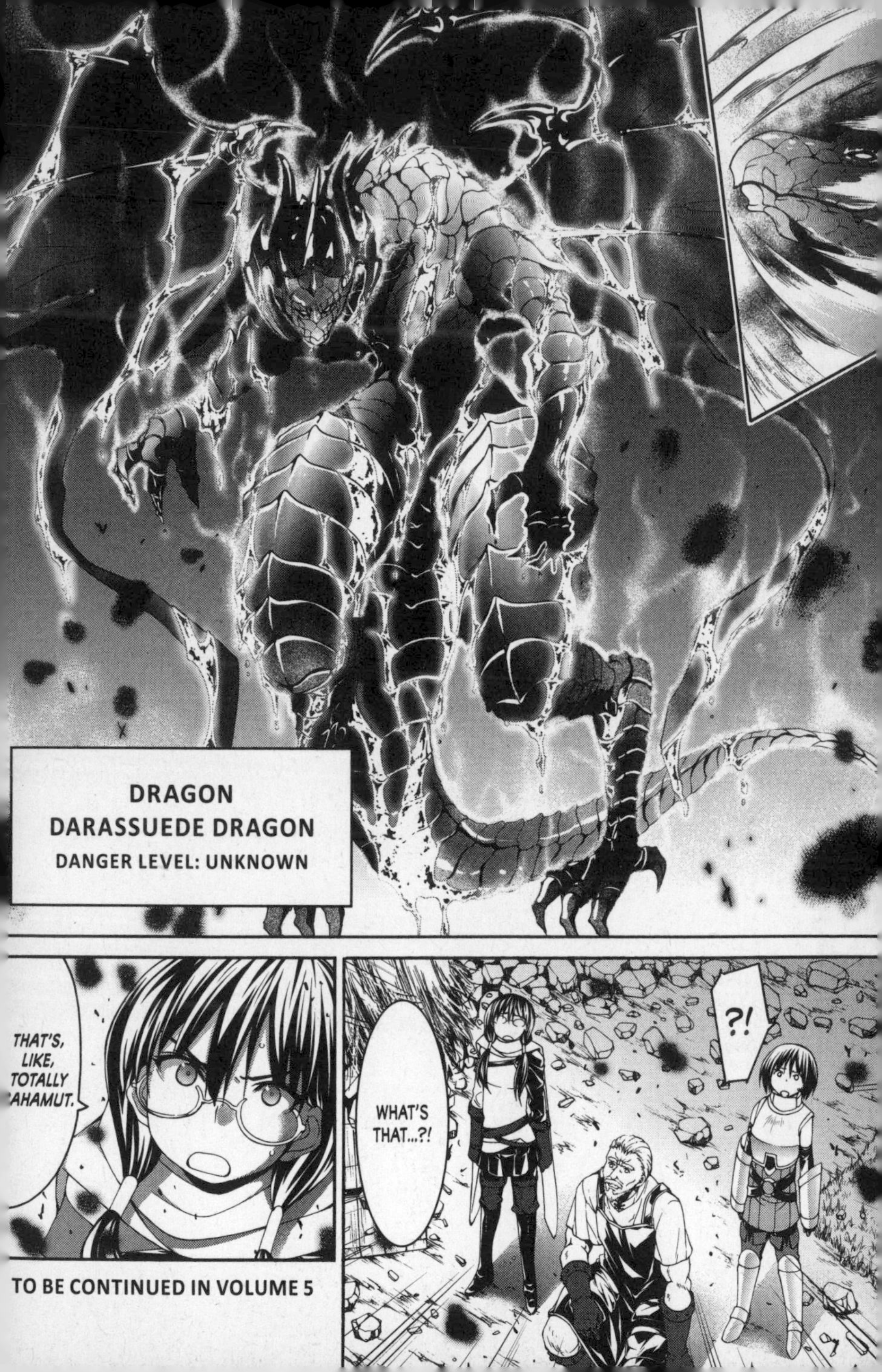
DRAGON
DARASSUEDE DRAGON
DANGER LEVEL: UNKNOWN
?!
WHAT'S THAT...?!
THAT'S, LIKE, TOTALLY AHAMUT.
TO BE CONTINUED IN VOLUME 5

I'M STANDING ON
A MILLION LIVES

■ ***Regarding disasters.***

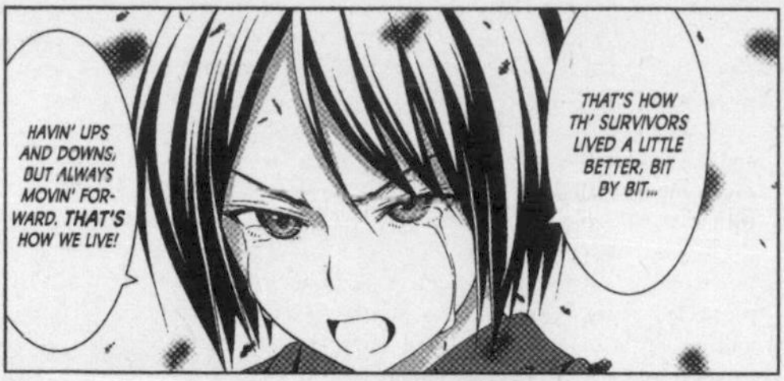
THAT'S HOW TH' SURVIVORS LIVED A LITTLE BETTER, BIT BY BIT...
HAVIN' UPS AND DOWNS, BUT ALWAYS MOVIN' FOR-WARD. THAT'S HOW WE LIVE!

In addition to current readers, this manga is being created with an eye toward future readers who might pick it up in a used bookstore someday. Most of this text is going to be common knowledge to people in our time, so feel free to skip it if it's not news to you.

In 2011, Japan had to face the Tohoku earthquake and tsunami, and in 2016, a couple of smaller-scale but still destructive quakes in Kumamoto. Moreover, scientists estimate a 70-percent chance that an earthquake will directly strike metro Tokyo within the next 30 years. Conventional wisdom also states that a "Nankai megathrust" earthquake—originating from the Nankai Trough that runs across the seas near south and east Japan—could be right around the corner. (Or maybe it's already happened by the time you're reading this? This was written in December 2017.)

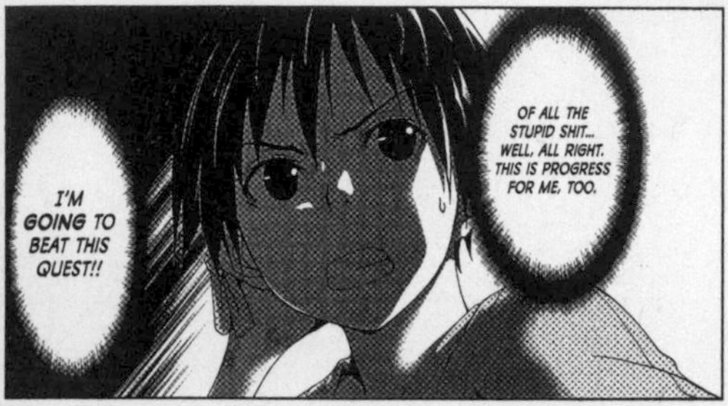
OF ALL THE STUPID SHIT... WELL, ALL RIGHT. THIS IS PROGRESS FOR ME, TOO.
I'M GOING TO BEAT THIS QUEST!!

People's awareness of public safety always goes up after a serious disaster, but everyone (including future generations) tends to forget these lessons over time. This tendency also influences the media: TV programs about disaster preparedness begin to see their ratings dip, and eventually cease to be aired. When people die because they didn't know about things which could've saved them, that means that lives have been needlessly lost to past disasters. Thus, I'd like to write a few things about disaster preparedness here.

■ ***Regarding earthquakes.***

Remember: There is a 70-percent chance of a direct strike on Tokyo within the next 30 years.

Hearing that, I think a lot of people's first response is along the lines of, "Well, things still seem all right to me." But if you remove that 30-year time limit, the chances go up to 100 percent. Sooner or later, near the tectonic plates, you are absolutely certain to see one. The only time they'll stop happening is when planet Earth itself no longer exists.

Japan is a series of islands built up from four of these plates, making it the second most earthquake-prone nation in the world (Indonesia is number one).

■ ***Regarding "Well, things still seem all right to me."***

This is a pretty natural thing to feel. Nobody alive and breathing, after all, has died from an accident or natural disaster. Those events only killed other people. Every summer in Japan, dozens of people die from water-related accidents, but I doubt any of them woke up on that morning and said to themselves, "Oh, man, I might drown today."

■ ***Regarding earthquake prediction.***

Japan has been conducting research into predicting earthquakes since 1880, but in recent years, we've started to conclude that it can't be done. Technically, it might be possible if we can perfectly trace plate movements, see how those link up with earthquakes from the past several dozen millennia, and input all that data into a supercomputer for processing. But in terms of the required tech, time, and budgets involved, it's far, far less expensive—and takes a lot less time—to just ask all of us to take more precautions.

Since the 3/11/2011 Tohoku quake, you sometimes see internet posts about people who can predict earthquakes, but these stories are along the same lines as occult tales of ghosts and time travelers. Please don't put much stock in them. Japan has around 5,000 earthquakes that register a 3.0 magnitude or higher every year, approximately 160 of which break 5.0. It's also worth remembering that predictions tend to be forgotten if they're wrong and remembered when they're correct. With some of the trashier news sites on the net, you pretty much only see stories about astonishingly correct predictions.

■ ***Regarding occult tales.***

The year 1995 began in Japan began an earthquake in January that struck the city of Kobe, killing approximately 6,000 people. This was followed in March by the Aum Shinrikyo cult's sarin gas attack on the Tokyo subway, which killed thirteen and still remains Japan's deadliest terrorist attack.

One way the cult was able to grow its membership was by preying on people's fears of earthquakes and other natural disasters; it offered salvation from such disasters to those who pledged their belief. Aum Shinrikyo's adherents have included graduates from Tokyo University and other prestigious schools, indicating that gullibility is in no way related to intelligence or lack thereof.

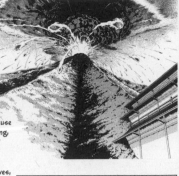

■ *Regarding volcanic eruptions.*
On the other hand, it *is* possible to predict some volcanic events.
A few months before a major eruption, magma begins to push up into relatively shallow depths beneath the surface, which actually makes the mountain swell up a little. Smaller-scale eruptions, however, cannot be spotted in advance. The 2014 eruption of Mount Ontake, which blew ash and projectiles that killed around 60 people, was one such "small-scale" event. Mount Fuji itself erupts in a cycle of approximately 300 years, with some believing that another eruption is imminent (there are several theories about this).
Sometimes you hear volcanoes referred to as "extinct" because they have pretty well tapped their magma supply. This term has fallen out of favor, however, since science has found that calling a volcano extinct simply because it hasn't erupted for several centuries is the geological equivalent of saying, "I haven't had a cold the past few days, so I doubt I'll ever get one again."

■ *Regarding tsunamis.*
In movies and such, you often see tsunamis depicted as just really big waves, like something a surfer could ride on. Even in this series, we've taken a few liberties in our depiction to make it easier to follow. But a giant tsunami doesn't come rushing in all at once. It's wide, not tall, so it's not a wave so much as the entire water level rising for several minutes or hours.
As a result, when a huge tsunami is on its way, you should worry more about getting higher than getting farther from the shore. If you stay on low ground, by the time you can see the tsunami with the naked eye, you're already too late to outrun it. For example, if a tsunami six miles wide and five yards high comes along and you want to get away from it, you'd need to run six miles inland to avoid it; meanwhile, if you can get five yards more elevation between you and sea level, you'll at least survive the event (assuming the ground under your feet holds).

TSUNAMIS AS SEEN IN DISASTER FILMS

N.Y.C.

← SHORT WIDTH →

TALLER THAN BUILDIN

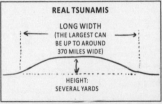

REAL TSUNAMIS

← LONG WIDTH →
(THE LARGEST CAN BE UP TO AROUND 370 MILES WIDE)

HEIGHT: SEVERAL YARDS

■ *Regarding "Did the shaking make a hole in the sea?"*
I figured I should explain this reference. Partly it comes from geocentric theory, i.e. the Ptolemaic idea that the Earth is flat and all the other celestial bodies revolve around it.
It's also a reference to the 2004 Indian Ocean earthquake and tsunami, when children marveled at the waters receding from the shore. They proceeded to walk deep offshore to the now-empty seabed. The fact that their parents didn't stop them indicates that they weren't aware of the telltale sign of a tsunami, either.

■ *Regarding "Tsunami Tendenko."*
This is a Japanese mnemonic, first devised in 1990, which boils down to:
"If a tsunami comes along, don't worry about anyone or anything else; just flee to higher elevation by yourself." If you can *see* a tsunami, you're already too late to avoid it. There's no time to come back and try to help other people.
During the 3/11/2011 quake, you saw people who made it to evacuation points (or had the time to) but died after coming back to help someone else. In some cases, the people they came back to save had actually already evacuated elsewhere and were perfectly fine. That's the sort of tragedy this mnemonic was invented to prevent. One particular event, the "Miracle of Kamaishi," took place in the Iwate Prefecture city of Kamaishi, which was severely damaged by the 2011 tsunami. 2,900 grade-school children in Kamaishi received education in "Tsunami Tendenko," and on March 11, every single one who attended school that day survived the event.

■ *Regarding typhoons.*
Severe typhoons and hurricanes are driven in part by high ocean temperatures, meaning that these storms will only become more powerful as temperatures rise worldwide.

Future Reader A: Hey, you know how the dude who wrote this acted like he was some kinda genius? Well, did you know that he died from ********* just ** years later?
Future Reader B: Holy shit! Really? lol

Text: Naoki Yamakawa

GAME MAST NOTES FROM TRANSLATE

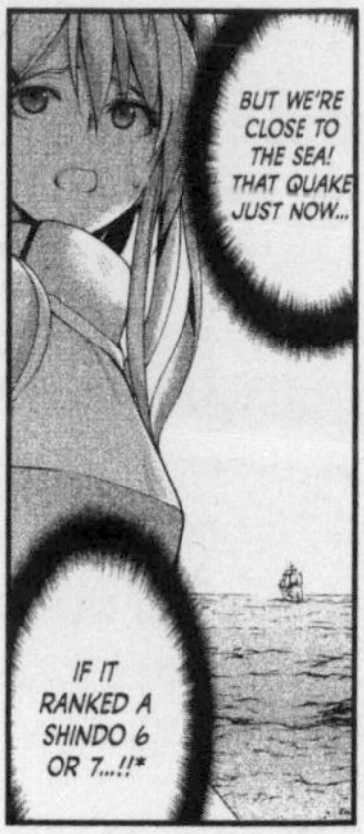
BUT WE'RE CLOSE TO THE SEA! THAT QUAKE JUST NOW...
IF IT RANKED A SHINDO 6 OR 7...!!*

PAGE 158: SHINDO SCALE

The *shindo* scale, more officially known as the Japan Meteorological Agency Seismic Intensity Scale, is used to measure the intensity of earthquakes in terms of the intensity of the shaking that results from it, unlike the more common Western scale that measures overall magnitude. A "*shindo* 7" earthquake is an extremely rare and powerful event, last recorded with the Tohoku earthquake and tsunami that killed over 15,000 people in 2011.

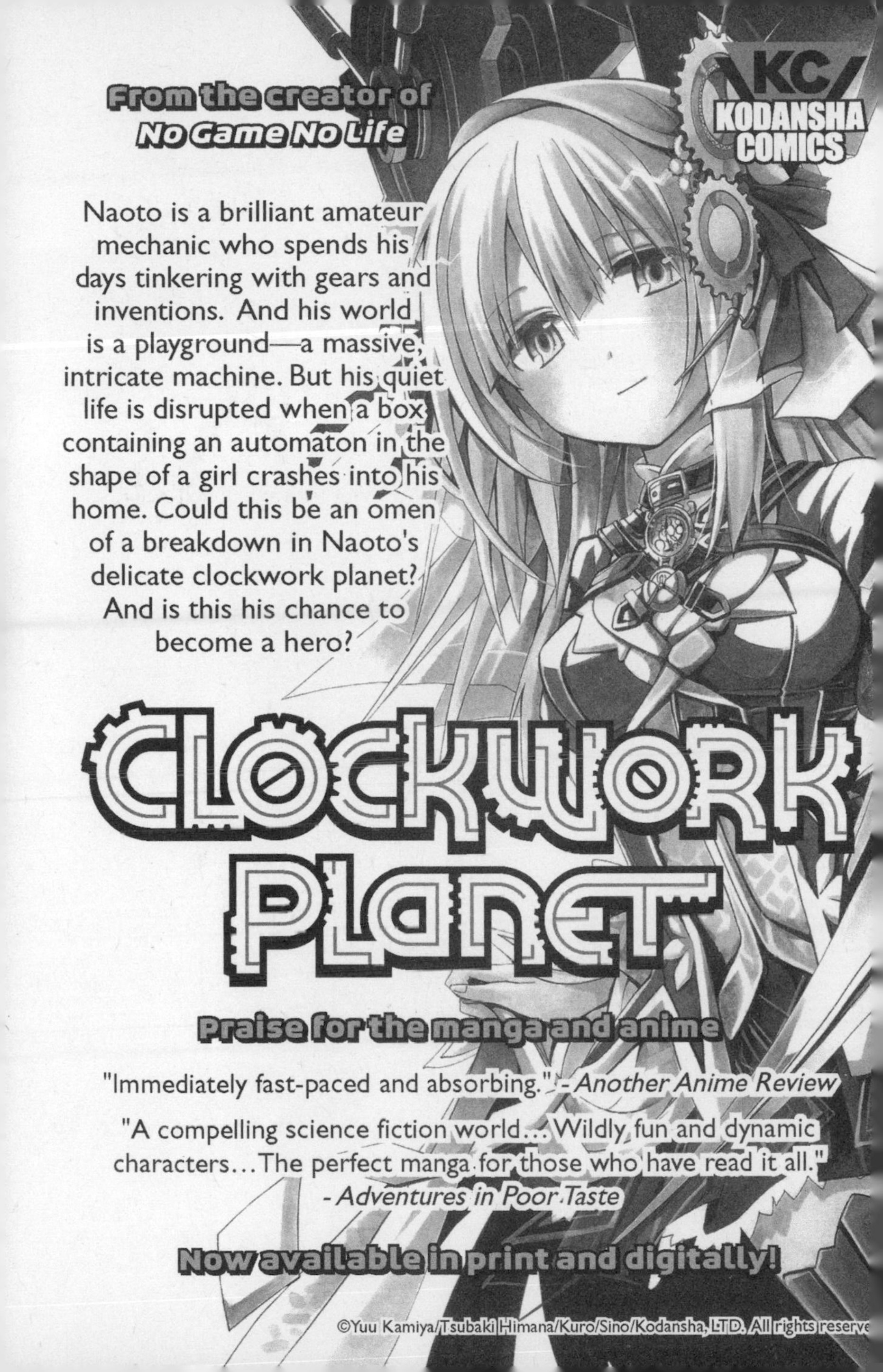
KC KODANSHA COMICS
From the creator of
No Game No Life
Naoto is a brilliant amateur mechanic who spends his days tinkering with gears and inventions. And his world is a playground—a massive, intricate machine. But his quiet life is disrupted when a box containing an automaton in the shape of a girl crashes into his home. Could this be an omen of a breakdown in Naoto's delicate clockwork planet? And is this his chance to become a hero?
CLOCKWORK PLANET
Praise for the manga and anime
"Immediately fast-paced and absorbing." - Another Anime Review
"A compelling science fiction world... Wildly fun and dynamic characters...The perfect manga for those who have read it all." - Adventures in Poor Taste
Now available in print and digitally!
©Yuu Kamiya/Tsubaki Himana/Kuro/Sino/Kodansha, LTD. All rights reserve

I'm Standing on a Million Lives 4 is a work of fiction. Names, characters, places, and incidents are the products of the author's imagination or are used fictitiously. Any resemblance to actual events, locales, or persons, living or dead, is entirely coincidental.

A Kodansha Comics Trade Paperback Original

Published in the United States by Kodansha Comics, an imprint of Kodansha USA Publishing, LLC, New York.

Publication rights for this English edition arranged through Kodansha Ltd., Tokyo.

First published in Japan in 2018 by Kodansha Ltd., Tokyo.

ISBN 978-1-63236-841-6

Printed in the United States of America.

www.kodanshacomics.com

9 8 7 6 5 4 3 2 1
Translation: Kevin Gifford
Lettering: Thea Willis
Editing: Erin Subramanian, Tiff Ferentini, and Nathaniel Gallant
Kodansha Comics edition cover design by Phil Balsman

KC KODANSHA COMICS

Publisher: Kiichiro Sugawara
Managing editor: Maya Rosewood
Vice president of marketing & publicity: Naho Yamada

Director of publishing services: Ben Applegate
Associate director of operations: Stephen Pakula
Publishing services managing editor: Noelle Webster
Assistant production manager: Emi Lotto